New Approaches to Rhetoric

Dedication

To Ray for his ongoing love and support
To Judi, Claire, and David, whose love and support sustain all my scholarly efforts

New Approaches to Rhetoric

EDITORS

PATRICIA A. SULLIVAN
State University of New York at New Paltz

STEVEN R. GOLDZWIG
Marquette University

SAGE Publications
International Educational and Professional Publisher
Thousand Oaks ▪ London ▪ New Delhi

For information:

Sage Publications, Inc.
2455 Teller Road
Thousand Oaks, California 91320
E-mail: order@sagepub.com

Sage Publications Ltd.
6 Bonhill Street
London EC2A 4PU
United Kingdom

Sage Publications India Pvt. Ltd.
B-42, Panchsheel Enclave
Post Box 4109
New Delhi 110 017 India

Printed in the United States of America

Library of Congress Cataloging-in-Publication Data

New approaches to rhetoric / Patricia A. Sullivan and Steven R. Goldzwig, editors.
p. cm.
Includes bibliographical references and index.
ISBN 0-7619-2912-6—ISBN 0-7619-2913-4 (pbk.)
1. Rhetoric. I. Sullivan, Patricia Ann. II. Goldzwig, Steven R.
P301.N48 2004
808—dc21

2003014618

Printed on acid-free paper

04 05 06 07 08 09 10 9 8 7 6 5 4 3 2 1

Acquiring Editor: Todd R. Armstrong
Editorial Assistant: Veronica K. Novak
Production Editor: Claudia A. Hoffman
Copy Editor: Dan Hays
Typesetter: C&M Digitals (P) Ltd.
Indexer: Molly Hall

Contents

Acknowledgments

We thank the contributors for their generosity and for their patience. We are deeply appreciative of the vital scholarly dialogue that made this volume possible. We are indebted to Todd Armstrong for believing in this collection.

We also wish to thank the reviewers of this project:

Sonja Foss, University of Colorado at Denver
David Henry, University of Nevada, Las Vegas
Robert L. Ivie, Indiana University
Janice Rushing, University of Arkansas at Fayetteville

Preface

The purpose of this collection is to provide fresh perspectives on the study of rhetoric for the twenty-first century. Although traditional approaches (e.g., neo-Aristotelian) to the study of rhetoric have utility for the twenty-first century, communication in a complex, mass-mediated postmodern age calls for new critical approaches. As professors, we struggle to help our students understand traditional critical approaches as well as cultural and ideological approaches that will help them "make sense" of communication in a complicated world.

This collection invites students to join rhetorical theorists and critics in an ongoing dialogue concerning what it means to study communication in a postmodern world. As rhetoricians struggle to articulate critical approaches to account for discourse in a multicultural world, they question the assumptions guiding their research. In a special issue of the *Southern Communication Journal* in 1998, scholars offered perspectives on the shape that the study of rhetoric would take in the twenty-first century. Raymie McKerrow argued that "Western Rhetoric, as currently fashioned via a male dominant language, is virtually incapable of being the 'site' from which to appraise rhetorics within a diverse world" (p. 315). John Angus Campbell urged scholars to recognize the legacy of neoclassical rhetoric as they seek critical perspectives for the twenty-first century. He suggested we return to our historical roots and recognize an important connection between neoclassical rhetoric and contemporary rhetorics. Neoclassical rhetoric shares with postmodern and deconstructionist rhetorics a recognition of "the importance of grounding theory in local conditions and is wary of the potential tyranny of universalizing perspectives" (p. 291).

Other scholars have addressed possibilities for bridging the "old" and "new" rhetorics in acknowledgment of conditions in a postmodern world. In responding to the fragmentation of culture, Michael Calvin

McGee (1990) argued that rhetoricians "make discourses from scraps and pieces of evidence" (p. 279). Maurice Charland's (1987, 1991) work has examined ways in which audiences rather than rhetors are responsible for creating discourses. In the early 1990s, Martha Solomon (1993), in an article published in *Communication Monographs*, speculated on the direction of rhetorical studies for the twenty-first century and proposed "continuing this process of questioning our taken-for-granteds and expanding our views of rhetorical processes" (p. 67).

A number of scholars have asked what it means to study rhetoric in an increasingly diverse world. Dana Cloud and Celeste Condit debated the roles of the ideal and the material in human communication. In *Critical Studies in Mass Communication,* Cloud (1997) and Condit (1997) expressed different philosophies concerning the limits of communication in bringing about social change. In a special issue of *Communication Studies* published in 1996 on "Theorizing Communication From Marginalized Perspectives," guest editors Sonja Foss and Eileen Berlin Ray suggested they strived to "advocate theoretic pluralism and an appreciation for different theorizing and methods that expand our explanatory lenses rather than constrain us by the myopia of dogmatic theory" (p. 253). Laura Gray-Rosendale and Sibylle Gruber (2001), editors of *Alternative Rhetorics: Challenges to the Rhetorical Tradition*, "emphasize multiplicity and fragmentation within and between different rhetorics and different traditions" (p. 5).

In identifying threads in contemporary approaches to analysis, and what he described as "the tangle of rhetorical culture," Dale Cyphert (2001), in a *Quarterly Journal of Speech* article, claimed that the study of rhetoric is undergoing profound changes. He summarized the ferment in approaches to rhetorical criticism as follows:

> The transcultural questions implied in our current threads of theory suggest the study of rhetoric is undergoing a more profound change—a paradigm shift, perhaps—that dissociates the study of rhetorical cultures from the normative presumptions of Western rhetorical tradition. (p. 390)

As we move into the twenty-first century, then, rhetoricians explore possibilities for bridging rhetorical studies of the past with rhetorical studies of the future. The essays in this collection offer guidance for professors who are attempting to address this paradigm shift in rhetorical studies. The essays challenge and expand the definitions, approaches, and assumptions governing rhetorical scholarship, but they do not reach consensus. The collection is divided into three parts: Part I: Rhetorics, Ethics, and Values; Part II: Rhetorics, Institutions, and Contexts; and Part III: Rhetorics, Cultures, and Ideologies. Each part begins with a brief introduction designed to frame discussion for students. Readers who are familiar with the critical approaches represented in each section may choose to bypass the introductions. Following Part III, Barry Brummett provides a response to all the essays in the collection. Professor Brummett highlights a key thread in the assumptions that have prompted these essays.

Part I

Rhetorics, Ethics, and Values

James Boyd White (1985) offers the following plea for the recognition of rhetoric's significance: "Whenever we speak or write, we should be prepared to ask ourselves what kind of community and culture we make, what kind of meaning they shall have" (p. 48). Klumpp and Hollihan (1989) have argued that the critic has the responsibility to be morally engaged. Hollihan (1994) summarizes this position and suggests that "critics who ignore the moral implications of rhetoric thus perform support for the mystery that preserves the social order" (p. 230). In a dialogue on communication and social justice, Frey, Pearce, Pollock, Artz, and Murphy (1996) argue that communication researchers have "dealt inadequately with the interests of those most in need in our society" (p. 114). They summarize the political dimensions of research as follows:

> Our argument is that research is never a politically neutral act. The decision to study *this* group rather than some other, to frame the research question *this* way rather than another, and to report the findings to *this group* or *that journal* rather than in some other forum privilege certain values, institutions, and practices. (p. 114)

Ono and Sloop (1995) also address the political dimensions of research. Although they recognize the importance of studying "documents of power" or influential speeches given by rhetors (e.g., Martin Luther King,

Jr.'s "I Have a Dream" speech and Abraham Lincoln's "Gettysburg Address") (p. 19), they make a case for expanding the scope of rhetoric:

> If we limit our attention to such documents available to the widest possible audience, documents that "shaped" the "history of society," then we are missing out on, and writing "out of history," important texts that gird and influence local cultures first and then affect, through the sheer number of local communities, cultures at large. (p. 19)

The essays in Part I address, in different ways, moral responsibilities of critics and their audiences. As you read this section, consider the following central question for scholars writing about rhetoric in the twenty-first century: How, and under what conditions, will moral arguments be articulated in the twenty-first century? You will see how each author answers this question and, in turn, responds to White's plea for recognition of rhetoric's significance.

James Darsey's essay, "James Baldwin's *Topoi*," is an inquiry into a cosmopolitan rhetoric examining the connection between place and epistemology in the postmodern world. Although Baldwin's work deals with issues that defined the United States in the 1950s and 1960s, his work suggests lines of argumentation that speak to contemporary issues in rhetorical scholarship. Darsey says that Baldwin, in the struggle to define where he belonged, developed a rhetoric that holds promise for helping us articulate moral arguments in our postmodern, postcolonial world.

In "*Ingenium*—Speaking in Community: The Case of the Prince William County Zoning Hearings on Disney's America," Kathryn M. Olson and G. Thomas Goodnight address the intersection of national and local rhetorics in argumentation grounded in values. A case study of local planning commission hearings on Disney's America project suggests ways in which the discourses of national institutions are reshaped through the discourses of local communities. In analyzing the discourse of the hearings, the authors acknowledge the importance of vernacular discourse or "speech that resonates in local communities" (Ono & Sloop, 1995, p. 20).

George Cheney examines the practical ethical implications for adopting one term or meaning rather than another in corporate or organizational discourses. Specifically, he studies market-oriented discourses as they frame discussions of the economy, work, and consumption. In

"Arguing About the Place of Values and Ethics in Market-Oriented Discourses of Today," he suggests that the dominance of the market metaphor elevates and naturalizes corporate interests and operations.

"Cultural Contracts Theory: Toward a Critical-Rhetorical Identity Negotiation Paradigm" defines cultural contracts as value-laden analysis. Ronald L. Jackson articulates a vision of identity negotiation as a rhetorical process through which individuals enter cultural contracts. Jackson emphasizes the importance of analyzing how identities are shaped by "everyday rhetorical transactions."

The essays in Part I highlight the place of values in attempts at rhetorical influence. Personal, local, organizational, and cultural identities are created and produced by rhetorical transactions. The essays clearly demonstrate that analysis and evaluation of both the rhetorical process and the rhetorical product are important.

1

James Baldwin's *Topoi*

James Darsey

I am a Frenchman in Germany and a German in France; a Catholic among the Protestants, a Protestant among the Catholics; a philosopher among the religious . . ., a mundane among the savants, and a pedant to the mundane; Jacobin among the aristocrats, and to the democrats a nobleman, a man of the Ancien Regime. . . . Nowhere am I at home!

—Adelbert von Chamisso to Madame de Staël

He loved no other place, and yet Home was no home to him.

—Samuel Taylor Coleridge

We often speak of taking an "argumentative position" or of "advocating a position," of persuading others to adopt our position, to see things from our place. In these efforts, we act as exponents (from the Latin *ponere*, "to place"). In his *Rhetoric*, Aristotle provides *topoi*, places to look for arguments, and Stephen Toulmin (1964) maintains that arguments may be grouped into "fields" based on the shared logical type of their backing or conclusions, that is, on commonality of their "grounds." These two modes of placement, the placement of the rhetor and the placement of the argument itself, are joined in Kenneth Burke's (1969a) pentadic element "scene," which is so powerful an element that it can be said to "contain" both agent and act. Similarly, Lloyd Bitzer (1968) argues that it is in the essence of rhetoric to be called forth by situations, from the Latin *situs* ("situation" or "site"). There is implied in these locutions a geographical dimension to rhetoric, a largely unexplored theoretical Antarctica. The very notion that the rhetor "holds a position" points to the consideration of his or her location as an element of *ethos*, *ethos* being related to *ethea* ("habitat").

Consider Daniel Webster's "Seventh of March Speech" (1850/1989) on Henry Clay's proposed compromise on the slavery issue. Webster begins the speech by placing himself above provincial and partisan concerns: "I wish to speak today, not as a Massachusetts man, nor as a Northern man, but as an American, and a member of the Senate" (p. 191). In this single sentence, Webster transcends parochial state and regional concerns and insists on identifying with *patria* and national office, a member of a body "not yet moved from its propriety [Kenneth Burke would no doubt point out here the propinquity of propriety and property], not lost to a just sense of its own dignity and its own high responsibilities" (p. 191).

Webster's strategy is, in Aristotelian terms, ethical; it is part of an attempt to project a particular character. In a moment of crisis and confusion, Webster, as he attempts to provide clarification, stands on firm ground, high ground, ground "not yet moved," solid and immovable ground. As long as Webster can ascend to this solid and exalted place, he cannot be lost—that is, he cannot be confused.

Webster's empyrean perspective seems lost to us in the United States today except as an object of nostalgia (from Greek, meaning "to return home"). To be sure, the rhetorical form lives on, as Arkansas Republican Asa Hutchinson demonstrated in his opening remarks to the House Judiciary Committee on the first day of the Clinton impeachment hearings. Describing how Arkansans felt about the Clinton-Lewinsky affair, Representative Hutchinson said that "as Arkansans, we prefer to change the subject," but "as Americans," the good citizens of Arkansas recognized their civic duty to look the issue squarely in the face. The character and consequent responsibility of Representative Hutchinson's constituency changes according to the geographical boundaries invoked to define it. The conceit may have floated in the heat of the moment, but as quickly as temperatures cooled, it shriveled and fell, exposed as the gaseous bombast that it was. Webster's solemn declaration that he speaks as an American fails, in a contemporary application, to elucidate.

There are precious few high and solid places now. At the dawn of the twenty-first century, homelessness and displacement are increasingly the characteristic features of life. Charlene Spretnak (1999) finds the provenance of our current rootlessness in modernism, which denigrates place "except as a springboard from which the salvific ideology of progress would launch its grand trajectory. Place was associated [in modernist thought] with constraint: the binding ties of community, extended family, and tradition as well as the local demands of nature" (p. 27). Spretnak goes on to indict modernist architecture and design for seeking to liberate itself "from the local and the vernacular by a fierce reduction to sterile minimalism that is truly cosmopolitan, reflecting no place and no culture, only an ideology of freedom through denial" (p. 27). James Clifford (1992) has gone so far as to suggest that the hotel, maybe even more appropriately the motel, be seriously considered as the primary locus of postmodern culture. A similar sense of contemporary dislocation is expressed by Akhil Gupta and James Ferguson (1997a):

> Today, the rapidly expanding and quickening mobility of people combines with the refusal of cultural products and practices to "stay put" to give a profound sense of a loss of territorial roots, of an erosion of the cultural distinctiveness of places. (p. 37)

With homelessness, transience, and displacement come a loss of identity and moral grounding coincident with diminished possibilities for community. "Place making involves a play of differences," write Gupta and Ferguson (1997b):

> The structures of feeling that enable meaningful relationships with particular locales, constituted and experienced in a particular manner, necessarily include the marking of "self" and "other" through identification with larger collectivities. To be a part of a community is to be positioned as a particular kind of subject, similar to others within the community in some crucial respects and different from those who are excluded from it. (p. 17)

Difference is a scarce commodity in a mobile world in which cultures intermingle in unprecedented ways; ethnic subcultures, women, and gays and lesbians "forget their place" and "get out of line;" trade and media are globalized; and people spend increasing amounts of time in the hyperspace of the World Wide Web. Everything is suddenly available everywhere. Everyplace begins to look very much like every other place. Geographical boundaries no longer serve the function of binding people and things to particular locales. Eva Hoffman (2000) describes life in our global village as "virtual indeed—dependent not on locality but on the detachment of knowledge, action, information, and identity from a specific place" (p. 46), and Pico Iyer (2000) describes himself as a "modern citizen of nowhere" living in a "mobile world" with "porous borders" (p. 43). The results of these multiple sources of dislocation can be both amusing and poignant. The sidewalk window advertising the "Rancho Il Wok de Paris, Tex-Mex Italian Asian French Cuisine" is a David Sipress (1999) cartoon in *Utne Reader* (p. 13), but in the neighborhood in which I live, the carryout run by Asians, catering primarily to African Americans, proudly advertising "Buffalo [NY] wings, Southern style," operates with no apparent sense of its incongruities and without evidence of ironic puckishness.

In the United States, and increasingly throughout the world, the ubiquitous shopping mall, with its Gap, Victoria's Secret, Camelot Music, Bath and Body Shop, and Pearle Vision Center, is, some have suggested, the quintessential postmodern public space, and it is stultifyingly homogenous and familiar wherever one goes. In Lubbock, Texas, or Bangor, Maine, Seattle or Savannah, enclosed, climate-controlled, filled with brand names, splashing fountains, and semitropical plantings recognized and trusted from coast to coast, these malls are not simply everyplace, they are everyplaces. And when Benneton, Max and Erma's, Pottery Barn, and Starbucks invade such formerly distinctive urban locations as Walnut Street in Pittsburgh, Pennsylvania, someplace threatens to disappear into no place in particular.

At this moment in history, we all are rapidly becoming cosmopolitans: If we do not leave home, home leaves us, or the world crushes in on us, forcing us into alien and often characterless ecumenical, multicultural proprieties. In an age in which exile has become a near-universal experience, we have, Eva Hoffman (2000) notes, "come to value exactly those qualities of experience that exile demands—uncertainty, displacement, fragmented identity" (p. 46). Hoffman continues,

> Exile gives perspective, making every emigrant an anthropologist and a relativist. To have a deep experience of two cultures is to know that no culture is absolute, to discover that the seemingly natural aspects of our identities and social reality can be arranged, shaped, or articulated in another way. (p. 47)

From a variety of quarters and in a variety of forms, among the most disturbing being the renascent fascisms in the United States, we see responses to a felt loss of common ground, the basis of social life. Lamentations over the current state of our public discourse are currently so numerous that we might better pile them into our own Wailing Wall than read them.

Can Hoffman or Iyer or the temporary resident of James Clifford's motel take a position? Do any of them have the foundation from which to forward a moral stand? Arthur Schlesinger, Jr. (1992), here representative of a rising chorus of spokespersons, popular as well as academic, from across the political spectrum, provides an expression of the starting place for this inquiry. "What happens," Schlesinger asks, "when people of different ethnic origins, speaking different languages and professing different religions, settle in the same geographical locality and live under the same political sovereignty?" (p. 10). One need not surrender to apocalypticism to recognize the truth in Schlesinger's dark warning: "Unless a common purpose binds [a people] together, tribal hostilities will drive them apart" (p. 10; see also Bellah, 1970; Bellah, Madsen, Sullivan, Swidler, & Tipton, 1985; Hirsch, 1987; Hughes, 1993).

A discourse different from that we most often find in the public arena is demanded here, one that can adequately reflect the pluralism that has long been the American ideal and is now, increasingly, the world's reality (Glendon, 1991). We know that neither the Scylla of pure tolerance—unmasked 30 years ago by Moore, Wolff, and Marcuse but revived in some understandings of multiculturalism—nor the Charybdis of rigidly enforced monolithic orthodoxies and purification schemes, either domestic or international, will do (Nussbaum, 1996, 1997, pp. 25-57). David Harvey (2000) casts the dilemma as a choice between "a relativism that suggests that for each cultural group there is some theory of justice that captures its ethical intuitions" and "moral universals that may be just as unpalatable even if they can be defined" (p. 542).

Hopeless as this loss of grounding may seem, there is encouraging evidence in the history of American public discourse that a tradition of cosmopolitan moral rhetoric already exists, a rhetoric that may have great utility in our current circumstances. A cosmopolitan rhetoric would be a rhetoric created by those, like Hoffman and Iyer, who have "left home," who have been alienated, sometimes multiply alienated, who have lost, left, or forgotten their place yet who somehow found new, transcendent places or struggled toward such places, and from these new places served as compelling moral spokespersons on significant public issues—rhetors who found a way, despite their displacement, to take a position.

James Baldwin is a prototypical American cosmopolite. Baldwin, self-described "transatlantic commuter" (Auchincloss & Lynch, 1969/1989,

p. 80; see also Terkel, 1961/1989, p. 15), a man whose recorded date of death is December 1 in France and November 30 in the United States, left home multiple times: the evangelical Christian church; his father's house; the black world of Harlem for the white world of Greenwich Village; the racist, antisexual, homophobic world of the United States for the more permissive, less anxious world of Paris (Darsey, 1999, p. 190; see also Dievler, 1999, pp. 161-183; Wright, 1999, p. 208). Baldwin, however, did not give up place in his multiple emigrations, not permanently at least. The state of being lost is an important theme in Baldwin's writing—"Nobody Knows My Name," "A Question of Identity," *One Day When I Was Lost*, *No Name in the Street*, "Stranger in the Village," "The New Lost Generation," *Just Above My Head*—but Baldwin's personal diaspora is temporary, part of what James Dievler (1999) identifies as an "exile cycle: a sense of homelessness at home; actual physical exile and a corresponding love experience; and a return to home with a detached awareness and maturity about the culture that caused the trouble in the first place" (p. 179). Baldwin uses his exile to escape various cages, various prisons and strictures, and to discover his true limits in an atmosphere of freedom. "And I love Paris," muses Baldwin's surrogate in *This Morning, This Evening, So Soon*, Paris becoming a synecdoche for all of Baldwin's emigrations: "I will always love it, it is the city which saved my life. It saved my life by allowing me to find out who I am" (p. 157).

From his new place, Baldwin, though he was dismissive of "the avowed aim of the American protest novel . . . to bring greater freedom to the oppressed" (1984, p. 18), at the same time held "the business of the novelist" (and presumably that of the essayist) to be that "power of revelation" that enables us to "find . . . ourselves and the power that will free us from ourselves" amid "this web of ambiguity, paradox, . . . hunger, danger, [and] darkness" (1984, p. 15; see also Baldwin, 1985, p. 315). Dwight McBride (1999) reminds us that

> Baldwin's life was committed to struggle. He resisted hegemonies in their myriad forms by fighting for racial equality, against elitism both in the United States and abroad, and against the forces of heterosexism both inside and outside the black community. (p. 1)

His exilic conditions notwithstanding, Baldwin finds a place to stand, a place from which he raises his voice in moral criticism of his home. "I love America more than any other country in the world," he writes, "and, exactly for this reason, I insist on the right to criticize her perpetually" (1984, p. 9).

Although his role as a spokesperson for the reform of racial relationships in the United States is today largely overshadowed by our memories of Martin Luther King, Jr., Malcolm X, Stokely Carmichael, and others, and although his role as a spokesperson for the reform of American sexual attitudes is often dismissed as half-hearted and timid, Baldwin was an eloquent and probative voice of conscience for a generation. On the occasion of Baldwin's death, Amiri Baraka (1987) wrote in the *New York Times*, "At the hot peak of the [Civil Rights] movement Jimmy was one of its truest voices" (Sec. 7, p. 27). It may be that the true value of that voice is only now being recognized. In a 1995 appreciation of Baldwin in the *Boston Book Review*, John Stevenson (1995) acknowledges that, while James Baldwin

> isn't much commented on these days . . . for a few years in the early 1960s he lit up the cultural landscape like a bolt from the heavens—a prophet of the decade's black liberation struggle who became one of the most widely read African American writers in this country's history.

"THE HARLEM GHETTO"

Baldwin is obsessed with place. "Even the most incorrigible maverick has to be born somewhere," he writes. "He may leave the group that produced him—he may be forced to—but nothing will efface his origins, the marks of which he carries with him everywhere" (Baldwin, 1993, p. 10). Baldwin's first two collections of essays, *Notes of a Native Son* and *Nobody Knows My Name: More Notes of a Native Son*, far from seeking to efface those marks of origin, embrace and highlight them, and many individual essays, in their titles, locate themselves: "The Harlem Ghetto," "Journey to Atlanta," "Encounter on the Seine," "Equal in Paris," "Fifth Avenue, Uptown," "East River, Downtown," "Down at the Cross: Notes From a Region of My Mind," Words of a Native Son." Baldwin's concern is always "the mores, morals, and morality of this particular and peculiar time and place" (Baldwin, 1985, p. 679).

Baldwin is obsessed with place because he is aware of its formative power. Although he is too subtle a thinker to commit the Burkean scenic, materialist fallacy whereby action is reduced to motion (Burke, 1969a, p. 131), Baldwin nonetheless recognizes the dominion of environment. Referring ostensibly to his own childhood, but in fact to his childhood as a synecdoche for all childhoods and especially for the childhoods of black Americans, Baldwin (1985) writes, "The fact that this particular child had been born when and where he was born had dictated certain expectations" (p. xvi):

> By and by older kids I knew finished school and got jobs and got married and settled down. They were going to settle down and bring more black babies into the world and pay the same rents for the same old shacks and it would go on and on. (p. 10)

The future perfect progressive—"They were going to settle down"—signals inexorability, a process already in motion, and "the same old shacks" signify the breeding ground, literally and figuratively, of conditions programmed to replicate themselves, an ineluctable circularity: "and it would go on and on." Geographical place overlays racial place: "All over Harlem, Negro boys and girls are growing into stunted maturity, trying desperately to find a place to stand" (Baldwin, 1985, p. 10). Harlem, "uptown," is Baldwin's most characteristic metonym for the place allowed blacks in the United States. "This is a white neighborhood, I don't rent to colored people," a landlady screams at Peter in "Previous Condition." "Why don't you go on uptown, like you belong?" (Baldwin, 1995, p. 91). It is during the summer of his fourteenth year that Baldwin realizes that he has been "produced by" the same circumstances that produced "the whores and pimps and racketeers on the Avenue" around him; that he "could become one of them" (1993b, p. 16); that he is at some level expected to; and that he will unless he finds a way out of this place. "The avenues, side streets, bars, billiard halls, hospitals, police stations, and even the playgrounds of Harlem—not to mention the houses of correction, the jails, and the morgue—testified to the potency of the poison" (1984, p. 106). Baldwin's circumstances, his society, his "poison" are the same as those that "produced and destroyed" Billie Holiday. That society "had not the faintest intention of producing her and it did not intend to destroy her; but it has managed to do both with the same bland lack of concern" (Baldwin, 1985, p. 178). It is the same society that created "the Negro leaders," "trapped as they are, in a no-man's-land between black humiliation and white power. They cannot move backward, and they cannot move forward either" (Baldwin, 1985, p. 260; see also

Baldwin, 1984, p. 59). It is the same society that "fixed bleak boundaries" to his father's life because of his father's blackness (Baldwin, 1984, p. 87). Baldwin's father is exemplary of the restrictive powers of place, their ability to circumscribe the exercise of personal power and talent. In a world in which public accommodations, public conveyances, and even drinking fountains and soft drink machines are segregated, the sin of racial trespass is always at hand. "Racist institutions," Baldwin (1985) declares, "—the unions, for one example, the Church, for another, and the Army—or the military—for yet another, are meant to keep the nigger in his place" (p. xvii; see also Baldwin, 1985, pp. 22, 320, 638, 671; Baldwin, 1993b, p. 85; Baldwin, 1993c, p. 81; Baldwin, 1995, pp. 97, 99-100).

The scenic impact of sexuality is not as prominent in Baldwin's writings as the scenic impact of race. Baldwin, like DuBois before him, views "the color line" as "the greatest moral and social problem" facing the United States (1993b, p. 103); he is absorbed with the opposition of "the black world" to "the white world," "a society mainly divided into black and white" (Baldwin, 1985, p. 179; see also Baldwin, 1993c, pp. 59, 63-65, 215). But Baldwin does acknowledge, when he moves from Harlem to Greenwich Village, that he suffered not only as a black man in a white world but as a "queer," a "pussy," a "faggot," whose existence "was the punch line of a dirty joke" (1985, p. 681). Sexual categories, especially the American construction of masculinity, are as limiting as racial categories (Baldwin, 1985, pp. 667-690; see also Baldwin, 1993c, pp. 155-162).

Often, race and sexuality, along with culture and nationality, are invoked "in a dizzying array of combinations" (Wright, 1999, p. 225), a discussion of one morphing into another or some conclusion regarding one broadening to incorporate the others. In speculating on the motives of white girls who go to bed with black men, for example—"to civilize you into becoming an appendage" or "to humiliate her parents"—Baldwin (1985) addresses the intricate dance of race and gender in the United States: "More than one white girl had already made me know that her color was more powerful than my dick" (p. 686).

It is, finally, about categories, the defining, restrictive, confining, delimiting, differentiating, sometimes debilitating structures in which we live. This is as much true for those dominant groups privileged to create the categories as it is for the powerless who become their hapless vassals. In what is ostensibly a review of "Porgy and Bess," Baldwin (1985) writes,

> The image one is compelled to hold of another person—in order, as I have said, to retain one's image of oneself—may become that

> person's trial, his cross, his death. It may or may not become his prison; but it inevitably becomes one's own. (p. 181)

White America, in its efforts to keep blacks in their place and to locate itself in distinction to that place, is trapped in the prison house of its own definitions. A fence or a wall prevents movement equally from both sides (Baldwin, 1985; see also Baldwin, 1985, pp. xvi, xx):

> Thus, what the house of bondage accomplished for what we will call the classic white American was the destruction of his moral sense, except in relation to whites. But it also destroyed his sense of reality and, therefore, his sense of white people had to be as compulsively one-dimensional as his vision of blacks. The result is that white Americans have been one another's jailers for generations. (pp. 672-673)

Place provides the footing for Baldwin's epistemology. What we (are allowed to) know depends on where we stand; "your sense of reality" depends on "where you find yourself in the world" (Baldwin, 1985, p. 403).

Powerful as place is in Baldwin's epistemology and his cosmology, it is not deterministic. Human agency is capable of transcending the places—geographical, racial, sexual, economic—to which we have been relegated by accident of birth and circumstance. "We do the things we do and feel what we feel essentially because we must," Baldwin (1985, p. 317) writes, testifying to scenic leverage, but the conclusion of the sentence sets up a Burkean contradiction between determinism and responsibility: "We are responsible for our actions, but we rarely understand them" (p. 317). Against puissant and inclement geographies, personal responsibility maintains a tenacious claim in Baldwin's thinking: "I was never entirely at the mercy of an environment at once hostile and seductive," he assures the reader in the introduction to his last published work, a compilation of his essays from 1948 to 1985, his valedictory collection (p. xi; see also Baldwin, 1984, p. xii). Sometimes, the very oppressiveness of place forces a choice between transcendence and annihilation. Baldwin (1993b; see also Baldwin, 1985, p. 305) recognizes clearly the nature of the choice:

> I was icily determined—more determined really, than I then knew never to make my peace with the ghetto but to die and go to Hell before I would let any white man spit on me, before I would accept my "place" in this republic. I did not intend to allow the white

> people of this country to tell me who I was, and limit me that way, and polish me off that way. (pp. 23-24)

"The world was bigger than the world they wanted me to live in," Baldwin writes (1995, p. 175). The fearful prohibition of his father notwithstanding, Baldwin transgresses the boundary that separates black aspirations from white: "I really *believed* I could do anything a white boy could do, and had every intention of proving it" (1993b, p. 26).

Baldwin's trespasses manifest themselves in four primary arenas. First, Baldwin, like DuBois before him, though not immediately a product of the American South, recognizes the provenance of African American culture in southern culture (Baldwin, 1993c; see also Baldwin, 1985, p. 398):

> Negroes in the North are right when they refer to the South as the Old Country. A Negro born in the North who finds himself in the South is in a position similar to that of the son of the Italian emigrant who finds himself in Italy, near the village where his father first saw the light of day. Both are in countries they have never seen, but which they cannot fail to recognize. (p. 98)

African American culture is exilic culture—from the African slave ships to the Underground Railroad, to the great migrations out of the South to northern industrial cities both early in the twentieth century and after the Second World War. This racial diaspora, beginning in slavery and moving toward freedom, provides both background and a model for Baldwin's personal emancipatory odyssey (Baldwin, 1993c, p. 84; see also Baldwin, 1985, p. 554). Second, Baldwin quits Harlem, "uptown," "the black world" and moves "downtown" into the white, then still largely Italian, world of Greenwich Village. Baldwin's life in the Village begins, significantly, at a very specific place, the apartment of Beauford Delany, 181 Greene Street (Baldwin, 1985, p. ix). Linked, temporally and psychologically, to the move from Harlem to the Village is Baldwin's decision to leave the pulpit, a decision he views as the betrayal of his role in the community (Baldwin, 1985, p. xvi). Abandoning the black community of Harlem and achieving only a limited acceptance in the white community, Baldwin finds himself without a home (Baldwin, 1985, p. xvi; see also Baldwin, 1995, pp. 99-100).

America's places are divided, starkly, into black and white, gay and straight, with no room for the uncomfortable ambiguities in between.

Therefore, as a black, gay man who refuses the places allowed black men and homosexuals in the United States, Baldwin must make his third migration, to Paris (Baldwin, 1985, pp. 307-313). It is in Paris that Baldwin finds a place open enough to allow him to dismantle the structures he has grown up with and to begin anew—a place large enough to allow the shedding of his "American confusion seeming to be based on the very nearly unconscious assumption that it is possible to consider the person apart from all the forces which have produced him" (Baldwin, 1984, p. 136). As adamant as Baldwin is about the reality of racial categories in particular and about their moral quality, it appears to be the effort of his fourth migration to arrive at a world without color, a world in which color is irrelevant. Baldwin (1985) celebrates the fact that "the people I love . . . cannot, usefully, be described as either black or white, they are like life itself, thank God, many colors" (pp. xvii-xviii). Of the habitues of the San Remo in Greenwich Village, he writes, "It seemed to me that I was no longer black for them and they had ceased to be white for me" (1985, p. 687; see also Baldwin, 1993b, p. 71). "Color is not a human or a personal reality," he declares, "it is a political reality" (1993b, p. 104).

Like DuBois before him, and consistent with his scumbling of racial categories, Baldwin exhibits a curious ability to speak in the voice of both polities: white America—"We (Americans in general, that is) like to point to Negroes and to most of their activities with a kind of tolerant scorn; but it is ourselves we are watching, ourselves we are damning or—condescendingly—bending to save" (Baldwin, 1985, p. 6; see also Baldwin, 1985, p. 20). Baldwin's first-person plural opposes "Negroes," and the third-person plural possessive "their" identifies Baldwin with a presumed white reader. "Our dehumanization of the Negro then is indivisible from our dehumanization of ourselves: The loss of our own identity is the price we pay for our annulment of his" (Baldwin, 1984, p. 25)—and black America—"There is not a Negro alive who does not have this rage in his blood," Baldwin broadly declares on the authority of his own blackness. "As for me, this fever has recurred in me, and does, and will until the day I die" (p. 94). "I picked cotton, I carried it to the market, I built the railroads under someone else's whip for nothing. For nothing," he proclaims, standing synecdochally for all black Americans, the Negro whose identity has been annulled (1985, p. 404).

Baldwin's racial transcendence involves a forsaking of his given places, which leaves him, temporarily, homeless, without any places at all, but it does not end there. Baldwin finds a new place, not his temporary refuge but a place that allows him to acknowledge, even embrace, his home at the same time that he adjusts his relationship to it (Baldwin, 1993c, pp. xii, 185; see also Dievler, 1999, pp. 165, 168; Wright, 1999, p. 212). In Michelle Wright's formulation,

> The transatlantic Subject's moment of forgetting is one that points not to the wholesale removal or erasure (however one might imagine it) of race but instead to a different frame of reference within which we can come to understand race (p. 216).
>
> He has not changed the structure of his transatlantic Subject; he is looking at it from another vantage point, from the point of view of the French—or more exactly, from the point of view of the American who comes to understand what it means to be an American by what is refracted back through his structures of meaning from the French point of view (Wright, 1999, p. 218).

As Baldwin (1993c; see also Baldwin, 1993c, p. 83) expresses it,

> The writer is meeting in Europe people who are not American, whose sense of reality is entirely different from his own. They may love or hate or admire or fear or envy this country—they see it, in any case, from another point of view, and this forces the writer to reconsider many things he had always taken for granted. (p. 9)

In order to see things as they are, Baldwin must first climb to the mountaintop, must spend his 40 days and 40 nights in the wilderness.

 "LETTER FROM A REGION IN MY MIND"

Although Baldwin cannot be released from place and, in fact, would not want to be, he consistently challenges his audience to realize that geographical place—and all the proscriptions, interdictions, and boundaries associated with it—holds only as much force as we allow it. Geographical place achieves sovereignty only in the absence of a secure, solid, spiritual inner place on which to stand, that is, only when one is not at home with oneself (Baldwin, 1995, p. 89). "The conquest of the physical world is not man's only duty," Baldwin reminds us. "He is also enjoined to conquer the great wilderness of himself" (p. 315), his "interior, uncharted chaos" (p. 318).

Just as the colored boundaries on a map of nations are the creation of the cartographer representing divisions that are more political and economic than geographical, exterior spaces are, in important ways, fictions (Harvey, 2000, p. 553). "You can *say* that," an exasperated Cass says to her husband Richard "—and in such a tone."

> She mimicked him: "Something women have dreamed up. But *I* can't say that—what men have 'dreamed up' is all there is, the world they've dreamed up *is* the world" (Baldwin, 1993a, p. 108).

In a world in which hegemonic ideologies are routinely exposed, articulated, deconstructed, and critiqued, it would be easy to dismiss Baldwin's insight of 40 years ago—that the world in which we live is the world as it has been created largely by white, Western European, heterosexual, Protestant men—but it would be presumptuous to do so. Baldwin's understanding is lived and practical, and he is able to supply the pathos missing from sterile theoretical formulations. Giving eloquent expression to internalized oppression, Baldwin (1985) writes,

> The object of one's hatred is never, alas, conveniently outside but is seated in one's lap, stirring in one's bowels and dictating the beat of one's heart. And if one does no know this, one risks becoming an imitation—and, therefore, a continuation—of principles one imagines oneself to despise. (p. 686)

In leaving the United States, Baldwin does not escape the forces that had kept him from knowing himself except through the lens of racism, economic elitism, and homophobia—"these forces had become interior and I had dragged them across the ocean with me"—but he is, through exile, at least able to separate the all-to-ready concurrence of place from his own self-abjuration and to begin to interrogate the latter. He finds himself "far freer in a strange land than he has ever been at home" (Baldwin, 1993b, p. 54; see also Baldwin, 1993c, p. xii; Baldwin, 1995, p. 149).

Baldwin brings us to a place that is essentially rhetorical, a place in which we must adjudicate the competing claims of the authority of the self against external realities. Although he argues that every person, especially those encumbered by oppression, must find his or her own place, his or her own "unshakable" authority (Baldwin, 1993b, p. 99) within, must confront "the necessity to remake the world in their own image" (Baldwin, 1993c, p. 29; see also Baldwin, 1993a, pp. 212, 220), Baldwin nevertheless allows that the object of this unshakable authority should be the determination of "what is really happening here." Those who find in Baldwin's essays only an "insistent subjectivity," a "personal drama" that sabotages the effectiveness of the essays as social commentary, do so only by ignoring an equally insistent ontology in Baldwin's writings (Anderson, 1998). Baldwin's identification with the form of the essay—the term "essay" with its etymological origins in weighing or balancing, its characteristic sense of exploration and exertion, and its highly personal style—is entirely consonant with his pilgrimage.

"THE TRUTH, AFTER ALL, IS THE TRUTH"

Baldwin the essayist struggles impressively and explicitly with this epistemological limbo, this incipient chaos. Describing the difficulties in coming to know the self, in finding the secure inner harbor, Baldwin (1985) writes of the high barrier "between oneself and one's knowledge of oneself":

> There are so many things one would rather not know! We become social creatures because we cannot live any other way. But in order to become social, there are a great many other things that we must not become, and we are frightened, all of us, of these forces within us that perpetually menace our precarious security. (p. 317)

This meditation on self-knowledge begins by providing the locus of struggle and defining the barriers, the boundaries that must be confronted in that struggle. The tension between our social selves, those selves that endorse their socially defined places, and our selves as individuals is an articulation of the tension between determinism and personal responsibility. Our fear of individualism at the expense of our "precarious security" is the fear of being alien, estranged, "alone"; it is the fear of homelessness (Baldwin, 1993a, pp. 44, 52, 60-61, 72, 78, 132, 172, 199, 290, 368). Baldwin (1985) continues:

> Yet the forces are there. We cannot will them away. All we can do is learn to live with them. And we cannot learn this unless we are willing to tell the truth about ourselves, and the truth about us is always at variance with what we wish to be. (p. 317)

It may be true that "the world in which people find themselves is not simply a vindictive plot imposed on them from above" (Baldwin, 1985, p. 155), that we helped to create it, but it is equally true that that world is not infinitely plastic and malleable. It makes irrefragable claims on us. Baldwin has no difficulty acknowledging facts. Even "extremely unattractive facts . . . *are* facts, and no purpose is served in denying them," he declares (1993c, p. 79; see also Baldwin, 1993c, pp. 76, 95). The failure "to look reality in the face diminishes a nation as it diminishes a person, and it can only be described as unmanly," he goads (1993c, p. 116), puncturing the racial delusions of both North and South. "The human effort," Baldwin concludes, "is to bring these two realities [the reality of human agency and freedom and the reality of the material world] into a relationship resembling reconciliation" (1985, p. 317). "I know that people can be better than they are," Baldwin avows. "We are capable of bearing a great burden, once we discover that the burden is reality and arrive where reality is" (1993b, p. 91). The circle is complete: We begin in an artificial and constricting social place, a system of definitions and categories designed to perpetuate the regnant order. To realize ourselves fully, we must escape this place; we must leave home, must refuse our place in the social order. This realization of self, however, requires an alternative foundation, some new place to stand, a view of reality unencumbered by social strictures.[1]

Baldwin the novelist occasionally uses his characters to play out the struggle that Baldwin the essayist presents to us. In his cruelest, most unsparing moments, Baldwin strips those characters of all but the most basal touchstones and leaves them there, naked, to stumble back toward a workable view of the world (Baldwin, 1993a):

> The coffeepot, now beginning to growl, was real, and the blue fire beneath it and the pork chops in the pan, and the milk which seemed to be turning sour in his belly. The coffee cups, as he thoughtfully washed them, were real, and the water which ran into them, over his heavy, long hands. Sugar and milk were real, and he set them on the table, another reality, and cigarettes were real, and he lit one. (p. 427)

His world shaken to the core, Vivaldo must start over from scratch; nothing can be assumed or taken for granted. It is a moment of liberation. It is also a moment of terrifying homelessness and personal struggle. "Any real change implies the breakup of the world as one has always know it, the loss of all that gave one an identity, the end of safety," Baldwin the creator moralizes (1993c, p. 117).

Baldwin's quest for a new place, as it turns inward, collapses the spatial and the temporal "in the beginning," the moment of origin, the point at which both time and space come into being (Baldwin, 1985):

> Go back to where you started, or as far back as you can, examine all of it, travel your road again and tell the truth about it. Sing or shout or testify to keep it to yourself: but *know whence you came*. (p. xix)

Echoing Emerson's epistemology, Baldwin (1993b) counsels his nephew James, "Take no one's word for anything, including mine—but trust your experience" (p. 8). "Know whence you came," he repeats (p. 8). Baldwin urges white Christians to recover the history of their role in racial oppression (p. 44), and he urges blacks to recover the history of "African kings and heroes" as a basis for "black pride" (p. 77). Among the things to be excavated and exorcised in this archaeology is an "inherited rage" in both races that defies experience and reason (Baldwin, 1993a, pp. 59, 61, 63, 67, 260). Moral authority cannot exist "in a country that had told so many lies about its history, that, in sober fact, has yet to excavate it history from the rubble of romance" (Baldwin, 1985, p. 222).

The narrative is familiar enough, especially to someone of Baldwin's Christian evangelical upbringing; it is the story of death, redemption, and resurrection. The deaths of Rufus in *Another Country* and of Giovanni in *Giovanni's Room* are literal, but for even more of Baldwin's characters, death is madness. "It was terrible, it drove me crazy," Eric tells Vivaldo in *Another Country* (Baldwin, 1993a, p. 335). And Cass, in the same novel, begins to think

> that growing just means learning more and more about anguish. That poison becomes our diet—you drink a little of it every day. Once you've seen it, you can't stop seeing it—that's the trouble. And it can, it can . . . drive you mad. (p. 405)

What Baldwin's characters most have in common is the need to empty the self, to die, before they can begin again. Baldwin himself goes mad, suffers "a species of breakdown," he calls it (1993c, p. 5). He provides a graphic statement of his relationship to his characters and their common madness when he writes of the artist, the demons, and the exorcism: "All art is a kind of confession, more or less oblique. All artists, if they are to survive, are forced, at last, to tell the whole story, to vomit the anguish up" (p. 179). This purging is as much a requirement in the lives of nations as it is in the lives of individuals, a "charged, . . . dangerous moment, when everything must be reexamined, must be made new; when nothing at all can be taken for granted" (Baldwin, 1985, p. 674).

"NOTES OF A NATIVE SON"

For Baldwin, the home of "the American Negro" must be sought in the United States, for "the Negro has been formed by this nation, for better or for worse, and does not belong to any other—not to Africa, and certainly not to Islam" (Baldwin, 1993b, p. 81; see also Baldwin, 1993b, p. 84; Baldwin, 1995, p. 167). Baldwin (1984) writes,

> And despite the terrorization which the Negro in America endured and endures sporadically until today, despite the cruel and totally inescapable ambivalence of his status in his country, the battle for his identity has long ago been won. He is not a visitor to the West, but a citizen there, an American; as American as the Americans who despise him, the Americans who fear him, the Americans who love him—the Americans who became less than themselves, or rose to be greater than themselves by virtue of the fact that the challenge he represented was inescapable. (p. 173)

"The American Negro," Baldwin insists, "deludes himself if he imagines himself capable of any loyalty other than his loyalty to the United States. He is an American, too, and he will survive or perish with the country" (1993c, p. 78; see also Baldwin, 1984, p. 42).

America's Emersonian newness is both its problem and its promise in Baldwin's estimation. On the one hand, that newness manifests itself as "relentless" parochialism and immaturity (Baldwin, 1985, p. 259). "This isn't a country at all," Cass complains to Eric. "It's a collection of football players and Eagle Scouts" (Baldwin, 1993a, p. 406; see also Baldwin, 1985, p. 673). America's newness and immaturity manifest themselves as instability and a consequent uneasiness regarding placement, what Richard Hofstadter called "status anxiety." In Baldwin's (1985) rendering,

> In America . . . life seems to move faster than anywhere else on the globe and each generation is promised more than it will get: which creates, in each generation, a furious, bewildered rage, the rage of people who cannot find solid ground beneath their feet. (p. 10)

America's embrace of "equality" as an ideal—even if, in reality, it may be only an equality in "misery, confusion, and despair" (Baldwin, 1993a, p. 301)—and its historical eschewal of class lines has led, Baldwin (1993c) observes, to the problem of status in American life: "Where everyone has status [Latin, *status*: a standing or position], it is also perfectly possible, after all, that no one has. It seems inevitable, in any case, that a man may become uneasy as to just what his status is" (p. 7). Insecurity and anxiety over status foster the motive for the creation, in the United States, of strict, stark categories—racial, sexual, and social (Baldwin, 1985, p. 672; Wright, 1999, p. 223)—and this insecurity and anxiety account for, in Baldwin's view, the exalted place of "property," geographical place as a surrogate for social place, in the American pantheon (Baldwin, 1985, p. 679).

On the other hand, even as we struggle to impose boundaries and build fences, this "fragrant, booming benevolent confusion called the Republic" (Baldwin, 1985, p. 14) is, precisely to the degree that it is inchoate, pregnant with potential (Baldwin, 1993c):

> American writers do not have a fixed society to describe. The only society they know is one in which nothing is fixed and in which the individual must fight for his identity. This is a rich confusion, indeed, and it creates for the American writer unprecedented opportunities. (p. 11)

This is true not only for the American writer but for all Americans. America is, in Emerson's phrase "always in the process of becoming." There is, in the United States, the opportunity, unparalleled anywhere in the world, or at least in the West, for "the creation of a new people in this still-new world" (Baldwin, 1985, p. 262; see also Baldwin, 1993c, pp. 93-94, 105-106, 214). Our anxiety over categories is precisely proportional to their amorphousness. Forty years ago, Baldwin tried to tell America something many refused to face until the wholesale corporate layoffs of the 1980s, something many refuse to face even today—that all across this country "there were boys and girls drinking coffee at the drugstore counters who were held back from [homelessness] by barriers as perishable as their dwindling cigarettes" (Baldwin, 1993a, p. 4). Although Baldwin's paramount division, when he is writing about domestic issues, is racial (see Baldwin, 1993c, pp. 13-55), in a lengthy essay on the 1956 Conference of Negro-African Writers and Artists held in Paris, he sets Africa and Europe in opposition with the United States occupying an ill-defined, nebulous third place and no consideration at all of Asia or Latin and South America.

The United States is Baldwin's place, his home, the ground from which he stakes out his argumentative positions, not the United States as it is empirically but the United States as it is in its ideals (Baldwin,

1985, p. 262). Baldwin challenges the American ideal of equality, daring it to overcome its opportunistic and nostalgic tendencies to measure all things against a false European idea of whiteness and to become instead truly cosmopolitan (Baldwin, 1985, pp. 406-407, 432, 669-670). Baldwin's vision of the dissolution of borders and the end of Western empire—"of the black and nonwhite peoples who are shattering, redefining, and recreating history—making all things new" (Baldwin, 1985, p. 673)—has proved to be astonishingly prescient. It is the destiny of the United States—because the United States is "the issue of the entire globe" (Baldwin, 1985, p. 679) and because the United States is, even now, the "new world," relatively pliable, relatively unencrusted with the barnacles of class or other hierarchies—to show the way in this postmodern, postcolonial reordering of the world. "We can make America what America must become" (Baldwin, 1993b, p. 10). American equality must, finally, be an equality of freedom, not a procrustean conformity (p. 16).

"AN HONEST MAN AND A GOOD WRITER"

The apparent paradox with which Baldwin presents us, the need to go into exile in order to discover himself—himself as an American in particular—is, in fact, no more paradoxical than the shibboleth "American individualism," indicating as this phrase does the solitary soul within a specific cultural context. Baldwin imagines himself as a participant in "the lonely activity of the singular intelligence on which the cultural life—the moral life—of the West depends" (Baldwin, 1993c, p. 26). The ethos he cultivates is that of the lonely cosmopolitan, not Nietzsche's superman unleashed, but rather more like Prometheus suffering for his dedication to humankind (Darsey, 1999, p. 189). Baldwin mourns the fact that Richard Wright "found himself wandering in a no man's land" without a platform from which to instruct America (Baldwin, 1993c, p. 215), and he chastises Norman Mailer for refusing the opportunity to help "excavate the buried consciousness of this country" (p. 238). The recovery of the standard of human freedom with which America began "demands of everyone who loves this country a hard look at himself," Baldwin counsels, "for the greatest achievements must begin somewhere, and they always begin with the person" (p. 116). "It took many years of vomiting up all the filth I'd been taught about myself, and half-believed, before I was able to walk the earth as though I had a right to be here," he reflects (1985, p. 227).

Baldwin calls for a Heidiggerean authentic self, but authentic in a way, that while it does not surrender to the "theyself," recognizes its provenance in and responsibility to a culture. It is the same dialectic reflected in the novel *Trans-Atlantyk* by Witold Gombrowicz, a Pole who found himself exiled in Argentina at the outset of the Second World War. In his introduction to *Trans-Atlantyk*, Stanislaw Baranczak (1994) writes of Gombrowicz's conception of the individual "suspended between the external ideas of Form and Chaos, between total subordination of the ego to the generally accepted patterns of behavior, logic, language, and so forth, and total liberation from all that is inherited or imitated" (p. xi). For Baldwin, as for Gombrowicz, total subordination is escaped, literally, by leaving home to see home more clearly—to, through experience in another culture, another landscape, separate the appurtenances of home from its essentials (Baldwin, 1985, p. 312). When Baldwin is arrested in Paris, he is somewhat shocked to realize that he is treated not as a black man nor as a gay man but as an American, unhappily "equal" to any other American in the same circumstances (Baldwin, 1984, pp. 146, 152). However unhappy this set of circumstances, his treatment reveals the provinciality, the contingency and arbitrariness, of certain American categories—race and sexuality in particular—as they are used to justify the differential treatment of American citizens in America.

The moral authority Baldwin seeks—an authority based on the "flesh, the defeats endured, disasters passed, and triumphs won" of those who possess it, "the only authority that endures" (Baldwin, 1985, p. 222)—is demanding and athletic. It requires that we forego the easy formulae and pat categories of the past (Baldwin, 1985, pp. 308, 689; see also Baldwin, 1993b, p. 68; Baldwin, 1993c, p. xiii)—that we come to the realization that "not many things in the world [are] really black, not even the night, not even the mines. And the light [is] not white either, even the palest light [holds] within itself some hint of its origins, in fire" (Baldwin, 1993a, p. 430). Baldwin's moral authority requires that we embrace the freedom entailed in ambiguity (Baldwin, 1985, p. 322; see also Baldwin, 1993c, p. 116), and in ways entirely consistent with the existentialist thinking prominent in Baldwin's time, it requires that we embrace the personal responsibility, the moral choices, that are the indissoluble burden of that freedom (Baldwin, 1993b, pp. 81, 90, 92; see also Baldwin, 1993c, p. 10; Dupee, 1986, p. 11). Old categories cannot be maintained in a world in which boundaries are disappearing. Western culture is remaking the world in its own image: "From the point of view of power," Westerners "cannot be . . . strangers anywhere in the world" (Baldwin, 1984, p. 165).

Most important, and most germane to Baldwin's vocation as a writer, the morality he seeks demands a new vocabulary, especially a new vocabulary of place. "Anyone who is trying to be conscious must begin to be conscious of that apathy and must begin to dismiss the vocabulary which we've used so long to cover it up, to lie about the way things are," Baldwin (1985, pp. 400-401) counsels his audience in 1964. "Safe streets," as in the Nixon-era Safe Streets Act, must be exposed as one of many euphemisms for "keep the nigger in his place" (p. 671). A new vocabulary must be able to express equality without invoking the false American ideal that "everyone should be as much alike as possible" (p. 6). If segregation along racial and other capricious lines cannot be countenanced, neither is absolute integration either feasible or desirable. Definition cannot be forsaken altogether without sacrificing the individual—the seat, for Baldwin, of all genuine knowledge—to chaotic, formless homogeneity; therefore, new ways of talking about position, status, rank, propriety, must be invented. "Equality" must come to mean that a black man or black woman can be black and still have access to all of the places to which white men and women have access. A false ideal of masculinity must be liberated from the chains of its own forging, opening opportunities for women and gay men, and for heterosexual men as well (Baldwin, 1985, pp. 678-683).

The invention of this new vocabulary, this new language, is at the heart of Baldwin's project. At the time of Baldwin's death, Amiri Baraka (1987) wrote, "Jimmy Baldwin was the creator of contemporary American speech even before Americans could dig that" (Sec. 7, p. 27). As part of the same tribute, Toni Morrison (1987) employed the following apostrophe, elaborating Baraka's assessment:

> You made American English honest—genuinely international. You exposed its secrets and reshaped it until it was truly modern, dialogic, representative, humane. You stripped it of ease and false comfort and fake innocence and evasion and hypocrisy. And in place of deviousness was clarity. In place of soft plump lies was a lean, targeted power. In place of intellectual disingenuousness and what you called "exasperating egocentricity," you gave us undecorated truth. You replaced lumbering platitudes with an upright elegance. You went into that forbidden territory and decolonized it. (Sec. 7, p. 27)

An international and decolonized speech, a contemporary speech appropriate to a world witnessing the breakup of Western empire (Baldwin,

1985, p. 673), a speech capable of disabusing America of its European pretensions and of expressing America's genuinely cosmopolitan nature (p. 432)—Baldwin the novelist has a conception of poesis that is ancient and almost mystical.

In the contemporary world, especially among "first-world" cultures, poetry no longer leads revolutions. It has, in Archibald MacLeish's famous expression, been reduced to the status of housecat. Baldwin's critics accused him of subordinating his artistry to didacticism, testifying to the rhetorical power of his work, and although he always referred to himself as a novelist, it seems likely that the essays will constitute the most enduring and important part of his legacy. In whatever form he works, however, Baldwin understands the profundity of the change he is fomenting; he understands that "a total revision of the ways in which Americans see the Negro" necessitates "a total revision of the ways in which Americans see themselves" (Baldwin, 1985, p. 216). In the aftermath of the Montgomery bus boycott, Baldwin observed not only the "cold hostility" but also the mystification and deep hurt of white people in Montgomery:

> They had been betrayed by the Negroes, not merely because the Negroes had declined to remain in their "place," but because the Negroes had refused to be controlled by the town's image of them. And, without this image, it seemed to me, the whites were abruptly and totally lost. The very foundations of their private and public worlds were being destroyed. (p. 249)

The myths that have sustained us for too long must be rewritten (Baldwin, 1985, p. 383). There must be a new idiom for talking about "home," one that salves the "spiritual disaster [of] those homeless Europeans who now call themselves Americans and who have never been able to resolve their relationship either to the continent they fled or to the continent they conquered" (p. 382) and at the same time recognizes at last the rightful place of black Americans in this homeland:

> Until the moment comes when we, the Americans, are able to accept the fact that my ancestors are both black and white, that on that continent we are trying to forge a new identity, that we need each other, that I am not a ward of America, I am not an object of missionary charity, I am one of the people who built the country—until this moment comes there is scarcely any hope for the American dream. (p. 407)

In his essay "Notes on the House of Bondage," published in 1980 near the end of his productive career, Baldwin (as cited in Baldwin, 1985; see also Balfour, 1999, pp. 75-99) provides an elegant summary of his mission:

> The irreducible miracle is that we have sustained each other a very long time, and come a long, long way together. We have come to the end of a language and are now about the business of forging a new one. For we have survived, children, the very last white country the world will ever see. (p. 675)

Baldwin is a man struggling to find his way home, using a map that resolutely denies that such a place exists, negotiating a geography that changes even as he traverses it. In this way, he is very much like all of us at the beginning of the new millennium. Baldwin, whose ethical ground rests in lived, personal experience, who reads particular events as symptoms of overarching conditions, is a synecdoche for the dislocation and disorientation of contemporary American culture. Being all that society denies and denigrates, he contains all that society embraces and values. Yet, amid change and confusion, Baldwin manages to maintain his moral bearings. He is able to talk about placement, including its prescriptive implications, its proprieties and improprieties, without provincial pieties.

Baldwin loved the United States, not as the white, Anglo-Saxon, Puritan Protestant culture it fashioned itself to be but as the cosmopolis it is in fact, and he sought a language capable of encompassing and celebrating that diversity. Addressing the United States in the 1950s and 1960s, Baldwin anticipated the state of the world half a century later. How can we make moral arguments that have universal force? How can we order the world in ways that are respectful of local differences? In 1996, the U.S. Congress passed into law the Federal Prohibition of Female Genital Mutilation Act of 1995, making criminal an ancient Muslim religious rite. In Colorado, a proposed change to the state's child abuse law would subject Christian Scientists who pray rather than seek medical attention for a child to criminal prosecution if the child suffers harm as a result of the "neglect." The Boy Scouts of America is under pressure from many quarters to allow openly gay boys and men to serve in the positions of Scouts and gay Scout leaders. On the world scene, former Yugoslavian President Slobodan Milosevic made his first appearance before the World Court in the Hague where he is to be tried before an international panel of jurists for crimes against humanity. Milosevic refused to enter any plea, denying the authority of the court. The world today cries out for new ways to talk about place, new ways to take positions. James Baldwin's cosmopolitan rhetoric provides some *topoi* worth consideration in our postmodern, postcolonial time.

NOTE

1. With this line of thinking, Baldwin anticipates debates among postmodernists regarding the collapse of the autonomous subject and the possibilities for human agency within the matrices of language, ideology, and the ascendancy of the commodified object and the spectacle.

2

Ingenium—Speaking in Community

The Case of the Prince William County Zoning Hearings on Disney's America

Kathryn M. Olson and G. Thomas Goodnight

Writing of his era of globalization, John Dewey (1927) wondered how American communities would survive the intervention of far-flung forces into the locally based deliberations of democratic civic culture. Despairing of the "great community," he found the public sphere—the crucial realm of citizen deliberation—to be fragmented, if not in a permanent state of decline. Our own time of globalization beckons similar reflection, as a vast congeries of national events and global interests test the capacity of local communities to initiate and sustain deliberations critical to community life. Indeed, the term *community* usually summons associations of unity and shared identification more easily than those of division and struggle. Actual communities, however, periodically experience unavoidable controversy, sometimes divisive enough to threaten their future viability. In a real-life community, rhetorics of unity and division intimately coexist and must be negotiated ingeniously if the community is to survive and thrive. Consequently, these complementary dynamics need to be appreciated, simultaneously and without subordinating one to the other. This essay examines the "vernacular" discourse—the speech of everyday rhetoricians called to the public platform as citizens of a community—to engage the uniquely textured discursive give-and-take of local communities (Goldzwig, 1998). As such, we take up Gerald Hauser's (1999) call to explore "vernacular exchanges" in which "rhetorically engaged actors deliberate over social, political, and cultural issues" (p. 88). The public hearings of September 10, 1994, featuring the speeches of citizens before the Prince William County Zoning Board, offer a site of vernacular discourse where the forces of global interests are instantiated in debates affecting the future of local community and, we contend, local citizens successfully enacted ingenious deliberation in self-fashioning a civic culture.

The case we examine was initiated by a controversy that rocked the nation but had high firsthand stakes for one local community: the Disney's America project. Late in 1993, Disney announced its plans to "create a unique and historically detailed environment celebrating the nation's richness of diversity, spirit, and innovation," a theme park designed to be "an ideal complement to visiting Washington's museums, monuments, and national treasures" ("Plans Unveiled," 1993). Thus, a plot of land in the vicinity of the Bull Run battlefield became the focus of powerful institutions that used all available means to influence local choice. Prince William County became a community struggling at once to demarcate lines between work and play, growth and preservation, and indigenous culture and global tourism. The proposed Disney project portended life-altering changes, both opportunities and risks, for residents of Prince William County, and the local planning commission was positioned to either block or facilitate Disney's grand plan via its zoning decisions. Individual community members shared a desire to act in Prince William County's best interest but were of strong and divided opinions on which course actually promoted that common goal.

Publicists from Los Angeles, Washington, and New York had upped the stakes of this site as a key contest in the culture wars. A vote for Disney was a vote for jobs, progress, tourism, and growth; a vote against was for class, "authentic" heritage, history, tradition, and "not in my backyard" visions opposing sprawl. Not only were the entertainment industry and the academy at odds and generating national publicity but also not all local citizens shared similar attitudes toward history, comparable economic status or interests within the community, purposes for dwelling in Prince

William County, or appreciations of Civil War history. For local residents, the stakes could not have been higher. The proposed $650 million, 3,000-acre project would substantially alter the way of life for residents of that county, as would publicly rejecting development offered by such an internationally visible company. Anticipated was a 400-acre theme park, as many as 6,000 housing units, 1,300 hotel rooms, 2 million square feet of commercial space, a water park, a campground, and golf courses—together attracting 6 million tourists a year and providing 19,000 local jobs (Kotz & Abramson, 1997). Audiotapes of approximately 16 hours of public hearings at which Prince William County residents deliberated their shared future before the local planning commission provide an extraordinary chance to analyze the vernacular discourse of a community negotiating unity and division as it struggled with a critical shared decision; community members testified fully knowing that, whatever the final outcome, they would need to continue their daily interactions with one another.

The debate among Prince William residents on September 10 resembles what Amy Gutman and Dennis Thompson (1996) identified as a "deliberative disagreement." Of course, the situation invites civic discourse: a public forum, a choice of future action, and an impending democratically derived, legally binding decision. Deliberative disagreement ensues, however, when citizens "differ not only about the right resolution but also about the reasons on which the conflict should be resolved" (p. 73). The spoken differences regarding the shared future featured alternative orders of moral premises within the community, some prioritizing jobs or the education of youth and others promoting a traditional way of life or reverence for the dead. Such contention, Gutman and Thompson assert, is likely "irresolvable" both because rejection of one set of values cannot be shown to be preferable and because the claims are incompatible and their assertion and defense may fragment the community. This debate provides a third outcome. Under pressure, local citizens found a way to articulate difference and to strengthen the life of their own civic culture through engaged argument (as distinct from Gutman and Thompson's suggestion that predicates norms of reciprocity on the weaker stance of respect due to "uncertainty" that one's own view is correct [p. 79]). This local community debate among ordinary, untrained rhetors deliberating their common future was a success by virtue of the *ingenium* of its participants, who found ways to resist the stereotypes of growth and no growth offered by publicists. Throughout the debate, citizens ingeniously found ways to articulate difference while enacting common decency through a discourse of reciprocal respect for fellow members of the greater Prince William community, which in this high-stakes, contentious debate appeared both as a prerequisite for deliberative address and as a remarkable collective achievement. Occasionally, the importance of ingenuity has been recognized within the rhetorical tradition. We suggest that it be reconsidered as a critical springboard for examining discursive communities rather than limited to its familiar role in oratorical pedagogy.

UNDERSTANDING INGENIUM AS A CRITICAL RATHER THAN PEDAGOGICAL CONCEPT

Surveying rhetorical scholarship, ingenium has been treated primarily as a lesser cousin of "invention." Plato's *Phaedrus* (p. 269) declared that rhetorical perfection necessarily required three elements: knowledge, practice, and natural power. Perhaps invention received the lion's share of attention because it was positioned early as a realm of organized, teachable commonplaces, *topoi*, *stases*, and modes of proof. As a canon, invention was the centerpiece of rhetoric's system of knowledge. Would-be orators could be armed with this system of how to generate arguments and their exercise of it honed through rigorous practice using its principles. This teachable system of knowledge, paired with the warning of the necessity for much practice, was a marketable *techne* or *ars* that could be packaged into lessons or treatises, sold, and its delivery verified (Clark, 1957, p. 5). As inventional systems and treatises proliferated, they eclipsed the importance of that indispensable but more elusive third leg of the triad: natural gift or faculty of ingenium.

Although Vico claimed that one's innate faculty of ingenium—quick wit, genius, and immediate sensitive and intellectual perception of unspoken relationships—may be coached via models and practice in the simultaneous exercise of "memory, imagination, and perception" (McKeon, 1973, p. 203), it cannot be captured effectively in, or taught as a skill via, a methodological system. Ingenium is "free" and so can be cultivated through exercises and practice but "opposes itself always to constraint" (Hidalgo-Serna, 1983, p. 235). Instead, ingenium has proved stubbornly concrete and localized, a current of discovery and creativity that cannot be reduced to (McKeon, 1973)

> a philosophy established by consensus concerning the nature of things, the powers or faculties of thought, the devices of arts, or the

> meanings or warrants of statements. It must be a pluralistic philosophy which establishes a creative interplay of philosophies inventing their facts, their data, their methods, their universes. (p. 207)

Ingenium's brand of practical "active" and original knowing, "whose common denominator is *inventio*, . . . emerges as a creative and essential answer that fills out the empty space of disorder. The immediate and existential character of necessity forces man to set his inventive activity in motion" (Hidalgo-Serna, 1983, p. 230). Ingenium insists on ambiguity; McKeon (1973) writes,

> The great problem of creativity is "creativity" itself. It is a commonplace, a meaningless word which assumes clear and fixed meanings in well-known commonplaces that express what everybody knows about it, or which preserves a productive systematic ambiguity from which new insights may be derived and new consequences constructed. (p. 208)

Perhaps because it cannot be contained systematically and effectively taught via abstract reason, ingenium is no more acknowledged now than it was in earlier times (Hidalgo-Serna, 1983, pp. 228, 230).

Although ingenium is still not teachable as a system to potential orators, the concept holds unrealized promise for rhetorical critics, especially those interested in examining the ordinary discourses of technically untrained, unpracticed rhetors thrust by necessity into public speaking situations. According to its accumulated formal definitions, ingenium refers to an inherent quality, natural ability or talent, or a certain cleverness, skill, or ingenuity; it implies a natural disposition, subtle inclination or mode of thinking, and a faculty for genius ("Ingenium," 1907, 1968). As Donald Lemen Clark (1957) summarized, ingenium mentally encompasses the imagination, intelligence, memory, and language aptitude that make for oratorical success; morally, it includes courage, prudence, justice, and temperance (pp. 4-5). Ingenium rests not on the knowledge of and ability to apply an abstract system but on the "'ingenious' grasping of resemblances and correspondences [that] is the essence of invention and is the indispensable element in rhetoric" (Hidalgo-Serna, 1983, p. 237). Thus, the concept of ingenium offers critical entrance into the meaningful inspection of vernacular eloquence born of commitment and circumstance rather than training.

In addition to its potential to show itself in untrained, unpracticed rhetors, ingenium is an appropriate rhetorical concept through which to view local community discourse because such discussions are often forced by outside necessity rather than initiated by the rhetors. The investment of ingenium's peculiar keenness or sharpness or acumen in invention originates in necessity because it relies on pressures emerging from the relative, the concrete, and the special (Hidalgo-Serna, 1983, pp. 228-229, 232, 236). In the crucible of community crisis, ingenium alone may be available to help individual community members muster their best arguments. Serna (1980) notes that "the imaginative and metaphorical language [that] proceeds from the fertility of ingenium . . . is dynamic, suggestive, and plastic. It directly stimulates the wheels of imagination and creativity in the human spirit" (p. 260). In so doing, ingenious concepts reexpress "the related, the individual, the relative, and the concrete," promoting comprehension that might evade or reject rationality's laws (Serna, 1980, p. 259). The rhetor exhibiting ingenium "digs with difference, and thinks that perhaps there is more than he first assumes; in such a fashion that the reflection arrives at a place where perception does not" (Gracián as cited in Serna, 1980, p. 252). Sometimes, admirable invention and its sought-after companion, eloquence, emerge from original conditions of disorder or necessity (Hidalgo-Serna, 1983, p. 229).

Third, in addition to focusing on uncoached imaginative rhetorical acts that are compelled by necessity, ingenium fits rhetorical criticism of local community discourse well because it inherently involves cultivating relationships and arguments. Ingenium is as open and nonabsolute as it is inventive. The "faculty of making new inventions, which are essential to satisfying human needs, belongs to ingenium and not to reason," wrote Hidalgo-Serna (1983, p. 230). Furthermore, the human needs that ingenium satisfies are not those that occur in isolation but those in relationships. Consequently, ingenium may better explain discourse in which preserving the fabric of one's community for the long term is as important as advocating one's individual preference passionately in the pressing controversy at hand. Hidalgo-Serna explained:

> [C]reativity in society and in the arts has its roots in a two-sided "ingenious" perception of relations and resemblance. At first man perceives the resemblance between his own experience of necessity and the necessities of his fellow human beings, who are similar to him. Second, it is *similitudo* that makes this possible; because human beings are connected through a commonality of situation (*communio rerum*), one can draw a comparison between one's own experience and that of other human beings. . . . The actual work of

> a keen *ingenium* is to go to the perception, "to direct attention to all things, to gather them together, and to arrange them among themselves." This "ingenious" grasping of resemblances and correspondences is the essence of invention and is the indispensable element in rhetoric. (p. 237)

Through images that evoke "living visions of similarities," ingenium in action thus appreciates "the most varied and distant relationships" not only among objects and ideas but also "between individual beings" (Serna, 1980, p. 260). The Disney's America hearings richly illustrate community members sensually sharing their experiences of Prince William County in ways that connect them meaningfully to others' experiences, clarifying personal similarities and argumentative positions in ways that promote community affiliation without insisting on homogeneity. Mooney (1985) noted that

> through the activity of the senses and imagination, our encounter with external realities is made into an experience; things acquire sensual and imaginative forms and so become real for us. Within this encounter, the work of ingenuity is the critical activity, giving unity to our experience and so making us truly aware of it. (p. 152)

Ingenium can enfold the "array of multiple discursive moments" on a shared concern that characterize vernacular discourse (Ono & Sloop, 1995, p. 34).

Finally, ingenium is relevant to rhetorical criticism of community discourse by virtue of its insistence that understanding, not only of ideas and experiences but also of one another, accompany advocacy. Following Gracián, Serna (1980) elaborated that ingenium involves the "'courage to understand,' whose victory is represented through 'that which is understood' (the concept). In this *understanding* we see the philosophical meaning of *ingenium* as a faculty which links one man cognitively with others and with the natural world" (p. 251). For Gracián, ingenium is "judgment's" reciprocal partner in forming "understanding" (Serna, 1980, pp. 249-251). Likewise, Vico asserted that ingenium, a "faculty of bringing together things that are disparate and widely separated" (as cited in Mooney, 1985, p. 151), is judgment's synthetic counterpart in generating "understanding." This emphasis on inventively balancing a unifying dynamic with analytically taking apart qualifies ingenium as critical equipment for apprehending and evaluating community discourse. With ingenium now resituated with an emphasis on rhetorical criticism rather than pedagogy, we sketch the larger situation of necessity that prompted Prince William County community members to speak and then analyze the contours of the local hearings that reveal ingenium in action in the service of community.

CONTOURS OF A MOUNTING CONTROVERSY

On November 11, 1993, Disney announced the advent of its new theme park, Disney's America, to be located in the Virginia countryside near several Civil War battlefields and just 30 miles west of Washington, D.C. (Turner, 1993, p. A2). The park's stated aim was to entice visitors to the Washington/Virginia area to include day trips to Disney's America in their plans; consequently, this theme park's conception and development would differ from those of Disney's existing "total destination resort" parks in California and Florida (Turner, 1993, p. A8). The theme for the park was geared to the location: American history. Disney proposed to bring the nation's past to life by making history as engaging for all ages as its EPCOT Center had made science. Promotional material (Achenbach, 1993) predicted that

> the wizardry of Disney's CIRCLEVISION 360 technology will transport visitors into the center of Civil War combat; outside, they may encounter an authentic re-enactment of a period battle or gather along Freedom Bay for a thrilling nighttime spectacular based on the historic confrontation between the Monitor and the Merrimac. (p. C3)

Disney cited the area's historicity as a reason for locating such a park at the former site of the Waverly Plantation in Prince William County; Disney Design and Development's Peter Rummell claimed that the area's "historical significance and proximity to Washington makes this the perfect home" for a historical theme park (as cited in Sloan, 1993, p. D1).

Virginia's Republican Governor-elect George F. Allen learned of Disney's plans for his state while on vacation at Disney World as his family unwound from the election campaign (Harris, 1993). He was thrilled. In the midst of Florida's version of the Magic Kingdom, Governor Allen (as cited in Singletary & Hsu, 1993) commented, "I think it'll be a money-maker for the state. Our administration will certainly kick down any hurdles" to Disney's proposed development (p. A18). Outgoing Governor L. Douglas Wilder (as cited in Singletary & Hsu, 1993) concurred: "We didn't have to bid for this. That's a rare, rare thing. How gratifying that Disney didn't subject us to a bidding war" (p. A18). Likewise, Prince William County officials promised to put Disney's proposal on a "fast-track zoning process" to be completed by July 1994 in time for Disney to begin construction by mid-1995 and open in 1998; this plan would collapse a process that normally takes at least 2 years into 6 months (Hsu, 1993a, p. A18).

Not willing to rely on its reputation and Allen's largess, Disney left few stones unturned in its effort to ensure success by garnering support and quelling opposition from all quarters. The company already had acquired the bulk of the land for the development—including the largest section from a defunct Exxon real estate venture (Eisner & Schwartz, 1998, p. 321)—using pseudonyms to avoid driving up property prices or arousing resistance to selling to a large corporation that intended to put a theme park there (Hilzenrach, 1993a, 1993b; Singletary & Hsu, 1993). It made sizable donations to organizations that were likely to oppose a Disney historical theme park at the Virginia location, such as the Association for the Preservation of Civil War Sites (Hsu, 1994i). Likewise, Disney neutralized the opposition of local and high-profile national historians, Civil War reenactment buffs, and ethnic minority leaders by hiring them as "consultants," purportedly to make Disney's portrayal of history as "authentic" as possible (Heller, 1994; Hsu, 1994f). In addition, the company retained Beveridge & Diamond, the first large Washington law firm to dedicate its practice to environmental law, and hired an adviser rated by an environmentalist publication as the "most influential man in America on the drafting of [environmental] legislation" (Hsu, 1994e, p. D3). In the Virginia General Assembly and in Washington, Disney practiced "saturation lobbying" to overcome national and regional barriers to the development. According to Charles Lewis, director of the Center for Public Integrity, Disney was "basically hiring Rolodexes" to push for approval on every front (as cited in Hsu, 1994e, p. D3).

Despite Disney's power, publicists, and pockets, controversy regarding the project could not be avoided entirely. Throughout the nation and the region, public debate raged over numerous issues. Some opponents were concerned about the development's negative impact on the environment and quality of life due to sharply increasing traffic on routes already loaded with Washington, D.C., commuters, promoting an upsurge of visitors to the relatively rural area, and precipitating the kind of surrounding "schlock" development that followed in Disney World's and Disneyland's wake (Odum, 1993). The Piedmont Environmental Council, whose members and major donors included heirs to the du Pont, Mellon, and Firestone fortunes as well as Knight-Ridder publishing heir Marie Ridder, Virginia Senator John W. Warner, and former first lady Jacqueline Onassis, announced a fund-raising goal of $1 million to fight Disney's America (Hsu, 1994e). The 18,000-member nonprofit American Farmland Trust, which enjoyed financial support from the Rockefeller family and the Ford and Richard King Mellon foundations, joined the forces arrayed against Disney (Hsu, 1994g). Some opponents focused on the trade-off between the economic boost Disney development brings and the exploitation of the workers or community created by Disney's usual demands for tax breaks, its propensity to create mostly low-skilled, low-paying jobs, and its drain on shared community resources (Hsu, 1994d).

Another topic hotly disputed was whether a historical theme park would desecrate the nearby battlefield sites and history through "Disneyfication" or whether this was a positive means for getting American children more interested in history (Twomey, 1993; Yardley, 1993). Submerged beneath the issue of this park's implications for American history was a broader dispute about the general propriety and "authenticity" of various possible tourist experiences. Well-heeled organizations, such as the Environmental Defense Fund and the Sierra Club, joined forces with existing preservationist groups such as the Save the Battlefield Coalition, which had blocked the development of a regional shopping mall near Manassas in 1988, and well-respected intellectuals such as filmmaker Ken Burns, who produced the landmark "The Civil War" documentary series for public television. Notable historians led by David McCullough, a Pulitzer Prize-winning historian and narrator of "The Civil War" television series, formed the Protect Historic America group specifically to squelch the Disney's America project (Baker, 1994a, p. D5; Bradley, 1994; "Film Maker," 1994; Hsu, 1993b, 1994i). As consumer advocate Ralph Nader observed of the national pro-Disney/anti-Disney showdown, "What you've got almost is the Establishment divided against itself" (as cited in Hsu, 1994e, p. D3; see also Bailey, 1994).

These larger interests on all sides sought to replicate their positions and rhetorical tactics in miniature in the local vicinity. For its part, Disney's strategic plan for securing local cooperation was as carefully prepared as any Civil War battle fought on that land. It methodically engineered a grassroots campaign in support of Disney's America. Although it reportedly did not provide financial or organizational backing, Disney "put in touch" with each other Prince William County's real estate agents, lawyers, and chamber of commerce members who favored the theme park's arrival; the resulting 25-member Welcome Disney Committee mounted a telephone and mail campaign to mobilize the "positive majority" of area residents supporting Disney (Hsu, 1993c, p. C7). Another Disney initiative was a phone bank commissioned to call citizens in the area to ask if they favored building Disney's America. If the call recipient responded affirmatively, the phone bank patched him or her through directly to his or her elected representative without first alerting the caller of the transfer; citizens' responses quickly forced Disney to abandon this tactic (Hsu, 1994c, 1994e). Finally, Disney warned area officials and citizens that they must accept the development proposal promptly and with few conditions or risk its withdrawal (Ayres, 1994; Baker, 1994b; "Disney: Now the Real Bargaining," 1994; "Virginia Approves," 1994). Coupled with this imminent deadline was the Disney practice of providing "scanty" initial information and low-balling projections about the final extent of development and cost to the community (e.g., the number of visitors expected per day, additional traffic lanes and other civic-funded needs, and the impact on environmental protections), projections that it later repeatedly revised upward ("Disney: More Dueling Statistics," 1994; Hsu, 1994a, 1994b; Mathews, 1993, p. A19). Together, the pressure for (and their premature promise of) a rapid decision plus the changing numbers made it difficult for county officials to be confident which decision would be in the community's long-term best interest.

Meanwhile, the national and regional anti-Disney forces lined up their own parochial allies. The Piedmont Environmental Council (PEC) mobilized a Virginia preservationist group (based outside Prince William County) to stir opposition through the aptly named Disney—Take a Second Look Campaign; this group opened a toll-free telephone line and hired a full-time organizer to lead the charge (Hsu, 1993b, p. E1; Odum & Hsu, 1993). Taking the fight to the airwaves, the PEC funded a $100,000, 85-spot radio and television ad campaign to present some anti-Disney's America reasoning (Hsu, 1994h; Mansfield, 1994, p. C5). A group comprised solely of Prince William County residents, Protect Prince William County, organized itself and allied with the PEC (Hsu, 1993c). Thus, the local planning commission hearings on the Disney's America proposal allow us to study how competing discourses generated by national institutions are absorbed, adapted, and resituated within the boundaries of a local community.

The public hearing took place on September 10, 1994, in the Prince William County government center, with some speakers "lining up as early as 3:30 a.m. for a marathon session of the county's planning commission" (Tousignant & Hsu, 1994, p. A1). Each speaker was to be allowed 3 minutes in front of the microphone, and although early newspaper reports of the meeting featured the debate involving more than 150 speakers as overwhelmingly in favor of Disney, later stories suggested that the debate was more balanced, as our reading confirms. This essay analyzes portions of these debates that we transcribed from tape recordings provided by Prince William County for September 10 and the September 21 follow-up meeting. This local public exchange exemplifies the power and coherence possible among ordinary community members, with neither rhetorical training nor extensive practice, when faced with a pressure situation, complicated by extensive extracommunity pressures, that necessitated a difficult decision risking the fate of the community. Area residents, many of whom noted in their statements that they never previously had spoken in public or even imagined that they ever would, came forward to testify to each other in ways that inventively resituated national arguments to give them meaning in the community whose future would be affected most directly, whether or not Disney came. Although the content of the issues raised was similar to that in the national and regional wranglings over the park, the tone and conduct of this community's debate make it notable. Each speaker turned his or her own experiences over in respect to a common future proposed for members of the community but not by them. Each advocate delivered and debated his or her best argument with an apparent intent to influence the commissioners while simultaneously acknowledging the grounds for fellow citizens with conflicting opinions to be recognized and accepted within their shared community. Thus, citizens were able to make known sharply different self-understandings of their own relationships to the community while at the same time opening a place for others with different views. The rhetorical notion of ingenium heuristically illuminates this community's passionate discussions as it contemplated its shared future in light of its common past.

INGENIUM IN A LOCAL COMMUNITY'S DELIBERATIONS

High-power persuasion strategies and recalcitrance characterized the national argument on Disney's America, although expressed differently in the strategic positions of the entertainment/tourism industry/

economic advisers and the historians/environmentalists/New York press. On the one hand, Disney's professional campaign used the latest in lobbying, highly visible publicity, and opinion-formation techniques to boost favorable opinions for development. In the process, the company pursued rhetoric as a techne. On the other hand, American historians and environmental preservationists poetically resisted with festivals, plays, readings, music, and other self-articulated gestures of respect for the area as sacred and an "authentic" national treasure.

At the local level, however, another kind of rhetoric took shape. The work of this deliberating community was to create a common ground that took into account other sides of the controversy in its refutations and reexpressions of the significance of argument in relation to community members who invented angles of vision by articulating common pasts and alternative futures. Speakers—male or female, young or old, self-identified as rich or poor, newly arrived or landed gentry—believed it necessary to both acknowledge a sense of place for their own discourse in relationship to others (fellow neighbors as well as planning commissioners) and fulfill the duty of articulating arguments that voiced decisive positions regarding the crucial choice that confronted their community. The speakers all exhibited a common awareness of both the importance of speaking effectively to the issues and the importance of being able to speak cordially with their neighbors long after and however the Disney's America choice was resolved. Routinely, speakers were able to invent ways to articulate a different opinion and yet accommodate with respect the genuine, if differently weighted, concerns of their neighbors. With so much at stake, as each side saw it, such necessitated creativity in the interest of sustaining community across all parties is a truly remarkable accomplishment. The following analysis shows how community speakers advanced arguments aimed to influence even while strengthening affirmative spaces for widening the range of public articulation.

When this debate is read against the state-of-the-art techne by highly experienced professional persuaders, one sees people largely naive to the techniques of public address. Their rhetoric built on their experiences within the locality and willingness to learn from one another as they struggled to make a good shared decision and, more important, to keep the community from being ripped apart in the process. As the local deliberation unfolded, speakers shared their own experiences in ways that made those experiences sensual and real to other members of the community and listened to others' accounts; this practice not only legitimates the right to speak but also fosters mutual understanding. Instead of being a stumbling block to decisiveness or authenticity, differences become connecting points for the community through the ingenious articulation of individual experience. Furthermore, in weighing the alternatives, the speakers imagined aloud various common pasts and visions of potential common futures inhabitable not only by themselves but also by a variety of mutually appreciated community members. This stance created space for respecting differences among fellow community members' experiences and positioning arguments that identified a speaker with the community as a whole while unrecalcitrantly advancing the relative merits of persuasive positions. Three particular qualities characterize the ingenium displayed by local participants in the Prince William County zoning hearings and are worth examining critically.

Community Membership Is Asserted as Grounding One's Right to Participate

In this local discourse, the right to speak and be heard is asserted on the grounds that one is a legitimate member of the community. Only those with a stake in the community's life (not merely an economic or academic interest), as established by participation and bearing the daily risks of the ongoing consequences of a choice on the shared future, are entitled to a voice in the community's local deliberation. The participants speak in a way that legitimates their right to advance arguments by suggesting "I am the community; here is how Disney's America would affect me and other community members with similar concerns." Although it is customary and sometimes required for those who speak at open local hearings to state their names and addresses, those who spoke at the Disney's America zoning hearings went far beyond that. From the retiree who had cut hay on the proposed development site and understood the implications of Disney's America through the lens of his war experience, his recent vacation to Orlando, and his work at Dulles airport to the 16-year-old girl who looked at Disney's potential to make her and her two younger sisters' required history education more interesting, the speakers located themselves, their reasoning, and their right to participate through their intimate, existing ties to the local community.

Almost without exception, speakers detailed their personal history as a member of the community. Special emphasis was placed on the length and proximity of one's or one's family's membership in the community; the geographical proximity to the proposed Disney development; and the detail, variety, and extent of roles one plays in the community's life. For example, Linda Myer explains that she owns a small horse farm, dating from the eighteenth century, located directly across the street from the proposed Disney's America site. Elizabeth Nekins establishes her right to speak to and on behalf of the community, saying, "I live on a small property about a mile away from the Disney project. My family settled in Virginia in 1669 and has held this homestead where I live since 1854." Betty Dooley is even more explicit about her family's long-standing place in the community and how the texture of this firsthand experience makes her more qualified to speak on the area's history and needs than the nationally recognized historians who cannot claim any link to the local community or concern for its common future. She comments,

> I live at 5798 Featherbed Lane adjoining the Manassas National Battlefield Park. Since the day my great-grandparents arrived at the Wellington railroad station in 1880 with six children, two cows, three horses, and a pig, there have been members of my family living right on the Manassas National Battlefield Park. Although—I must add, there are nine children in my family—and I am not recognized by any national board of historians or any other scholarly panel, I believe that my opinion on Disney's America is even more valid than some high-profile historians that have appointed themselves guardian of the Battlefield but who do not know anything about what is important for the future of the area in question as well as this county. Prince William County has more history than Civil War history.

Dooley continues by emphasizing that shared history is not limited to a single, poetic, authoritative version producing a carefully restricted "proper" experience of it but is alive, dynamic, and the property of diverse members of the community who will experience it on their own terms and put it to various uses.

Dooley and many others defend their right to speak and their credibility in this deliberation on the grounds of being a community participant, actively downplaying qualifications of professional status or technical expertise. Dooley continues,

> Some of these historians have recently spoken out about Disney's destroying national heritage that is kept alive by the battlefields. Who are these historians? Maybe I'm one. Their families have not

> lived in Prince William County for multiple generations, and they are not my neighbors. Neither are they on this commission. They have no right to dictate the use of 3,000 acres of privately owned land that is more than 5 miles away from the nearest plot of the Battlefield. Besides, it is awfully presumptuous to say that the Disney park will destroy the Battlefield. It is my belief, by living there, that the tourists pay for the Battlefield, so why shouldn't they be able to use it?

For her, history is not abstract and monolithic but situated, flexible, multifunctional, shared, and open to a variety of interactions in the present and future. As a result, it is a sustained relationship with the community whose future will be most affected, rather than professional expertise, that gives one the right to speak and be heard on the matters at hand. Lillian Boaz concurs:

> Members of the commission, please . . . don't be negatively influenced by a core minority of Disney opponents who have national clout. A great number of these people don't even live in this area. As a resident of Manassas, I find it an insult for such people to come into our area where I live and to have them think they can dictate to us what we should or should not build and to tell us we don't know what we are doing.

Those outside the community who have not "invested" themselves in its common life do not have the right in this forum to have their concerns weighted on par with those of long-time members.

Another aspect featured in establishing one's right to speak and be listened to rested on presenting the multiple and indispensable roles that one plays in community life. The nature and number of ways one's life intersects the community's buttress one's right to speak for it and to it. One speaker introduces her remarks, stating "Mr. Chairman and members of the Commission, my name is Sherry Yates. I live in Prince William County 1 mile from Haymarket. As the mother of two small children, a commuter, a Christian, and a county resident, I take pride in supporting Disney's America." Another introduces herself and establishes her right to speak as follows:

> My name is Shirley Davis. And I'm a mother and a wife and a business owner here in the county. My family has been in this county

> for over 100 years. But if you don't remember anything else about me today, I want you to remember that I'm a born-again Christian. I'm the mother of two children, and as I raise my children up in this county the thing I try to install [sic] in them most is good values and love for their fellow man.

By elaborating their roles contributing to the texture of local community, the speakers indicate that their comments are not grounded in selfish, individualistic interests. Instead, their concerns are offered as a shared resource revealing a unique perspective on the community's pressing common business that stems from experiencing and taking part in the community's ongoing life.

The right to speak as a community member also implies the right to be heard respectfully, to be listened to by other members of the community, and to have one's concerns taken into account. The treatment of hearing witnesses exhibits affirming care in the face of differences of opinion. For example, when an elderly woman with a soft voice could not be heard after her opening ("Please listen to my concerns"), various auditors can be heard in the background calling out instructions to help her operate the microphone. When this speaker runs out of time because she is having difficulty reading her notes in the hearing room's light, she gently resists being silenced by the moderator before she has finished her say. Auditors chuckle approvingly when she apologizes to the moderator as she leaves the microphone after finishing her speech, saying "Thank you. I'm sorry if I ran over [my 3 minutes], but this light is not good enough for me." She joins the ensuing laughter with a delightful chuckle. She has been heard.

Another community member fears that she can speak but will not be heard because she both opposes Disney's America and is a fox hunter; there has been talk that the fox hunters are elitists and so not adequately appreciative of other community members' needs and experiences. Kitty Smith confronts the possibility and explicitly seeks to overcome barriers to others, including her concerns in their consideration of the issue. After offering her reasons for opposing Disney's America, she defends before her neighbors her right to be heard openly in the face of claims that selfish "elitist" concerns were blocking the opportunities that Disney's America offers for "ordinary" citizens. Through the story of her personal history in the locality, Smith reminds other community members that, if only for the sake of preserving community, the individuality of debate participants must not be allowed to dissolve into the stereotypical and broad-brush labels of elitism and class struggle evident in the national debate. Such a practice wrongly excuses the easier but mutually isolating tack of tuning out the concerns of those members different from oneself and refusing to appreciate other participants' experience of the location and community. Voice breaking with emotion, she says

> I have lived in Fauquier County and Louden County all my life, and, yes, I'm a fox hunter, and I'm proud to say so today. I'm third generation of my family to fox hunt in that area, and I know we've been called elitist snobs. But I lived on a dairy farm in western Louden County, and we had 50 cows to milk twice a day, every day, 7 days a week, 365 days a year. And if there was any time left over and any money, we went fox hunting. My mother sold every pony and every horse off of our farm so she could send three children to college as a single parent. We didn't consider any of this very elitist living. But what draws us to this area? Is it the fox hunting? No. It is the land. It is the land. It is the rural character of this land that draws us to this area. It is a sense of strong community. It's a sense of community and place and pride in that place. That's what draws us to this area.

She reminds listeners that individuality and differences are superseded by a common commitment to each other and their space. The mutual response of appreciating and respecting the divergent, unique experiences that community members express in exercising their right to participate points to a second quality of this genuine discourse—its "both-and" quality.

Simultaneously Affirms and Confronts Others and Their Perspectives

Possibly the most noteworthy aspect of Prince William County's zoning deliberation was its transcendence of the dichotomy that rhetoric can either be affirming but ineffectual in arguing a position or effective but combative and destructive toward those whose initial stands differ. These speakers passionately advance arguments intended to persuade fellow community members, but they simultaneously affirm each others' different but equally legitimate experiences of that community and locale. The result is a discursive persuasive practice that asserts one's own right to both address the community and speak on its behalf while acknowledging that other community members have the same right to speak to and on behalf of the community, even if their experiences and recommendations differ radically from one's own. Given the stakes, every advocate argues as convincingly as he or she knows how, but the importance of preserving a community feeling of affiliation upon the debate's conclusion ranks with advancing arguments intended to move others toward one's preferred outcome.

The both-and dynamic is expressed in multiple ways. For instance, although she objects to the PEC's coercive tactics, Sherry Yates reaffirms the bond of community that unites her with and gives her the chance to meet with and hear the concerns of her neighbors, both those who support the PEC and those who do not. She closes her comments with the following remark:

> If anyone had told me a year ago that I would be speaking before you here today, I would have laughed. Many like myself could not sit back any longer in the face of frivolous lawsuits and lame press releases. I would like to thank the PEC for introducing me to politics and my neighbors from one end of this county to the other. Thank you.

Similarly, Ione Dusenberry acknowledges that mutual goodwill among even members with strongly held opposing opinions is taken for granted within a community. Demonstrating faith in her community's bond, she recommends imagining a common future broadly in light of the strengths of an imagined common past. She comments,

> Everyone in this room, I am sure, wants the very best for our children and future generations. In order to do this, we need to honor the past and to borrow the best from our ancestors. However, if we are to go forward with wise stewardship of this land, I wonder that we haven't heard more innovative ideas.

She gently encourages drawing on common ingenuity to generate broader possibilities than those currently available, to imagine options that may better address the concerns of and facilitate cooperation among those on all sides of the issue. Perhaps citizen Ben Rickets best expresses the mutuality of genuine discourse at work. After encouraging citizens to be alert to the "backdoor" political activity that he perceived Disney, a community outsider, to be using to leverage its selfish interests, Rickets encourages community members to listen to each other carefully and weigh everyone's concerns in reaching a decision:

> I'm an ardent supporter of Virginia, and I think that we need to realize that everyone who wants the Disney project or who opposes the Disney project are good people with serious concerns who really do care about what's going on in Prince William County. And when all is said and done, I hope that no one burns bridges. I hope the Disney company and the Prince William County government realizes the concerns, from the old lady who spoke earlier to the corporate business tycoons of Orlando. Make sure that everyone has a complete understanding and appreciation of each other's viewpoints.

Another man expressed his pro-Disney's America perspective and supporting arguments and then closed with a reaffirmation of the sense of community, whatever happens with Disney's America:

> In closing, I'd like the planning commission and everyone else, regardless of which side of the fence you're on [regarding Disney's America], please come to our annual Haymarket Day, next weekend, Saturday, September 17. We're going to have parades, food, fun, games for the kids, and wholesome fun for the whole family.

Yet another speaker focused on pursuing the American Dream explicitly. He calls for listeners to resist any arguments or efforts that risk dividing the community; they are not worth whatever gains they bring.

Each speaker thus acknowledged the importance of other community members and their concerns while seeking to argue persuasively as one member of that community on how the Disney's America decision would affect his or her life-in-community. Their positions are neither moralistic nor totalizing. They allow for a variety of experiences of community and room for difference. Others are not ridiculed or dismissed because they differ, nor are they urged to conform. Instead, there are requests for cooperation and fairly weighing everyone's concerns—others' as well as one's own—to create a shared deliberative climate that embraces the range of community members' interests and experiences.

Exhibits Concern for a Community Imagined Beyond One's Own Interests and Life Span

The third telling feature of these local hearings was the participants' willingness to imagine multiple common pasts and shared futures.

Speakers imagined a variety of common futures on the landscape of their community, with and without Disney's America, some positive and some negative. These futures were grounded in various imagined pasts. In the spirit of the inclusiveness previously discussed, no one insisted that his or her view was the only possible or proper one, even as he or she tried to win others over; there was room for varying views of the community's life together through time. The imagined futures and imagined pasts were peopled not only with present community members but also with future generations and ancestors; concerns expressed were for the community envisioned beyond any single member's individual interests and life span. For instance, a community member with a soft Southern accent points out that the Disney's America decision must be made with a focus on shared concerns rather than individual self-interest; the decision has implications for a nested set of communities about which the speaker apparently cares deeply. She comments,

> My support of Disney's America as well as those whom I represent—and I am representing the "Friends of the Mouse," which is a grass-roots organization in the community—has nothing to do with personal considerations but has everything to do with what's right for my community, for the Commonwealth of Virginia, and for our democratic system.

Participation in and concern for common pasts and shared futures energizes the debate's vernacular.

Imagined common pasts included immediate and distant ones. One participant called listeners to remember the community's recent past and persistent hardships. She expressed a pressing concern for the community's economic development, although the whole of her remarks imply that she personally is employed:

> It saddens me that the opposition has manipulated our county to the point of defending the thousands of jobs that Disney is offering us, and, in the same breath, they attack Disney for paying the people who create them. Have we forgotten so soon the families who lost their homes, the students who couldn't find work, the companies forced to lay off workers, the empty storefronts, or the feeling of early retirement? Have we forgotten the projects in Prince William alone that dissolved before our eyes? IBM is gone. Contel, absorbed. Atlantic Research, cut in half. The list goes on. For those

> of you here today whose lives are removed from the reality of a recession, I would like to expose you to the facts. Last year alone 23,640 households in Prince William County were more than 30 days behind on their electric bills. The Prince William County Sheriff's Department evicted 5,809 families between 1990 and 1993. This, ladies and gentleman, is real. Disney's America is needed in Prince William County.

Similarly, Calvin Hackerman, immediate past president of the Prince William County-Greater Manassas Chamber of Commerce, directs his comments to various constituents within the community and frames them around three reasons, each focusing on preparation for the whole community's continued existence and growth. He previews his remarks:

> There are many reasons that the citizens, the business community, and the government leaders in Prince William County should enthusiastically support this proposed rezoning application related to Disney's America project. In the interest of time, I am going to focus my comments today in three areas. One, growth is coming to Prince William County, with or without Disney's America. Number two, existing citizens and existing traffic demand road improvements now, with or without Disney's America. And three, there are significant benefits to be realized by attracting the tourism industry to Prince William County and to northern Virginia.

In forecasting the shared future of diverse community members and subgroups, Hackerman stresses that past choices have made the advent of development inevitable; the trajectory has been set by previous community decisions. To him, the shape of the future centers on what shape the inevitable development takes. He argues,

> As we heard earlier in the staff presentation, much of the property that makes up the Disney's America property has already been zoned for development. . . . The choice is not between 3,000 acres of undeveloped, virgin, rolling countryside versus Disney's America. The choice is between Disney's America and some unknown, but virtually certain development. We believe the proposed Disney's America development presents a highly desirable use for this property consistent with the county's comprehensive plan.

Small business owner Donna Bolton envisions a future for the area that not only cradles her in retirement but also equips the upcoming generation of community youth with job skills, a sense of responsibility, and school money:

> But I'm here today for all of those kids who will need a seasonal or part-time job, those going to George Mason Institute in Manassas or the Northern Virginia Community College at Manassas. Getting an opportunity from Disney for the training and ethics, manners, dress code, and people skills that they will need after they get that education to get those high-tech, high-paying, railroading jobs that the opposition keeps talking about. As a Virginian, I can see the generation of jobs in manufacturing. . . . Someone's going to have to bake all those hot dog buns and ground [sic] up all that hamburger.

Disney's arrival frequently was debated on the ground of what kind of neighbor the speaker imagines Disney will be, if allowed to join the community, and what it will contribute to or subtract from future shared life. One speaker pointed out that Disney's actions to date reveal it to be an "untrustworthy neighbor." Conversely, in her self-proclaimed first foray into open community discussion, Pam Macauslin, a first-grade teacher, draws on her experience as a local educator. She expresses her and her colleagues' "elation" at the prospect of Disney joining the community because it will be "an asset to our community and an excellent community partner." In knitting together her version of a common past and future, Macauslin recounts a personal experience with one young student who saw the battlefield as merely "a nice place to go fly her kite and have a picnic." With Disney's assets and expertise, she then asserts, a theme park would bring history to life and offer opportunities better preparing the community's children for the future. She concludes by envisioning a common future made different and better if existing community members embrace Disney:

> If Disney's America were here, I would have been able to help her experience the events of the Civil War and Manassas' place in history. I am sure our schools and all those around us will take advantage of the educational opportunities that this partner will extend to us. Our area bands, drill teams, ROTC units, and choral groups will be given an opportunity to perform at events hosted by Disney right here in their own community. . . . I'm sure some of the

> educational programs that they already have implemented will be available to our community as well. These include scholarships, antidrug programs, curriculum materials to be used by teachers when they go on a field trip, and the American Teacher Award recognizing excellent teachers. Disney deserves an A-plus for their dedication to education, to family, and to the American spirit. We don't want to fail our community and its future generations by letting Disney's America slip through our fingers.

The theme of realizing the American Dream by living in this community also permeated the debate, linking imagined futures to members' pasts. A woman who opposed the theme park's development stated,

> I cannot afford to pay for the roads, although my tax dollars are going there. I cannot afford to pay for water or sewer, because I don't have those things now. I do pay $3,400 a year in taxes. I do not have public water. I do not have sewer. I don't even have an electric light out there, but I'm paying more than my share because I wanted the American Dream. And that was to have a beautiful home in a peaceful and quiet neighborhood, and now Disney threatens me. . . . They pay for their popularity. . . . [T]his is not right, that we work for the American Dream, and Disney can come in and well afford to blow it out the window. It's not right. If Disney comes, we might as well move to D.C. Not a pretty picture. I want to stay in Prince William County because I love it; it is a beautiful county, not with Disney coming in and spoiling the environment.

On the opposing side, a man who favors Disney's America claims, "The dream is in the people, not in the land." One mother with a 3-year-old daughter imagines a community including Disney's America as "a future full of hopes and dreams," a way to build a shared future that is environmentally aware, has lower tax burdens, keeps hopes alive, and is populated with children curious about history. Another mother, however, who dedicates her speech to her young daughter Amanda Nicole, opposes Disney's America because she moved from a crime-ridden, urban location to this area specifically to raise her child in a more crime-free, greener location that was also rich in history.

Others stressed the relevance of an imagined past to this decision about the future. For example, Linda Myer notes that the importance of preserving the unique and sacred history of the region is not in dispute, as Disney's opponents at the national level have asserted; instead, she sees the conflict as one over which means can preserve the area and its common past most effectively to enrich the shared future. She supports Disney's America on the grounds that only through comprehensive planning can the community's past and its future be secured:

> Disney offers a concrete proposal to preserve the area through a historical theme park reflecting the rich and sacred past of Virginia and beyond. I hear no counterproposal from the historians to buy the Waverly property. I hear no proposal from PEC and Protect [Historic America] to buy the Waverly property. There is silence from the opponents of Disney as to alternatives. Stopping Disney is not an alternative. I would like to see a comprehensive alternative devoted to preserving for future generations the rich past of the region, devoted to green belts and controlled growth, and devoted to sound corporate citizenship that will provide jobs and tax revenue. Disney offers this possibility. As to an equally comprehensive plan for the Waverly property, the historians and PEC constituents offer only silence. This silence has led me to ask, which group really wishes to preserve the region: those with a comprehensive plan or those who have no plan and who have refused to engage in any real effort to work cooperatively with the citizens of Prince William to find a solution which will preserve while creating hope for future generations of citizens? . . . I like that kind of initiative. That is the American way. That is what was fought for at the two battles of Bull Run and that's why I support Disney.

Still other participants used the past to derive recommendations for the future. For some, shared past complications offered resources for rejecting Disney's America. An elderly woman described how she taught the children of Franklin Roosevelt's brain trust during World War II and then used that aspect of the common past to draw a lesson for the future:

> At the end of the war, we dropped an atomic bomb on Hiroshima and on Nagasaki. The bomb got out of control, and today we are frightened with thousands and thousands of these bombs. Now, is Disney's America safe? [She is interrupted by the timekeeper.] . . . It merely reflects on the fact that we have to look ahead of [sic] what is coming to us, that we are not just ignorant people. We know that the world changes, and it doesn't go backward. So, I just want

> to finish: Your vote on this matter would forever change the character of western Prince William's County and will be the most important decision you may ever make. . . . Deny Disney its application.

The community's decision will irrevocably affect its existence through time, she concludes. To this speaker, a broader common past offered an analogous lesson of uncontrollable nuclear proliferation, a parallel aimed at making sure others realized that this development decision was irreversible and would have consequences throughout the community's existence. It must be considered with the utmost care and solemnity.

This third quality worked with the other two as ingenium. The speakers integrated sense, imagination of alternative futures, and memories of recent and long-ago pasts ingeniously express differences but at the same time identify and value all community members as of sustained worth and concern. In so doing, they brought to life visions of the community and its potential through time, often focusing on a framework beyond their individual life spans and interests. Their visions of the past and future included other community members, dead as well as generations yet to come. Such discourse exhibits the ability to simultaneously affirm and contest other members' perspectives while still asserting the right to speak and be heard based on one's proven commitment to the community's shared life through time.

On September 21, the local planning boards approved $130 million in road improvements and endorsed the company's plans (Fordney, 1994). One week later, Disney shelved the project of its own volition (Harris & Sanchez, 1994). The press announcement by Peter Rummel read, "We recognize that there are those who have been concerned about the possible impact of our park on historic sites in this unique area, and we have always tried to be sensitive to the issue;" Disney thus avoided a fight that, despite the local vote, promised to be "long, litigious, expensive, and messy" (Bailey, 1994). At the national and regional levels, Disney's opponents strutted and claimed responsibility for this "victory." Predictably, national spokespersons absorbed and transformed the meaning of the local victory into a national trajectory predicting "a new determination among Americans to prevent the loss of historic land to development" (Fordney, 1994). Meanwhile, Disney vowed to develop a historic theme park elsewhere but quickly moved on to other projects. For Prince William County, it was only a battle, not the war, that was over. Subsequently, residents of the region have been engaged in a succession of debates on development ranging from a proposed automobile racetrack on the Brandy Station battlefield to an onslaught of giant Wal-Marts (including one slated for the farm on which George Washington grew up as a boy) and the road expansion such development requires (Kotz & Abramson, 1997).

CONCLUSION

Viewing Prince William County's planning commission hearings on Disney's America from the perspective of ingenium offers one close critical analysis of a vernacular discourse. The debate of September 10 provides fresh insight into rhetoric's role in "how community relations are interwoven and how communities are contingent" (Ono & Sloop, 1995, p. 21). In the case of Disney's America zoning hearing, we observed ingenium at play in the articulation of pasts, presents, and futures that included community members in imagined frames of experience linked to both interest and responsibility. That these imagined temporal lines varied could be expected because the community exhibited knowledge of and respect for different lines of experience. Such differences frequently emerged from how a speaker offered his or her own temporal perspective based on family history and age. Facing a common future, with or without Disney, also provided a decision point for judgment that oriented individual participants' perspectives and drew forth telling arguments. Thus, a community addressed itself in diversity and unity, with respectful accommodation of differences as well as forceful points of view.

Given ingenium's inherently concrete, relative, and localized nature, the conclusions that may be drawn from this controversy are limited necessarily. The conceptual and political contours of larger global controversies are visible in the struggles between and among competing institutions, including the state and private agencies whose spokespersons sometimes present themselves as guardians of the nation's heritage and education and sometimes as innovators in community development and entertainments. Each community and local moment of controversy invites, even as it resists, an ingenium that challenges the vernacular to articulate civic culture. To translate nationally circulated, divisive, institutionally generated arguments into discourses that sustain local community while testing choices is difficult. Because the local is a site at which global institutions struggle for reach and advantage, vernacular discourse is challenged to absorb, translate, and transform these tensions into enactments that, it is hoped, strengthen rather than weaken a particular civic culture. It would be surprising to find any two outcomes of such controversy, any two debates, exactly alike. Because topics vary in local encounters, different communities and even diasporic groups will respond differently to common tests. Different localities at different points in time, however, are capable of creating trends, models, or movements that influence a public sphere's development in a given era. For example, Hauser's (1999) powerful reading of the vernacular was highly influenced by the local revolutions of Eastern Europe ending the Cold War. Even now, contemporary publics may persist as reticulate or even fragmented entities, "a discursive space in which strangers discuss issues they perceive to be of consequence for them and their group" (p. 64). On September 10, 1994, however, it was "neighbors" and not "strangers" who constituted a local public, and the full power of wit and invention was used to portray the ample passions of advocates while resisting the divisiveness of contention.

The local Disney's America debates suggest that rhetors can sometimes find inventional resources that nourish a community in the face of external and internal pressures. Francois Rochat, in his 2002 study of why some communities preserved their own standards of neighborliness despite official pressures to persecute or stand by as onlookers during World War II, identifies what he calls a "dynamic of common decency"—a refusal to do anything other than to regard one's neighbors with concern relative to their needs. Although the speakers of the Disney's America hearing did not rise to the desperate heroism of rescuers, we nonetheless note the decency of members of the Prince William community who held in regard the opinion of others, who responded favorably to others' need to be heard, and who articulated common decency as a strong core of ingenious public debate—strong enough to resist, at least for this day, the fragmenting sources of global interest. It is encouraging to find evidence that the deliberative norms of civic culture may indeed be strong and not brittle, may find "harmony" in democratic public expression rather than persist only in an underground (Hauser, 1999, p. 58) or outlier, and may usefully forward one's own opinion in the gesture of respect for others. The diverse, impassioned speakers of that hearing appeared uniformly sensitive to difference and determined to avoid replicating the stereotypes of anger, fear, suspicion, and greed—the overly negative or positive images sometimes offered by professional public relations in stereotyping advocates and advocacy. Such debate indicates a route to public genius available in ordinary deliberations of average local community members, a route that we suspect is more common than routinely imagined in mass-mediated spaces.

In the face of global pressures and debates, a local civic culture can turn contentious, divisive, and fragmentary. It can become a collection of individualistic strangers bound together by legal rule, force, or sheer indifference. Occasionally, however, difference turned to debate may strengthen rather than splinter a community. Key to this moment is the ingenious enactment of a discourse that simultaneously expresses difference within recognition. Ingenuity is a necessary ingredient to perform this deliberative feat, and such communal accomplishments challenge the critic to bracket generalizations, methods, and expectations about the public sphere to seek out and explore "the products of creativity [as] acquired insights, made things, planned actions, composed statements" (McKeon, 1973, p. 208). The creativity and originality of the local, the vernacular dimensions of a civic culture, will be cheated unless familiar expectations of rhetoric at work are "brought into contact with the transformations of innovation" (p. 208). Thus, rhetorical inquiry into such situated vernacular can serve as a useful critical means for recovering actual instances of ingenium and developing a better understanding of the relationship between rhetoric and community and of the rhetorical practices that make a community under pressure resilient.

3

Arguing About the Place of Values and Ethics in Market-Oriented Discourses of Today

George Cheney

If there is a single saying that crystallizes my concerns in this essay, it is today's popular expression "just business." This simple phrase accomplishes two important pragmatic results: It elevates commercial activity to the status of a supreme human endeavor, and it protects that which is placed under the rubric of "normal business activity" from careful ethical scrutiny. In both respects, "It's just business" highlights the ways in which business can be thought to be either inherently ethical or moral ("Let the market decide") or amoral—that is, not available to ethical analysis ("All's fair").

AUTHOR'S NOTE: I acknowledge Shiv Ganesh, Sara Hayden, and Mary Simpson for their helpful feedback on the manuscript.

PURPOSE AND BACKGROUND

Building on the work of numerous others and some of my own, I reflect on important implications of market-oriented discourses today. Specifically, this essay considers the various ways in which ethics are "located" in or excluded from prevailing discussions of the economy, work, and consumption, especially in the United States but also to some extent in other areas of the world. From this standpoint, markets are seen as basically amoral.

At the broadest level, when the market actor is granted sacred and almost supernatural status, its inner workings are deemed to be beyond question. The market is celebrated and justified for the choices it affords us, acting as consumers, but the a priori choices about the structure and logic of the market, protections for corporate interests, or concentration of power are little examined (Schmookler, 1993). In this case, it is the market as a whole that is treated as being "natural" (e.g., President Clinton stated that "free trade is a rising tide that will lift all boats" in his pitch for the North America Free Trade Agreement in 1993 and 1994) or ethical ("The best system that we can imagine") and in need of preservation ("We must promote market-oriented thinking in order to advance the goals of democracy"). At the same time, we frequently hear insistence on the market's functional neutrality and instrumental design. Such a move is often coupled with an invocation of Adam Smith's (1776/1986) *Wealth of Nations*, even though Smith himself granted enormous roles to values, morals, and sentiments (such as compassion and empathy; see Werhane, 1991).

Enter Communication

The Microsoft monopoly case, and its many legal spin-offs, is not only about the proof or denial of imperialistic or "predatory" corporate practices but also about which sorts of discourse and which set of definitions will have the upper hand. That is, how Microsoft has appealed a December 1999 U.S. Justice Department ruling and an April 2000 U.S. District Court decision against its linkage of a Web browser to its widely used operations package centers on the values of "innovation and entrepreneurship" and "future orientation" in the face of charges that it succeeds in squelching innovation by other firms and effectively denies consumers the range of options they might otherwise have. For several years, Bill Gates has been taking Microsoft's case to the U.S. people with full-page ads in major newspapers emphasizing values such as innovation, freedom, and cooperation. Such battles over terminology and labels have important practical consequences not only in terms of attitude change but also with respect to decision and policy making, whether we are talking about the Enron et al. accounting scandal of 2001 and 2002 or the conflict-of-interest issue (or, rather, nonissue) with respect to certain U.S. companies rebuilding Iraq in 2003 and 2004.

At the same time, the transformation of the citizen to the consumer tends to make certain practices, such as labor or human rights abuses, less immediately relevant than they might be from a different point of view. A shift in labeling here also signals a change in perspective. That is, the symbolic umbrella of "the consumer" is less likely to cover some human activities than it is others, although it, like other abstract points of reference, is changeable. A *New Yorker* cartoon (July 21, 1997, p. 5) depicts the political-ethical implications of the eclipse of the citizen very well. Two heads of state are seated at what is obviously a summit meeting. One turns to the other and says, "My government is concerned about your government's torture and maiming of potential customers."

A Qualification

None of these trends are univocal or monolithic, however. Currently, there is considerable symbolic play at work under the headings of "free/fair trade" and "consumer rights." There are complex interrelations between symbolic and material forces when we enter the realm of the rhetoric of economics and business. Thus, this essay balances a modernist, value-based critique of such discourses with postmodern realizations of the open-endedness and "undecidability" (Derrida, 1976) of symbols such as the consumer. For example, there are currently movements on some campuses and in some cities to advance the idea of what we might call "conscientious consumption," by which consumption regains some of its antiquated waste-oriented meaning and a newer sense of ethical commitment and responsibility.

The Bottom Line

These and related trends bear a closer analysis, especially from the standpoint of rhetorical and communication studies. For too long, economics, finance, and commerce have maintained a mystique that has left them seeming impermeable to analysis by a so-called "softer" discipline, such as communication. Many advocates of free-market supremacy adopt a neorealist stance in which they would deny the persuasive, rhetorical, or discursive dimensions of their own advocacy, insisting that their vision of the world is not only the best but also, in fact, offers a direct response to "the way things are." As Aune (2001) notes, much free-market promotion today tries to deny its own subjectivity and "discursivity." The shroud of certainty and legitimacy, however, has been lifted partially off of economic reasoning in recent years by various forms of practitioners (Gray, 1998; Korten, 1999) and theorists (Sen, 1992). The centrality of economic activity ànd discourses about it in the contemporary world demand that we not only critically examine "the market story" but also explore alternatives to it. The market has taken on the status of an overarching framework in its attempt to explain all sorts of major questions and has been used to organize nearly every domain of life, from health care to education, the environment, and religion.

Questions of Power

As Foucault (1984) insightfully observed, especially in his later essays, the workings of power are at their height when power succeeds in masking its own mechanisms, much like the U.S. empire denying it to be such. Therefore, it is the arguments in corporate boardrooms and legislative assemblies and trade negotiations that often turn on the apparent factuality of claims to interpret "progress," "efficiency," "innovation," or "economic growth." If arguments about the "way things ought to be" (prescription) can be effectively disguised by or collapsed into arguments about "the way things are" (descriptive realism), the advocate has a tremendous rhetorical advantage over any opponents in effectively "translating" what should be an ethical discourse into a purely instrumental one.

Overview

In the remainder of this essay, I provide an examination of some of my basic assumptions about communication, discourse, organizations, economics, and ethics. Second, I explore the variety of ways values are expressed and used in contemporary organizational discourses. Third, an examination of the various "placements" of ethics vis-à-vis the market are presented. Fourth, the essay offers insights about ethics and the market from a seven-year case study of worker cooperatives turned multinational corporations in the Basque Country of Spain. Finally, I suggest a few practical lessons from an examination of the rhetoric of the market and its implications for ethics.

KEY TERMS AND ASSUMPTIONS

Rhetorics of Economics

The rhetoric of economics has begun to draw more interest among communication and rhetoric scholars, largely because of how references to economic ways of thinking now dominate the cultural landscape in the United States and in many other industrialized societies. Especially since the publication of McCloskey's (1985) *The Rhetoric of Economics*, scholars in and outside of the field of communication studies have examined more closely connections that were previously not much investigated. In the process, some of the mystery surrounding economics has been dispelled in terms of both scholarly and popular discourses on the topic. In the research literature of the 1980s and 1990s, at least three distinct senses or areas of analysis appeared under the broad heading of "the rhetoric of economics":

- The analysis of "implicit" rhetorics within the discipline of economics, along with the acknowledgment of similar persuasive dimensions in other disciplines, such as psychology, sociology, and even physics (Desilet, 1999; Gaonkar, 1997). The central idea in this approach is that any discipline, being a vocabulary and a corpus of principles, has a rhetorical dimension, regardless of its protestations to the contrary. This position is not to say that any discipline is nothing but rhetoric but that it is *at least rhetorical* in the ways it makes choices about what to study, how to study it, and how to represent that which is under investigation.

- The analysis of persuasive dimensions of popular economic discourses, such as discussions of the market as an agent or the superordinate value of efficiency (as "the biggest bang for the buck"), especially in terms of their influences on other domains (e.g., politics, work, and leisure) (Aune, 2001; Cheney & Christensen, 2001; Conrad, 2002). The key proposition here is that popular economic discourses should be examined not only with respect to their specific content (e.g., claims about the relationship of one economic indicator, such as stock performance, to another, such as the unemployment rate) but also in terms of the explicit and implicit persuasive strategies employed.

⋙ The analysis of the interrelations of economy and symbols (e.g., considering the dematerialization of money vs. the materialization of symbols) (Coulmas, 1992). That is, there are certain ironies to our accustomed division between the symbolic and nonsymbolic worlds. Recent popular economic articles have emphasized how money and exchange are becoming increasingly less "grounded" in the material as the "plastic economy" takes hold. Also, the making of money with other money (as in the financial services industry) and with apparently nonmaterial enterprises (such as "dot.coms") reinforces a sense that the economy is floating in air, far abstracted from its old footing on terra firma. At the same time, certain symbols become markedly more material in their popular usage, as we see in the current controversies regarding proper treatment of the U.S. flag and the very notion of the market, both of which are reified to the extent that it is often difficult to examine them in an open manner. We should also consider the ways in which the material world places constraints on persuasive endeavors (such as social movements by disadvantaged classes or nascent labor unions) and how the symbolic world comes to shape the material one (consider the persistent myth of relative classlessness in U.S. society: only recently has it begun to break down as increasingly more citizens admit to being non-middle class) (Cloud, 1994, 1996).

Communication, Discourse, and Ethics

This essay is concerned with all three senses of the rhetoric of economics discussed previously, although the second and third concern us much more directly than the first. The reference to "implicit rhetorics" is important as a background assumption insofar as we can subject academic discourses on economics to the same sort of deconstructive focus as done with popular discourses on the economy. As a prelude to my analysis, here I explain in brief my perspective on the concepts of communication, discourse, and ethics:

- Communication should be understood on multiple levels, from discrete symbol to broad discourses, but communication is not all there is. We must therefore look to material constraints, recalcitrance of material on symbolic, and vice versa (Burke, 1950/1969b). Also, we should consider "translations" with respect to the relationship between the material and the symbolic; that is, we should scrutinize the ways both material and symbolic aspects of our existence become represented within discourse (Cooren, 2000; Latour, 1993). In this regard, Burke's (1962) hierarchy of symbols is helpful, including symbols for things, symbols for relationships, symbols for ideologies, and symbols for the metaphysical or supernatural.

- Discourse refers to broad patterns of communication, including verbal messages, numerical calculations, social situations, and architecture. From this standpoint, discourse includes "orbits" or "constellations" around key symbols, worldviews, and Zeitgeist. For example, as Foucault (1978, 1984) explains, a key organizing symbol for discourses of the modern Western industrialized world is the idea of the "unique individual." Ironically, however, this very individualism is underwritten and maintained by a great deal of conformity—conformity to the ideal that individual free choice reigns supreme in all activities, just as it appears to do so in the supermarket.

- Ethics should be examined in terms of both specific ethical positions/judgments and ethical "space" in discourse. Thus, we may try to prescribe a minimum length for a notification period by a corporation of impending layoffs for its employees. We might consider the ways in which personal investment could be tied to support for certain socially responsible corporate practices. At the same time, we may move to a level of analysis at which ethics are "framed" or "contained" in broad discourses about work, consumption, production, business, and the market.

With these assumptions in mind, we next examine the multiple ways in which values (or value-related terms) and ethics (explicitly or implicitly) function within the discourses of contemporary management, business, and the market. In the following section, the vagaries of language are especially important in allowing for values to "do" so many different things and to occupy so many places in discourse.

THE PLACE OF VALUES IN CONTEMPORARY CORPORATE DISCOURSES

Values are all the rage in today's organizations. They are centerpieces of mission statements. They are seen in terms of positioning a company in its market. They are employed as inspirational tools. They are widely seen as lacking and therefore in need of promotion and earnest quests. Values are also framed in strategic terms, thus linking the notion of "added value" to the promotion and perhaps internalization of values by groups of stakeholders, including employees. Value expressions are in some cases denounced as completely inauthentic commitments that should be avoided by organizations, lest even greater cynicism among employees and other constituencies be fostered (Larkin & Larkin, 1994). A survey of the relevant academic and popular literature reveals at least 14 different ways that values are "used" by organizations. These are distinct although sometimes overlapping categories of usage. My list is not exhaustive. I offer the "catalog" of values in discourse in the spirit of the tradition of the philosophy of pragmatism to pose the following question: What difference does it make, practically speaking, to adopt this term or that meaning?

Talk about values and "valuing" in contemporary organizations reveals the following configurations of meaning and usage:

1. Values in a hierarchy of commitments (e.g., "People first"): This sense of values relates closely to the pioneering work of Rokeach (1973) by considering every value as an abstract principle that is of greater, lesser, or equal importance with respect to other values. Organizational mission statements often list their "core" values.

2. The advocacy of specific values (e.g., "customer service"), especially with new campaigns: For instance, in the early 1980s, General Motors Corporation made a major announcement that henceforth "safety" would be their primary concern.

3. The celebration of simply having values (as in political discourse: "family values"): In fact, while participating in such discourses, it may well be to the rhetorical detriment of any organization to specify the meaning of a phrase such as "financial integrity" (Cheney & Frenette, 1993).

4. Values as mimesis or in the imitation of other organizations (e.g., "They have excellence; we need it, too!"): Values as parts of mission statements, identity packages, image management, and corporate issue advocacy are often contagious in the sense that organizations belonging to a single industry or even to diverse industries will seek to be in vogue by mimicking what value terms are in ascendancy (Christensen, 1997).

5. Values as premises for decision making and as building blocks of future persuasive efforts (e.g., in issue management: establishing common ground and "common sense," often with only vague or implicit references or images): By establishing one value or value premise, such as "We are all about customer service," certain practical implications may follow, such as a comparative neglect of employees' concerns or a redefinition of employees as, alternately, customers and suppliers of one another (per the notion of "internal markets").

6. Correspondingly, value premises can serve as means of employee motivation and (apparently) horizontal control in organizations ("concertive" organizing around visions, missions, etc.). Values have become a staple in managerial philosophy and practice, particularly since the corporate culture craze of the 1980s (Bullis & Tompkins, 1989; Tompkins & Cheney, 1985). The inculcation of value premises in an organization, such as "Give 110%," can function as a means of peer-based control (Barker, 1999) once the premise is internalized across the workforce.

7. Values as representing or encapsulating the tradition of an organization (such as in appeals to founding principles): Values in this sense are meant as symbolically transcendent means of linking present employees and customers to the history and especially the founding of the organization. This persuasive strategy helps to give the organization an air of solidity, timelessness, and mystique. This notion of corporate values was well conveyed in Watson's (1963) tribute to IBM, *A Business and Its Beliefs*.

In contemporary terms, values are central to corporate branding, identity, and reputation. Values have become prominent in corporate advertising, public relations, and marketing (Cheney & Christensen, 2001):

1. Values as undefined master symbols or sacred points of reference: Values and value-based slogans come to command great allegiance for decision making even when their multiple meanings and practical senses

go unexplained. Thus, a proponent of organizational change today can have the upper hand in a discussion simply by arguing for change. This is just one example of the strategic use of ambiguity in organizations (Eisenberg, 1984). Value-related or value-implicative terms are thus indexes for entire domains of meaning and as simultaneously devoid of meaning. Values therefore often serve as emotionally charged labels (e.g., "family friendly organization"). In this way, value expressions can operate as means of pacification and denial of problems (e.g., "We are all equal"). The currently popular trend of "diversity management" is subject to this same critique because the sheer celebration of diversity can be used as a substitute for more tangible progress in the area.

2. Values as inappropriate assertions of consensus, as measured against value diversity (e.g., "We at Acme all believe"): Here, we encounter the gulf between spokespersons' assertions of values for an organization and its members and the reality of diversity of opinion within that organization (Dahler-Larsen, 1998). Thus, the letters from CEOs that frequently appear inside the covers of annual reports will proudly announce certain value commitments possessed by "we" rather than "I."

3. Values as checks or benchmarks against which performance is evaluated: Values become benchmarks of performance when they are quantified and placed in the domain of calculation and accounting, broadly conceived (Zbaracki, 1998). The connection between the value expression, such as "quality," and its operationalization is often tenuous, however; it is always, in a sense, arbitrary (Xu, 1999).

4. Values as sites of resistance (e.g., in employees' subversive use of the organization's mission): To the extent that values and value-related terms are abstract and able to be mutated or even inverted, they offer opportunities for those who would resist the dominant trend or order in an organization or society (Fairhurst, Jordan, & Neuwirth, 1997). This is exemplified in practice by a case in a New Zealand public-sector agency in which an employee at a "customer service workshop" shouted, "Well, if we're all customers here—we're not going to buy this shit anymore!" (Gedye, 1999).

5. Value-based logic as the rationality of the organization (e.g., in reflexive organizations that revisit their own values or the idea of organizational integrity): This is the Weberian (1978) notion of a values-based logic whereby periodic, collective self-reflection characterizes a type of

organization that seeks to overcome the pitfalls of excessive reliance on more purely instrumental or formal rationality.

6. Values as embedded in social practices (e.g., journalistic objectivity as enacted by ritual): Journalism in the United States and a number of other countries has long tried to instantiate and routinize certain values, such as objectivity, through specified practices of reporting (Breed, 1960). In this way, an entire set of procedures comes to stand for certain values: In practice, the procedures narrow the vision of the professionals in certain ways so as to make some interpretations of what counts as "news" more likely than others. Relatedly, values are often implicit in or inferred from entire patterns of behavior or whole relationships (e.g., trust).

7. Transformation of values, both "within" or "under" key terms and across them (e.g., the evolution of the term *consumer* in the twentieth century): Value terms become a kind of symbolic putty in practice. They are not infinitely changeable, but they can take a variety of forms, even under the same label, as measured against time. The remarkable elevation of "consumption" from its wholly negative connotations at the turn of the twentieth century (referring to tuberculosis and to waste) is a case in point (Gabriel & Lang, 1995).

This brief but broad catalog of uses of values in business and organizational discourses shows not only that values and value-related terms can occupy a variety of positions in such discourses but also that the very question of what counts as a value can be ignored, highlighted, or contested in any given case. As we shift our discussion to the question of ethics in market-oriented discourses, we should keep in mind the lessons of this survey of value-related terms, especially concerning the capacity of language in use to recast any idea in terms that may be quite distant from original intent or from traditional usage. Ambiguity is an inherent dimension of language; thus, we should not seek its eradication but, rather, pay close attention to the resources of ambiguity (Burke, 1950/1969b). In fact, the more important the idea, typically the more abstract will be its formulations and, consequently, the more possibilities there will be for pragmatic and ideological implications under the umbrella of "freedom" or "free enterprise." Popular symbols, such as freedom, efficiency, or teamwork, will be shaped and stretched like putty: Their forms are not limitless in number, but the possibilities are many.

Another way to state the matter, metaphorically speaking, is in terms of certain meanings becoming "stuck" or "unstuck" to nodal points in public discourse on an issue of importance (Mouffe, 1992). Certain associations emerge as commonplace and are compelling in the public mind, such as "government" and "bureaucracy" today in the United States and some other industrialized countries. So powerful are such linguistic bonds that it can be difficult to pry apart two terms or images bound together by repeated invocation.

Another key dimension of the issue is how the "market" of ideas about values has been flooded with messages about them, thus potentially reducing the importance (i.e., the currency) of any particular message that asserts values or value-based commitments. This postmodern predicament of a simultaneously expanding and shrinking universe of discourse (Baudrillard, 1983) is best represented by a cartoon that depicts a person stranded on a tiny tropical island. As she prepares to throw a bottle with a message in it into the sea, she discovers to her great dismay that the sea actually consists of nothing but bottles with messages in them. Thus, how is a value best asserted or demonstrated by an organization, even when its leaders' intentions are sincere? How do we discern authenticity in value-based commitments by corporations and other organizations? After awhile, does anyone really care what organizations are saying about values (Christensen & Cheney, 2000)?

Next, we discuss a common lens through which values in organizations are seen and interpreted today: the market. The market today is simultaneously a reservoir of "value" and an arbiter of "values" in that it both determines worth and functions as an overarching framework within which values must contend for recognition. Thus, we may somewhat playfully speak of "getting value in," "added value for," and "the values of." We examine the multiple ways the market operates in popular discourses today. We ask, Is a market "framing" of values invariably reductionistic, or are there ideational or discursive ways out of this apparent dilemma?

THE PLACE OF ETHICS IN CONTEMPORARY MARKET-ORIENTED DISCOURSES

The market has come to be a supreme organizing symbol in many domains of human experience, and this has been all the more true since the fall of the Berlin Wall in 1989, a moment that for many dramatic commentaries signaled the functional end of the twentieth century and the beginning of the twenty-first century. As Cassidy (2000) writes with glib self-assurance, "If there are two things most people can agree upon these days, they are that free-market capitalism is the only practical way to organize a modern society and that the key to economic growth is 'knowledge'" (p. 44).

From this secure argumentative position, one might see the need for a close examination of the many roles "the market" *qua* symbol plays in economic discourses. Still, if we take the free-market call for competition seriously, then we should seek out and not just tolerate competitors to the market story of our development and achievement as a society (Cheney, 1999; Cooren, 1998). With an interest in promoting "entrepreneurship" and "diversity" among discourses, I list and explain briefly each of a number of different places occupied by the master symbol of the market in contemporary discourses. This exercise is valuable enough alone if it encourages self-reflection about who we are, what we do, and where we are headed as a society, even if one grants the victory of contemporary corporate and financier-centered capitalism.

What follows is a heuristic classification of the semantic and pragmatic functions of the market term, as it appears in today's public discourses—popular, academic, or other. I invite you to consider these categories, scrutinize them, consider their areas of overlap and distinctiveness, and especially reflect on ways in which this scheme may be biased, incomplete, or otherwise insufficient. After all, the degree to which we have accorded significance to the market as a master symbol for our society calls for our careful attention.

1. The market as the best way: This position simply asserts the market's superiority, often in a taken-for-granted manner. This conception of the market is based largely on the logical and moral priority of a self-interested, "rational, calculating individual, whose goal is to maximize 'utility.' This premise says everything and nothing, since it is true by definition in all cases" (Kuttner, 1997, p. 41).

2. The market as exigence, pressure, "because of" motive: Here, I appeal to Schutz's (1967) phenomenology, in which he distinguished between "because of" and "in order to" motives, thus signifying the difference between something one speaks of as moving himself or herself versus something one sees himself or herself as moving toward. The market term as a because of motive is best demonstrated by the comment of a manager or financial analyst that "the market made us do it." From this point of view, the market comes to symbolize and consolidate

pressures from the outside, an amalgam of social forces translated into economic terms that is captured in succinct terms in response to the questions, "Why this policy?" "Why reduce staff?" and "Why change course again?"

3. The market as victor over socialism/communism; the market as "the end of history": This is simply the post-Cold War position that the market has triumphed over socialist and communist economies. With this position, capitalism is usually equated with democracy, such that mentioning one neatly accounts for the other, and writers and speakers comfortably slide back and forth between the two terms (see Almond, 1991, on the complex relationships between capitalism and democracy). Perhaps most interesting is that there is seldom any mention of the possibility for alternative, as yet unimagined economic systems, except for some politically pragmatic talk of a "third way" in North America, Western Europe, and Australasia (Chatterjee et al., 1999; Giddens, 1998).

4. The market as god; the market as an answer to ultimate questions: To the extent that the market is posed as an answer to fundamental, even ultimate questions, it comes to function as a religion in Durkheim's (1933) terms. This positioning of the market has been observed explicitly by sociologist of religion Cox (1999), who has commented on the tendency today to view nearly every domain of human activity (including, sometimes, even religion) through a market lens. Echoing Marx's famous formulation of capitalism's drive toward expansion and absorption of everything around it, Cox writes,

> Divine *omnipotence* means the capacity to define what is real. It is the power to make something out of nothing and nothing out of something. The willed-but-not-yet-achieved omnipotence of The Market means that there is no conceivable limit to its inexorable ability to convert creation into commodities. (p. 20)

5. The market as a frame within which value questions will be excluded; the market as amoral: This idea brings us back to the phrase "just business," with its way of dividing the world into domains within which moral judgments will be entertained and those within which they will not be seen as relevant (Daly & Cobb, 1994). Of course, if one takes the position that market functioning is a moral institution, representing not only a pragmatic choice but also an ethical one for human beings, then the position of "just business" is enclosed within a wider framing

that sees unencumbered functioning of the market to be, ultimately, a moral necessity (Friedman, 1962).

6. The market as a domain of human expression, activity, and relationships: This positioning of the market harks back to the notion of a marketplace as an arena in which relationships between buyers and sellers are paramount in any consideration of exchanges. In some respects, this is a romantic conception of the market, conjuring up images of the ancient Athenian agora, the Turkish bazaar, or farmers' markets throughout the world. A conception of a market that is constructed not only of economic self-interest but also an interest in the social bonds that underwrite trade, however, is actually a key element in Smith's (1776/1986) *Wealth of Nations*.

7. The market as an arena of consumer choice; the market as an inherently democratic institution: One way in which marketing has positioned itself as a preeminent business function since approximately 1990 (consider "the marketing organization," in which all employees are enjoined to be "customer conscious") is through its apparently democratic ethos (Halal, 1996). Marketing relies heavily on a supermarket metaphor of consumer choice, but it actually encourages superficial forms of engagement and fosters methodological artifacts, such as when marketers virtually force respondents to express attitudes toward products or services about which the consumers know nothing or have no real concern (Laufer & Paradeise, 1990).

8. The market as a network of interorganizational relationships; the market as global commerce: This conception of the market locates it not so much at the level of interpersonal relationships but at the level of interorganizational ones. White's (1981) definition of the market as "a self-producing social structure among specific cliques of firms who evolve roles from observations of each others' behavior" (p. 518) expresses this idea of the market very well.

9. The market as an arena of investment and symbolic play: This approach to the market treats it as an arena for play and profit, within the realm of stocks, bonds, venture capital, and financial leveraging. From this standpoint, the driving force of today's market is neither production nor consumption but financial speculation, particularly as money managers represent whole segments of "the investment community" in applying pressure on corporations to change their policies in ways that will maximize stock prices (Weisberg, 1998).

10. The market as the "real-world" domain of competition: In discussions of institutions ranging from shoe manufacturing to airline travel, new technologies, and education, market competition is celebrated as the best way to ensure hard work, innovation, and attention to customers.

11. The market as a story, as myth, as metanarrative, as propaganda: In this case, the market is positioned as a grand narrative, a way of telling our story as a modern people. Here, I use Frye's (1957) definition of myth as story plus ideology. To the degree that it crowds out other possible interpretations of our "success," even denying their serious consideration in the court of public opinion, the market story functions as a kind of propaganda.

12. The market as everyday social practice; consumers as "modern-day hunters and gatherers": This view of the market sees it as something within which we all participate and something we all do. Ethnomethodological and ethnographic approaches to activities of consumption may well reflect this perspective by naturalizing, but also making slightly foreign, the everyday practices of consumption (de Certeau, 1984). The loci of such participation are therefore the shopping mall, television, and the much-heralded e-commerce, with their many different variations.

13. The market as constraint and domination: Here, I describe briefly emerging protests about and counterformulations of the market. By movements ranging from Internet organizing against the World Trade Organization (WTO) to local economies based on barter, the revocation of corporate personhood in some communities, and socially responsible investing, the hegemony of the market is being challenged from both within and without.

The lessons of this preliminary survey of possible meanings and pragmatic sensibilities for the market are many, and point of view determines which will be emphasized. My own perspective calls into question not only the material excesses of the market (e.g., a widening gap between rich and poor, the mindless proliferation of stuff such as Beanie Babies, and overdone packaging) but also symbolic dimensions by which the market, in effect, takes over lives. These include the equation of the good life with material affluence, the message of personal inadequacy that underwrites nearly all advertising (Parallax Pictures, 1997), the reduction of human value to "added value" to work processes and products, narrow notions of the bottom line in accounting and assessments of corporate performance, and the takeover of alternative discourses and other domains of discourse (politics, culture, and social relations) by market-oriented notions.

Thus, our very formulations of value and values are heavily influenced by market conceptions today—and not only in the realm of business or commerce. In the following section, I discuss an important contemporary case in which the struggle between social values and market-oriented ones (although, admittedly, they cannot be cleanly separated) is on display for us. The case is a good empirical example because it is at once foreign and distant to our concerns but surprisingly familiar in some key contours and tendencies. The case concerns the development of the Mondragón worker-owned and -managed cooperatives in the Basque Country, Spain. With this case, I illustrate how a variety of notions of value(s) and ethics are manifest in a set of organizations working out their own economic and social destiny.

THE CASE OF MONDRAGÓN

Significance

This case study began as a search for a model organization, specifically a for-profit business that was large, financially successful, and enduring but consistently adhering to core democratic values. In a sense, this quest is an age-old one in organizational studies, regardless of the sector considered. Weber (1978) was deeply concerned about the extent to which any large, complex organization, even in the arenas of charities, social movements, or religious denominations, could well hold on to their basic values. For shorthand purposes, we can call this issue "organizational integrity." Some observers have even argued that there was an implicit fourth type of authority and, by implication, organization in his scheme but that it remained underdeveloped at the time of the theorist's death in 1920. From Weber's standpoint, of course, it is the social logic of relations at work (including how control is exercised and how decisions are made) that is the defining feature of any organizational arrangement. Thus, to an extent, we may speak of an organization's "character" as being its predominant logics of authority and rationality, with the options being charismatic, traditional, legal-rational, and perhaps also value-based (Rothschild-Whitt, 1979; Satow, 1975). In a way, much of the work of critical theory (especially with Habermas, 1989) may be viewed as a working out of the question of what place noninstrumental, values-based logics of social relations can and should have in modern institutions, especially when we include notions of intersubjectivity and empathy.

Parallel to this theoretical question is a practical one: To what extent can any value-based organization, particularly in the for-profit sector, hold on to its core values in the face of an expanding and pressure-ridden global market? This question is being posed in many different ways and in all corners of society today as conservatives and liberals alike are coming to question certain runaway aspects of high-tech corporate capitalism and financial networks (Gray, 1998; Greider, 1997a, 1997b; Hawken, 1993; Kuttner, 1997; Moody, 1997; Soros, 1997).

Ironically, one practical effect of a globalizing economy is that diverse communities and regions throughout the world are seeing their own common interest in resisting the trend toward distant control over their capital, labor, and economic development. Indeed, this is one reason why the tensions within the Mondragón cooperatives are applicable to many other organizations, peoples, and places: In trying to balance a "rhetoric of efficiency" with a "rhetoric of social commitment" (Taylor, 1994), the cooperatives offer important lessons for the study of values and ethics in market-driven organizations today (Cheney, 1995, 1997, 1999). The Mondragón cooperatives offer an exceptionally interesting case for examining the roles of values and ethics in today's market not only because they have a strong social tradition but also because talk about values is such a prominent part of worklife within the co-ops. That is, the social values of solidarity, democracy, and equality have important roles in the discourses of the co-ops, just as they do in the surrounding communities. The term *solidarity* has at least seven distinct meanings in the everyday practices of the co-ops, referring to a range of things from camaraderie to an egalitarian wage scale, institutional support, and bonds with the larger community (Cheney, 1997). The corporate values of consumer service, efficiency, productivity, and globalization are coming to have increasing importance through the workings of new management programs under the labels of total quality management (TQM), total participative management (TPM), and constant improvement (or *Kaizen* in Japanese, as it is even more widely known). The case offers a window on the social processes at work in renegotiating social values in the prevailing market-driven terms of today.

I had the good fortune to explore this case in-depth by spending a total of 7 months at Mondragón in 1992, 1994, and 1997. Data were gathered from more than 150 formal interviews, hundreds of informal conversations, corporate documents, training sessions, a survey, and general assembly meetings.

History

The Mondragón cooperatives are one of the oldest, most successful cases of worker ownership and self-governance by workers in the world. They are based in the heart of the Spanish Basque Country, 1 of 18 autonomous communities created under the 1978 Spanish Constitution. They were founded in 1965 through the efforts of a quiet but charismatic Basque priest, Don José María Arizmendiarrieta, and five young engineers from an old steel mill who were committed to a "third way" between the excesses of unbridled free-market capitalism and the constraints of centralized state socialism. Having begun with a small cooperative to make gas appliances, the cooperatives now number more than 150. Also, there are approximately 45,000 worker-owners or *socios* (associates).

The co-ops are represented by two different corporations: the Mondragón Cooperative Corporation (MCC), which with total sales in 1999 exceeding $8 billion ranks as the 10th largest private firm in Spain, and Grupo ULMA, which consists of five co-ops that broke away from MCC in early 1992 due to issues of corporate restructuring. ULMA, with more than 1,200 employees, is among the top 25 firms in the Basque Country.

Many of the cooperatives are in the industrial sector, making products ranging from machine tools to auto parts and packaging and warehousing systems. For example, one of the largest single cooperatives in MCC, FAGOR-Electrodomésticos, is the leading manufacturer of refrigerators and several other household appliances in Spain. There is also a large superstructure of "second-tier" cooperatives, including a cooperative bank (the Caja Laboral), health care services, provisions for social security, and a complete educational system (which now features a technical university).

Equity is held almost entirely by associates; the cooperatives have no outside owners and sell no stock. Typically, 70% of profits go into individual capital accounts to accrue dividends for employees, pay out salaries, and to be held until the time employees end their association with the co-ops. Approximately 20% of the firms' profits are invested in joint or intercooperative projects (including training and marketing), whereas approximately 10% of the money is used to support community projects. Today, the intercooperative projects, such as marketing, are taking on greater importance as the co-ops, in the words of top managers, "try to respond to the market with a single voice."

The co-ops employ a complex system of direct and representative democracy whereby each co-op elects a president and a governing council. The governing council, in turn, appoints a general manager, and together they hold most of the power for practical, day-to-day decision making. Each co-op also maintains a social council, which is designed to counterbalance the bias of management and the governing council toward productivity with a social vision. Typically, social councils focus on such issues as safety, hygiene, and the adjustment of job indexes for pay and benefits. In some of the cooperatives, participation in the social councils is vigorous and independent-minded. In others, the social councils are weak and ineffective, without much practical authority.

All the individual co-ops that form MCC combine to form a Cooperative Congress, in which there is proportional representation according to the sizes of the cooperatives. The congress is the highest decision-making body for MCC and its constituent co-ops; it must approve major changes in policy or strategy.

Direct democracy can be seen in the form of the one-person, one-vote principle embodied in the organs that govern the life and direction of the cooperatives. At the same time, representative democracy is employed to deal with the constraints of size and to ensure that various segments of the workforce in each cooperative are fairly represented by members of key decision-making bodies. The system then exists in a dual relationship with appointed management, both at the level of individual co-ops and at the level of each cooperative corporation (MCC and ULMA). In practice, the management of a co-op, often in conjunction with the governing council, initiates new plans and programs.

Change From Without, Change From Within

There can be no doubt that the Mondragón cooperatives are under pressure from the larger market, although it is difficult to assess the actual extent of pressure. Even with the elimination of trade barriers within European Union countries in 1992 and the resulting free movement of capital across national borders, there is still a question about how much the co-ops really need to change internally in response to the larger market forces. Although the cooperatives have chosen to compete in sectors such as automobile parts that place them in direct competition with other international firms, this may not mean that the cooperatives have to fully imitate the trends and structures that prevail in other firms.

Top management of the cooperatives, for the most part, see themselves as responding in inevitable ways to demands from an increasingly global market. As one manager said to me, "We must internationalize, internationalize, internationalize." Upon further probing, however, through both interviews and examination of the corporate house organ, *Trabajo y Unión* ("Work and Unity"), I found that the argument for internationalization of the co-ops was basically tautological: "We must internationalize because we must internationalize." The idea that the firms might venture into some sectors that could keep a local or regional profile was pushed entirely out of sight and out of discussion.

Consider the use of the ambiguous but powerful term *quality* within the cooperatives, as in many organizations today. On the surface, the value is unassailable: It is an unquestionable good because all organizations today wish to be "quality organizations." Wilkinson and Willmott (1995) wrote, "Arguably, its vague, but nonetheless positive associations make the appeal of quality immediate and extensive" (p. 2). In many of today's organizations, however, quality is not being considered so much as the organization's striving to meet increasingly higher standards of excellence as it is simply a direct response to perceived customer demands. Wilkinson and Willmott note that quality means "the development of 'uniform and dependable' work practices that are congruent with delivering products or services at a low cost with a quality suited to the market" (p. 3). Thus, the pursuit of quality as such can ironically mean an organization's subordination of its own expertise to some external and popular point of reference.

While "continuous improvement" is being applied to the elimination of product defects and other errors in production, it is seldom being used to reassess the areas of hygiene, safety, and employee relations. In these ways, the co-ops are effectively surrendering part of their own internal mission and autonomy in an effort to meet the presumed customer demand in the markets in which they have chosen to compete with some of Europe's largest multinationals. Despite their long and impressive history, the co-ops are not depending on their own earned wisdom. In Goll's (1991) terms, top management is appropriating an ideology that takes for granted market pressures and uses them as a reference point in promoting a new managerial ideology, one that echoes dominant managerial trends elsewhere. In rhetorical terms, management adopts a set of terms, principles, and practices that appear to be "the best way" or "the only way" for corporate survival and success, using a reference to the market as an overriding policy justification and as a frame within which the organization's tradition and values will now be seen. In the process, local wisdom and an internal locus of control are overtaken by alignment with ideologies and practices from without.

Important internal changes have occurred within the co-ops in recent years, and several have occurred within the context of debates over social values. The changes include

- the growth of a managerial superstructure at the top of the cooperatives, especially in MCC;
- the centralization of many functions, especially strategic planning and marketing;
- the restructuring of clusters of co-ops within MCC away from regional or local groupings and toward functional sectors that are defined by specialization; and
- the departure from the traditional flat wage scale (it began as 1:3), whereby some top managers' salaries can now increase to 70% of those of their market counterparts.

Other important policy changes include participation in joint ventures with noncooperative corporations; the acquisition of numerous noncooperative forms on other continents as part of a capital expansion effort; and increased reliance on contract-based, nonowning employees to give the cooperatives greater flexibility during economic fluctuations.

A number of these changes are contested within the cooperatives. For example, the "sectoralization" or regrouping of co-ops was a significant reason for the breakaway of the ULMA Group of co-ops in early 1992; they sought to maintain ties to the local community. The change in the historic wage index propelled the growth of a quasi-union within the co-ops (officially, unions are outlawed because they are viewed as having no place in a structure in which capital and labor are not divorced), even though the actual salaries of the approximately 25 top managers covered by the new policy are little more than 50% of those of their market counterparts. In this case, the symbolic power of the shift as a threat to the core value of solidarity is enormous. One worker-member told me, "This change in the wage system represents a violation of trust, or our common commitment to the cooperatives."

One of the most important changes, however, is a practical shift under the rubric of the cherished value "employee participation." This deserves special attention as we ponder the interrelations of language, the market, values, and ethics. During most of the history of the cooperatives and certainly until the early 1990s, "participation" referred mainly to the system of direct and indirect democracy described previously. It stressed voting and employees' capacity for collective influence over the course of the firms.

Competitive pressures and their interpretation have led to vigorous attempts to reorganize work processes and "revitalize" participation, relying mainly on borrowed notions of TQM, TPM, and *Kaizen*. Partly as a result, the familiar labels of efficiency, quality, and customer service are fast becoming slogans in the cooperatives, such that their variety of meanings or the diverse ways they may be implemented are not always considered deeply. For example, some of the co-ops are using an efficiency index to calculate indirectly the "added value" of an employee or a work team to the production process; whereas in the past the same term referred mainly to the comparative advantage of working in a cooperative as opposed to being an employee of a traditional capitalist firm. The tectonic shift in meaning under the rubric of participation is captured by the words of one of the surviving founders of the cooperatives, Jesús Larrañaga, in an interview with me in 1994:

> Today, we need a form of neo-cooperativism. Participation means something different and more than voting on policies; it must be real participation in daily work, and not something legal or political in nature. . . . We have to participate for reasons of competitiveness and expansion of the market. And, the kind of participation we most need is not something up in the clouds, dealing with abstract issues, but something continuous and concentrated in one's job.

Practically speaking, neo-cooperativism means that the fundamental rationale for participation has shifted from a largely internal locus to a largely external one. Whereas in the past, employee participation was justified on both practical and moral grounds as a main benefit to employees in guiding the direction of the firm, the emerging and perhaps now prevailing view is that participation is a requirement of all employees at the level of job and work team because all are enjoined to bind their thoughts and actions to the image of the customer. In this way, the market becomes the point of reference by which formerly internal values are reshaped and recast, although remarkably (in this case) under the same rubric. Along the way, worker-owners are being relabeled and redefined alternately as customers and suppliers within the firm. This is an extraordinary shift in meaning and practice, as conducted under the cover of a central value term: The change is all the more amazing because it has been authored in part by some of the organization's founders and presumably the guardians of tradition.

At the same time that market pressures are being exerted and interpreted by management in the co-ops, other cultural and social changes are affecting the firms and their surrounding communities, including

- a major decline in formal religious observance in the post-Franco era (from 1976 to the present);
- an increase in both careerism and consumerism, especially among the younger generations;
- the substantial movement of women into the workforce; and
- the awakening of environmentalism.

All these trends implicate values and talk about values. For my purposes, however, the rise of consumerism and careerism is the most important because it signals a fundamental change in the ways Basque citizens conceive of themselves, their relationship to the larger society, and worker-owners' relationships to the co-ops. In principle, we can imagine three broad possibilities for the degree of social change in the co-ops (or in any other organization, community, or society). These distinctions are crucial for any type of analysis that seeks to characterize the nature and degree of change within an organization, institution, or broader social setting:

- "Washing over" or "floating above": Here, we find a comparatively superficial change in which discourses of global management and the market are adopted in official communications, but most everyday social and cultural practices inside and outside organizations remain untouched.
- Cooptation: The same popular business and economic discourses and ideologies are adopted by organizations and communities but in ways that conform significantly to local knowledge, preference, and practice.
- Transformation: In this case, the changes being undertaken in light of the importation of global discourses by managers, workers,

and consumers are fundamental in terms of impact on worldview and social practice (Zorn, Christensen, & Cheney, 1999).

My observations at Mondragón lead me believe that the last and most sweeping of these types of change is occurring; however, at the same time, I see evidence of the other two in some quarters, given trepidation and dissent within the co-ops regarding their current policies and strategies.

The redefinition of the person in consumer terms has tremendous implications for values and ethics, although it is not a monolithic trend and it may well yield some surprises in the future. For instance, acting as consumers, new waves of worker-owners may demand more avenues of participation as benefits from the firm (Derber & Schwartz, 1983). This would be an ironic twist to the end of an "era of self-sacrifice," as one founder of the co-ops, Alfonso Gorroñogoitia, described to me the recent changes in the culture surrounding the co-ops.

CONCLUSION

In terms of the broader scope of this essay on values, ethics, and market-oriented discourses, the following conclusions can be drawn from the case of the Mondragón cooperatives:

- Even in an organization with strong humanistic commitments (e.g., to social solidarity and democratic decision making), contemporary market-oriented values can overtake tradition. This is especially the case if the organization ceases to rely on its own tradition, expertise, and wisdom as beacons. Although the line between internal and external values is necessarily a fuzzy one in all instances, we can observe how a removed point of reference such as the market comes to be taken as a rationale for social change even when it has been little analyzed in its deeper implications.

- If the market becomes the dominant frame for organizational values, notions of efficiency, productivity, and customer service are likely to override more social concerns for employees' rights. Although highly social and ethical conceptions of the market certainly exist as rhetorical resources and can well be embraced by organizations (e.g., some moves toward business for social responsibility), the dominant ethos of market-driven notions of business and management tend to privilege short-term, pragmatic, and decontextualized articulations of decisions.

Thus, it is important to examine cases of resistance today, which include employee demands of employers, alternative trade organizations, business for social responsibility (in some forms), and local economies, for efforts to advance more socially inspired versions of the market or to challenge its dominance altogether:

- If the market is defined as a given by top management, then questions of "should" or "ought" take a backseat to an overwhelming sense of inevitability, necessity, and urgency, underwritten by the metaphor of a global race. In this way, globalization loses much of its social, cultural, and ethical textures, becoming a knee-jerk rationale for moving quickly, boldly, and without much reflection on broader or longer-term consequences for action. The worship of global management gurus plays a major role here, as does organizational imitation or the contagion of "cutting-edge" trends.

- Value transformations occur not only as ostensible shifts from one value to another but also as major shifts in meaning under the terminological umbrellas of key value-oriented labels (such as participation). Ambiguity is grounds for control and struggle. Old terms will inevitably be reshaped and reoriented, new terms will appear to treat old ideas and practices, meanings will be appropriated and co-opted even from some unsuspected sources, tensions over meanings will sometimes have their roots in practices, and changes in practices will sometimes follow shifts in meaning. Some of these changes (or advocacy for change) will deliberately be made within the market frame or context, as with Hawken's (1993) insistence that corporations fully calculate waste and environmental costs in pricing products and services. In other cases, attempts will be made to move out of the market frame or pose a dialectical alternative for the estimation of value (Gibson-Graham, 1996).

- Ironically, an emphasis on short-term profit maximization and heightened efficiency may undermine the very social foundation that allowed these organizations their financial success. In lay terms, we might contrast a short-term, high-profit perspective on organizational performance with a longer-term stability + growth perspective. Even this contrast, however, does not fully capture the tension between mainly market-driven versus more socially inclined values as points of orientation. Inattention to issues such as individual job social satisfaction, group cohesion, and overall purpose can lead an organization away from being self-sustaining and down a path of economic and social disintegration.

(Interestingly, an economist made this point before I did in observing the evolution of the Mondragón cooperatives; see Moye, 1993.)

Regardless of the prevailing cultural and symbolic winds, we may expect further transformation in the key values of democracy, productivity, and consumption. As individual consumer-workers change their outlook, motivations, and practices, and as management tests new approaches to eke out greater productivity and efficiency, there will be some surprises and some repackaging of past events. In this regard, it will be crucial to observe future changes in the development of the consumer metaphor and its associated practices (de Certeau, 1984). None of these terms or concepts have reached their final destinations in terms of associated meanings and practices; moreover, new terms and ideas will develop to reference and consolidate different clusters of significance and actions. Such musings and reformulations should be encouraged, if only because the market calls for competition. Such competition should include the ways we "tell our story," determine value, and make decisions about the good life (Lane, 2000). Therefore, we should not only be alert to the ways that current market-speak devalues or dismisses ethics but also be attuned to ways to reinvigorate economic analysis with profound ethical concerns. Deconstructing the notion that the market is an end in itself is a good place to start.

4

Cultural Contracts Theory

Toward a Critical-Rhetorical Identity Negotiation Paradigm

Ronald L. Jackson II

> *The identity negotiation theory focuses on the motif of identity security-vulnerability as the base that affects intercultural encounters. . . . It explains how one's self-conception profoundly influences one's cognitions, emotions, and interactions. It explains why and how people draw intergroup boundaries . . . it also maps out the factors that contribute to identity shock.*
>
> —Ting Toomey (1999, pp. 26-27)

AUTHOR'S NOTE: A version of the cultural contracts theory introduced here was presented at the Eastern Communication Association conference in Pittsburgh, Pennsylvania, in April 2000 and has been published by both the *Howard Journal of Communications* and the NCA/AAHE initiative titled, "Included in Communication," edited by Judith Trent. A special thanks goes to the Research Alliance Collaborating for Equity (RACE) for support of this manuscript.

Aristotle has been noted for stating that rhetoric is the faculty of observing in any given case every available means of persuasion. Rhetoric has been studied as a means by which orators or speakers articulate persuasive arguments and express personhood that resonates or is consubstantial with the realities of those to whom one is speaking. Consequently, every area of rhetorical inquiry, in some way, links rhetoric to how one views the world; therefore, an analysis of rhetoric is an analysis of one's identity as implied by the rhetor. If it is true that identities are negotiated in everyday interactions with others (Hecht, Jackson, & Ribeau, 2003; Jackson, 1999a, 1999b), then this identity negotiation process must be understood as a rhetorical phenomenon.

The analogic relationship between identity negotiation and cultural contracts deserves further clarification. As with any contract, a cultural contract is a binding agreement between two or more parties. This quid pro quo agreement seeks to disclose expectations concerning some exchange. Often, the exchange is related to goods or services or both in an ordinary contract, but in a cultural contract the exchange is related to values and worldview as much as the relationship between all parties. So, essentially, we as interactants have our own distinctive backgrounds and experiences that lead us to relate to people in different ways. Often times, those who hold positions of power have what I call "ready-to-sign" contracts. In other words, metaphorically, it is as though when you meet them, they pull out a ready-to-sign contract that suggests their expectation that you will assimilate to their perspective or set of values. Ultimately, if you choose to "sign" (or agree with) the "contract" (or perspective or value system), then that defines the parameters of your relationship with that person. It also says something significant about both your acceptance of the perspective and your compromise of certain values you held prior to signing the contract. In this situation, according to the cultural contracts theory, you will have negotiated your identity.

Communicologist Stella Ting Toomey has devised an identity negotiation theory that is founded upon the principle that identities are malleable and sometimes fragile. So, the key question within her research is: How do identities shift and why? Moreover, once shifting has occurred, how does the new ontic position influence behaviors and cultural worldview? There are multiple implications for rhetorically motivated movement and growth of identities. One of the concerns of contemporary identity theorists and cross-cultural psychologists alike is adaptive and protective behaviors that become automatically engaged as a psychological or cognitive reflex to a perceived threat. The vulnerability Ting Toomey mentions in the quotation that opened this chapter is directly related to identity development. At a less developed or less mature stage of identity, the self is much more vulnerable and perhaps more susceptible to change. Unlike symbolic interactionism, cultural contracts theory seeks to explore issues surrounding value shifts and the effect of those shifts on one's collective and personal self-definition. Although society, self, and mind are entwined as in symbolic interactionism, social acts can be defined trivially from a symbolic interactionist perspective, but with cultural contracts theory the only social acts explored as units of analysis are culturally and/or politically motivated. Social movement analysts might argue that this is the point at which protest rhetoric can be most penetrating and effective.

Critical rhetorical studies scholars who consider themselves to be postmodernists, feminists, afrocentrists, or postcolonialists suggest that the power differentials among interactants interrupt harmonious and equitable relationships even when assimilation occurs. This is an important point because often times within inequitable relationships, artificial congruence in opinion and behaviors seems awfully real. It seems logical that a speaker can effectively persuade an audience of an idea without impinging on their identities, but this logic does not take into account the humanistic aspect of rhetorical communities that form on the basis of ingroup similarity and outgroup divergence. So, if linguistic code switching is enacted properly by a subordinate in a supervisor-subordinate relationship, for example, then on the surface everything may appear intact. But beneath the surface, the identity negotiation that has taken place has inhibited freedom of expression and negatively impacted the subordinate's identity by lowering his or her self-efficacy and detaching himself or herself from an indigenous rhetorical community. This is only one possible identity effect. Generally, identity negotiation refers to a conscious and mindful process of shifting one's worldview. During this process, cultural contracts (or worldviews) are exchanged and implicitly managed. Values, beliefs, norms, patterns of communicating, and ways of viewing the world are at stake. A shift in any one or any part of one of these aspects of identity constitutes the signing of a cultural contract.

Everyone has signed at least one cultural contract in his or her life, and with every significant encounter, one or more cultural contracts are negotiated. The term *cultural contracts* refers to the end product of identity negotiation; hence, every signed or agreed upon cultural contract has a direct impact on one's identity. The effect on identities, whether it is a shifting or solidifying move, depends upon the nature of the identity negotiation process or the significance of the incident that initiated the negotiation. The word "cultural" in cultural contracts is deliberate. It is impossible to exist without culture. Even if one is unable to articulate the particularities of the cultural value system to which he or she subscribes, there are still cultural patterns of interaction, rules, and norms that guide everyday behavior (Calloway-Thomas, Cooper, & Blake, 1999). So, with this cultural contracts paradigm, there is no such thing as a noncultural or culturally generic contract, and everyone has at least one cultural contract.

As with any negotiation, one can either choose to abide by an existing contractual arrangement or sign another contract. Naturally, there are penalties associated with breaches or early withdrawals. Although the concept of identity negotiation is simple, it is not always clear what is being negotiated, especially since identities are nonmaterial. The cultural contracts paradigm is being introduced to make sense of what is actually being negotiated. Hecht et al. (2003) contend that identities are relational and negotiated in everyday interaction with others. Furthermore, they assert that "identity is defined by the individual and is co-created as people come into contact with one another and the environment. As people align themselves with various groups this co-creation process is negotiated" (p. 41).

Everyone has identified or aligned himself or herself with others throughout his or her life. This alignment can be behavioral or cognitive or both. Cultural contracts are most concerned with sustained alignments, whether short or long term. For example, you may choose to align yourself with a stranger to achieve desired ends, such as with a teacher in a classroom or a supervisor at work. You may not agree with, question, or even like the designated leader; however, you will remain within that context and continue to sustain and coordinate the relationship (Jackson, Morrison, & Dangerfield, 2002) if the ends outweigh the means. Essentially, you will have agreed to a ready-to-sign cultural contract, and in doing so you have placed a portion of your cultural values, norms, beliefs, or all three aside. There are many motivations for engaging in cultural identity negotiation. In this case, you may have done so to preserve harmony. This and other motivations will be explored later.

In this essay, I relate cultural contracts to rhetoric and identity negotiation, explain and define cultural contract types, discuss contract assumptions and propositions, explore several motivations for signing cultural contracts, and conclude with implications for the study of rhetoric and recommendations for future research.

RELATING CULTURAL CONTRACTS TO RHETORIC

Often times, rhetoricians approach a text from either an audience- or a speaker-centered perspective. Yet, rhetorical analyses can and should represent both audience- and speaker-centered perspectives, and this can be accomplished via cultural contracts theory. In applying this paradigm rhetorically, it is essential to ask and answer several central questions:

1. What are the exigencies for the rhetor engaging the audience?
2. What are the values implicit in the rhetorical situation?
3. How do the speaker (originator of the message) and the audience expose their values via their discourses?
4. Is there an alignment between speaker and audience value expectations? What are the cultural contracts that emerge?
5. Is there ever a shift from one cultural contract to another?

To further explain this, consider the post-September 11, 2001, brouhaha concerning the design of a monument in remembrance of the lives lost on that day. First, as a rhetorical analyst, I must discuss the exigencies. In this case, the exigence is defined by the perceived need to publicly memorialize the lives lost during this tragic occurrence in New York City. Second, I would need to address the values implicit in the rhetorical situation. The rhetor or speaker would be the originator of the idea to build such a monument, and the audience would be the citizens who countered one design by presenting another. Both parties would most likely be responding to a call for communal togetherness, American patriotism, family remembrance, and overall resilience. Third, to fully ascertain the implicit values, there would need to be a mapping of the emergent themes within the discourses. Thus, for instance, the New York City authorities recommended that the faces and bodies on the monument should reflect the death toll. Because more White firefighters died, there should be more White firefighters represented. Many New Yorkers were outraged by this suggestion and countered by recommending a design that included one Black, one White, and one Latino person. In this situation, values related to fairness and diversity were questioned via their discourses. The fourth "investigative" question now arises: Is there an alignment between speaker and audience value expectations? What are the cultural contracts that emerge? Clearly, the values are somewhat divergent. They may agree that there should be some public monument, but they are debating over the representations. We can discern the cultural contract types by examining the mapped text searching for points of value alignment or misalignment but also for the end resolution. Did the city scrap the whole deal and decide to start over or not to do any monument at all, or did it use the initial plan, the new plan, or devise a compromise?

In an effort to extend what Foss and Griffin (1992) call an "invitational rhetoric" or a rhetoric of balance and mutual valuation, I have devised a trialectic paradigm known as cultural contracts theory. Cultural contract is a metaphor for how identities are negotiated in rhetorical situations. Thus, when negotiating cultural contracts, one is negotiating or exchanging values that reflect one's identity. The three cultural contract types are ready-to-sign, quasi-completed, and co-created contracts, which refer to assimilation, accommodation, and valuation, respectively. The co-created contract is virtually synonymous with invitational rhetoric. In the case of the public monument design, if the end result is that the speaker/city decides to use its initial plan, then the audience/citizens may perceive that they are being handed a ready-to-sign contract that they are expected to agree with against their will. If the city truly engages in a deliberation that permits some compromise between the two perspectives, then the contract type would be a quasi-completed contract. If the city scraps the whole project and invites the citizens to fully participate in every step of the design, this invitational rhetoric is indicative of a co-created contract. If the city scraps the whole project permanently without any agreement with the citizens to do so, this could be regarded as a gesture indicating the city's interest in forcing its hand or exercising its legitimated state authority, which is clearly related to a ready-to-sign contract. Keep in mind that the audience also has its own values and cultural contracts that orbit around its own discursive formations. If these values and cultural contracts are misaligned with those of the speaker, then the effects on identity and rhetorical community can be quite deleterious unless one of the parties shifts perspectives.

RELATING CULTURAL CONTRACTS TO IDENTITY NEGOTIATION

Cultural contracts theory is a rhetorical paradigm that is about locating and understanding values, which are constitutive parts of identities.

Identities are negotiable via cultural contracts at every stage of relationship development, irrespective of context, from initial interaction to relational termination. The following three premises to identity negotiation must precede any in-depth conversation about the process or outcome of this daily engagement or both: Identities require affirmation, identities are constantly being exchanged, and identities are contractual.

Identities Require Affirmation

Although there are multiple ways to think of identity, it essentially refers to a self-definition that is communicatively affirmed or validated by others (Jackson, 1999a). This is what has come to be known in critical cultural and critical rhetorical studies circles as the "I-Other" dialectic. Postcolonialist and psychiatrist Frantz Fanon (1963) goes so far as to say that "to speak is to exist for the other," which suggests that there is an interdependent function to human interaction. The I, acting as subject, has a direct relationship to the Other, which functions as the dialectical object; therefore, each comes to understand the self by knowing what the self is not. In other words, we know what it means to be rich by contrast to what it means to be poor. We know what is right by also acknowledging what is wrong. Foucault labels this the principle of exteriority—the idea that external observations and representations of the self facilitate the ontological development of the interior. Similar to this "oppositional discourse" perspective, Burke theorizes rhetorical dialectics in terms of a cluster-agon approach through which identified god and devil terms help rhetoricians to understand how words "tell on us" by signifying value judgments.

Identities Are Constantly Being Exchanged

It is well-known that communication is inevitable and happens all the time. Even when we think we are not communicating, we are. It is this enduring feature of interaction that sustains identity negotiation as both a personally and a socially developmental activity. It is simple to suggest that humans communicate constantly, but it is much more complicated to argue effectively for how one exchanges identities or portions of identities while interacting. As Cui, van den Berg, and Jiang (1998) explain in their analysis of cross-cultural adaptation, ontological difference implies a need for relational coordination. The cultural competence literature presumes that racial coordination should occur unilaterally from the most powerful to the least powerful, which then forces adaptation. Ting Toomey (1999) disagrees with this slippery claim and correctly asserts that it is faulty to think that a stranger should always adapt to a host, regardless of context. Likewise, in environments in which cultures cohabitate, such as in the United States, it is nonsensical to assume that Latinos will never need to adjust to a Black relational context. There is not one clear host, unless we are to presume that Whites are the hosts in every situation.

We would like to believe that we are simply exchanging conversation, but within every interaction we are also rhetorically exchanging codes of personhood. It is this premise that is primarily responsible for the vulnerability mentioned by Ting Toomey. The frequency with which human beings interact increases the likelihood that identities will either concretize or become highly unstable and unaware over time. Each has its price.

Identities Are Contractual

There is a socially, politically, and culturally binding feature to all cultural contracts enacted via rhetoric. Consequently, there are penalties incurred when one breaches the contract by asserting values that work against the expectations one party has for another. Likewise, there is a commitment to the contractual arrangement that must be acknowledged. Naturally, social rules and laws govern behavior and become guideposts for acceptable and normal interaction. Essentially, these restrictions are socially agreed upon, and complicitous behavior confirms your signature on the contract. McPhail's (1994a, 1998) rhetorical paradigm is called complicity theory and explains that complicitous behavior affirms essentialist ways of knowing. The severe danger inherent in agreeing to disagree is the possibility of human oppression, structural and political constraints, and inhibited social transformation.

Although identities are contractual, negative social and political practices can be rehabilitated in a climate of resistance rather than complicity. One fascinating critical analysis of complicity is that of Dreama Moon (1999), who contends that "to achieve and maintain 'good (White) girl' status, White women must be willing to be, if not actively engaged with, at least complicitous with the reproduction of White supremacy" (p. 182).

Moon (1999) goes on to suggest that Whites experience a racialized enculturation process at home, which only reaffirms the bourgeois status of Whites and subordinate citizenry of non-Whites in the United States. This assertion not only has ethical significance but also denotes a contractual relationship to maintain what education theorist Christine Sleeter (1994) calls "White silence." Nakayama and Martin (1998), among others, have taught us that when privilege, in whatever form, is codified according to skin color, as is whiteness, the discursive signifiers such as "American" or "whiteness" protect the beneficiaries from having to acknowledge or think about privilege. Their identities are normalized and treated as nondescriptive aspects of the wider culture. Complicity is reified once again.

The three premises of identity negotiation mentioned previously are foundational principles for all cultural contracts. By comprehending these, alliance building is facilitated, and relational coordination is better understood.

CULTURAL CONTRACT TYPES

Cultural contracts theory is a rubric of identity negotiation. The identity negotiation theory explicated by both Ting Toomey (1999) and Jackson (1999a, 1999b) offers a general structure for the cultural contracts theory; therefore, it functions as a metatheory for the introduction of this cultural contracts paradigm.

Before presenting the assumptions and propositions, it is important that the different contract types be discussed. Ready-to-sign cultural contracts are prenegotiated, and no further negotiation is allowed. For these persons, signing or relational coordination may or may not be the goal. They may not even be aware that their whiteness is a marker of normality and privilege. There is no such thing as not having a contract; hence, they have either directly or indirectly chosen to contract with themselves. To say that one has no cultural contract is to say that one has no culture or understanding of how to function in the culture in which he or she lives. One cultural contract is with whiteness, which is often defined by an interest in maintaining privilege, although it may also be defined by a resistance to retaining privilege, as in the case of self-proclaimed antiracists (Wray & Newitz, 1997) or white abolitionists (Ignatiev & Garvey, 1996). Quasi-completed cultural contracts are partly prenegotiated and partly open for negotiation. These persons are not ready to fully co-create and not necessarily ruling out maintaining their own worldview. These persons "straddle the fence" in terms of their commitment to reorder privilege. They would rather maintain some measure of control. Arguably, this is due to a perceived sense of vulnerability. This is perhaps the least long-lasting contract. Finally, co-created cultural contracts are fully negotiable, with the only limits being personal preferences or requirements. This is often perceived as the optimal means of relational coordination across cultures because the relationship is fully negotiable and open to differences. If a cultural contract is co-created, there is an acknowledgment and valuation of cultural differences. These cultural differences are not ignored but do not become the only reason why the two relational partners are together. The emphasis is truly on mutual satisfaction rather than obligation. Metaphorically, each contract type is a result of how identities have been personally and socially constructed and explored.

OUTLINING CORE THEORETICAL ASSUMPTIONS AND PROPOSITIONS

Assumptions

Assumption 1: Human beings cannot exist without culture; culture is the basic organizing unit of social processes (Ting Toomey, 1999).

Assumption 2: Cultural contracts are necessary for the sake of preserving, protecting, and defining the self; hence, everyone has at least one. (There is no such thing as not having one, although you may not be aware of what your contract requires you to do. All contracts have fine print that may be overlooked without careful reading.)

Assumption 3: Cultural contracts can be either temporary/episodic or long-term/enduring.

Assumption 4: Cultural difference among human interactants presupposes a need for coordination that is manifested in cultural contracts (Cronen, Chen, & Pearce, 1988).

Assumption 5: Although important, there is not necessarily a mutual interest in relational coordination, identity negotiation, or intercultural competence among all human interactants (Jackson, 1999a). With these persons, signing is not the goal.

Assumption 6: Identities are dynamic, not static, and they are influenced during interaction with others (Hecht, Collier, & Ribeau, 1993).

Assumption 7: Every time people communicate, they are communicating their identities by expressing how they view the world (Hecht et al., 1993; Ting Toomey, 1999).

Assumption 8: Communicators' personal histories and antecedent interactions influence the degree to which they are open to entering into identity negotiations with others (Jackson, 1999a, 2000a; Jackson et al., in press).

Assumption 9: Because multiple identities are functioning simultaneously within communicative contexts, they may also be negotiated simultaneously (Collier & Thomas, 1988).

Assumption 10: The attempt to function as a "free agent" and "join" another culture or accept an alternative value system is not always as profitable as it sounds; it is often stressful, shocking, and isolating (Ting-Toomey, 1999).

Assumption 11: A contract will only be completed or "tendered" if there is a strong desire or perceived need for it, even if it is forcibly signed for the sake of survival (Jackson et al., in press).

Propositions

Proposition 1: When there is unequal power among interactants, strategic communication will occur (Giles, Mulac, Bradac, & Johnson, 1987).

Proposition 2: There is a direct and proportionate relationship between power and self-efficacy (Moon, 1999; Orbe, 1994, 1998; Ting Toomey, 1999).

Proposition 3: If there is no perceived need to relationally coordinate, then there will also be greater resistance to co-creating cultural contracts (Orbe, 1998). (These persons will either expect you to sign their contract or have none at all.)

Proposition 4: As cultural loyalty increases, so does the likelihood that ready-to-sign cultural contracts will be prepared for other cultural relationships in advance (see Gallois, Franklyn-Stokes, Giles, & Coupland's [1988] discussion of ethnic vitality).

Proposition 5: There are at least three types of cultural contracts: ready-to-sign (i.e., not budging; closest to win-lose), co-created (i.e., win-win and interdependent self-construal), and quasi-completed.

Proposition 6: If contracts are breached, there are penalties associated with this "rule" violation, one of which may be the cost of community ostracism. (Of course, there are "escape clauses" in the fine print.)

Proposition 7: When a breach or violation occurs, one of three actions will occur in varying degrees: termination or rupture of the relationship, tendering of a new or revised contract, or settling without penalty due to the perceived high value of the relationship and low assessment of damage.

MOTIVATIONS FOR SIGNING CULTURAL CONTRACTS AND BREACHING THEM

Motivations vary according to which contract type is being negotiated and the context and conditions under which they may be signed. Organized by contract type, the following sections present reasons why people sign cultural contracts.

Cultural Contract Type: Ready-to-Sign (Requires Assimilation)

Motivations

- To preserve an artificial harmony (interested in being one with another)
- To achieve desired ends (interested in accomplishing goals and objectives)

Rhetorician Roderick Hart (1997) identifies the "melting pot" concept in the United States as an identity myth—an ill-founded belief often told to guide or solidify a group around a given practice or worldview. The melting pot concept was an attempt to get Americans to view themselves as more alike than different. Generally, Hart argues, myths are the substance of culture and serve five functions: to heighten a sense of authority, continuity, coherence, choice, and agreement. That is, myths are historical truths that shape how we view authority and politics. They also help us to link ideas with experience, establish connectedness, facilitate ethical choices, and structure consensus.

Both the melting pot concept and the previously mentioned motivations are exemplified by the 2000 U.S. census, which revealed that approximately 7 million Americans opted to identify themselves as multiracial by checking more than one box on the census form. This number is equal to one half of all Americans age 18 or younger. Americans age 18 or younger represent one fourth of all U.S. citizens. The census results have many profound implications—political, economic, cultural, and rhetorical. Here, I focus on the cultural and rhetorical implications. One of the most effective ways to merge these two constituent parts is to frame the discussion as a critical-rhetorical one. According to McKerrow (1998), critical-rhetorical studies emphasize the confluence between discourse, culture, power, and identity. The discursive and cultural implications refer to the ways that identities are marginalized on a daily basis via the language we use to frame our conversations about race and culture. Implicit in this framing is the notion of power as an interceding variable in all asymmetrical interracial encounters.

Because the data reveal that Latinos now represent more than 12% of the U.S. population, a percentage exceeding that of Blacks, America seems much more diverse. Keep in mind, however, that as major news outlets such as the *Washington Post*, CNN, and the *Chicago Tribune* have reported (Page, 2001),

> Of the 13% of Americans who said they were Hispanic, for example, only about half (6%) called themselves White. Another 5.3% curiously checked "other." Many wrote "I am Hispanic" next to the race question, officials said. Does that mean that those individuals thought they belonged to a race other than the listed choices of White, Black, Native American Indian, Asian or Pacific Islander, and multiracial? Or did it simply mean that none of the offered choices had any meaning to them?

According to *Washington Post* columnists Cohn and Fears (2001), if the label "Hispanics" were added to the census form, an additional 126 categories would have to be included. On paper, the multiracial categorization effort has reinforced the idea that America is a diverse melting pot with multiple cultures blended together, although they still have to negotiate the unique "flavor" that distinguishes them from cultural others. In other words, nothing has really changed except the fact that we now know for certain what we already suspected: Americans have overlapping ancestries, and there is really no utility to naming races. The U.S. Census Bureau has not statistically controlled for race within the multiracial category, so it can report only a raw number that indicates those who chose to self-designate as multiracial. *Chicago Tribune* columnist Clarence Page (2001) posits,

> New racial and ethnic numbers in the 2000 U.S. census show an increasingly complex picture of the way we Americans look at ourselves. It also shows the job of counting by race and ethnicity to be about as precise as grabbing a handful of Jell-O.

I have noted these census numbers and concerns because they are illustrative of the ready-to-sign cultural contract. The melting pot concept is grounded in an assimilationist perspective. The more people blend their identities to match those of (proto)typical Americans (i.e., Whites), the more likely we are to be a more harmonious nation. The Republicans were in favor of the multiracial categorization initiative because by noting that one is of multiple origins, the monies designated for improvement of culturally specific, proportionately underrepresented communities and districts are redistributed into a larger, culturally indiscernible community. Eventually, monies allocated for culturally specific communities will disappear. Although this appears to be political on the surface, the rhetorical implication is that the melting pot gets reconfigured. The melting pot has been denounced among many U.S. citizens because it conceptually eliminated cultural particularity, but as long as Hispanics are given few other choices besides identifying themselves as Whites or others, some mixed-heritage Hispanics will continue to choose "White," and this label will merge their Latino identities with that of mainstream Americans. The consequence is a reinvention of the melting pot and the signing of a ready-to-sign cultural contract.

Cultural Contract Type: Quasi-Completed (Requires Partial Commitment to Value Difference)

Motivations

- To avoid conflict (interested in maintaining comfort)
- To gain cultural pride or cultural consciousness (interested in being a part of something that seemed more familiar and easier to relate to)

Collier and Thomas (1988) note that "Blacks seem to employ different rules [and] role prescriptions differ in that Blacks note cultural role prescriptions with Whites" (p. 133). Orbe (1997) concurs and suggests that Blacks are constantly "playing the part." This type of behavioral code switching or style shifting strategically escapes conflict with established norms. That is, if a code is a way of expressing one's relationship with and to the world, then code switching refers to the shifting of one's relationship to the world given certain rhetorical exigencies. A person may also be motivated to code switch so that he or she can be appreciated or valued for being a part of the in-group. During focus group interviews with Blacks at a predominantly White East Coast university, Jackson (1999a) found that the respondents resisted complicity with hegemony. One student responded to a question about whether she negotiated her cultural identity in the different-race educational context. Although acknowledging that behavioral code switching is sometimes appropriate, she stated, "If you keep on changing yourself for other people, after awhile, you won't know who you are . . . and those people you are trying to be like will not respect you" (p. 83). This statement was affirmed by others in the group and suggested an acute awareness that how one labels and identifies oneself culturally is critical.

This awareness is linked to the second contract type, quasi-completed contracts. Giles et al. (1987) explain that accommodating behavior is directly correlated to one's level of ethnolinguistic commitment or in-group vitality. In cases of low vitality, one's core self can be altered more easily for the sake of gaining a higher level of vitality and, hence, cultural pride. In this act of rhetorically framing identity, interactants avow themselves to a rhetorical community that shares values, norms, and beliefs. Likewise, as long as they do not have an ethnocentric orientation toward other cultural groups, this can serve as a stabilizing force that allows cultural interactants to appreciate others because they are grounded in their own cultures. The less one is grounded, the more likely he or she is to assimilate. Of course, it is possible to move back and forth between contracts as one identity shifts, matures, and is influenced by critical incidents.

Cultural Contract Type: Co-Created (Requires the Most Work Because Each Person Seeks to Fully Value the Other)

Motivations

- To genuinely learn to value the other person (e.g., interracial relationship)
- To prove one is an ally
- To resist marginalization

This final contract type is best illustrated by a conversation moderated by Susan Page (1997) of *USA Today*. The participants featured here are Wade Henderson (Leadership Conference on Civil Rights), Ward Connerly (American Civil Rights Institute), and Ralph Reed (Christian Coalition). They are all responding to President Clinton's call for racial reconciliation:

Henderson: I thought the president's speech was a very important beginning. At the same time I think the likelihood of a success from dialogue alone is probably limited, because I think there is an extraordinary denial on the part of American people. Americans in general have an attitude about racial problems which says that racism is not a problem, but if it is a problem, not significant. And if it is significant, we're not going to deal with it.

Connerly: I think we can have a candid discussion about race, but it's one that all of us have to be willing to be very honest about. Black people have to be prepared to come to the table and discuss their biases as much as everybody else.

Reed: A lot of things we debate, a lot of other issues that might on the surface appear unconnected to race, there is a subtext of race in each of these issues, whether it's crime, drugs, welfare, or education we're confronting. The one

> thing that I would say that I was disappointed about in the president's speech is that of race, and I don't think his commission is fully inclusive of the diversity of views either. But at least he started. (p. A1)

This conversation is a perfect example of co-created contracts. Each statement gives a critique or comment that indicates a mutual respect and valuation of other cultures and perspectives. Likewise, it is important to note that Connerly is attentive to the idea that co-creation is a mutually vulnerable position. It requires sacrifice and self-abnegation among all parties involved. Henderson insightfully suggests that co-creation involves a willingness to acknowledge faults, oversights, and limitations as obstructions to real relationship building. Finally, Reed epitomizes the ideal co-created cultural contract by indicating the importance of being "fully inclusive." He uses the word "full" twice to imply that there is a fragmented effort to solve a whole problem. To completely address the issue of diversity, diversity must be represented. By signing a co-created cultural contract, interactants are obligated to see one another so that difference is not invisible. It is apparent, substantial, important, and valued. For those readers who know the ideologies of each of these individuals, this conversation seems almost unreal. Their views range from quite conservative to at least centrist or slightly left of center. Therefore, although they ideoogically differ, the example given is an important illustration of how individuals may articulate certain values in one setting and different ones in others. It does not mean the person is necessarily contradicting himself or herself but that human beings are complex. We have multiple ideas that are not always consistent on the surface but may need to be contextualized to make sense. I might support affirmative action for minority contractors who historically are excluded from the competition for federal grants, but I might be against affirmative action for college admission policies in which Whites are given financial aid for attending a historically Black college or university. This says something about the kinds of cultural contracts I am willing to sign in certain rhetorical situations.

There are as many motivations for signing cultural contracts as there are conditions and contexts. Here, I provided seven reasons to introduce the impetus for engaging in the identity negotiation process. I have provided a more thorough review elsewhere (Jackson & Simpson, 2003). Nonetheless, cultural contracts are a way of life, a means for functioning in any given society. People occasionally breach them and are often penalized for doing so. There are also escape clauses and fine print not discussed here. These features complicate the cultural contract even more because interactants do not always know what they are getting themselves into when they sign. Sometimes, people do not know why they are in a given group or relationship and choose to opt out of it. This reminds me of Tiger Woods, who was labeled a sellout to Black culture because he chose to label himself "Cablasian." He chose not to approve the ready-to-sign Black cultural contract to behave and identify himself as the "African American community" wanted. He chose to view the African American community as a diverse set of communities that represented the best of individuality rather than a collective will of a cultural faction of the United States. This was perceived by many to be a breach of a contract Blacks thought Tiger had signed or would sign because he was visibly Black. The fine print of Tiger's self-labeling was that being American supersedes being African American, especially in circumstances in which one is performing as an athlete in and outside the country and representing the entire populace of Americans. He escaped the contract, and the community has frequently embraced him for his talents but spoken poorly of him as a confused person.

IMPLICATIONS AND RECOMMENDATIONS FOR FUTURE RESEARCH

Culture is rhetorically transmitted on an everyday basis and is fundamentally public property, historically situated, and socially bound. You may be a member or representative of this entity called culture, but it is not entirely yours to negotiate. It is property shared with others who have sizable investments in it. It is not that you are negotiating your share of it. Actually, you are negotiating to retain access to a cultural collective or rhetorical community rather than give that access away, and every negotiation is a rhetorical one. Much of the social identity literature assumes that you are an ascribed member of a given culture for life, however culture is learned and avowed, whereas such social tropes as race are ascribed. Although there are core components of one's cultural personality that tend to remain stable over time, these aspects are still potentially negotiable items. Essentially, identity negotiation is about giving oneself permission to be despite having one's being consistently called into question.

As critical rhetoricians or cultural critics, it is imperative that paradigms such as cultural contracts theory are produced to help make sense of how we as communicators have our identities affected by everyday rhetorical transactions. Future research might examine the intersections of race, sexuality, class, gender, identity, or all these. It would be ideal to have studies concerning a critical-rhetorical analysis of Latino masculinity as a marginalized identity or of homosexual sexuality and identity effects as a result of cross-cultural discourse.

Perhaps identity negotiation is a social requisite of all human survival. Even when one claims that he or she is not a participant, this may be a matter of not acknowledging a subconscious proclivity for redefining oneself within every interaction. According to Foucault (1972), self-transformation begins with discursive regularities being disrupted by "interplays of difference" (p. 37). This process is doubly intensified when the need to redefine emerges from the demand for cultural homogeneity rather than difference. When this ontological pressure is applied, the threat of self-erasure becomes vividly real, and the struggle to retain the self ensues. The paradigm of cultural contracts is useful for exploring how relationships and identities are formed, coordinated, rejected, or terminated and how this process occurs rhetorically. The optimal relationship allows asymmetry only when reciprocated. The reality is that cultural interactants want to be valued. Leslie Reese (as cited in Jackson, 2000b) said it best: "Introduce me to a world where I don't have to miss myself."

Part II

Rhetorics, Institutions, and Contexts

Whereas the essays in Part I focus on articulating rhetorical responses to ethics and values, Part II features four case studies that will encourage you to focus on neglected dimensions of rhetoric that require attention in the twenty-first century. Consider the following questions as you read the essays: What are the functions of rhetoric in specific institutions and contexts? What new interpretations of generic requirements seem useful?

In "Remembrance of Things Past: A Postcolonial Critique of the Human Genome Diversity Project," Marouf Hasian and Emily Plec, in the spirit of scholars who have offered critiques of dominant discourses with the goal of empowering the disempowered (Hasian & Flores, 1996; Hegde, 2001; Shome, 1996a, 1999), focus on responses of national and international communities to biotechnology movements. In their study of the Human Genome Diversity Project, Hasian and Plec offer an analysis that advances cultural communication scholarship by addressing global issues. As Shome and Hegde (2002) suggest,

> A quick look at interdisciplinary critical cultural literature from various publishing houses and journals in the last 5 to 10 years shows that globalization is precisely the point around which a great

deal of cutting-edge cultural work is being produced, theorized, and interrogated. (p. 173)

Two essays in Part II are case studies that point to possibilities for bridging "old" and "new" approaches to rhetoric by extending genre theory. Genre theory, according to Karlyn Kohrs Campbell and Kathleen Hall Jamieson (1978b), is a useful tool for the critic because "rhetorical forms that establish genres are stylistic and substantive responses to perceived situational demands" (p. 9). Although the emphasis on situation has defined generic critical approaches, William Benoit (2000) has called for more complex generic approaches to account for "the inherently complex rhetorical acts" (p. 178). "The Life of the Party: The Contemporary Keynote Address," by John M. Murphy and Thomas R. Burkholder, argues for the significance of keynote addresses in authorizing political parties as agents of collective action in a democracy and the keynote as a genre. The keynote address defines the party, rather than a candidate, and as a genre speaks to the continuity of political parties as institutions. Victoria J. Gallagher examines the relationship between public memory and social action through a generic study of visual rhetoric. In "Memory as Social Action: Cultural Projection and Generic Form in Civil Rights Memorials," she addresses the extent to which the memorials, as sites of tourism, function rhetorically to instruct visitors to frame their responses in terms of particular racial ideologies.

The final study in Part II focuses on entertainment, in this case film, as rhetoric rationalizing institutional policy. George N. Dionisopoulos analyzes John Wayne's film, *The Green Berets*, as a rhetorical justification for U.S. efforts to shape the world following World War II. *The Green Berets* functioned rhetorically to justify U.S. policy in Southeast Asia. The film is still available and may serve as a cautionary tale to remind viewers that when patriotism is reduced to simplistic "right versus wrong" messages, the consequences may be tragic. Dionisopoulos reminds readers that film is a powerful medium of communication, and that it has the power to shape audience perceptions of public policy.

In Part II, the authors draw from a variety of rhetorical contexts and genres, including biotechnology, the political keynote address, a civil rights memorial, and a film, in an effort to ground their analyses and extrapolate new knowledge about our rhetorical environment.

5

Remembrances of Things Past

A Postcolonial Critique of the Human Genome Diversity Project

Marouf Hasian, Jr. and Emily Plec

> *The conquest of the earth, which mainly means the taking it away from those who have a different complexion or slightly flatter noses than ourselves, is not a pretty thing when you look into it too much. What redeems it is the idea only.*
>
> —Joseph Conrad (1988, p. 282)[1]

In recent years, a growing number of scholars within the discipline of communication have been interested in exploring the influence that ideology, power, and discourse have within international and national spheres. Aligning themselves with an interdisciplinary movement known as postcolonial studies, such critics have actively searched for critical and theoretical approaches to understanding that engage and promote the voices of subalterns throughout the world (Hasian & Flores, 1996; Shome, 1996b; Steyn, 2001; Supriya, 1996; Wander, 1996). Employing various Foucauldian, deconstructive, and feminist approaches in their interrogations of imperial and colonial practices, postcolonial theorists and critics search for ways of simultaneously critiquing dominant discourses and enabling the disempowered.[2]

In this essay, we join in this conversation and provide a possible site of intervention by examining the ways in which various national and international communities are coping with some of the issues raised by global, biotechnology movements. In June 2000, reporters commenting on the famous Human Genome Project announced that scientists had finished mapping the "book of life" in the form of human genetic codes and warned about the possibilities of genetic discrimination (Goodman, 2000). We focus on just one aspect of these complex genomic debates, explicating some of the critical rhetorical problems associated with the loosely affiliated Human Genome Diversity Project (HGDP).

Defenders of the HGDP have noted that the more famous Human Genome Project provided us with important clues about the genetic makeup of Western communities but precious little about the genetic diversity that exists in other human populations. Some population geneticists and biologists claim that we need a much broader collection of blood and tissue samples from more diverse populations if we are going to truly get a picture of human similarities and differences. In the spring of 1997, a geneticist at the University of Maryland explained that "you can't go gene hunting in Chicago" for information on the genetic maladies of groups such as Native Indian tribes, so scientists need to examine "remote populations that make perfect laboratories" (as cited in Salopek, 1997, p. I8). Confirming this claim, other scientists and researchers ruminated that without the genomic data from countries such as India and China, the Human Genome Project "could more aptly be called the 'Western Nation Genome Project'" (Smaglik, 2000, p. 912).

Promoters of the HGDP viewed the project as the next logical step in our progressive understanding of the relationship between genes, populations, and linguistic communities (Cavalli-Sforza, 2000). They also argued that the "gift of blood" will help us learn a great deal about the genetic structure of both "developed and 'primitive' societies" (Dickson, 1996, p. 11). In the initial planning stages, the advocates of the project wanted to analyze the genetic data that would be collected from approximately 500 "geographically isolated or culturally or linguistically unique populations" (Crigger, 1995, p. 2; Pennisi, 1997, p. 568). The arguments advanced by advocates of the HGDP have been considered to be problematic for a number of reasons, not the least of which is the way in which they discursively position indigenous or "isolated populations" as "perfect laboratories."

Throughout the 1990s, hundreds of indigenous communities and their allies attacked both the feasibility and the desirability of the HGDP, and they successfully slowed the pace of government funding for the project. Detractors contend that the HGDP is a "vampire project" that poses several problems, including the possible expropriation of intellectual property from the poor, the potential violations of indigenous rights and societal norms, the lack of consent or consultation that accompanies some gene "mining," and the creation of unreasonable expectations on the part of communities that suffer from daily deprivations (Central Australian Aboriginal Congress [CAAP], 1994; Crigger, 1995). Glantz, Annas, Grodin, and Mariner (1998) note that people in "developing countries" are often placed in vulnerable research positions "because of their lack of political power, lack of education, unfamiliarity with medical interventions, extreme poverty, or dire need for health care and nutrition" (p. 39).

In this essay, we argue that part of the reason the disputes over the HGDP were so vehement is due to the fact that both critics and advocates of the project walked into a discursive minefield laden with the sedimented layers of racial and colonial ideologies. McGee (1990) notes the ways in which even finished discourse may be composed of fragments that are constructed by audiences, readers, and critics. This view of discourse is especially important to consider in postcolonial situations in which the colonizer and colonized may have ambivalent feelings and anxieties about the introduction of genetic benefits into what some have called the "Third World." Reardon (2001) argues that the HGDP could not move from the planning stages because advocates of the project were unable to exert control over the intertwined social and scientific issues. By coproducing a natural and social order, she argues, the project organizers might be better equipped to deal with such "emotionally and politically charged discourses" (p. 357). In contrast, we look to the responses of the project's critics, specifically the perspectives and public statements of individuals and organizations claiming to represent the indigenous populations initially targeted by the HGDP. We do this so that we can understand why some viewers have characterized the HGDP as an imperialist or eugenical project.

To understand some of the complexities of this rhetorical situation, we divide the essay into three major sections. In the first section, we frame the essay by outlining some of the basic assumptions of postcolonial criticism. In the second and largest section, we briefly review some of the scientific and cultural debates that have prefigured the controversy surrounding the attempted popularization of the HGDP[3] and then delve into some of the specific rhetorical claims made by each side in the controversy. Here, we compare and contrast some of the indigenous and Western scientific arguments that were deployed in the discursive conflicts over the meanings of the HGDP. This move is somewhat precarious because we invoke a binary opposition (between supporters and critics) in a way that is characteristic of colonial discourses; that is, the analysis has the potential to fix identity and exclude the possibilities of hybridity (Bhabha, 1994). The contrast, however, allows us to unveil "the Eurocentrism and imperialism in Western discourses" that postcolonial criticism engages (Shome, 1996b, p. 41). By privileging the perspectives of subalterns, we seek not to reinforce a colonial model wherein academics give voice to "communities of zero workers" (Spivak, 1988) but, rather, to expand critical terrain, especially around the rhetoric of science, and expose contemporary colonial and imperialist discourses. We conclude the essay by providing a heuristic assessment of the potential for postcolonial studies as a critical perspective on future genomic questions.

INTERROGATIONS AND INTERVENTIONS OF POSTCOLONIAL THEORIES AND PRACTICES

When academicians use the term *postcolonial*, they may be talking about an intellectual paradigm, a particular period in history, political movements of resistance, or a generic form of writing. Despite its "short history as a practice in the Western academy," notes Moore-Gilbert (1997), postcolonialism has had a "major impact upon the current modes of cultural analysis, bringing to the forefront of concern the interconnection of issues of race, nation, empire, migration, and ethnicity with cultural production" (p. 6). Unlike Orientalist projects that are Eurocentric in nature, postcolonial interventionists are willing to interrogate the taken-for-granteds of imperialist tales. Thus, instead of assuming that the advance of civilization or the progress of science depends on the dissemination of particular knowledges from West to East or North to South, postcolonial scholars are skeptical observers who monitor the impact of globalization practices. Moreover, postcolonialism calls into question the articulation of such ideographs as "progress" and "science" as well as the assumption that civilization is advancing. Shome (1998) argues that postcolonial theorizing involves the "theoretical project" of examining the "relations and problematics of colonialism" while simultaneously paying attention to the conditions that have emerged "after the end of territorial colonial occupations" (p. 205). These conditions warrant the skepticism of many indigenous communities opposed to the HGDP.

The postcolonial posture is an important position to take in trying to illuminate some of the discursive dimensions of the modern genomic controversies because it calls attention to the ideological and rhetorical nature of claims about nationalist progress or beneficence. For example, some beleaguered promoters of the HGDP have tried to stave off some criticism of the program by creating alliances with genetic researchers and supporters in developing countries, thereby giving the impression that such research trajectories are inevitable and beneficial (Salopek, 1997). Spivak (1999) contends that capitalists need discourses filled with commentaries of "uniformity and rationalism" because these structures can be mobilized to justify "changes in patent laws" and the monopolization of "novel gene combinations" (pp. 398-401). The uncritical adoption of the language of liberal multiculturalism creates a situation in which class issues and subaltern positions are forgotten as new alliances are formed by those who share the profits and symbol systems of the West (Spivak, 1999).

Although many participants in genomic research promote a dichotomous world that separates the science of genetics from its social application, postcolonial critics contend that such rhetorical maneuvers hide power relationships, marginalize indigenous voices, and deflect normative criticisms of research project lines. Whitt (1998) argues that the promoters of the HGDP use the "conjunction of value-neutrality and value-bifurcation" to dismiss "the radical critiques of Western science" and mute the "charges of material oppression and conceptual domination" (p. 71).

Genomic studies, which offer the tantalizing hope of providing many cultures with the proof that we are all basically alike underneath our epidemiological, morphic structures, are claimed to be a value-neutral way of approaching the problems associated with racism and misunderstanding. This is an especially problematic assertion for postcolonial critics because such ideologies are seen as benign supplements to existing nationalistic tales of incremental development and economic growth. Communities that once celebrated the importance of "decolonization" now have researchers who are becoming willing participants in Western-oriented programs (Spivak, 1999).

To understand how these changes have taken place, we need rhetorical analyses that can trace some of the fragments that make up such complex ideologies. Said (1979), in the introduction to *Orientalism*, argues that there are times when "biology" and other academic disciplines can be accused of complicity in the "imperialist view of the world" (p. 14). The question then becomes, What should members of the "First World" do when some subalterns or their self-appointed representatives choose to participate in biotechnological enterprises? We need a postcolonial lens that can encompass some of these ambivalencies and tensions. If colonization means much more than simply the expropriation of physical wealth from other countries and peoples, then critics need to be attentive to the ways that hegemonic ideologies are fabricated, embraced, and denied in today's world. Sometimes, this involves decoding what Gandhi (1998) calls colonial "amnesia," the conscious or unconscious repressions that are involved in the traumas of ideological struggles.

RACIAL CLASSIFICATION, EUGENIC DIFFERENTIATION, AND THE POSTCOLONIAL DEBATE REGARDING THE HUMAN GENOME DIVERSITY PROJECT

Numerous genealogical fragments have historically influenced the ways in which we think about race, inheritance, and cultural differences. Since time immemorial, many Western communities have been fascinated by the role that inheritance plays in the configuration of our physical, mental, and moral well-being. For example, Plato wrote about how the Greeks needed to accept the fact that nature had created human beings who were made up of "gold," "silver," and "bronze" materials, and that the state needed to ensure that the right parents supervised the development of these various classes. In the Christian Bible's gospel of Matthew, readers are reminded that "a good tree cannot bring forth evil fruit, neither can a corrupt tree bring forth good fruit," and Exodus instructs, "God visits the iniquity of the fathers upon the children and the children's children unto the third and to the fourth generation" (Mayer, 1930, p. 3). The human body was considered to be a container filled with both possibilities and perils.[4]

During the sixteenth through eighteenth centuries, many Europeans were fascinated by such questions as the distinctiveness of human "species," the relationship between the cells of primates and humans, and the positioning of certain animals in the "Great Chain of Being" (Marks, 1995, pp. 3-5). Researchers from a variety of fields, such as Agassiz and Buffon, began searching for taxonomies that would give them some clues about the limits of human similarity and difference and formed racial hierarchies on the basis of presumed hereditary characteristics. Lock (1999) notes the ways in which scientists continue to be implicated in racially coded eugenic logics:

> That these classifications persist is politically significant because the majority of biologists, geneticists, and anthropologists, even though they assisted until the middle of this century in legitimizing the race concept, have now abandoned this type of classification as scientifically valid. . . . Prior to the discovery of genetics, it was often the idea of "blood"—its purity or mix—that provided the biological justification for lineage making. Blood, language, religion, caste, and other forms of distinction constitute genealogies that in turn become the basis for economic exchange and solidarity among groups. (pp. 86-87)

Long before the arrival of the HGDP, many Western explorers, missionaries, medical officers, and other global travelers carried with them imperial and colonial ideas about the "inequality" of "groups, of peoples, nations, classes, and races" (de Rooy, 1990, p. 9). Those who popularized eugenic creeds often commented on how either Mendelian or neo-Lamarckian ideas about inherited traits had much to tell us about racial fitness or character (Hasian, 1996). William Smith, writing in *The Nation* at the turn of the century, was certain both imperialism and race hatred came from the post-Darwinian acknowledgment that "blood will tell" (as cited in Matthews, 1964, p. 633). The future hopes of humanity rested on "modern science" grounded in a single principle: "perfecting the strong, not strengthening the weak" (Matthews, 1964, p. 622). Today, some of these arguments are often considered nonsensical and pseudoscientific, but for decades they circulated as foundational epistemes of Western cultures.[5] These ideological sedimentations do not disappear simply because proponents of development projects have more sophisticated understandings of the interrelationships between environmental and genetic influences on humans.

As Montagu (1967) notes, the relationship between race and blood has a checkered past, and innumerable writers and researchers have advanced theories about the genetic origins of both social and biological behavior. In the interim period between World War I and World War II, decolonization efforts were taking place at the same time that scientists were trying to reform eugenical projects (Kevles, 1985). Audiences throughout the world were invited to reconsider the wisdom of recirculating eugenic colloquialisms, such as "blood will tell," "the sins of the fathers," or "like always produces like." In fact, one of the many ironies surrounding the HGDP stems from the fact that many of the epistemic assumptions and goals of the controversial program were influenced by antieugenical movements. In the early 1990s, some of the most prominent researchers involved in the HGDP asked the "geneticists and public to collaborate now in collecting sufficient material to record human ethnic and geographic diversity before this possibility is irretrievably lost" (Cavalli-Sforza, Wilson, Cantor, Cook-Deegan, & King, 1991, p. 490). Several years later, some of these same advocates suggested that the "genetic diversity of people now living harbors the clues to the evolution of our species" (Gutin, 1994, p. 72).

Some of the very same regions that once held the covetous gaze of imperial nations are now considered to be "genetic goldmines" because their populations have relatively little geographic mobility (Cohen, 1996, p. 12). India and China, in particular, were targeted by geneticists as areas that could provide a wealth of material on complex diseases and disorders, including diabetes, asthma, cancer, and heart disease. Hence, Orientalist visitors to such regions no longer go on safaris or explorations to map the Dark Continent: Now they are "gene hunters" seeking blood samples from various indigenous groups. In India, for example, population geneticists try to collect material from high-caste brahmins, low-caste harijans, and hunter-gathering tribes called kadar (Jayaraman, 1996, p. 13).

Some geneticists, linguists, and physical anthropologists who supported the HGDP viewed the project as a modernist program that would help improve our understanding of genetic similarities and end semantic confusion, eventually dispelling racial fallacies or at least reducing racial prejudices. According to the initial plans of the organizers, trained groups from throughout the world would be collecting "samples" from "peoples in danger of cultural and physical extinction" (Butler, 1995, p. 373). The HGDP would be a "collaborative" program that examined the "generation of cell lines" in places such as the central African republic of Zaire (Cavalli-Sforza, 2000, p. 69). The sampling strategy of collecting blood samples for cell immortalization was supposed to be a way of illuminating our knowledge of human diversity, both biologically and culturally

(Friedlaender, 1993). The project's advocates believed that once the more educated members of the sample populations understood that ethical codes and legal contracts had been prepared to protect their human rights, the HGDP would face fewer obstacles. Moreover, the HGDP was to be a voluntary project that would not involve any draconian practices. Cavalli-Sforza, one of the original proponents of the program, suggested that those who objected to the reductive nature of this research were not really scientists but, rather, "cultural anthropologists" and "philosophers or social critics" (as cited in Gutin, 1994, p. 74).

From a postcolonial perspective, the problems associated with the HGDP involve more than semantics and the provision of improved ethical codes. The proponents and critics of the project face complex colonial and imperial ideologies filled with tales of blood, race, and oppression. Early in the project's history, proponent Calli-Sforza spoke publicly of the importance of studying "African 'tribes'" as well as "European 'ethnic groups'" (as cited in Gutin, 1994, p. 72). His terminology "revealed a disturbing glimpse of a colonial mentality at the highest level of the project" (p. 72). In fact, the HGDP's expressed purpose was to target "isolates of historic interest" (Calli-Sforza as cited in Hamilton, 2001, p. 622). From a postcolonial perspective, the nominalist rhetoric of some of the HGDP supporters reinforces a view of Third World Others as less civilized than their European counterparts and as property, objects, or relics.

Groups such as the United Nations Educational, Scientific, and Cultural Organization (UNESCO), the Onondonga Council of Chiefs, Rural Advancement Foundation International (RAFI), and the World Council for Indigenous Peoples (WCIP) openly opposed the HGDP. Connor (2001) highlights some of the major arguments advanced by the indigenous Others targeted by the HGDP. Those in opposition to the project, mainly critics "from North and South America," argued that it "intends to collect and make available our genetic materials which may be used for commercial, scientific, and military purposes" (Connor, 2001, p. 3). Although he describes the project's critics as dismissive and includes various examples of "disappearing peoples" in an effort to relate the potential importance of the HGDP, Connor also cites the "typical refrain" of indigenous critics: "You want to preserve our genes . . . but you don't want to preserve us" (p. 3). This statement highlights the tragic irony of the HGDP, a project designed to capitalize on the decimation of whole ways of life. Butler (1995) summarizes the conclusion of UNESCO's International Bioethics Committee, noting that the "HGDP has 'expressed urgency' in collecting samples from peoples in danger of cultural and physical extinction, [but] it had not expressed concern about their extinction per se" (p. 373). In a similar vein, Aroha Mead (as cited in Hamilton, 2001), a Maori activist opposed to the project, suggests that science is

> only of use if it improves the quality of life and society. Without that, it serves no useful purpose to humanity, only a purpose for a minority exclusive group of Western professionals, possibly at the expense of the unity and survival of indigenous communities struggling to remain intact. (p. 635)

Organizations such as RAFI have constantly warned communities targeted for gene hunting, and alliances have been created by indigenous community members, environmentalists, and scientists who have their own reservations about projects such as the HGDP (Dickson, 1996, p. 11). RAFI's research director, Hope Shand, expresses the organization's concern regarding the patenting of cell lines, and another member points out the lack of international legal statutes that would prevent unscrupulous abuses of the genetic data (Gutin, 1994). For example, the blood of "asthmatic inhabitants of the South Atlantic Island Tristan da Cunha" was sold first to a California company and then to a German pharmaceutical manufacturer for $70 million (Hamilton, 2001, pp. 627-628). The indigenous groups from which genetic material is taken rarely see even a fraction of a percentage of the profits reaped by Western corporations and scientists.

The most disturbing evidence of some lingering connections between colonial mentalities and modern biopiracies is found in the practice of patenting genetic material or cell lines of other individuals. Although supporters of the project contend that their scientific investigations have nothing to do with the commercialization of this genetic material, their detractors emphasize the fact that these proponents have little control over the future use of this research. Both RAFI and the WCIP protested the U.S. government's 1993 application for a patent on the cells of a Guaymi Indian woman whose consent had not been granted. Amid the controversy, a European parliamentary resolution temporarily banned the patenting of human genetic material. The U.S. government later disclaimed its patent on the cell line of a man from Papua, New Guinea, under similar pressure from international and indigenous rights groups. Critics contend that this potential marketing of cell lines calls into question some of the spiritual beliefs of many people in developing countries (Hamilton, 2001).

Others note that colonialist ideologies have similarly shaped "bioprospecting," the practice of seeking native, geographically isolated plant and animal life (and now human genetic material) for medical and pharmaceutical research. As Hamilton (2001) notes, "The current trend in Western science involves harvesting not just indigenous peoples' knowledge and resources, but their genetic material" (p. 619). Although Cavalli-Sforza and colleagues attempted to downplay the amount of criticism that was leveled at the project, major differences in ideological perceptions spurred hundreds of organizations throughout the world to assert that this was the newest form of piracy and "scientific colonialism" (Gutin, 1994, p. 71). Critics of the HGDP pointed out the ways in which such genomic projects "occupy a position on a continuum of cultural imperialism that seeks to exploit indigenous communities while offering almost nothing in return" (Hamilton, 2001, p. 641).

The increasing power of the Internet has simply magnified the critiques of the HGDP.[6] Postings about U.S. patents on the cell line of the "Hagahai man" from Papua, New Guinea, the intellectual property rights claims of citizens of the Solomon Islands, and the position of the World Health Organization on some of the shortcomings of existing ethical protocols publicized opposition to the project (RAFI, 1996). Debra Harry (1995), one of the project's most prominent critics, asks some of the questions at the heart of a postcolonial critique of the HGDP:

> On the assumption that these groups are headed for extinction, scientists are rushing in to gather DNA samples before they disappear. . . . But why the tremendous interest in saving the genes of indigenous people and not the people themselves? Who really stands to benefit from this endeavor? What are the dangers and long-term implications of biotechnology and genetic engineering? These are questions indigenous people must ask themselves in order to protect their interests in the face of such a mysterious and well-funded effort. . . . Indigenous people must be aware that it may be extremely difficult or impossible to recover or repatriate samples of our blood, tissues, or body parts, once they are removed from our bodies and stored elsewhere.

Harry, who coordinates the Indigenous People's Coalition Against Biopiracy, also points out the fact that the questions at the heart of the HGDP such as Who are we? and Where do we come from? are not relevant for most Indian communities (Petit, 1998, p. A5). Other critics worry that the collection of blood and tissue samples from indigenous peoples simply "confirmed peoples' feelings that they're regarded as experimental animals" (Mathews as cited in Kahn, 1994, p. 720). Their suspicion is corroborated, and their position as "isolates of historic interest" confirmed, by the Morrison Institute's[7] response to a frequently asked question about the cloning or re-creation of sampled populations:

> "Growing" humans (or even dinosaurs) from DNA samples is science fiction and will remain that for many decades to come—and quite possibly forever. And, even if that were possible, someone who wanted to do it probably would not want to collect DNA samples through the open and public method of the HGD Project.

By comparing the sampled populations to dinosaurs, the promoters of the HGDP effectively resign their research subjects to hopeless extinction, acknowledging only the value of their genetic material for scientific endeavors. Moreover, they suggest that individuals who did seek to re-create people from genetic material, were it possible, would not be interested in re-creating the indigenous populations sampled as part of the HGDP. Thus, apart from procedural safeguards and ethical protocols, the symbolism involved with the movement of genetic materials out of one community and into another poses another problem. Rodrigo Contreras, a representative for the WCIP, stated that the "assumption that indigenous people will disappear and that their cells will continue helping science for decades is very abhorrent to us" (as cited in Kahn, 1994, p. 721). Other critics of the program, including UNESCO's International Bioethics Committee, worried that the HGDP would reinforce some of the "prejudice that gives rise to racist and eugenic attitudes" (Butler, 1995, p. 373).

When both scientific and lay indigenous communities began attacking some of the goals and methods of the HGDP, the defenders of the program responded in several ways. They magnified the potential benefits of the program, created alliances with representatives of genetic programs in other countries, tried to trivialize the claims of their opponents, and then modified their claims about the types of populations that would be targeted for genetic sampling. At the same time, the advocates for the program presented themselves as dispassionate scientists who distance themselves from the "possible disputes about patent rights" and "commercial sponsors" (Dickson, 1996, p. 11). All these strategies bolstered Cavalli-Sforza's claims that detractors of the program exaggerated the dangers of the program (Butler, 1995, p. 373).

HGDP advocates argued that if cultural critics were really concerned about the adverse effects of racism, then they needed to support the project instead of attacking it. For example, Ken Weiss, a molecular anthropologist, averred that "if we don't go ahead with this, then in 10 years when the Human Genome Project is done, a Navajo, say, will look at those results and ask, 'Why did they bother? How well does that represent me?'" (as cited in Gutin, 1994, p. 72). Studying genetic diversity, then, was a scientific and moral imperative. If "non-Caucasians aren't studied," noted Ken Kidd of Yale University, they "won't benefit as much from biomedical advances . . . we're not trying to exploit people; we're trying to include them. It's racist to avoid the totality of humans" (as cited in Kahn, 1994, p. 721). Cavalli-Sforza proclaimed that the new data would show that there were "no separate races" (as cited in Lehrman, 1996, p. 14).

Although the HGDP failed to garner any major U.S. federal funding and the full support of international genetics communities, the debate initiated by its advocates continues to be significant. Hank Greely, one of the key legal consultants for the project, admitted in April 2000 that their "lack of funding is a huge issue" but also stated that "rumors that the HGDP has died, or is in a comatose state, are exaggerated" (as cited in Smaglik, 2000, p. 912). In the near future, we may witness more regional planners who willingly collect blood, hair, or saliva samples from diverse human populations than were mobilized in support of the HGDP. In fact, the public/private HapMap Project, which began in October 2002 with a price tag of $100 million, involves the collecting of blood samples from "Yoruba in Nigeria, Japanese, Chinese, and Americans of Northern and Western European descent" (Brower, 2002, p. 10).[8]

POSTCOLONIAL PERSPECTIVES ON GENOMIC DEBATES

If we took a classical liberal Western approach to the consideration of the HGDP, we might contemplate the possibility that there are ways of constraining the pernicious influence of eugenic ideologies while simultaneously creating national and international laws to protect both the humanitarian and economic rights of the targeted populations. This is the approach taken by several other writers (Hamilton, 2001; Juengst, 1996; Reardon, 2001; Resnik, 1999). Juengst, for example, openly extols the "diversity of perspectives" present in traditional "policy-development vehicles" (p. 94), such as grantee consortia, commissioned expert panel studies, advisory task reports, interagency workshops, public consultations, and conferences. The approach he and others advocate assumes that the promise of medical care for participation in research equals "voluntary" involvement, that the "rule of law" can function in a manner that differentiates between biotechnology and biopiracy, that scientists can police themselves, and that transnational corporations are benevolent and co-equal entities.

Building on essentialist notions of rights and duties, as well as naïve faith in the altruism of corporations and formal institutions, this classical liberal approach justifies the involvement of the Unites States' National Research Council (NRC), which in 1997 joined the ranks of those organizations that gave their qualified nod to the HGDP. Using traditional Western models for cost-benefit assessment and bioethical protocols, the NRC—after a purportedly thorough review of the arguments presented by both supporters and detractors of the HGDP—determined that the project was worthwhile and should receive public and private support (NRC, 1997; see also Cavalli-Sforza, Bodmer, & Dausset, 1997).

The 17 members of the Committee on Human Genome Diversity who wrote the 81-page NRC text presented themselves as objective, neutral observers who understood both the importance of scientific progress and the historical dangers of eugenics. In a chapter titled "Human Rights and Human-Genetic Variation Research," the committee acknowledged the cultural critiques of race and genetic exploitation, and they attempted to address arguments about the potential misuses of human population genetics. Most of the document, however, was written in a tone that did not question either the efficacy or the legitimacy of the HGDP. Nor did the authors take seriously the cultural complaints that were being voiced by indigenous communities that pointed out the potential neocolonial dimensions of the project. For example, representatives of RAFI, along with indigenous peoples from Colombia and the Solomon Islands, testified before the NRC, calling attention to the ways in which the project might violate some of the cultural or religious beliefs of disempowered indigenous populations.

The protocols outlined by the committee involved elites working in conjunction with sympathetic local denizens in the creation of the rules and regulations that would prevent the abuse of genetic information. At the same time, the anthropologists, medical doctors, geneticists, and bioethicists who constituted the committee identified existing and potential threats to the collection of genetic material. They pinpointed the culprits who had been sowing the seeds of dissension around the globe. In one key passage, the Committee on Human Genome Diversity (NRC, 1997) claimed that conflict

> is particularly likely to occur in situations in which, for example, expatriate or immigrant communities of some social group's location [sic] have caused it to think about participating in research in a different way from members of their group who live elsewhere. *We think it is too extreme a position to require both group and individual consent to DNA collection for genetic variation research. Nonetheless, researchers will have to make sure that their participants understand both the objections of their community and the rationale for them as part of the informed-consent process and, when doing research that is opposed by a specific community, will also have to take into account the possible impact of doing such research on the likelihood that other communities will cooperate with other genetic-variation researchers in the future*. (p. 64)

This thinly veiled attack on indigenous or postcolonial critics assumes that it is only isolated individuals who could possibly object to the HGDP. The members of the "expatriate or immigrant communities" are rhetorically characterized as obstructionists, whereas the local supporters of the project are configured as the true representatives of the needs of indigenous communities. The implicit argument is that one of the primary causes of disputation over the HGDP derives from the massive misperceptions indigenous people hold about science and scientific motivations. Genetic exploitation is treated as a rare occurrence, something that can be prevented by a cooperative venture that brings together enthusiastic local participants and benevolent, objective researchers who are working to ensure global biodiversity. In other words, the HGDP offers a missionary model of scientific data gathering that rhetorically marginalizes the perspectives of those outside the fold.

From a postcolonial perspective, the classical liberal analysis neglects the disparate material relationships that exist between the West and the East. Engaging in multiple forms of collective amnesia, the authors of documents such as the NRC report treat the massive economic, social, and political problems of colonialism as bygone events, often ignoring the eugenic fragments that are embedded within their discussions of biodiversity. For example, the rhetorical valorization of the "gene hunter," the geneticist interested in obtaining tissue samples, builds on the historical characterization of the great white hunters and explorers who also claimed to be involved in benign forms of imperialism or colonialism.

The dismissal of informed consent at the group or community level allows the committee to evade the problems posed by the likelihood that some indigenous groups do not participate in the logic of legal consent. Informed consent as defined, for example, by the Council of International Organizations for Medical Sciences,[9] requires that participants understand the nature and purpose of the research. As we have seen from the debates surrounding the HGDP, proponents and critics differ substantially on matters of both purpose and risk. Critics of the project advance positions informed by the postcolonial context of these genetic debates. They highlight the racism undergirding the eugenic movements of the past, question the motives of corporations and governments, and call attention to issues of agency and consent. They also critique the colonialist discursive legacy evidenced in the rhetoric of the HGDP, and they assert the primacy of indigenous survival over the legacy provided by indigenous genes.

As long as subalterns are denied the right to critique, evaluate, and reject genetic research programs, there will be a continual need for postcolonial critiques that decode the hegemonic discursive practices of empowered rhetors. Spivak (1999) explains that the opposition to the mining of the "subaltern body" and "indigenous knowledge" involves more than simply a question of "transnational literacy" (p. 403). As long as Western researchers can frame the genomic discussions in ways that bracket out many of the key complaints of their potential subjects, then we have few genuine, inclusive conversations. For example, when supporters of the HGDP in Australia were trying to decide which "aboriginal" communities were going to be identified for "immortalization," the CAAC (1994, p. 88) noted that the scientists involved did not consult any aboriginal groups or any members of the National Health and Medical Research Council.

This essay is limited to a critique of the HGDP grounded in the perspectives of those subalterns who can speak (through the Internet, popular magazine articles, scientific conferences, news media, and academic journals). Future studies using ethnographic methodologies might better capture the vernacular discourses of the various transplanted and indigenous peoples opposed to biopiracy. Because, as Spivak (1988) notes, original subaltern identity is unrecoverable from the violent play of colonial discourses and practices, we must be especially attentive when any group or individual claims to represent the rights and interests of indigenous peoples. In addition to exposing the logics and rhetoric of neocolonialism, postcolonial critiques of contemporary genetics research proposals offer ways of anticipating, and thereby intervening in, the production of potentially oppressive scientific projects and cultural formations. Such critiques also call on us to remember the eugenic past and the ways in which early population biology research served the interests of colonizers at the expense of indigenous peoples. It is precisely, and perhaps only, this remembrance of our collective eugenic history that stands solidly in the path of Western science's unbridled desire to satisfy biotechnological curiosity.

NOTES

1. In Conrad's (1988) *Heart of Darkness*, Marlow, in contrast to the antihero Kurtz, has the capacity to both participate in and critique the logic of colonialism in which he is also ideologically invested. The opening quote illustrates Conrad's acute awareness of the shifting but enduring features of colonial racism.
2. Said (1979), Bhabha (1994), and Spivak (1988), respectively, exemplify these approaches.
3. For a more in-depth discussion and analysis of these debates, see Hasian and Plec (2002).
4. Lock (1999) explains that "until the sixteenth century, in those regions that came under the Judeo-Christian sphere of influence, the idea of race was closely associated with genealogical lineages" (p. 85). For an illustration of how the phrase "sins of the fathers" became a part of even nineteenth-century discussions of human and social evolution, see Huxley (1893).
5. For studies that have examined the popularity of eugenics in Europe (especially England), see Jones (1986), McKenzie (1981), Searle (1976), and Stoler (1989, 1997).
6. Examples of the Internet discussions surrounding the HGDP can be found at http://bioc09.uthscsa.edu/natnet/archive/nl/9510/0331.html and http://bioc09.uthscsa.edu/natnet/archive/nl/hgdp.html.
7. See Stanford University's "Morrison Institute for Population and Resource Studies" Web site (http://www.stanford.edu/group/morrinst/hgdp/faq.html) for more information and examples of the project committee's rhetoric.
8. The protocols that will be used by the researchers of the HapMap Project reflect close consideration of the concerns about informed consent expressed by critics of the HGDP (Brower, 2002). See Hamilton (2001) for an extended discussion of the debates over informed consent and the HGDP.
9. The council defines consent as "informed when it is given by a person who understands the purpose and nature of the study, what participation in the study requires a person to do and risk, and what benefits are intended to result from the study" (as cited in Hamilton, 2001, pp. 625-626).

6

The Life of the Party

The Contemporary Keynote Address

John M. Murphy and Thomas R. Burkholder

In a cover story for *The Nation*, eminent electoral authority Walter Dean Burnham (2000) wistfully admits that the 2000 primary season "produced its expected result" (p. 11). The expected matters little to Burnham, however; his title screams "Whole Lotta Shakin' Goin' On" and the subtitle asserts, "A Political Realignment Is on the Way." Senator John McCain's insurgency, Burnham declares, "left a notably disturbed political atmosphere in its wake" (p. 11). That atmosphere, combined with the decline of political parties and the decline in voter turnout, suggests that the "equilibrium" of our current party system is "more unstable—hence, vulnerable to sudden and explosive overthrow—with every election" (pp. 12-13).

There is a paradox at the core of Burnham's (2000) argument, one that plagues other studies of party decline and partisan disaffiliation in U.S. politics. As scholars announce the growing irrelevance of parties, they simultaneously establish the salience of party identification to voting behavior or, as does Burnham, assume that party realignment somehow matters even as political parties seem to matter less (Abramson, Aldrich, & Rohde, 1999, pp. 164-190). The expected happens in elections, and yet explosions will occur. Turnout declines in 1996 to its lowest level since 1924 and yet party affiliation increases in that same year (pp. 62, 167).

W. Lance Bennett (1996) discerns a crisis that ruptures the ties between citizens and institutions, but party organization studies establish the centrality of parties as institutional actors in American elections (Beck, 1997; Burns & Sorensen, 1999, p. 70). Change and continuity lie down with each other and students of electoral behavior puzzle over the paradoxical signs.

Although one short essay cannot resolve such contradictions, we suggest that the widely trumpeted decline of political parties and, as many argue, the so-called disappearance of political community need to be interpreted in a broader context (Bennett, 1996; Hart, 1999; Jamieson, 1992). One does not have to accept the "fragmentation" of contemporary society or the end of the "metanarrative" to acknowledge that something is happening (Lyotard, 1991; McGee, 1990). Anthony Giddens (1994) suggests a more modest thesis than the advocates of a hyperreality. He argues that we are "the first generation to live in a thoroughly post-traditional society, a term that is in many ways preferable to 'postmodern'" (p. 83). Giddens claims that the impact of globalization, the transition to an information age, the growth of instant communication, and the profoundly significant social movements of the past half-century have combined with the previous impact of modernity to destabilize tradition. If, as Arendt (1993) argues, tradition works by "fettering each successive generation to a predetermined aspect of the past" (p. 94), then Giddens is correct. Little is predetermined in Arendt's sense of the term, and few seem fettered by their past political choices.

Giddens (1994), however, does not postulate a society without tradition; he believes instead that we live in a time "in which tradition changes its status. In the context of a globalizing, cosmopolitan order, traditions are constantly brought into contact with one another and forced to 'declare themselves'" (p. 83). When faced with traditional norms, people "have to ask themselves, and are asked by others, why" (p. 84). Such a querulous society demands "social reflexivity" from its members; Giddens notes that we use "information about the conditions of activity as a means of regularly reordering and redefining what that activity is" (p. 86). For instance, few people accept marriage as it was meant, and those that do find themselves defending their choices. Arguments about the condition of marriage redefine the activity of marriage; that which was "normal" changes, and marriage becomes a contingent, not a "natural," act. He concludes, "Tradition more and more must be contemplated, defended, sifted through, in relation to the awareness that there exists a variety of other ways of doing things" (p. 83).

Political parties cannot secede from their posttraditional societies. In this context, political identity is no longer a "fact of life" or a "given" aspect of the natural order. Rather, much as Giddens (1979) has said of all institutions, political parties are "patterns of relations constituted in agents' practices and put into place by their chronic reproduction" (p. 177). Political parties craft themselves through their chronic discourse and justify their existence to a socially reflexive electorate. Those people no longer take party affiliation for granted; instead, they sift through that identity not only in terms of other parties but also in terms of other outlets for political action—unions, social movements, churches, interest groups, and so on. Michael Schudson (1998) views this as a change in the idea of citizen. For years, we enshrined the Progressive ideal of an informed citizen as the key to democracy. Today, however, he says that citizens have a "monitorial obligation":

> Monitorial citizens scan (rather than read) the informational environment in a way so that they may be alerted on a wide variety of issues for a very wide variety of ends and may be mobilized around those issues in a large variety of ways. (p. 310)

Among the means for mobilization are political parties. As one of many options for political activity, parties exist in a reflexive and contingent universe. They must convince these monitorial citizens to accept the identity of partisan and to act through the parties and in support of their ends.

As a result, parties increasingly deploy discourses designed to create identity in a contingent world. We suggest that one place to search for such discourse is at the party conventions and, in particular, in the genres of rhetoric that characterize those conventions. Thomas Patterson (1993) notes that, in a candidate-dominated era, "the national conventions stand alone during the election as something resembling a true party affair" (p. 227). At these nationally televised gatherings, parties possess a priceless opportunity to reproduce themselves amid a large audience.

The typical means of discursive reproduction are the genres that endure but adapt from convention to convention. Karlyn Kohrs Campbell and Kathleen Hall Jamieson (1990) suggest that genres work to create and sustain institutions by deploying discourses that meet recurring needs; simultaneously, however, genres as discursive entities possess the potential to adapt to shifting social conditions. Mikhail Bakhtin (1986) states that genres are the "drive belts from the history of society to the history of language" (p. 65). Genres interpret changing conditions through enduring forms, and by so doing, generic rhetoric assures people that enduring institutions, given public form by the genres, can cope with changing times.

Finally, within conventions, the genre most concerned with party is the keynote address. Other genres connect candidates to party (nominating speeches) or turn candidates into potential presidents (nomination acceptance addresses). The keynote address, however, is concerned more with party than with candidate and, as such, is the ideal site for the analysis of party rhetoric in a posttraditional world.

In this essay, we argue that keynote addresses authorize political parties as agents of collective action in a democracy. In a contingent society, each election demands that parties reproduce their authority to act in the name of the people. Such functions are apparent in contemporary keynote addresses, those delivered since 1960, due not only to the growth of a posttraditional society in general but also to the forms such social change has taken in the campaign arena since that election: the rise of the primary system, the resultant change in the role of national conventions, and the influence of the mass media.

In this essay, we first develop a generic orientation toward keynote addresses, one that attempts to explore seriously the recurrent, institutional demands placed on such orators. We then discuss the historical development of keynote addresses, their place in party conventions, and the ways in which their purpose has changed as political traditions have become contingent. We follow with an analysis of the three key elements that coalesce within keynote addresses and authorize political parties as democratic actors in the public sphere. We conclude with reflections on the keynote address and the American political community.

GENRE

The term *genre* means type, sort, or category. Generic critics begin with the idea that all discourse invites comparison to other discourse. Without some understanding of the language community as a whole, rhetors would find specific encounters far too much work. As Bakhtin (1986) says, "If speech genres did not exist and we had not mastered them, if we had to originate them during the speech process and construct each utterance at will for the first time, speech communication would be almost impossible" (p. 79). As a result, Campbell and Jamieson (1990) contend that all criticism is, in one sense, generic criticism because all linguistic acts request us to view them as one sort of act or another: "To deal with anything at all without classifying or typing it, without remarking on similarities or dissimilarities to other like or unlike things is simply not possible" (p. 7).

All comparisons are not created equal, however. Generic critics focus on those similarities that affect the ends sought by a community and the means chosen to achieve those ends. As Campbell and Jamieson (1990) explain, "Generic analysis studies the links between function and form" (p. 8). The strategies employed in a genre, no matter how common to other discourses, coalesce in the genre to accomplish a particular end. For instance, communities demand the completion of recurrent linguistic tasks, such as the mourning of a loved one, much as they require the achievement of recurrent material tasks, such as the production of food.

Of course, the problems differ in kind. The symbolic needs of communities develop not solely as material demands but also as "social constructs" that flow from a common "definition" of a situation (Miller, 1984, p. 156). By defining a situation as a recurrent type, rhetors engage it "in a socially recognizable and interpretable way" (p. 158). Genres develop linguistic strategies and lines of argument to meet the typified situational demands posed by community. As Campbell and Jamieson (1995) write,

> In other words, a genre does not consist merely of a series of acts in which certain rhetorical forms recur; for example, it is conceivable that parallelism and antithesis might recur jointly without establishing a generic similarity. Instead, a genre is composed of a constellation of recognizable forms bound together in an internal dynamic. (p. 403)

Generic analysis possesses a bias for the routine; that dynamic recurs in interaction with a common definition of a situation. Bias, however, does not deny the differences between members of a genre. First, only knowledge of the genre allows one to note, for example, that Grant's second inaugural address violates the norms. Second, generic critics recognize that various linguistic choices may enact similar strategies; the inaugurals of Jefferson, Lincoln, and Kennedy select, deflect, and reflect cultures with different standards for a "high" style and are thus different speeches (Campbell & Jamieson, 1990, pp. 14-36). They are great inaugurals, however, and they invested the person in question with the office of the presidency. It is the bias for that "routine" social act that makes generic criticism valuable, particularly for a project of this sort. If critics are to chart the possibilities for party, politics, community, and commonality in a posttraditional or postmodern age, then it is to a common rhetoric that we should turn. A generic perspective explores rhetorics that we have in common, those "mystic chords of memory" that make of diverse individuals an at least occasionally united community or, in our case, political party. The interaction between speaker, genre, and party allows each to influence the other and all to meet the evolving communal needs of changing times.

PARTIES, CONVENTIONS, AND KEYNOTE ADDRESSES

Parties evolved in response to the communal need to regulate competition for public resources. Many scholars attribute the legitimation of parties to Martin Van Buren (Ranney, 1975; Silbey, 1994). He "argued for a system of competitive, equally legitimate political parties" (Greenstone, 1993, p. 154). Although each party was to be

> divided from its opposition on basic principles, each party was to be united by the willingness of its members to compromise with each other, by the combined support of the members for the party's nominees, and by an equitable division of patronage. (p. 154)

Parties would "restrain ambitious politicians who lacked partisan loyalty" and serve as a means to satisfy "individual preferences in a large polity" (p. 159). Political parties would unify the squabbling factions that worried Madison in Federalist No. 10, moderate conflict, and nurture consensus (Ranney, 1975, p. 41). They would do so by inculcating loyalty to a quasi-public institution, rooted in civil society and accountable to its members. Through parties, the narrow interests of factions would be distilled into compromise programs for the public good.

Coincident with the rise of political parties was the national convention. Parties and conventions seemed a natural fit. If candidates were truly to represent the entire party, and not just a faction, then representatives of the entire party, and not just its congressional wing, needed to agree on the nominees and the platform (Davis, 1983, pp. 24-27; Smith & Nimmo, 1991, pp. 26-30). Conventions became the heart and soul of nineteenth-century political parties. Joel H. Silbey (1994) says their authority was "total, as they represented the place where major decisions were made about all things" (p. 8).

The keynote address, however, was not part of the program until 1896. The Democratic Party, riven over monetary policy, rejected the "gold" chairman proposed by the National Committee. Instead, the silver delegates elected Senator John W. Daniel of Virginia and, as the July 8th *New York Times* reported, instructed him to make an address "that should be a keynote for the silver crusade" (as cited in Miles, 1960, p. 26). The July 8th *Raleigh News and Observer* reported that he did so "in a ringing speech" (as cited in Miles, 1960, p. 26).

From that point onward, the keynote address occupied a central role in party conventions. Delivered by the temporary chair of the convention until 1952 in the Republican Party and 1972 in the Democratic Party (when the position was eliminated), the speech set the tone for the party's fall campaign, as the musical metaphor indicates (Farrell, 1978, p. 293; "National Party Conventions," 1995). Changes in the nominating process, however, especially the rise of the primary system, altered the keynote address.

Most scholars divide the history of conventions into two eras, with the first characterized by the decision-making power of the convention to select the nominees and the second characterized by the legitimation function of the convention as it ratifies the choices made in the primaries (Davis, 1983, pp. 24-37; Smith & Nimmo, 1991, pp. 26-30; Trent & Friedenberg, 1991, pp. 36-45). Although the dates of the break range dramatically, we suggest that 1960 marks the key rupture. John Kennedy demonstrated that primary wins would result in the nomination. It was not until 1972 that a majority of delegates was available in the primaries; however, with the exception of Hubert Humphrey in 1968 (a nomination that provoked a civil riot, a political outcry, and, ultimately, party reform), contenders felt compelled to reveal their appeal in the primaries. The winner of the majority of the primaries inevitably secured the nomination.

The increasing importance of the primary system altered the keynote. Before 1960, delegate selection constituted an act of fealty to the party. Party delegates were invested with the authority to take collective action in the name of the common good (i.e., the choice of candidates and platform). In such circumstances, the nature and identity of the party were taken for granted. Certainly, the party's stance on a variety of issues was debated ferociously, but as a plaque bequeathed to one of the authors from his grandfather reads, "Democrat born, Democrat bred and, when I die, I'll be a Democrat dead." Party loyalty was expected—to the extent of being a "Democrat dead" in Chicago elections, no matter the nominees.

Beginning in approximately 1960, however, delegate selection became an act of fealty to candidates or, in Madison's term, to factions. Multiple visions of the party were available on a regular basis, not just in divisive years such as 1912. Candidates gained prominence and disdained "party politics." The party, in turn, seemingly disappeared from the process. Intense media coverage of politics accentuated this trend. Primary battles lent themselves to a frame that emphasized individual conflict and not party process. For instance, Theodore H. White's classic, *The Making of the President 1960,* shaped a view of a presidential campaign not as a collective party decision for the public good but as a "search for a once and future champion, his defeat of an evil opponent and, thus, the making of a president" (Murphy, 1998, p. 30). White's view, as Timothy Crouse (1973) and Thomas E. Patterson (1993) argue, set the contours for contemporary coverage of presidential campaigns.

This frame should not come as a surprise: Todd Gitlin (1979), Herman Gray (1989), and Bonnie J. Dow (1996) note that television programming has a consistent tendency to turn political inequities into personal struggles. A strong and decent person, not a powerful and capable party, is the key to political achievement in the eyes of many. Such a Romantic view of the political process, as Roderick P. Hart (1999) notes, leads to disappointment. The television viewer sees a candidate as an individual, shorn of party, even as a romantic (lowercase "r") partner: "The politician opens up his heart. We are drawn in. He or she then does something obnoxious or stupid—an inevitability in politics. We jump back, scorned, again. We declare the lot of them toxic waste" (p. 26). Whether as once and future king or as once and future spouse, politicians increasingly appear to us as individuals, people not only apart from party but also even tainted by party.

The keynote address seeks to remedy this situation. In a posttraditional, candidate-centered environment, keynote addresses aim to restore the place of parties in the polity. The legitimation of the party as an authoritative political actor does not occur in the primaries; it happens at the convention. Conventions persist, as Hart (2000) argues, "because an unratified politics cannot be a functional politics and because only a ratified politics can command authority" (p. 105). That authority, in turn, is created by oratory; paradoxically, television's distaste for conventions, manifested by the major networks' unwillingness to provide "gavel-to-gavel" coverage, has enshrined the speeches, by process of elimination, as the most salient events. As the first major speech of the convention, as the only speech directly concerned with party, and as the speech that marks the transition from intraparty conflict to interparty conflict, it falls to the keynote to perform a critical act of authorization.

KEYNOTE ADDRESSES

We have argued that critics should view political parties as institutions that seek to gain electoral power, mediate among factions, and construct a platform for the public good. The rupture of continuity, however, poses difficult challenges for parties. As a consequence, they perform party identity and affirm the efficacy of the party in each and every election. As a key institutional genre, the keynote takes as its social act, its internal dynamic, the authorization of the party as the agent for political action in a democracy. The keynote draws its character from this need for authority; each element establishes the efficacy of the party in time, and taken as a whole, the elements knit the ruptures imposed by the changes of time. The party endures, as it has endured and will endure, to serve the needs of its people. The genre deploys three elements to achieve this end: Keynote addresses define the times in which we live, create a people to be served by the party in these times, and visualize the bright vistas that will result if only the people will perform the identity offered by the party. By situating parties as agents through time, keynote speakers authorize parties in time for their election.

Defining the Times

The importance of definition has not escaped the notice of rhetorical critics. Zarefsky, Miller-Tutzauer, and Tutzauer (1984) note that "to choose a definition is to plead a cause. Language is not a neutral instrument; to name an object or an idea is to influence attitudes about it" (p. 113). Keynote speakers name the times. If people accept a party's definition of a particular moment, then an election victory, not to mention continued party authority, is within sight.

This move partly accounts for the partisan tone of keynote addresses. Each party attempts to associate itself with the "good times" and dissociate itself from the "bad times" (Perelman & Olbrechts-Tyteca, 1969, pp. 415-426). Nonetheless, it is possible to overemphasize the partisanship and miss the broader rhetorical strategy. As keynote speakers praise their party and blame the other, they affirm the efficacy of both parties. Parties matter because they have made a difference, for good or ill, in the real world.

We use the term *real world* because keynotes begin with what Robert Hariman (1995) identifies as a gesture typical of realism: Speakers disdain the genre to contrast the empty words of others to their realistic assessment of the nation's condition (pp. 17-19). Walter Judd (1960) begins with an acute appreciation of his rhetorical task:

> As we meet tonight in this Republican National Convention of 1960 I do not believe you want me to indulge in the traditional keynote speech, blaming the other party for everything that is bad, taking credit to ourselves for everything that is good, and promising that if you voters will just elect us to office this fall, we will solve every problem. . . . The times in which we meet are too serious for that. (p. 646)

Similarly, Barbara Jordan (1976) states, "I could easily spend this time praising the accomplishments of this party and attacking the Republicans but I don't choose to do that" (p. 1931).

Of course, those who devalue the perceived responsibilities of a keynote speaker proceed, in a form of paralepsis, to fulfill them. Jordan (1976) continues,

> I could list the many problems which Americans have. I could list the problems which cause people to feel cynical, angry, frustrated: problems which include lack of integrity in government; the feeling that the individual no longer counts; the reality of material and spiritual poverty; the feeling that the grand American experiment is failing or has failed. (p. 1931)

She could make such claims, but she chooses not to do so. Mario Cuomo (1984) asks permission of the audience to "skip the stories and the poetry" and then delivers perhaps the most poetic keynote in the contemporary era (p. 1781).

Easy as it is to enjoy this gesture, we must recognize its serious rhetorical effects. First, as Hariman (1995, pp. 16-18) argues, it naturalizes the definitions of the world and grants a text the authority of fact. The keynoters' words are not mere rhetoric; they reflect our condition. Second, realism assumes that "political texts are necessarily incomplete, awaiting realization in a material world" (p. 17). The keynote speech is not enough. It must be "realized" in the fall campaign; the party must have the authority to act. Its very recognition of "reality" works to achieve that end.

After signifying their realism, keynote speakers use the authority gained to define the times. Although they use many strategies to accomplish this goal, two stand out. First, they tell the story of the past 4 years, emphasizing evidence that demonstrates the verisimilitude of the narrative. Second, they use "depiction" or what Michael Osborn (1986) calls "strategic pictures" that "linger in the collective memory of audiences as representative of their subjects when rhetoric has been successful" (p. 79). The two strategies work together or separately to name the age for the audience. That age, in turn, has been created by the actions of political parties.

Thomas Kean, the 1988 Republican keynoter, frames the story of the Reagan years as a "voyage" and says that historians "must report the facts." Kean (1988) states that "they will report that today 17 million more Americans have jobs than just 8 years ago" and that "the leader of the Soviet Union went on television and admitted that communism has failed" (p. 7). Howard Baker, as Farrell notes, interprets the story of Watergate as a "crisis of faith" that "the Republican party had the strength to survive" and, in so doing, "raised the country's expectations for honorable government" (Baker, 1976, p. 2310; Farrell, 1978, pp. 295-296). Evan Bayh (1996) rehearses the war between a Republican congress and a Democratic president and says that when Republicans "threatened our values" and "shut the government down, the president said no again, we [the Democratic Party] stood with him again and the American people won" (p. 715).

Depiction provides people with visual images of the times, pictures that a community can test against its own experience. A powerful example derives from Mario Cuomo's 1984 address. Despite calling this section a "Tale of Two Cities," Cuomo provides little traditional narrative structure. He paints pictures:

> In this part of the city there are more poor than ever, more families in trouble, more and more people who need help and can't find it.

> Even worse: There are elderly people who tremble in the basements of the houses there.
>
> And there are people who sleep in the city streets, in the gutter, where the glitter doesn't show.
>
> And there are ghettos where thousands of young people, without a job or an education, give their lives away to drug dealers every day. (p. 1781)

Cuomo places the responsibility for these conditions on the Republican incumbent, Ronald Reagan. Reflecting the divisions of 1968, Daniel Inouye (1968), defending forces of "responsibility" against the "flags of anarchism," portrays students who have "publicly burned draft cards and even the American flag" (p. 709). Unfortunately for Democrats, the implicit logic of Inouye's speech is clear: Their party created this difficulty. These "strategic pictures," however skillfully or dubiously employed, linger in the memory of the audience and become portraits of a world.

Whether through narrative, depiction, or another strategy, keynote speakers name the times. While doing so, they identify political parties as the agents responsible for the country's condition. If parties have acted during the past 4 years, then they must act now to cope with the dangers. Such a stance heals the ruptures of time; the world is comprehensible—the problems of the present have resulted from the political choices of the past and thus can be remedied by the political choices of the future. The first element of the keynote coheres well with the second: If the times demand political agents, then parties must create a partisan people as political agents.

Creating a Partisan People

It has become a truism in criticism that audiences are, at least in part, "fictive." From Edwin Black's (1970) "second persona" to Michael Calvin McGee's (1975) "people" and Maurice Charland's (1987) "constitutive rhetoric," we have come to accept the notion that the people are conjured into being with and through the discourse accepted as authoritative. Such a stance denies the existence of a transcendental subject. Rather, the subject is always already a rhetorical effect of a particular set of discourses, an asserted people without whom the political program or party based on their needs could not exist.

Keynote speakers, confronted with the always present threat that the party will wilt away, strive to constitute subjects that embody the party.

To paraphrase Charland (1987, p. 134), the subject of a keynote address is not persuaded to join the party; rather, support for the party is inherent within the audience posited by the discourse. Keynoters invent a party out of the scraps of past experience and contemporary culture, weaving them together and presenting a stable but contingent identity—a people conjured out of verbal magic and one that might hold together long enough to win election to office.

As Black's (1970) analysis would lead us to believe, however, Republicans and Democrats go about this differently. If discourses imply an auditor, that audience, in turn, will be enmeshed within an ideology. One of the best ways into that ideology/identity is through stylistic tokens. Republicans present themselves as heirs to enduring principles by relying on deductive arguments from accepted values and leaders. In its rhetoric, the Republican Party is the word made flesh, and the audience sees the word and feels its impact. As conservatives, they are a people of the book, and the book does not change. Alternatively, Democrats use enactment and synecdoche by presenting themselves as a people whose voices percolate through the convention, the country, and our national history. As liberals, they are the party of the people, and the people have changed even as they have endured.

If the Republican Party is the word made flesh, then the word and the flesh are most often those of Lincoln. Thomas Kean (1988) is well aware of this fact:

> Our purpose was sounded more than 100 years ago by a man who said America means a government whose "leading object is to elevate the condition of men—to lift artificial weights from all shoulders—to afford every person an unfettered start, and a fair chance, in the race of life."
>
> Those words were Abraham Lincoln's. And, my fellow Republicans, his creed is our creed. When we have followed it, we have succeeded. When we have deviated from it, we have failed. (p. 7)

Phil Gramm (1992) tells a story of Lincoln's: A father and son go camping, the boy is frightened by shooting stars, and the father tells him to look at the fixed stars. Gramm, quoting Lincoln, says, "if America [is] guided by the fixed stars, the fixed stars of freedom established by the Founding Fathers, [then] all [will] yet go well for America" (p. 2550). Katherine Ortega (1984) proclaims, "We Republicans still see our nation through Lincoln's eyes" (p. 2119). Colin Powell (2000), after twice citing "the mantle of Lincoln," turns to another Republican president: "Our greatest strength is the power of our [the United States] example—to be that shining city on the hill that Ronald Reagan spoke of and that the world looks up to" (p. 653). Mark Hatfield (1964), generalizing the formula, says that "the Republican Party is committed to a set of principles. The commitment is an act of unwavering faith in the American people in the cause of freedom, in the eternal principles of morality" (p. 652).

In keynotes, the Republican Party assumes form as the "eternal principles of morality," the "fixed stars of freedom," and the "mantle of Lincoln." Republicans announce themselves as a fulfillment of past words. This strategy provides the assurance of prophecy to the constitution of the audience. In uncertain times, traditions still hold, prophecies still come true, and the people, whatever the changes made apparent by skirts and dark skins, are still fundamentally the same. They believe. The audience is the word. Daniel Evans (1968) says of another Republican hero,

> Dwight D. Eisenhower once defined America's goal in these eloquent words: It is, he said, "lifting from the back and from the hearts of men, their burdens of arms and fears, so that they may find before them a golden age of freedom and peace." We have come to Miami to make that vision come true. (p. 679)

In the Republican universe, visions come true and the people of the book endure.

Democrats eschew such strategies. Unlike the Republican tactic of relying on the word made flesh, Democrats cite leaders as models who enacted their partisan principle: Jordan (1976) states, "We are an inclusive rather than an exclusive party. Let everybody come" (p. 1932). After imbuing his audience with the "courage and confidence" to believe that the "wagon train" can "make it all the way with the whole family intact," Cuomo (1984) notes that "we" have believed that

> ever since Franklin Roosevelt lifted himself from his wheelchair to lift this nation from its knees. Wagon train after wagon train. To new frontiers [Kennedy] of education, housing, peace. The whole family aboard. Constantly reaching out to extend and enlarge that family. Lifting them up into the wagon on the way. (p. 1781)

Cuomo (1984) reads the roll of great presidents, but they are models of action rather than prophets—the parents, in a sense, of the American family as they "lift" each new generation of citizens "into the wagon," enacting and creating an ever more inclusive polity. The combination of familial and western metaphors creates a mythic audience of Ward Bonds—"wagon masters" imbued with the values of the past but acting in the present to lift immigrants, blacks, women, and, indeed, all citizens into the political process.

Thus, Democrats seldom stay in history, nor do they hold still. They enact or personify the party of today. A famous example is Jordan's (1976) claim that "my presence here is one additional bit of evidence that the American dream need not forever be deferred" (p. 1931). John Pastore (1964) refers to his immigrant heritage in ways that foreshadow Cuomo's use of his life story as the story of a party that is also the story of America (p. 706). These speakers personify, rather than enunciate, the principles of the party and enact its past success.

One of the most creative efforts to make Democrats derives from Zell Miller. Using his voice as a synecdochal figure, Miller (1992) begins,

> Listen to this voice. It's a voice flavored by the Blue Ridge, a voice straight out of the peaks and hollows of the Appalachian mountains, a voice that's been described as more barbed wire than honeysuckle.
>
> That this kind of voice could travel here from a forgotten corner of Appalachia is a testament to the grace of God and the greatness of the Democratic Party. (p. 2116)

Miller's voice, undeniably heard by the audience, offers evidence of the impact of the Democratic Party. Miller, however, does not leave the figure there. He (1992) continues to weave his story together with the nation's story and the party's story: "I made it because Franklin Delano Roosevelt energized this nation; I made it because Harry Truman fought for working families like mine; I made it because John Kennedy's rising tide lifted even our tiny boat" (p. 2116). In a conclusion that asks us to hear the Democrats as the voices of America, he says,

> We will fight your fight, we will carry your cause, we will ease your burden, we will hear all the voices of America from the silky harmonies of the gospel choirs to the rough-edged rhythms of a hot country band, from the razor's edge rap of the inner city to the soaring beauty of the finest soprano, we hear your voice, America. We hear your voice. We will answer your call. We will keep the faith. And we will restore your hope. (p. 2116)

These finely etched voices become the voices of the party, and if you speak in these tones, the party will "answer your call." It does not matter what faction, what state, or what race, the Democratic Party speaks as you, is you, and will "restore your hope." The audience can easily see and hear itself in this chorus, and the rhetorical and political genius of this constitutive figure lies in its contrasts. In contrast to "the people of the book," the visible differences between people (skirts and dark skins) are not merely irrelevant markers that mask an underlying belief in the "eternal principles" of the book. Rather, the differences between people are constitutive of the nation; a chorus relies on difference to achieve harmony. We are different, but together we make beautiful music.

For the party to restore our hope, it must be given power and, of course, the other party must be denied power. Often, the modes of political attack in these speeches flow from the auditors the party establishes. Speakers attack through contrast. Republicans attack Democrats as an incoherent party, fading away as it abandons principle. Susan Molinari (1996) quips, "This speech is a lot like a Bill Clinton promise. It won't last long and it will sound like a Republican talking" (p. 681). Democrats attack Republicans as a deaf party, unable to hear the people. Ann Richards (1988) says, "And, for 8 straight years, George Bush hasn't displayed the slightest interest in anything we care about" (p. 2061). Although circumstance can dictate a change in strategy (Democrats could not help but notice the discord among Republicans in 1964), the trends are clear. Attacks serve not only to deny the people of the opposition but also throw one's own party into stark relief as the only conceivable subject.

Again, however, the attacks, as well as the deductive arguments and personifications, highlight the party as the primary political identity available to the audience. Such strategies accentuate the parties, making them palpable and visible as agents of democracy in a televisual age—the word is made flesh, and the party lives in the figures appearing at the rostrum. As the party assumes visible form, it becomes the most viable form of political action.

Visualizing the Future

If the people become the party when they face an "hour of decision," then marvelous results should be expected. It is in the last element of a keynote address, the need to "go forth and shout the good news" (Lugar,

1972, p. 2172), that the influence of another rhetorical genre, the jeremiad, can be seen clearly, in a manner analogous to nomination-acceptance addresses (Bercovitch, 1978; Ritter, 1980). Keynote speakers visualize a bright future, painting a picture of the nation not as it is but as it will be, if we choose well. The cultural authority of a rhetorical icon, the Reverend Martin Luther King, Jr.'s "I Have a Dream," too often, perhaps, influences this section of keynote addresses. Edward Brooke (1972) claims that "I see an America . . . " (p. 2172). Howard Baker (1976, p. 2312), Reuben Askew (1972, p. 1749), and Thomas Kean (1988, p. 10) have dreams—dreams that are deeply rooted, not surprisingly, in "our American dream." The results are pallid.

Imitation is not Platonic flattery, however; as institutional rhetoric, keynotes often result in "triteness—a stale repetition of past addresses" (Thompson, 1979, p. 274). Although speakers wish to avoid the pejorative "stale," the repetition secures a key rhetorical end. The imitation of past linguistic formulas demonstrates that the party has endured from past to present, and that it has kept its commitments. It also suggests that the future bodes well. Much as the jeremiad assures the faithful that the created people will prosper if they adhere to their covenant with the Lord, so too does this element of a keynote assure success if only the people adhere to their party. It has happened in the past; it will happen in the future. The "easily predictable discourse" that marks the genre reassures the audience that, in uncertain times, the party can manage the future as it has the past (Henry, 1988, p. 107).

There are resources for eloquence, however, often when the speaker makes the future concrete. The rhetor's presence becomes a warrant for the claim that past success can continue if the party summons the energy. Given Democratic reliance on enactment and personification, they tend to create more stirring visions of the future. Republicans tend toward tired metaphors. The word, after all, does not change; thus, we are required only to maintain what Kean (1988) called "our generation's watch on deck" (p. 10).

Democratic keynotes reveal more inventive strategies. Richards (1988), for instance, begins her speech by recalling "summer nights when we'd put down what we called a Baptist pallet and we listened to the grown-ups talk" (p. 2061). She says that "it was back then that I came to understand the small truths and hardships that bind neighbors together" (p. 2061). At the end of the speech, she returns to that pallet along with "one nearly perfect granddaughter named Lily." The two "roll a ball back and forth" and she teaches Lily as Richards herself was taught. The continuity of life, its truths and hardships, and the strength of America will "never, ever be forgotten" as long as we keep our promises to the next generation (p. 2062; see also Dow & Tonn, 1993). Miller (1992), in the passage cited previously, weaves his voice in with other citizens, a musical riff that changes, but continues, throughout time. If the vision is to be effective, it must emerge naturally out of the speech and the speaker's experience.

CONCLUSION

We have argued that parties occupy a precarious place in contemporary culture. Like all traditional affiliative bodies, parties find themselves perched between past and future, justifying their existence to a reflexive and skeptical electorate composed of monitorial citizens. The three elements of the keynote coalesce to address such concerns. By defining the times as produced by party action, speakers situate parties as effective agents in time. By crafting a subjectivity, speakers create parties as the most appealing of the many groups competing for the energy of the people at this time. By visualizing a future, speakers reveal the successful covenant between party and people that carries through time. In other words, keynote addresses authorize parties as agents of collective action and weave out of the threads of past tradition and contemporary culture a powerful but contingent collective identity.

The fact that the identities differ substantially should give pause to those who believe that voters have a choice only between Tweedledee and Tweedledum. In the tradition of conservative thought, the Republican keynoters view differences only as surface manifestations of an underlying unity. Through deductive arguments, they establish themselves as a people of the book. The community offered by Republicans is a kind of hermeneutic enterprise; all are welcome, but they need to orient themselves to those "fixed stars of freedom." Democratic keynoters, as illustrated by Miller's (1992) speech, cast difference as constitutive of the nation. It is the differences that create the harmony. Multiple voices are allowed in the belief that they produce "silky harmonies." No Tweedledee and Tweedledum here.

The difference between the parties, as Black would suggest, emerges out of contrasting stylistic choices that manage to accomplish the same rhetorical end. That is, in keeping with Bakhtin's concept of genre as a "'form-shaping ideology'—a specific kind of creative activity embodying a specific sense of experience," the speakers craft a communal sense of political experience as made by parties (Morson & Emerson, 1990, p. 282). Whether it is a party of the book or a party of harmony, the party crafts U.S. political life. Differences between party beliefs emerge out of the similarity among party functions; the two exist, as genre theory suggests, in a dialogical relationship. Whatever the difference between parties, the institution of the party matters even in a posttraditional society.

To explore the symbolic charge of the keynote address, we have developed, in turn, the productive link between genre and institution proffered by Campbell and Jamieson. It seems likely that a generic perspective on discourse, biased toward the stability and common sense of a polity, will be productive when it explores the links between public rhetoric and institutional maintenance. Indeed, if the perspective elucidated here is correct, genres will play an ever more critical role in the production and reproduction of institutional identity. Much as Hart's (1987) analyses of the presidency suggest that people now see speaking the job as doing the job, so, too, with political parties. In a posttraditional culture, the place to search for party identity and affiliation is not necessarily in voting behavior, although this is useful, nor in the money that fills party coffers, although this, too, is useful. Rather, critics should focus on public performances of party identity: They should turn not only to the keynote address but also to the remainder of the genres common to national party conventions as well as other party communications, such as their Web sites. In the contemporary era, institutions exist as chronic rhetorical reproductions. Genres of political rhetoric, in turn, serve this end well and deserve renewed attention as a key means for the creation and maintenance of political parties.

Finally, in a posttraditional society, Bennett's (1996) observation that our ties have begun to disintegrate is probably correct. Tradition no longer "fetters" us to a seamless political community. Communities continue to exist, however. This analysis suggests that solidarity, rather than transcendental identity, is a more likely source of community today. Giddens (1994) notes that when the traditional way becomes one among many, the question is one of generating an "active trust—trust in others or in institutions (including political institutions) that has to be actively produced and negotiated" rather than accepted (p. 92). Such negotiation exists in the genres that chronically reproduce those institutions and, in a broader sense, create communities as people confront social tasks. In our time, the fragility of cultural and technological innovations easily attracts attention; the contingent stability of rhetorical genres and political institutions often escapes notice. The genres of a community, as staid as this perspective seems to many, offers a promising approach for exploring the generation of an active trust in a posttraditional time.

7

Memory as Social Action

Cultural Projection and Generic Form in Civil Rights Memorials

Victoria J. Gallagher

In my hometown paper, there was a story about a group of people embarking on a civil rights heritage tour. The tour was organized by the Raleigh Martin Luther King Resource Center and began on April 4, the 33rd anniversary of Martin Luther King, Jr.'s (MLK) assassination at the Lorraine Motel in Memphis, Tennessee (now the site of the National Civil Rights Museum). The travelers on this tour were described as being on a "pilgrimage into the past" and "bonded by their hunger to see civil rights landmarks firsthand" (Starling, 2001, p. 1D). Although this story caught my attention because it involved civil rights-related memory sites, the linking of memory and tourism struck me as particularly interesting. If, as Danielle Rice (1992, p. 231) notes, "tourism in modern industrial societies helps people to define who they are and what matters in the world," the proliferation of museums, memorials, and sites of memory in the past two decades takes on added significance for scholars interested in examining how culture is communicated rhetorically.[1]

At the same time, the past decade has seen an increase in the scholarly attention devoted to, as Donna Graves (1992) notes, identifying and analyzing the "symbols and patterns that characterize attitudes toward race and difference in American culture" (pp. 215, 217). Graves argues that analyzing the built environment, including public memorials, monuments, and museums existing in the public spaces of urban America, is essential to understanding how cultural artifacts create, sustain, and reproduce racial ideologies.[2]

The relationship between public memory and social action such as tourism and also the creation and reproduction of racial identities and ideologies are the motivating themes of this essay. It represents one piece of a larger project devoted to discovering and explaining the defining characteristics and social action inscribed in a genre of memorial discourse, which both honors the accomplishments and reminds us of the tragic losses accrued during the civil rights movements of the 1950s and 1960s in the United States. Due to the complexity and divisiveness of race relations in the United States—characteristics that translate into how space is allocated, who lives where, and the "good" and "bad" parts of cities—civil rights–related memorials and museums are essentially complicated, unfinished texts. At the same time, however, these material artifacts provide stability in response to the uncertainties and complexities of racial identity and a means for portraying a positive image of subordinate groups to the larger culture.

The goal of this essay is to "describe and theorize the patterns of regularities" (Freedman & Medway, 1994, p. 3) in the rhetorical discourse of four civil rights memorials and museums in the southeastern United States. Although not exclusively linguistic in nature, these artifacts combine layers of oral, written, visual, and spatial elements to form a complex whole, simultaneously symbolic and material in nature. As I will demonstrate, they reproduce and "quote" each other's forms even as they provide differentiated experiences to visitors. Drawing on theories of cultural projection, memory, and genre, my analysis illuminates the extent to which these particular sites of memory provide the linguistic and extralinguistic elements through which visitors perceive recurring situation types and are thereby instructed in how to interpret their own and others' identities, motivations, and goals in light of racial ideologies.

THEORETICAL FRAMEWORK

In his book, *Representing Black Culture: Racial Conflict and Cultural Politics in the United States,* Richard Merelman (1995) asserts that there is a growing debate about American (read United States) national identity due to changes in American (read United States) culture. These changes, in turn, are brought about by what Merelman refers to as cultural projection: "the conscious or unconscious effort by a social group and its allies to place new images of itself before other social groups, and before the general public" (p. 3). There are differences, however, in a group's cultural projection based on whether it is a dominant or subordinate social group. Also, according to Merelman, the relative economic status and degree of authority in social and political institutions that a given group possesses determine its dominant or subordinate status. To wit,

> A politically, economically, and socially subordinated group engages in cultural projection when its allies put forth new, usually more positive pictures of itself beyond its own borders. By inviting respect, commendation, debate, and engagement, these new images contest the negative stereotypes that dominant groups typically apply to subordinates. For its part, a dominant group engages in cultural projection when it and its allies develop a newly positive set of self-images, and put forth such images to subordinate groups. These new images not only contend that dominant groups deserve the right to rule, but also ask subordinate groups to approve rather than resist or distrust rule by dominants. (p. 3)

Merelman (1995) argues that the past 30 years have witnessed a growth in black cultural projection, particularly with regard to entertainment media, schools, universities, periodicals, research foundations, and, to a lesser extent, government. Thus, according to him, "the scene is set for a struggle between a changing American culture—in which black cultural projection plays an increasing role—and white domination exerted through the normal processes of American politics" (p. 25). The key question for Merelman is

> why this power struggle among a dominant white and subordinate non-white racial groups, especially blacks, should take on a *cultural* dimension, as opposed to traditional forms of economic struggle (over, say, the distribution of income) or political struggle (over, say, the distribution of elected representatives). (p. 26)

He addresses this question by describing five conditions that he believes "favor the transformation of dominant-subordinate racial group struggles into cultural forms" (p. 27): increased social contact between middle-class whites and blacks, the increasing place of cultural capital in the American economy, the persistence of racial domination despite the fact the tenets of liberal democracy were legally broadened to include blacks, divisions among white intellectuals over multiculturalism, and the growing impact of the mass media.

Merelman (1995) develops a template of the following four basic types of cultural projection and reads various events and artifacts, including the establishment of the Martin Luther King, Jr. national holiday, through this framework:

1. Syncretism occurs when "dominants accept some of the subordinate cultural projection, and subordinates accept some of the dominant projection. . . . Syncretism is thus a form of mutual projection. By incorporating subordinate imagery, syncretism may weaken the cultural foundations of political domination in a society."
2. Hegemony occurs when "dominant groups control the flow of cultural projection. . . . Dominants enjoy hegemony when their point of view becomes a 'common sense,' shared widely both within their own group and beyond. Hegemony thus undercuts the ability of subordinates to resist domination."
3. Polarization occurs when cultural projection fails and increases the opportunity for conflict. "Groups that experience the pain of having their own projections rejected by others, and who must simultaneously struggle to fight off the projections of these same others, will become angry and embittered."
4. Counterhegemony occurs when "subordinates and their allies convert dominants to subordinate versions of the world. The result of counterhegemony is that many dominants gradually become

> more accepting of subordinates. In so doing, dominants adopt to some degree a worldview which immediately and definitively questions their right to hold power, and which demands they cede power to subordinates" (pp. 5-6).

The proliferation of civil rights–related museums and memorials in the past 15 years seems to support Merelman's (1995) contention that there is an increase in the number and type of images of blacks being put forward in the culture, which invite "respect, commendation, debate, and engagement" rather than negative stereotyping. Significantly, the images presented both visually and verbally at or in these sites are of black people engaging in political action in the face of great opposition and danger. This is in contrast to what Merelman claims are the areas in which black cultural projection has more typically been found, such as in entertainment media, sports, and music. Thus, one way to analyze these sites of memory is to determine, based on the previously discussed template, the type of cultural projection they offer or evoke. As Merelman suggests in his analysis of the King holiday, however, a particular cultural "text" often has elements of all four and thus can be read in multiple ways. Thus, for example, we might initially argue that civil rights–related museums and memorials do not seem to fit the description of polarization because they tend to be explicitly sanctioned or accepted by representatives of the dominant group (namely white persons in positions of political authority or social influence). My experience of who actually visits such sites—for example, the majority of visitors to the King Memorial in Atlanta during my four visits were African Americans and other people of color—suggests that there is still a tendency to understand these sites as by, about, and for black people rather than by, about, and for all citizens (Gallagher, 1995).

Whereas Merelman places cultural projection at the center of the debate on a changing American culture and thus a changing American identity, historian Michael Kammen (1993) views public memory as central to a nation's identity. He writes,

> Public memory, which contains a slowly shifting configuration of traditions, is ideologically important because it shapes a nation's ethos and sense of identity. That explains, at least in part, why memory is always selective and is so often contested. Although there have been a great many political conflicts concerning American traditions, ultimately there is a powerful tendency in the

> United States to depoliticize traditions for the sake of "reconciliation." Consequently the politics of culture in this country has everything to do with the process of contestation *and* with the subsequent quest for reconciliation. (p. 13)

In the United States, a cultural commitment to progress provides the rhetorical means for moving from contestation to reconciliation. Local communities, such as the city of Birmingham, extol a "tradition of progress" that seems absolutely central to the community's evolution, in this case from Bombingham to the city of medicine (Gallagher, 1999, pp. 315, 317). According to Kammen (1993), members of social and political elites become "tourists of the past, seeking justification in history" and the "lucrative profits available to those who invest in the 'heritage industry'" (p. 691). Social and political elites are not the only tourists of the past, however. As Kammen points out, the dramatic increase in tourism since the 1960s and the lucrative nature of the tourism industry have led to the democratization of tradition by making it more accessible. The result is the creation of sites of memory that provide visions of a timeless past, "of stable evolutionary change, and of history with a minimum of conflict and a maximum of aesthetic and patriotic appeal" (p. 691).

The development of a shared vision of the past can be elusive, however. As Edward Linenthal (1995) suggests, "The more volatile the memory, the more difficult the task to reach a consensual vision of how the memory should be appropriately expressed, and the more intense become the struggles to shape, to 'own' the memory's public presence" (p. 52). Social diversity within the United States means that there are multiple memories rather than a monolithic, collective memory. How and to what extent do civil rights–related museums and memorials evoke memory and contestation, amnesia, and reconciliation? How do they account for, reconcile, represent, and construct multiple versions of the past? Can a coherent vision be presented without moving into a progress narrative of some kind?

Theories of genre provide one way to address the difficulties that confront creators, critics, and, ultimately, audiences of public discourses of memory. Although the explicit discussion of genre has been somewhat absent from communication journals in recent years, generic approaches are still evident.[3] One of the areas in which this is particularly true is in the criticism of material rhetorics, including memorials, history sites, and other places and artifacts of cultural memory. In her 1986 essay on the Vietnam Veterans Memorial (VVM), Sonja Foss argues that memorials and sites of memory are rhetorical artifacts deserving of examination by rhetorical critics at least in part because of the generic function(s) they perform. Her analysis of the VVM is based primarily on examining the extent to which it embodies epideictic form, function, and substance. Foss's analysis of the VVM is important because it was one of the first in what has become a growing tide of critical essays in communication journals devoted to analyses of memorials, monuments, and other public sites of memory. Interestingly, it also echoes the earlier work of Karlyn Campbell and Kathleen Jamieson (1978a), who, in their efforts to establish generic criticism as a legitimate method, focused on how form, substance, and context both constrain and provide opportunities for particular rhetors. In recent analyses of memorials and sites of memory, however, the emphasis has changed from understanding the constraints and opportunities of form, context, and substance on rhetors to an emphasis on how audiences perceive, respond to, and understand these material forms of rhetoric (Gallagher, 1995). This shift marks a move from similarity in situation or occasion as a key characteristic of genre to shared social construction of meaning and public construal of situation types as indicators of genre.

Indeed, genres appear to be most serviceable in our attempts to categorize our experiences in day-to-day interactions with one another. In our discussions of films, speeches, television shows, novels, and even food, generic classification helps us to make claims about and to share with others our interpretations of and responses to all kinds of communicative experience. It helps us to define the situations we face by providing some level of predictability in our lives and the resources for modeling and inventing appropriate responses. This is important, given the contemporary concern with instability, indeterminacy, and the lack of stable categories. As Carolyn Miller (1984) points out, "It is possible to arrive at common determinations of material states of affairs that may have many possible interpretations because . . . our stock of knowledge is based upon types" (p. 156). This is true not because situations reoccur in any objective fashion, or even because perceptions reoccur, but, rather, because situations are social constructs that result from definition. Therefore, what recurs is "not a material situation (a real, objective, factual event) but our construal of a type" (p. 157). Thus, despite the fact that we are "in an age of 'marked instability' . . . [when] typical patterns are not widely shared . . . and motivation is 'liquid,' . . . and the whole matter of genre has become problematic" (p. 157), critics can and should pay attention to how people rhetorically work together to define experiences and situations in ways that are shared and thus recurrent.

Critics have already begun the process of determining the kinds of conventionalized social motives that memorials and sites of memory may evoke. As indicated previously, claims have been made regarding the epideictic and deliberative functions of the VVM. In his account of the 15-year struggle to create the Holocaust Museum in Washington, D.C., Linenthal (1995) argues for understanding the museum as therapeutic, a generic claim echoed in other work on Holocaust memorials, the VVM, and the Aids Memorial Quilt. Elsewhere, I have argued that civil rights–related memorials function at least in part as apologia, as a way of reclaiming moral high ground for a community or nation by providing a means for coming to terms with the wrongdoings of the past (Gallagher, 1995, 1999). Finally, critics and theorists have asserted an overarching social motive bound up in and evoked by narratives of progress (Kammen, 1993).

To develop a better understanding of how particular conventional social motives and racial ideologies come to prevail in the experience of audiences, a critic must also analyze the form, substance, and context of artifacts. In terms of museums and memorials, this means paying particular attention to the material nature of the artifacts. Because of their "assiduous materiality," the issue of context, including location, is particularly important. As Carole Blair (1999) suggests, unlike speeches or written texts, memorials "remain in our perceptual fields as long as we are nearby. They do not fall silent . . . nor are they put away" (p. 17). Instead, they have a recalcitrant presentness that, as Radley (1990) suggests, both impacts and is dependent on a physical setting or location. In the case of civil rights memorials and museums, location (or place) and form interact in particularly profound ways, such that even the most architecturally modernist, seemingly functional structure can never be taken at face value. Consider the National Civil Rights Museum, constructed within the remaining shell of the Lorraine Motel in an area of Memphis that is historically and politically charged. In and of itself, the museum is an unfinished text. It draws from outside its own structure to form the character of that structure.[4]

The Martin Luther King, Jr. Memorial in Atlanta, the Birmingham Civil Rights Institute, the National Civil Rights Museum in Memphis, and the Montgomery Civil Rights Memorial are four artifacts that share features in common but enable the social construction of distinct experiences, definitions, and lessons. The following section provides a brief comparative description of these four museums or memorials. An analysis of the four sites follows, which (based on the previous theoretical discussion) addresses the following questions:

1. What social action(s) is performed through the experience of these civil rights memorials? What are the consequences of their materiality, particularly in terms of cultural projection?
2. To what extent are the memorials and monuments as well as the responses to them shaped by generic elements embedded within the institutional discourse of which they are a product? How do these generic elements shape, particularly in terms of contestation and reconciliation, the re-creation and representation of multiple versions of the past?
3. What are the multiple contexts (economic, physical, and built environments) from which these memorials emerge, and how do they shape the re-creation and representation of racism and civil rights?

DESCRIPTION OF ARTIFACTS

Martin Luther King, Jr. Memorial and Center for Non-violent Social Change

The Martin Luther King, Jr. Memorial and Center for Non-violent Social Change is located in the Sweet Auburn district of Atlanta, a once thriving black middle-class community that is now a historic district and, curiously, a national park—an island of memory in a sea of urban decay. Visitors to the area can tour the birth home of Martin King, the Ebeneezer Baptist Church where both MLK and his father pastored, and the memorial plaza with its modernist buildings surrounding a central courtyard. The courtyard is defined by three additional structures: the Chapel of All Faiths, the Freedom Walkway, and a reflecting pool. At one end of the rectangular pool, adjacent to the Chapel of All Faiths and easily accessible from the street, King's stone casket sits on a stone dais, elevated slightly above water level. Located directly across the sidewalk from it is an eternal flame set into the brick terrace. The Freedom Hall at the opposite end of the pool houses a display of artifacts associated with Martin and Coretta Scott King as well as a bookstore/gift shop and an auditorium.

Prior to 1996, the view across the street, looking out over the eternal flame and away from the casket, was of public housing apartment buildings and an empty lot. In preparation for the influx of visitors in conjunction with the 1996 Summer Olympics, the National Park Service constructed a new visitors' center and the Ebeneezer congregation built a new sanctuary directly across the street from the original memorial and center. These structures and the plaza surrounding them reflect a different aesthetic. Compared to their built environment, they appear larger than life, very new and very lush. As a result, there is a kind of disconnect between the two sides of the street. The old sanctuary and the birth home, although carefully restored and maintained, appear old and a bit seedy, fraying around the edges as even the most tenderly cared for garment will do when it is has been handed down several times. At the new visitors center, uniformed park rangers greet visitors. In the King Center, the birth home, and the original Ebeneezer sanctuary, members of the community and the church serve as hosts. The new structures reflect the economic and political shifts as Atlanta has become the queen city of the New New South.[5] The older structures are linked to the once thriving neighborhood of the past. There is another gift shop located in the visitors center as well as a display room with picture, text, and video displays recounting King's role in the movement. The centerpiece of this display is a freedom walkway with life-size statues marching together on a road that begins at ground level and angles upward toward a wall of tempered glass windows. Located by the entrances to the display room are memory books and writing implements. Visitors are invited to write comments, reactions, and reflections.

Birmingham Institute

The Birmingham Institute was designed by the same architect who designed the Martin Luther King, Jr. Memorial and Center for Nonviolent Social Change, but the two have different structural features. The institute takes up one fourth of a city block and faces Kelly Ingram Park, the unofficial boundary between the black and white sections of the city in the 1950s and 1960s. Its external architecture is red brick with some classical elements, including a rotunda entrance, with white concrete steps ascending up to it. Directly to the left of the entrance is a well-stocked bookstore/gift shop.

The museum part of the institute consists of 10 galleries that take visitors from the era of segregation in Birmingham through the events of the

Civil Rights movement, both in Birmingham and throughout the nation, and finally to current struggles for human rights throughout the world. The promotional video for the institute describes a visit to the museum as "a self-directed journey through the Civil Rights movement and the history of African American life in Birmingham." The journey begins with a film titled "Going up to Birmingham," which describes the origins of the city (the city was founded after the Civil War as a desirable place for industry due to vast mineral resources in the area), the contrast between the experiences of whites and blacks during the early years, and the self-contained culture that black people built in response to the strict color line that emerged in the city. After the film, the screen rises and visitors walk through galleries depicting life in segregated Birmingham prior to the movement. As a segue between these galleries and the ones devoted to the events of the movement, there is a room of hanging Plexiglas panels etched with representations of Birmingham citizens of the 1950s (e.g., a black woman in a nurse's uniform, a white man in a suit, a black man in a suit and hat, and a white farm worker). A tape of voices plays continuously as visitors walk among the images so that each of the figures appears to be talking about his or her beliefs or experiences regarding civil rights, segregation, and racism. At the end of the room, on a black wall, loom the figures of Ku Klux Klansmen dressed in white robes.

Displays in the next section of the museum include a statue of Rosa Parks on a bus, MLK's Birmingham jail cell, the charred remains of the Freedom Riders' burned-out bus, and newspaper clippings, photographs, film footage, filmed interviews, and other artifacts and texts. The visitors move through these sections of the exhibit until they find themselves in the midst of a group of marchers commemorating the march on Washington. The marchers have jubilant expressions, and for the first time since the beginning of the movie, visitors experience a flood of natural light as they celebrate the successes of the movement, moving, literally, out of the darkness of legal segregation into the light of legal equality.

The rest of the museum section of the institute marks specific milestones in achieving legal equality in Birmingham and ends in a gallery devoted to international human rights. It features life-size images and audio narratives of individuals throughout the world who have experienced oppression and racism due to their gender, ethnicity, or religious beliefs and who are involved in movements to end such oppression.

National Civil Rights Museum

The National Civil Rights Museum in Memphis is located in the shell of the Lorraine Motel where Martin Luther King, Jr. was assassinated. The external courtyard and part of the façade of the building have been carefully reproduced to look much as they did the day King died, including parking spaces with two 1950s era cars, external walkways, and the original motel sign. Exhibits begin on the ground floor, and as visitors move through them, they proceed along a path that gradually spirals upward and deposits them, ultimately, at the reproduced and restored second-floor rooms King and his friends were occupying on the fateful day.

The main exhibits in the museum are vignettes capturing key elements of the Civil Rights movement and are organized around the constitutional issues the movement sought to test. Photos, audio recordings, documentary footage, life-size statues, and artifacts help to create the look and the feel of the era and provide a more experiential, process-oriented (as opposed to static) perspective on history. The 16 exhibits include many of the same events reproduced in the Birmingham Institute, such as the *Brown v. Board of Education* decision, the Montgomery bus boycott, student sit-ins, the freedom rides, King's Birmingham jail cell, the march on Washington, the march from Selma to Montgomery, and the Memphis janitors strike. The final galleries are quite different, however. The Memphis museum culminates at the rooms 306 and 307 displays, where visitors view the re-created hotel rooms through Plexiglas windows and look out onto the hotel's balcony where King stood before he was assassinated. The unmade beds, the dishes holding the remains of a meal, and the hotel façade suggest an attempt to put visitors into a moment in the past, to both evoke and instill memory.

As with the King Center in Atlanta and the Birmingham Institute, the Memphis museum is located in a neighborhood that, prior to the 1960s, was a center for black commerce and culture and is now a site of urban decay, targeted for urban renewal. In addition, when the building was purchased and reconstructed, inhabitants were displaced. One of those displaced was Jacqueline Smith, an African American woman who has staged a continuing protest, a sort of countermemorial, directly across the street. Her memorial is made up of an old couch on which she sits with her belongings, displaying hand-lettered signs. Ms. Smith's signs declare that, contrary to being honored and preserved by the museum, King's vision and legacy have, in fact, been betrayed by the museum. Visitors must pass by Ms. Smith to enter and exit the museum.

Montgomery Civil Rights Memorial

The Montgomery Civil Rights Memorial is perhaps the most unique of the four, particularly in form and substance. Although its published literature indicates an intended educational function, similar to that of the museums previously described, it is symbolically more open and ambiguous. The memorial is located in downtown Montgomery on a plaza in front of the Southern Poverty Law Center (SPLC), a modern concrete and mirrored glass structure with a resulting black-and-white appearance. Directly behind the memorial and center is a large green-and-mauve building, the Alabama Center for Commerce, which looms over the center and the memorial. Ironically (or, perhaps, significantly), most downtown buildings have a white exterior appearance, made all the stronger by the hot southern sun reflecting off white marble and white concrete. In fact, buildings that are "colored," such as the Dexter Avenue Baptist Church, where the Montgomery bus boycott was launched, with its red brick exterior and stained-glass windows, or the Commerce Center, which is money-green colored, stand out markedly from the surrounding built environment.

The memorial is composed of two structures: an inverted asymmetrical, conical pedestal of black granite (referred to by SPLC staff and the designer, Maya Lin, as a table) and a convex, curved wall of black granite with the inscription "Until Justice Rolls Down Like Waters and Righteousness Like a Mighty Stream." There are 53 inscriptions on the tabletop, the majority of which (32) name 40 individuals and the circumstances of their death (e.g., "15 Sep 1963. Addie Mae Collins. Denise McNair. Carole Robertson. Cynthia Wesley. Schoolgirls Killed in Bombing of 16th St. Baptist Church. Birmingham, AL"). The other 21 inscriptions, spread out in no particular pattern other than chronological, relate various civil rights activities (e.g., "5 Dec 1955. Montgomery Bus Boycott Begins"), legal decisions (e.g., "9 Jul 1965. Congress Passes Voting Rights Act of 1965"), and violent confrontations (e.g., "3 May 1963. Birmingham Police Attack Marching Children with Dogs and Fire Hoses").[6] In addition, both the table and the wall have a water element. On top of the table, water bubbles up from a well located in an off-center position and spreads over the full surface of the table so that every part is evenly coated in water. The water falls over the edge and disappears into a drain at the base of the cone. Water also rushes down the side of the wall, apparently from a pool above, and into a drain that runs along the entire base of the wall. Because of continual death and bomb threats directed at the staff of the SPLC, who, often successfully, try legal cases against hate groups, the top portion of the memorial and the entrance plaza to the center are roped off and guarded. As a result, most people are not able to view the top part of the memorial, an absolutely still pool of water made of uninscribed black granite.

The memorial is situated in such a way that it interrupts the sidewalk; anyone walking on that particular part of the street must move around the memorial and if there is a breeze will feel the mist from the water flowing over the edge of the table. In addition, the surrounding built environment contains several sites commemorating Civil War and pre-Civil War life in Montgomery, including the preserved and restored White House of the Confederacy and the location of the auction block where slaves were bought and sold.

ANALYSIS

1. What social action(s) is performed through the experience of these civil rights memorials? What are the consequences of their materiality, particularly in terms of cultural projection?

As suggested previously, all four of these artifacts have a strong educational function, both in terms of their creators' goals and purposes and in terms of their audiences' experiences. Indeed, the notion of heritage tourism is based on an interest in learning about the past, not simply through reading history but also through "experiencing" it via multiple modes. As the previous descriptions indicate, all the sites appeal to multiple senses, particularly hearing and touch in addition to sight, and they seek to form emotional identification through physical layout, personalized narratives, and juxtaposition of symbols and artifacts. In addition, each of the sites distributes brochures that emphasize the educational function the museum or memorial is meant to serve. These printed materials suggest that learning about the past through visiting the sites can help visitors (and through them, society as a whole) to avoid repeating mistakes while promoting better understanding of the dynamics of racism and racial hatred. The educational function of these memory sites is considered particularly important by both staff and visitors because of the comparatively limited availability of information about civil rights history and the role of African Americans and people of color in American history (Hacker, 1995). The bookstores at the King Center, the Birmingham Institute, and the Memphis museum work to fill a gap in availability of popular works and scholarship in these areas.

In addition to the educational function and related issues of form, these sites differ functionally and, as a result, provide somewhat different cultural projections. The MLK memorial has some of the formal elements of a mausoleum, housing the remains of the dead by an eternal flame and chapel of all faiths. Combined with the educational buildings and the visitors' center, these elements suggest that the memorial as a whole is highly functionalist in its materiality (Gallagher, 1995). In terms of cultural projection, the location of the memorial in the historic district, the designation as a national park, and the visitors' center run by the park service all suggest syncretism, a form of mutual projection by dominants and subordinates. The addition of the visitors' center after the fact, as it were, its invasiveness, and the newness and upscale look contrast markedly with the original memorial and Center for Non-violent Social Change, however. The coupling of the memorial with the center inscribed a relationship between the act of remembering King and the attitude of being committed to social change. The new visitors' center disrupts this, suggesting elements of hegemony and perhaps even polarization. A rejection of the old for the new, the wrong side of the street for the right side of the street, and local memory for nationally sanctioned memory may be read into the memorial as a result.

In the Birmingham Institute, educational, remembrance, and preservation functions are articulated in various ways (Gallagher, 1999). The materiality of the museum is imbued with visual argument, establishing the narrative of progress for Birmingham. In terms of cultural projection, the institute and its sponsors envision the museum as having a counter-hegemonic function, and it does do a good job of presenting the world and the worldview of African Americans in Birmingham—but always in the past and always in terms of the progress narrative. This progress narrative is more consistent with hegemonic projections because it is central to white perspectives on civil rights, particularly regarding how and to what extent those rights have been achieved. For example, one such perspective suggests that the legal remedies of the 1960s effectively solved the problem of unequal opportunity, and therefore there is no longer a need for affirmative action or other reparative initiatives. Because of its interactivity and its visual and verbal depiction of history as a process rather than an entity made up of discrete moments, the institute may also be viewed as having a counterhegemonic effect on white visitors, who are guided to an understanding of a subordinate group's experiences and viewpoints. Ultimately, the institute is strongly syncretic: Positive images of blacks are presented throughout the museum, and the strong emphasis on the successful accomplishment of legal integration yields an equally compelling set of positive images of the prevailing political system and its dominant group, namely, whites.

In addition to its educational function, the National Civil Rights Museum also evokes remembrance and preservation, but its shrine-like features make it distinctive. The materiality of the museum is characterized by a strong tension between the preservation of the shrine to King and the enactment of these other functions. Some scholars have argued that, given the physical layout of the building (ascending up through the history of the movement and ending at the assassination site), the museum creates a material inability to move beyond the assassination (Wilson, 1999). Interestingly, the museum is planning a full-scale addition that would include a gallery devoted to covering human rights on an international scale, similar to the final gallery of the Birmingham Institute. In terms of cultural projection, the narrative of progress is much less prevalent in the National Museum; thus, a counterhegemonic message, which questions the dominant political structure and its positive representations of whites, may tend to be experienced more strongly. The presence of Jacqueline Smith disrupts this, however. Her protest suggests a reading of the museum as hegemonic, as reinforcing the dominants' position that society is basically good and just needs some tweaking now and again (Armada, 1998). Ironically, the planned addition mentioned previously would most likely lead to the further displacement of Jacqueline Smith or, at the very least, provide a means for visitors to avoid having to experience her protest memorial (one set of plans calls for an enclosed walkway going from a parking area across the street directly into the museum).

Although the Montgomery memorial appears to be the most distinctive of the four discussed here, it serves and evokes some similar functions, including educational and remembrance. The inscriptions on the table draw attention to actions, tragedies, and people of the past as worthy of memory, but unlike the strong progress narrative in the institute or the shrine elements of the national museum, the memorial does not resolve the tensions indicated by the incomplete time line or the heavy security at the site. Compared to the functionalism of the other sites, the memorial's materiality is thus highly symbolic. In this sense, the memorial may be the most counterhegemonic of the artifacts, particularly in its association with the SPLC. Indeed, Blair and Michel (2000) argue that the memorial creates "a clear discontinuity between past and present in terms of the 'solutions' it symbolizes" while suggesting "the continuity between past and present is racism" (p. 48). It may also be experienced as syncretic, however, given that the attorneys of the SPLC are mostly white, and that they work through existing political institutions even as they take some power (usually monetary) away from some whites and attempt to distribute it to individuals of various subordinate groups. The cultural projection of the memorial may also polarize, particularly if it is perceived as a threat to the status quo of Montgomery (and the nation as a whole), a possibility suggested by my interaction with two women at the city of Montgomery's visitors center who, when asked for directions to the civil rights memorial, were quick to assure me that there were other sites more worthy of my time and attention.

2. To what extent are the memorials and monuments as well as the responses to them shaped by generic elements embedded within the institutional discourse of which they are a product? How do these generic elements shape, particularly in terms of contestation and reconciliation, the re-creation and representation of multiple versions of the past?

As indicated previously, the MLK memorial draws on modernist sensibilities of function over form more clearly than any of the others. The continued preservation of the Sweet Auburn district, the "birth home," and the old Ebeneezer church mimics other restored neighborhoods and homes. These features, coupled with the National Park designation and trappings, indicate tourism as a likely shared social motive for visitors. The displays in the new visitors' center quote the conventions and forms found in both the Birmingham Institute and the national museum: In all three, there are statues of marchers with which the visitor is invited or obliged (to continue passage through the museum or site) to join. In addition, all three use similar videotape footage, labels, and news coverage to tell the stories of the movement.

Another common aspect (to all four sites) is the rhetorical and material "presence" of King in the narratives of public memory. Each site features him in a slightly different way, with the first three highlighting his participation in the events of the movement, especially events that occurred in their respective cities. In the Montgomery memorial, King's words are engraved on the water-covered wall, and the inscriptions on the table end with the record of his assassination. The King memorial emphasizes the life story of King and his family to a much greater extent than any of the others, and there is a display devoted to his wife, Coretta Scott King, that provides a time line of her active involvement. Her voice and participation are nearly, if not completely, absent in the other sites. The inclusion of spaces where people may sit and write their comments and reactions in the new visitors' center at the King memorial allows individuals to enter their own voices into the story, a marked change from memorials of the past, which both materially and symbolically were set in stone, unchangeable. Some critics trace this type of participatory element in contemporary memorial sites to the traditions that developed at the VVM, such as visitors leaving personal artifacts or making pencil rubbings of names on the wall.[7]

Similarly, the Birmingham Institute appears to draw on the recent popularity of highly interactive, "hands on," contemporary museums in which history is represented as a process rather than as a collection of static objects and events. The institute's displays stimulate multiple senses and allow for a more active visitor role, particularly in creating identification and a type of multivocality. The national museum also mimics some of these interactive museum-like functions, particularly in its coverage of the freedom riders (the burned-out bus is re-created in both museums) and King's Birmingham jail cell (again, both have a re-creation of the cell). As previously indicated, however, it is most strongly influenced by the shrine: King's room and that of his colleagues and friends are left exactly as they were, funeral wreaths stand outside and in, and visitors are materially and symbolically enjoined to experience what is was like on that day and to consider what the assassination meant and still means today. Whereas in the Birmingham Institute visitors start in the dark and journey to the light, in the national museum, visitors start at ground-floor level and spiral upward through the history of the fight for freedom for black Americans, culminating at the two rooms. Although the museum experience ends here, the planned addition, which will continue the experience with a focus on international human rights, conceptually mimics the gallery devoted to these issues in the Birmingham Institute.

In fact, all four of the memorials and museums examined for this study contain strong symbolic and material elements that suggest, even prescribe, a journey or pilgrimage. At the Birmingham Institute, as indicated in the description, visitors are explicitly instructed that their visit to the galleries constitutes a journey from the very origins of Birmingham as a segregated city through the events of the movement and to the "bright" present and future of a legally integrated southern city. At the King memorial, the freedom walkway in the original memorial complex begins at the tomb and chapel of all faiths and continues up the side of the reflecting pool to the Freedom Hall complex, where educational programs take place. In the new visitors' center, the display hall is dominated by the marchers on the road leading to the wall of windows and the lush landscaping outdoors. In the Memphis museum, visitors begin at the lower level of the museum and spiral upward, following the path of the movement, reaching the shrine at the end of their pilgrimage. The placement of the Montgomery memorial in the path of the sidewalk and the three ascending elements of the site (the table at ground level, the wall looming above, and the still pool at the top) also suggest a journey upward to a future that is, as yet, uninscribed.

The prescribed ending of the journey at each of the sites symbolically and materially indicates four somewhat different visions of the tools, tactics, and goals for civil rights in the present and future. The journey or pilgrimage at the MLK memorial (the original side of the street), ending as it does at the Freedom Hall, points to education as the essential tool or goal. The road in the visitors' center has a less clearly defined end and, thus, may suggest that the journey is the important lesson or goal. The Birmingham Institute, through the use of space and lighting cues and the manner in which the story is told, suggests that legal and political integration combined with the rehabilitation of a city as it moves toward economic viability are essential goals for the present and future. As currently configured, the pilgrimage evoked at the national museum seems to offer memory of past wrongs as the guide for future action, culminating in what might be viewed as an admonishment to never forget. Regarding the Montgomery memorial, Blair and Michel (2000) argue convincingly that the uninscribed pool at the top of the memorial represents the future, and that its materiality suggests a break with tactics and strategies, as well as results, of the past. Accordingly, they suggest that the memorial "harbors as part of its rhetoric moves toward a coalitional politics of diversity and what bell hooks has named a 'deconstruction of the category of whiteness'" (p. 48).

The generic aspects discussed here provide evidence for the argument that each of these sites possesses rhetorical elements through which history and tradition are democratized by being made more accessible. Whether they also provide visions of a history with, as Kammen (1993) suggests, a "minimum of conflict and a maximum of aesthetic and patriotic appeal" is less clear. All the sites stress conflict, but they do so in a manner that leads to reconciliation of conflicts and that seems to argue for evolutionary rather than revolutionary change as the desired norm. Certainly, there is irony in the fact that none of these sites explicitly examines current issues of race and racism within the cities in which they are located. The physical coupling of the Montgomery memorial with the SPLC, the coupling of the MLK memorial with the Center for Non-violent Social Change, and the protest of Jacqueline Smith at the national museum, however, make it difficult for conflicts to be completely hidden and thus reveal a potential for overcoming the public amnesia that reconciliation narratives tend to create.

3. What are the multiple contexts (including the economic, physical, and built environments) from which these memorials emerge, and how do they shape the re-creation and representation of racism and civil rights?

Particularly in light of the recent successful efforts to site a memorial to Martin Luther King, Jr. on the Mall in Washington. D.C.,[8] it is interesting to note that all four of these sites are located in southern cities, in areas that were and are largely populated by black citizens and that have been, in at least three of the four cases, targeted for urban renewal. As indicated previously, the complexity of racial issues in the United States and the resulting impact on allocation and use of space, particularly in urban areas, make these civil rights commemorative sites particularly, even radically, contextual. These factors give added weight to Dell Upton's (1999) arguments regarding the goals of civil rights–related commemorative efforts. In his essay comparing the Montgomery Civil Rights Memorial and the commemorative sculptures located in Birmingham's Kelly Ingram Park, he writes,

> the creators of civil rights memorials seek to define the nature of southern society at the end of the twentieth century and the South's place in the twenty-first. These monuments, set in landscapes devastated by urban renewal, depict a South purged of its troubled past and ready to compete in a new global economy. (p. 23)

Just as the Sweet Auburn district in Atlanta is no longer sweet, at least in terms of the economic realities of its neighbors, so, too, the neighborhoods surrounding the national museum and the Birmingham Institute contain empty lots and shop windows even as they are touted as the means for revitalizing their communities. As Upton (1999) notes,

> In ways the black middle class may not have envisioned, their world was destroyed by the Civil Rights movement. . . . As downtown services and accommodations were opened up to African Americans, black merchants could not compete, the black banks and insurance companies that financed urban development declined and collapsed, and the former black business district was transformed into a "blighted" landscape ripe for redevelopment. The devastation of the landscape that was so painstakingly built through the efforts of the black middle class is shocking. The few churches and commercial structures that survive among the open fields and parking lots—and even more appropriate, the fields and parking lots themselves—constitute another kind of monument to the movement, for it is commemorated at the site of its significant events, but in a setting that bears virtually no resemblance to its historical self. (p. 31)

The urban landscapes and the economic realities of these communities return us to the role that tourism (and the lucrative nature of the heritage industry) plays in these sites and, ultimately, to how we understand race and racial identities as a result. These memorials and museums may provide a place where conflict is remembered and brought to the fore, but they do so in spaces whose forms and functions are consistent with the consumerism of tourism, engaging us in social but not necessarily political action.

Again, the Montgomery memorial is an exception. Although the urban landscape in which it is located has changed much since the Dexter Avenue Baptist Church was built on the street next to the capitol in 1885, the memorial's neighbors are mostly public buildings that, during the expansion of state governments in the 1960s and 1970s, according to Upton (1999), "spilled out of Goat Hill [the location of the state capitol] and consumed the residential neighborhoods near the capitol" (p. 25). In addition, the fact that the SPLC, and thus the memorial, is heavily guarded—that most visitors and passersby never get to see the full memorial (they are unable to ascend to the top of the stairs to view the still pool)—means that the experience of the memorial is charged with a heightened sense of conflict. Indeed, Blair and Michel conclude that the memorial is an example of critical public art "that is frank about the contradictions and violence encoded in its own situation, one that dares to awaken a public sphere of resistance, struggle, and dialogue" (Mitchell, 1994, as cited in Blair & Michel, 2000, p. 31).

CONCLUSION

What role do these sites of memory play in our understanding of our identities both as individuals who are "raced" and as a nation whose identity is tied to its cultural discourse? We are instructed by each of these museums and memorials to experience the Civil Rights movement of the 1950s and 1960s vicariously—to reflect on its impact in and for our own lives within established cultural generic forms, narratives, and places. In terms of cultural projection, the Birmingham Institute, with its strong narrative of progress, and the MLK memorial, with the addition of the new visitors' center, are perhaps best defined as syncretic: Dominants are provided the rhetorical means for identification and are thus led to accept some of the subordinate cultural projection, and subordinates accept some of the dominant projection that change is evolutionary, that progress occurs over time, sanctioned by the dominant culture, and, as a result, that reconciliation is important and necessary. In turn, the national museum, with its focus on the assassination and the ongoing protest by Jacqueline Smith outside its walls, and the Montgomery memorial are more likely to evoke contestation and memory rather than reconciliation and amnesia.

Thus, civil rights–related memorials and monuments inspire, educate, encourage, and even provoke us. Do they also provide the inventional resources necessary for dealing with our own issues of race and racism? Certainly, they make us more aware that current discourses related to who has political power, who lives where, who goes to what school, and who has what job are permutations of past arguments that were joined but never fully resolved. In providing the space, the material, and symbolic resources for confronting these issues, civil rights commemorative sites are places that instruct us in "the mutual, cultural knowledge that enables individuals" to "communicate as competent participants" in our culture (Miller, 1994, p. 72). This includes understanding that as individuals, we are distinct from one another but able to identify with each other, that we define experiences similarly but experience different realities, and that we can be moved to share power in certain ways and instances but have a strong tendency to leave the status quo intact and entrenched in others. Together, however, these sites provide us with more. In their varied depictions of the civil rights journey and its ends, they provide a composite vision of the ongoing nature of racial identity development: education, remembrance, self-reflection, participation, and, paradoxically, a break with the past.

NOTES

1. Rice's (1992) examination of the Rocky statue in Philadelphia provides an excellent sense of how tourist sites symbolize key cultural values, such as the rights of an individual defined more broadly as the pursuit of liberty.

2. Graves's (1992) analysis of the monument to Joe Louis in downtown Detroit demonstrates how visual, material images "become especially charged when applied to the public spaces of urban America" (p. 217).

3. The lack of attention paid to genre and genre analysis in communication journals is particularly noticeable when compared to the number of articles and books dedicated to genre authored by scholars in composition and rhetoric. See the journal *Written Communication* and edited collections such as Freedman and Medway (1994) and Duff (2000).

4. For additional discussion of this notion, namely that a material artifact may function as an unfinished text drawing from outside itself to determine its character, see Blair, Jeppeson, and Pucci (1991).

5. In his excellent comparative discussion of the memorial sculptures in Kelly Ingram Park and the Montgomery Civil Rights Memorial, Dell Upton (1999) argues that the commemorative activity surrounding the Civil Rights movement of the twentieth century promotes a rehabilitation agenda similar to the creation of the "New South" at the end of the Civil War period. He writes, "A century later, southern leaders frame the Civil Rights movement as a second painful rebirth—'the payments our history required,' in the words of one tourist publication—that transformed the New South into a New New South. Its memorials are tombstones of racial strife and heralds of a new order. Taking their cues from the spectacular economic success of Atlanta, which billed itself during the Civil Rights movement as 'The City Too Busy to Hate,' southern urban leaders herald the birth of a (non)racial order that fulfills the 'nations commitment to liberty and justice for all' and forms the social basis for a reinvigorated, globalized regional economy" (p. 32).

6. For an excellent, thorough description and analysis of the Montgomery memorial, including pictures and additional examples of inscriptions, see Blair and Michel (2000).

7. There is also a tradition of visitors inscribing themselves onto a memorial space in European antimemorials (Young, 1992).

8. For additional information about the approval of the site and the winning design, see Tuttle (2000) and Fogerty (2000).

8

John Wayne, *The Green Berets*, and the Containment Doctrine

George N. Dionisopoulos

[The Green Berets] wasn't really about Vietnam, it was about Santa Monica.

—Michael Herr (1977, p. 188)

Released during the summer of 1968, approximately half way between the Tet Offensive and the American presidential elections, John Wayne's film, *The Green Berets*, immediately became a "focus for the intense passions that had come to divide America" concerning Vietnam (Hellman, 1986, p. 91). Barbour (1974) observed that the movie made those sympathetic to Wayne's view quite happy and those who opposed literally livid with anger (p. 122).

Critical reaction to the film was almost universally negative. Schickel (1968) wrote that *The Green Berets* "is, of course, just as stupid—ideologically speaking—as you were afraid it would be and far worse—as an action film—than you suspected it could be" (p. 8). Morgenstern (1968) observed sarcastically that it could have been shortened "if everyone simply said 'yes' instead of 'affirmative'" (p. 94). The *New Yorker* said that its "serious moments are tough to bear, but its sense of humor is worse" (Gilliatt, 1968, p. 46), and Mohr (1968) predicted that when *The Green Berets* was shown in Vietnam, it would "leave even the Saigon commandos (rear area troops) and the Red Cross doughnut girls laughing" (p. 49). *New York Times* critic Renata Adler (1968a) was among the harshest, telling readers that the film was

> so unspeakable, so stupid, so rotten and false in every detail that it passes through being fun, through being funny, through being camp, through everything and becomes an invitation to grieve . . . for what has happened to the fantasy-making apparatus in this country. . . . It is vile and insane. On top of that, it is dull. (p. 49)

The public drama surrounding the movie even made it to the United States Congress. Senator Strom Thurmond defended Wayne, saying that he was many things, "but never dull" (as cited in Pitts, 1984, p. 146), whereas New York congressman Benjamin S. Rosenthal (as cited in Madden, 1969; see also Barbour, 1974; Carpozi, 1979; Shepherd, Slatzer, & Grayson, 1985) charged that the U.S. Army had subsidized the movie as a

> useful and skilled device employed by the Pentagon to present a view of the war which was disputed in 1967, when the film was made, and . . . largely repudiated today. . . . [The] glorified portrayal of the Vietnam war, which is the heart of this film, raises serious questions about the Defense Department's role in using tax funds for direct propaganda purposes. (p. 23)

Since the beginning of the project, *The Green Berets* had caused some concern for people connected with it. Several major filmmakers had shelved plans to make a movie about Vietnam. One of them, Stanley Kramer, pointed out that it was "literally impossible to make a film about the war without a point of view" (as cited in Windeller, 1967, p. 41; White & Averson, 1972). Director Mel Shaverson noted that any such point of view concerning Vietnam would potentially alienate those who did not agree: "Hollywood can't take sides, because if it does it can't sell tickets to the other" (as cited in White & Averson, 1972, p. 240; see also Suid, 1981). As Spark (1984) noted, during the war, Hollywood was "paralyzed, caught between the pressure for prowar films from successive administrations, and the reality of a predominantly youthful cinema, growing steadily more hostile to the conflict" (p. 36).[1]

Even after the movie was completed, studio executives, fearing a hostile reaction to the film, decided to "forgo the kind of elaborate premier that usually accompanies the openings of spectaculars and instead simply started continuous showings at noon, without any special fanfare" ("Glory," 1968, p. 24). The advertising campaign for *The Green Berets* was described as "restrained—almost defensive," with advertisements depicting the film as "just another war movie with no particular political viewpoint" (p. 24). Even Wayne was restricted in the press releases to some low-key statements to the effect that the film was filled with the type of action and adventure that audiences like (p. 24). During production, the media carried several statements from both John Wayne and his son Michael, who produced the film for Wayne's production company, Batjac Productions, maintaining that *The Green Berets* was an entertainment film and not a political statement (Barthel, 1967; Gold, 1967).

The avalanche of negative critical opinion that greeted the movie prompted Roberts and Olson (1995) to comment that it seemed as though the reviewers had "attacked the film as if it was the primary cause of the war" (p. 548). Although this observation contains some truth, *The Green Berets* was, indeed, at its base a political statement and, as such, acquired "an importance it otherwise would not have" (Cook, 1968, p. 453).[2] As a filmic effort to "help make the war comprehensible" ("Far From Viet Nam," 1968, p. 84), *The Green Berets* was an "ideological fiction," employing the narrative form of a motion picture to persuade an engaged audience "of the 'correctness' of a particular way of interpreting the world" (Suleiman, 1983, p. 1; Spark, 1984). White and Averson (1972) labeled such movies "message films" and observed that they

> indicate a recognition of the potential of motion pictures for more than diversion. Incorporating but going beyond the pleasure principle of mass entertainment, they utilize the film medium for expressing social commentary with the intention of drawing public attention to various social issues. They are purposely, and in the broadest meaning of the word, propaganda films; and their producers, directors, and writers can indeed be called social persuaders armed with a celluloid weapon. (p. viii)[3]

This essay examines *The Green Berets* for three interrelated reasons. First, this movie can be viewed as an important part of Cold War rhetoric because it was grounded in a contested vision of the United States' role in the post–World War II era. Critical examinations of Cold War rhetoric have most often focused on the pronouncements of presidents. During this time period, however, major institutions in American life, including the entertainment industry, were "engaged in the effort to influence popular opinion" (Barnet, 1990, p. 292). During the Cold War, some popular mediated texts, such as a message film, adopted a given ideological perspective that then had to be negotiated by contemporary audiences. *The Green Berets* is a case study of a particular rhetoric used to justify American efforts to shape the world after World War II. The post–Cold War/post–September 11 world currently finds the United States, often described as the only remaining superpower, engaged in "nation building" in Iraq and Afghanistan. As governmental decisions move the country toward more global intervention, we may be well served to examine the rhetoric of another time in which Americans were compelled to accept the fashioning of a "new world order" as part of their destiny.

A second reason for undertaking this analysis is that *The Green Berets* "was and remains the only prowar Vietnam movie to come out of Hollywood" (Roberts & Olson, 1995, p. 555). This concern is further exemplified when one considers that the filmic images of the war in Vietnam are some of the most easily accessible "popular history" concerning the conflict. Just as the young soldiers who served in Vietnam carried with them the motion picture representations of past American wars and heroes, often exemplified by John Wayne, future generations will learn about Vietnam from movies such as *The Green Berets* (Adair, 1989; Auster & Quart, 1979, 1988; Devine, 1995; Hillstrom & Hillstrom, 1998).[4]

It might be tempting—with the benefit of several years of reflection—to agree with Representative Rosenthal and dismiss the political message of *The Green Berets* as being an atavistic throwback to another era. It is important to remember, however, that when it was released, this film spoke to and for a great many Americans. Although critically condemned and picketed in New York, Los Angeles, and several college towns, *The Green Berets* was one of the top 10 movies of 1968. Wayne's film, with its simple message of right versus wrong, "tapped into the smoldering resentments of the working classes" (Roberts & Olson, 1995, p. 551), a group Richard Nixon would later appeal to as the "great, silent majority" of Americans.

The third reason for undertaking this study is to examine the importance of John Wayne as a political figure. Although Wayne was not in the common sense a politician, he was, by every measure of the concept, a political being. As Gary Wills (1997) observed, it would have to be "a very narrow definition of politics that would deny John Wayne political importance." The Duke "did not just have political opinions. He embodied a politics . . . of large meanings" (p. 29). He represented that "large politics" in an on-screen persona grounded in a particular vision of America, including its "proper" role in the post–World War II era. In both his 1960 film, *The Alamo*, and 1968's *The Green Berets*, Wayne attempted to define "the duties of Americanism in the 1960s," as he articulated "the power and resolution of America" after World War II (p. 191).

In this essay, I first provide a contextualization for the message of *The Green Berets* by examining the U.S. Cold War policy of "containment" and how U.S. efforts in Vietnam were viewed as a test case for that policy. Next, I argue that John Wayne became both a representation of and a powerful spokesperson for the worldview encompassing that policy. Then, I examine *The Green Berets* as a rhetorical effort to justify U.S. policy in Southeast Asia against a backdrop of the danger of Communist expansion. This examination is conducted by addressing how Wayne's worldview combined with government "assistance" to influence the film's message and how this message was developed through the film's characterizations of Americans and Vietnamese. Finally, I close with some conclusions and implications of this study.

COLD WAR CONTAINMENT AND JOHN WAYNE'S AMERICA

Several scholars have observed that the Cold War policy of containment was premised on the idea that Americans had some responsibility for ordering the world (Barnet, 1990; Campbell, 1986; Schwabe, 1986). Its beginnings trace back to the period following World War II when Americans became "particularly sensitive to the crusading tone of Moscow's communism with its early calls for 'world revolution' and its later maneuvering under Stalin's ruthless leadership to expand its control wherever this appeared feasible" (Smith, 1986, p. 46). As early as 1947, Truman's undersecretary of state Dean Acheson "formulated the 'domino theory' which Truman's successor, Eisenhower, later made famous and handed down as wisdom to his successors" (Thornton, 1977, p. 258). Following the "loss of China" (Newman, 1975) and the heavy fighting between American and Chinese troops on the Korean peninsula, "it could be tenably argued that China and the Soviet Union were in league with one another—and they were on the march" (Smith, 1986, p. 46).

As Barnet (1990) noted, there was no serious debate within or outside of the government regarding this perspective or the strategies that emerged from it. It became an orthodoxy that was, unfortunately, "like any set of ideas about national security . . . a simplification of reality. Official truth necessarily rested on selective attention to the extraordinary turmoil of the immediate postwar era and summary judgment about the significance of complex events" (pp. 293-294). Once this perspective became the received view governing American actions (Smith, 1986; see also Newman, 1975),

> it became difficult to change. On the one hand, there was the argument about "credibility" and warnings that should the United States default on its obligations to one party the entire structure of political commitments of which it was a part would be put in doubt. On the other hand, there was the domestic constituency for being "tough on communism," so that each president had to weigh what it meant for him and his party should [they] be in office when another country was "lost" to communism. (p. 47)

Given the set of seemingly unchallenged "realities" that emerged from this outlook, it is understandable that for many Americans, expressions of postwar colonial nationalism lost their charm when their movements received recognition and aid from "avuncular friends in Moscow" (Thornton, 1977, p. 259). In "containing" the spread of communism, we "imposed the American *cordon sanitaire*;" enacted through, among other methods, "alphabet alliances" throughout the world and direct military intervention in Korea (under the auspices of the United Nations), Guatemala, Lebanon, Cuba, the Dominican Republic, and Vietnam (p. 258). Pursuit of the containment doctrine saw the United States attempting to "preempt a potential rival by assuming a position of domination in a given area" (Schwabe, 1986, p. 16). This course was to have dramatic consequences in several areas throughout the world, probably none more tragic than in Southeast Asia.

As Thornton (1977) noted, policies such as the containment doctrine can, at any time, bring abstractions to life:

> Swaths of jungle, desert wadies, unheard-of valleys can be suddenly heard of, indeed promoted to worldwide prominence so that in the name of one or another national interest men may be ordered to take and hold them at all costs. (p. 25)

That was certainly the case in Vietnam, in which a "country which not 1 in 10,000 Americans of Franklin Roosevelt's day could have found on a map" (Thornton, 1977, p. 225) was suddenly "a test case" of American will in the Cold War (Wesseling, 1986, p. 6; see also Hellman, 1986).

As time went on, however, American efforts in Southeast Asia embroiled us deeper and deeper in what many considered to be the internal affairs of another country. As Thornton (1977) stated, as long as official policy stays

> close to common sense, men will do as they are told. When it does not, they will not. A man who will fight for "king and country," or its equivalent, does not willingly die for an abstraction he cannot attach to anything he knows. In the late 1960s citizens of the United States of America, whose foot was caught in the gin trap of an undeclared war in an unknown country, experienced this revulsion. Since their purpose was not clear, their self-image came under an attack fiercer than any mysterious enemy could mount. (p. 25)

When Vietnam caused Americans to question their role in "ordering the world," it concomitantly threatened the democratic consensus necessary to "impart authority and legitimacy to foreign policy" (Melanson, 1983, p. 186; see also Dionisopoulos & Goldzwig, 1992; Hoffman, 1978; Melanson & Thompson, 1985). Rhetorical attempts to reestablish the domestic consensus took many forms. One particular effort in this regard was John Wayne's movie *The Green Berets*.

THE MAKING OF THE GREEN BERETS

To understand the ideological message of *The Green Berets*, it is first necessary to examine two factors that combined to influence the final product. The first is the political worldview of John Wayne, particularly his views concerning Vietnam and the "danger" of the "Communist conspiracy."

John Wayne became both a representation of and a spokesperson for "the particular definition he gave to 'being American'" during this time period (Wills, 1997, p. 27). As his screen image became an embodiment of what it meant to be an American, many looked to him as "the pattern of manly American virtue" (Wills, 1997, p. 27).[5] In 1971, Bentley observed that Wayne had become

> [t]he most important American of our time. . . . In an age when the image is the principal thing, Wayne's is the principal image, and if the soul of this image is *machismo* . . . its body is the body politic, and its name is anti-communism. (p. 155)

Wayne was an ardent "Cold warrior" who "accepted the domino theory" (Roberts & Olson, 1995, p. 536) and "made the Viet Nam war his personal crusade" ("John Wayne as the Last Action Hero," 1969, p. 53). His views concerning Vietnam were "carved in stone. . . . The war was in the best interests of the United States and the free world." He was "convinced that the war was winnable, that the U.S. military effort could stem the Communist tide in Indochina" (Roberts & Olson, 1995, p. 537).

Unlike other moviemakers, who had abandoned projects about Vietnam, John Wayne believed that "filmmakers *had* to take a side" (White & Averson, 1972, p. 240) and was "never in doubt about his point of view. . . . It's my country, right or wrong, and pure as the driven snow" (Windeller, 1967, p. 41). As the star, coproducer, and director of *The Green Berets*, Wayne was in a powerful position to determine the film's "message," and "from the very beginning [his] own views on the conflict in Vietnam gave the script and ultimately the movie its focus" (Suid, 1977, p. 109). As Smith (1975) wrote, *The Green Berets* was "entirely a reflection of [Wayne's] will, containing no image he did not expressly desire or permit" (p. 95).

Like many Americans of the time, Wayne's views concerning Vietnam were part of a larger worldview premised on containment. He saw American action in Vietnam as "a noble effort on the part of the American people to protect the rights of a small nation which was being attacked by outside, Communist-inspired forces" (Barbour, 1974, p. 121). A *Time* magazine article, written while *The Green Berets* was in production, said that Wayne was "preoccup[ied with] Communist expansion. . . . Today his cause is Vietnam" ("Stars: The Duke," 1967, p. 67). A similar article in the *New York Times Magazine* (Barthel, 1967) quoted Wayne's views at length:

> If you go into any depth on it—the war—it has to be almost that you're for it; if you're a decent person you can't let people be so oppressed, particularly when you've told them and the rest of the world that you'll stop it. . . . We've been doing this for years, and it's about time we kept our word. . . . I have seen what's going on over there, and I have seen the guns and ammunition that our boys are

> getting killed with. Well, it's a Communist conspiracy. . . . As far as I'm concerned, they are our enemy. The Communists are our enemy, not the Russian people. The Communist conspiracy is our enemy. (p. 29)[6]

Wayne's defense of the U.S. policy in Southeast Asia is grounded in the moral certainty of the cause and slips facilely between the war in Vietnam and the Communist conspiracy—a message that also permeates his film.

Bound up with Wayne's concerns about Vietnam and communism were his views of Americans who threatened domestic consensus by opposing U.S. efforts in Southeast Asia. As Smith (1975) wrote, Wayne was in

> a state of permanent war against America's enemies—not so much the physical enemies outside the gates as the psychic enemies within. Wayne's war was against doubt and doubters, against those Americans who wished to step outside the straight and narrow. (pp. 92-93)

His worldview marginalized those who could not or would not recognize the importance of Vietnam for stopping communism. He was equally enraged by protestors who marched carrying the Vietcong flag and all the "liberal politicians" who had "stuck their noses" into a policy that, in Wayne's view, was "out of their bailiwick" (Barthel, 1967, p. 29). It genuinely puzzled him how a person could "be so swayed to the opposite side" on a matter of such obvious clarity (Wayne, 1971, p. 86). Senators such as Robert Kennedy and J. William Fulbright, and "all those goddamn 'let's-be-sweet-to-our-dear-enemies' guys," were just "helping the Reds and hurting their own country" (Wayne as cited in "Stars: The Duke," 1967, p. 67). From this perspective, the "Communist menace" was "an imperative, not a choice, and a matter of patriotism, not politics" (Shepherd et al., 1985, p. 248).[7]

The second important factor influencing the film was the cooperative relationship between the filmmakers and the U.S. government. Wayne was said to have been "enthralled" by Robin Moore's (1965) best-selling book *The Green Berets*. After Columbia Pictures dropped its option on the book, Wayne purchased the screen rights and set out "to do what no other Hollywood producer had dared to do—make a picture about the Vietnam fighting" (Carpozi, 1979, p. 218). Before he could start filming, however, he had to secure government assistance for the endeavor.

Wayne had previously received technical assistance from various branches of the U.S. military on several of his war movies. The military's caution about assisting filmmakers, however, had increased dramatically after the 1964 release of such movies as *Doctor Strangelove*, *Fail Safe*, and *Seven Days in May*—all showing either "the military or its technology out of control" (Smith, 1975, p. 18). Although Wayne had not been associated with such films, he began the project taking no chances, and in late December 1965, he wrote to President Johnson regarding the movie. In his letter, Wayne (1965) stated that although he supported the administration's policy in Vietnam,

> I know it is not a popular war, and I think it is extremely important that not only the people of the United States but those all over the world should know why it is necessary for us to be there.
>
> The most effective way to accomplish this is through the motion picture medium. Some day soon a motion picture *will* be made about Vietnam. Let's make sure it is the kind of picture that will help our cause throughout the world. . . . We want to tell the story of our fighting men in Vietnam . . . in a manner that will inspire a patriotic attitude on the part of fellow-Americans—a feeling which we have always had in this country in the past during times of stress and trouble.

In an interesting aside to one of his earlier pictures, Wayne left no doubt concerning the importance of Vietnam to containment:

> Perhaps you remember the scene from the film *The Alamo*, when one of Davy Crockett's Tennesseans said: "What are we doing here in Texas fighting—it ain't our ox that's getting gored." Crockett replied: "Talkin' about whose ox gets gored, figure this: A fella gets in the habit of gorin' oxes, it whets his appetite. May gore yours next. Unquote [sic]. And we don't want people like Kosygin, Mao Tse-Tung, or the like, "gorin' our oxes."[8]

A memo from Jack Valenti (1966) to President Johnson recommended "we give Wayne permission to make the film." Valenti observed that although "Wayne's politics are wrong"—he was a "rapping Republican" ("John Wayne as the Last Action Hero," 1969, p. 53) who had supported Nixon in 1960 and Goldwater in 1964—as far as Vietnam was concerned, "his views are right." Valenti went on to emphasize the potential power of a motion picture to disseminate the administration's perspective concerning Vietnam:

> If [Wayne] made the picture he would be saying the things we want said. Moreover, a commercial film about Vietnam, with popular stars in it, would probably have a more beneficial effect, and [be] seen by more people than any film the government could make, or any documentary other people would make.

In a reply to Wayne, special assistant to the president, Bill Moyers (1966), said that although government cooperation would depend on the script, the president did "indeed remember the film *The Alamo*, and like you, understands that ox-goring has a way of whetting an aggressor's appetite."

By February 1966, Batjac Productions had hired James Lee Barrett, "an extremely competent writer to start work on the screenplay" (Wayne, 1966). Barret's selection calmed some Pentagon worries that Robin Moore would do the screen adaption of his novel. Suid (1977) noted that Moore had "alienated the Defense Department by including in his book information about American actions in Vietnam which he had not cleared with the military and the Pentagon wanted nothing to do with him" (pp. 108-109).

In a letter to Moyers, Wayne (1966) sketched out the "message" of his movie. The developing screenplay

> will show the American people the extent and importance of this war to the Vietnamese. We want to enlighten them as to some of the facts: That more Vietnamese have been killed in this war than we lost in World War II, so they certainly are not lackadaisical about winning as a number of reports from overnight visitors would lead us to believe. That the Commie guerillas are ruthless, have killed twenty thousand civic leaders and their families during these years of slaughter.
>
> We want to show such scenes as the little village that has erected its own statue of liberty to the American people. We want to bring out that if we abandon these people, there will be a blood bath of over two million souls.
>
> We want to show the professional soldier carrying out his duty of death; but also, his extracurricular duties—diplomats in dungarees—helping small communities, giving them medical attention, toys for their children, and little things like soap, which can be so all-important.

In June 1966, Wayne went on a 3-week hand-shaking USO tour of Vietnam to "get a feel of the place and what was happening there" (Shepherd et al., 1985, p. 270). He promised the troops that he would make a film that would let "the American people know what's going on over there" (Barthel, 1967, p. 29). At a press conference on his return, Wayne expounded "on the threat of international communism and his opposition to admitting Red China to the United Nations" (Shepherd et al., 1985, p. 270).[9]

Following another research expedition to the JFK Special Warfare Center at Fort Bragg, North Carolina, Wayne wrote to several senators, including Richard Russell and J. W. Fulbright, advocating continued support of the government's policies in Vietnam. He reminded the senators that if guerrilla warfare was successful in Southeast Asia, it could also occur in South America, and he suggested that criticism of American policies in Vietnam might "damage our government's present policy and destroy the freedom which is being bought by the blood and lives of the people of Vietnam, the United States, and her proven allies" (as cited in Suid, 1977, p. 110).

Final clearance for Department of Defense cooperation was granted during the summer of 1967, and filming got underway at Fort Benning, Georgia, on August 9 of that year. Batjac Productions submitted an eight-page list of required equipment, including "jeeps, captured Viet Cong weapons, American rifles, machine guns, carbines, parachutes, mortars, trucks, tanks, armored personnel carriers, bulldozers, ambulances, helicopters, cargo aircraft, and scout dogs" (Fulbright, 1970, pp. 117-118). To accommodate Wayne's need for "troops of Oriental descent who could pass for Vietnamese" (Smith, 1975, p. 126), the Army obligingly located a platoon of Hawaiians "training at Fort Devens, Massachusetts, and put them on [administrative] leave status so that Wayne could bring them to Fort Benning to be in the picture" (Fulbright, 1970, p. 118; Suid, 1977).

Army support for *The Green Berets* was "one of the most extensive cooperations of the armed services and Hollywood in history" (Roberts & Olson, 1995, p. 544). It also gave the film a degree of technical expertise that would have otherwise been unavailable.[10] In fact, the technical excellence was recognized by some of the critics who otherwise found almost nothing of value in the film ("Far From Viet Nam," 1968). The Army's cooperation, however, also meant that the final product had to "put the military in the best light possible" (Fulbright, 1970, p. 117) and that the government was free to demand changes in the script.[11] Thus, one can safely assume that when *The Green Berets* was released in

1968, it contained no images that policymakers in Washington would find objectionable.

THE GREEN BERETS AS COLD WAR RHETORIC

The film can be viewed as containing three distinct parts. The first takes place in America, where Green Berets Colonel Mike Kirby (Wayne) forms two A teams for Vietnam—"where the action is." Once in Vietnam, the film script draws loosely on two incidents from Moore's (1965) novel: an enemy attack on Special Forces Camp A-107 and the kidnapping of an enemy general. The balance of this essay focuses on how the film portrays Americans and the Vietnamese and what these portrayals communicate concerning the American "mission" in Vietnam.

There are two characterizations of Americans in *The Green Berets*. There are the members of the Special Forces, led by Colonel Kirby, and there is reporter George Beckwith (David Janssen), representing significantly both the media and those Americans who do not support U.S. efforts in Vietnam. The Beckwith character adds almost nothing to the narrative progression of the movie—and, indeed, does not resemble any character in the Moore (1965) novel—but his presence is important to the political message of the picture. Roberts and Olson (1995) observed that the

> unifying focus of the movie is the awakening of George Beckwith . . . a liberal journalist, to the real nature of American involvement. At first, Beckwith is skeptical; he doubts the domino theory, the threat of communism, and the viability of the government of South Vietnam. But after observing a series of heinous Vietcong atrocities and following the activities of Green Beret Colonel Kirby, he reverses his earlier opinions. (p. 547)

The rhetorical importance of Beckwith is illustrated in the film's opening scene. At a public demonstration of the capabilities of the Green Berets, Sergeant Muldoon (Aldo Ray) tells the civilian visitors that he and Sergeant McGee (Raymond St. Jacques) have had, between them, three tours of duty in Vietnam: "That makes us experts. So we've been ordered to volunteer to answer your questions." In the ensuing question-and-answer period, the Green Berets share the feelings they have formed "out there" and offer their articulate justifications of American policy in Vietnam.

Sergeant McGee assures the audience that he can understand "the killing of the military" but not the "extermination of the civilian leadership, the intentional murder and torture of innocent women and children." When someone points out that the answer does not mean "they need us or even want us," McGee puts it

> in terms we can all understand. If the same thing happened in the United States, every mayor in every city would be murdered. Every teacher, every professor you ever heard of, every senator, every member of the House of Representatives and their combined families, would all be tortured and killed. And a like number kidnapped. But in spite of this, there's always some little fellow out there willing to stand up and take the place of those who've been decimated. They need us, Miss Sutton, and they want us.

When a woman who identifies herself as a housewife asks why we never read of this in the newspapers, Sergeant Muldoon replies, "Well, that's newspapers for you, ma'am, you could fill volumes with what you don't read in them."

Beckwith then asks the sergeants how they are so sure we should be fighting for a South Vietnamese government that has not held free elections or produced a constitution after 6 months of effort. Muldoon replies,

> The school I went to taught us that the 13 colonies, with proper and educated leadership, all with the same goal in mind, after the Revolutionary War, took from 1776 to 1787, 11 years of peaceful effort, before they came up with a paper that all 13 colonies would sign; our present Constitution.

After the applause subsides, a noticeably angry Beckwith tells Muldoon that the war is "between the Vietnamese people. Let's let them finish it." "Let them finish it, Mister Beckwith?" replies Muldoon incredulously. He then offers an argument that places the war within its larger defining context. Retrieving captured weaponry from a display board behind him, Sergeant Muldoon drops each on the table in front of the doubting reporter:

> Chi-com K-50. Chinese Communist. Soviet-made SKS carbine, Russian Communist. Ammunition, Czechoslovakian Communist. No sir, Mister Beckwith, I don't need a lead weight to fall on me, or a hit from one of these weapons to know that what's involved here is Communist domination of the world.[12]

Beckwith is unconvinced and goes over to talk with Colonel Kirby. Beckwith tells Kirby, "Your brainwashed sergeant didn't sell me" on the idea that "we should be involved in Southeast Asia." Kirby asks if the reporter has ever been to Southeast Asia. When Beckwith mumbles a defensive "no," Kirby walks away.

This opening scene makes "clear that [*The Green Berets*] is not so much about winning the war against the Vietcong as it is about winning the hearts and minds of the American public" (Smith, 1975, pp. 133-134). First, this scene previews many of the rhetorical arguments that will be developed in the balance of the film. One of the most important is that those who have been to Vietnam know best, with the unspoken implication that those who know best should decide policy. For example, Muldoon's remark about being "ordered to volunteer" draws some laughter from the audience, but his expertise—certified by his having been to Vietnam—is never questioned and seems to be accepted at face value. In fact, the very structure of this scene reinforces this message. The relevant facts about American involvement in Vietnam are presented by two army noncoms, not officers. Theirs is a working-class expertise grounded in the primacy of personal experience rather than the intellection one might expect from college-educated officers. In fact, in the encounter between Beckwith and Colonel Kirby, the officer offers no argument at all. Instead, once the reporter admits he has not been to Southeast Asia, the colonel simply walks away, dismissing as unimportant, uninformed, or both anything further Beckwith might have to say.

This message concerning the primacy of experience is reinforced after the story moves to Vietnam. After Beckwith has witnessed the aftermath of a particularly brutal atrocity committed by the Vietcong, Kirby speaks to him as one of the "enlightened" to another: "You know, it's pretty hard to try and explain this country to someone until they see it for themselves."

Second, this scene also previews how the movie will present the Wayne persona. During the Vietnam era, John Wayne was more than just a movie star: He was a cultural icon. As Mohr (1968) observed, Wayne was "an important part of the folk culture of the young Americans who [fought] the war in Vietnam, a kind of reference marker for fictional toughness" (p. 49). Playing the "big tough boy on the side of right" ("Star: The Duke," 1967, p. 67), Wayne was always "a strong man defending right and the weak against a larger, more powerful evil group" (p. 137). This could have presented a problem for bringing "Waynism" to Vietnam, a war in which America had become the powerful group bringing unparalleled levels of destruction to a peasant nation. As David Halberstam noted, this switch in roles "was a terribly difficult thing for John Waynism" (as cited in Suid, 1977, p. 118; see also Suid, 1981). The solution to this problem is previewed in Sergeant McGee's observation that "there's always some little fellow out there willing to stand up and take the place of those who've been decimated." By making Wayne a member of the Special Forces and situating most of the action at a firebase in the middle of "Indian country," an area controlled by the Communists, he could again be on the side of right, surrounded by the same evil hostiles he had been fighting for decades.

Third, the opening scene makes clear that the film will address the domestic divisions caused by the war in Vietnam. The scene establishes the antiwar attitude of the character of George Beckwith while simultaneously undermining his credibility by pointing out that his strongly held opinions are based on something other than firsthand experience. His designation as a reporter is significant in that many people blamed media coverage for exacerbating antiwar sentiment during this time (Hillstrom & Hillstrom, 1998; Paletz, 1999).[13] Sergeant Muldoon's observation that one could "fill volumes with what you don't read in [newspapers]" serves to further undermine any information that may conflict with the perspective being offered.

Finally, the opening scene previews the characterizations of the Vietnamese that will be played out in the balance of the film. The expert accounts offered by Sergeants McGee and Muldoon portray a savage enemy that systematically murders and tortures innocent civilians. In contrast, the South Vietnamese are courageous in their opposition to the oppressors and in their fledgling attempts to engage in what American politicians such as Vice President Hubert Humphrey called nation building (Wakefield, 1968).

After the opening sequence in the United States, the movie shifts locations to Vietnam.[14] It is here that the characterizations previewed in the opening scene are fleshed out to complete the message of the film. The character that is probably the most important from this perspective is Beckwith, who travels to Southeast Asia to experience it firsthand.

"Experiencing" Vietnam converts Beckwith from opposition to support of the American effort there.

As the film's only representation of both the media and domestic antiwar sentiment, Beckwith's conversion is vital to viewing *The Green Berets* as a message film. As Smith (1975) observed, Colonel Kirby had only to kill the enemy, whereas Beckwith had "to kill his own doubts about America's destiny in Southeast Asia" (p. 134). His conversion is certified in his last scene when Kirby asks him what he will write "for that newspaper of yours." He responds, "If I say what I feel, I may be out of a job." When Kirby says that the Green Berets will provide one, Beckwith responds, "I'll probably do you more good with a typewriter." The Warner Brothers–Seven Arts press kit for the film states that Beckwith, a "former skeptic about the war . . . leaves [Vietnam] to write about the heroic exploits of the American and South Vietnamese forces" (Adler, 1968a, p. 49).

Beckwith's conversion conveys important elements of the film's message. First, as stated previously, the opening scene establishes that Beckwith's passionate antiwar stance is based on no firsthand experience in Southeast Asia. Once he sees the "Truth," he comes to believe in and, indeed, proselytize for American involvement in Vietnam. This further reinforces the earlier message that only those who have been there and seen American policy being carried out can really understand it. Beckwith's final statement that if he tells the truth of his firsthand experience, he may be out of a job adds an ominous, almost conspiratorial, quality to the earlier comment concerning "what you don't read in [newspapers]." The obvious implication is that not only are the American media not telling the real story about Vietnam but also any reporter who supported the American effort there would be fired. If it were true that "all those biased newspaper accounts of the war came from men who didn't know what they were talking about" (Smith, 1975, p. 134), it might explain why so much of the mediated environment was full of negative news concerning Vietnam.

The final interesting element of Beckwith's conversion is that it does not seem to have been based on analysis of any issues dealing with American military involvement in Vietnam. Indeed, while in Vietnam, Beckwith is not shown doing anything other than living day-to-day with the Green Berets (James, 1989). Instead, his conversion is based on witnessing firsthand the brutality of the enemy, especially the rape and murder of a young Montagnard girl he had befriended. As Smith (1975; see also Carpenter, 1990) observed, depicting the enemy killing and raping defenseless children is

> a time-honored device that goes back to anti-Hun movies of the Great War. . . . Following the rape-murder of the girl, Janssen stops nit-picking about the justice of the war. The unspoken assumption is that Americans never rape or murder, and that simply showing a reporter what the enemy does will guarantee agreement that we should be involved in the war. (pp. 134-135)

The Vietnam scenes also flesh out the film's depiction of the Green Berets. The most important exemplar of the Americans is John Wayne. His character, Colonel Mike Kirby, is the kind of war hero audiences had come to associate with Wayne, and most of the movie revolves around his on-screen presence. As Slotkin (1992) observes, "the plot, the dialogue, and the framing of sequences and even of individual shots all emphasize the absolute centrality of Wayne's character, Colonel Mike Kirby, to the successful prosecution of the war" (p. 521). As the iconographic representation of America on the side of good, Wayne's presence helped to advance the message of the film.

The portrayal of the Americans with Colonel Kirby is also important. As demonstrated in the movie's opening scene, these men were articulate in their argumentative defense of foreign policy. In Vietnam, we see that they are also kind and paternal toward the good Vietnamese and masterful at fighting the enemy. They voice no skepticism or doubt about their mission and move with skilled proficiency between holding a daily sick call for local Montagnards and preparing their camp for an attack by an overwhelming force of enemy soldiers. In essence, they perform the same types of heroic actions American audiences had come to expect from celluloid war heroes.[15]

The film's heroic portrayal of the Green Berets dovetailed well off the public image that had been assiduously cultivated for the Special Forces since the days of the Kennedy administration (Gustainis, 1989; Spark, 1984). As part of the message of the film, however, this depiction of the heroism involved in the American mission takes on added importance. As Bass and Cherwitz (1978) indicated, rhetorical defenses of such missions have long relied on the myth of the cultural hero, struggling and suffering through adversity to bring salvation and enlightenment to less fortunate races of people.

Interestingly, the film's portrayal of the Americans contrasts sharply with that offered in the novel on which it was based. Although the Green Berets in Moore's (1965) book were also dedicated, they trafficked drugs with the Vietnamese, gave money and guns to Cambodian bandits, and disregarded international borders and laws outlawing torture (p. 22). Undoubtedly, including these elements from the novel would have led to conflict with the Department of Defense and clouded the film's message concerning America's purpose in Vietnam.

The Americans are not the only heroes in *The Green Berets*. The film also portrays good Vietnamese who recognize the altruistic benevolence of the American involvement and are committed to keeping their country from falling to communism. For example, the South Vietnamese army commander at the Special Forces camp, Captain Nihm (George Takai), vows to return to his home in Hanoi after he has killed "all stinking Cong." He is a dedicated, fearless man who leads patrols and fights to defend the camp when it is attacked. His counterpart in Moore's (1965) book spent most of the time hiding in his bunker. In fact, Moore's Green Berets demonstrated a "cynical unconcern for the lives of [their] allies" (Gold, 1967, p. 3). They did not respect the South Vietnamese because they were corrupt and would not fight the enemy. As one Green Beret in the novel stated, even the Vietcong know that "there isn't a battalion commander in the ARVN that would take a chance on getting himself or his officers shot" (Moore, 1965, p. 121). In the novel, the South Vietnamese officers dealt in opium, encouraged desertion to steal the deserters' pay, sold peasant children into slavery, and dropped unexpended bombs on Montagnard villages. The extensive corruption of the South Vietnamese army and government meant that security was always a problem, forcing the Americans to hide as much from their allies as from the enemy.[16] Again, however, images such as these would conflict with the intended message of brave South Vietnamese engaged in "nation building" and would have prompted questions about why we were expending so much blood and treasure to prop up such a corrupt regime. Instead, film audiences saw cooperative harmony between the Americans and the South Vietnamese. Novel author Moore said that this decision was a strategic "concession we had to make to the Defense Department. We couldn't have made the film without their approval" (as cited in "Glory," 1968, p. 27).[17]

Another interesting Vietnamese character in the film is Hamchuck, an orphan boy adopted by the Green Berets. He lived with missionaries until they were assassinated. It is not stated who killed the missionaries, but within the context of the film the clear implication is that they were murdered by Communists. It is Hamchuck who serves as the focus for the film's most emotive moments, first when his dog is killed during the enemy attack on Camp A-107 and then in the film's final scene when

Colonel Kirby has to tell him that Peterson, who had vowed to take care of the orphan, was killed on the film's final mission. Thus, twice orphaned, Hamchuck asks the colonel, "What will happen to me?" and Kirby responds, "You let me worry about that, Green Beret. You're what this is all about."[18]

This emotional dialogue is pointed because it, albeit unintentionally, encapsulates the relationship between the Americans and the South Vietnamese portrayed in the film and thus serves as "a perfect allegory of the ideological rationale for American engagement in Vietnam" (Slotkin, 1992, p. 524). The Americans will worry about what is right for the Vietnamese and will do what is necessary to secure them a better way of life. Gilliat (1968) described the film's portrayal of this relationship:

> Vietnam is treated as if it were a little savage, in dire need of moral upbringing. . . . As the picture sees things, all the appalling butchery carried out by the Americans in it is for Vietnam's own good. The Vietnamese haven't had our advantages; they don't know what's best for them. (p. 44)

Wakefield (1968) echoed this idea in his observation that many Americans felt a duty to spread our

> "way of life," as embodied in government as well as economics and religion, to less favored peoples of the earth. . . . The sincere belief that their country is bringing a better way of life to the Vietnamese people is one of the things that sustains many soldiers in their service there, and the evidence which they bitterly experience in the lack of appreciation or hostility of many of the people can be justified by the fact that they don't know what's good for them. (pp. 203-204)

When scriptwriter James Barrett went to Vietnam to do research for *The Green Berets*, he was impressed by the attitude of an officer who told him "these people don't want to be free, but by God, we're going to make them free." Barrett believed that the idea of forcing people into a better way of life was a "new and exciting concept" (Wakefield, 1968, pp. 204-205).

Of final importance here is the film's portrayal of the enemy. The enemy is depicted mostly through its acts of brutality against the Green Berets and against the helpless civilians. This depiction of the savage nature of the enemy is contrasted with the benevolent Americans described previously. This Manichean juxtaposition made the movie a simple melodrama of harshly contrasting characterizations (Barthel, 1967; Edelman, 1979; "Far From Viet Nam," 1968; Morgenstern, 1968; Smith, 1975).

The portrayal of the enemy serves important functions for the film's message. First, it reinforces the heroic nature of the brave Americans and South Vietnamese who will stand up to these monsters and, in the words of Sergeant McGee, "take the place of those who've been decimated." Second, the savage portrayal of the enemy reinforces the reason for American commitment. Finally, and most important, it shows American audiences the true nature of communism and thus reinforces the danger of allowing it to expand. As Shepard et al. (1985) noted, *The Green Berets* was really "a film about the international Communist conspiracy. Like the real conflict, it just happened to be set in Vietnam among the Vietnamese, whose national problems, like personal problems, were insignificant if not irrelevant to that greater evil" (p. 272).

Some important elements of the enemy are omitted from the film, however. The enemy's defining characteristic seems to be its willingness to terrorize the locals into supporting its cause. According to Moore (1965), however, the principal terrorist technique used by the Vietcong was assassination of village leaders, which could be done "without alienating the population." This contrasted sharply with the effects of allied air strikes, which turned "hamlets of loyal peasants into VC sympathizers overnight" (p. 122).

Also omitted is any serious consideration of what might be motivating the enemy, beyond its ideological drive for "Communist domination of the world." This is all the more problematic because most of the enemy soldiers in the film are very brave. During the attack on Camp A-107, they advance relentlessly across open ground directly into withering small-arms fire, through a minefield, over booby-trapped barbed wire, and across a punji-staked ditch. Like much American introspection into Vietnam, this movie showed little interest in what motivated "the millions of Vietnamese . . . who willingly sacrificed their lives and livelihood in resisting America's imperial agenda for postcolonial Vietnam. . . . [Nor did it ask] why 'their' Vietnamese fought so hard and so long and for so little material reward" (Vlastos, 1991, p. 72). A more developed characterization of the enemy might have posed some uncomfortable questions concerning the U.S. agenda and what the Vietnamese really wanted regarding their future.

CONCLUSION AND IMPLICATIONS

The Green Berets confounded many of the industry experts and film critics and proved to be a box office success. Shot with a production budget of $6.1 million, the film made $7 million during the first 3 months of its release ("John Wayne as the Last Action Hero," 1969, p. 56) and $20 million within 18 months.[19] Although the film was a moneymaker, its ability to, in Wayne's words to President Johnson, "inspire a patriotic attitude" on the part of contemporary audiences was more problematic.

Although there were undoubtedly several very complex reasons for this, I suggest the following. First, critical examination suggests that part of the movie's message seemed to work against itself. In an effort to delegitimate the swelling chorus of protest against American involvement in Vietnam, the movie advances from its first segment, an argument that only those who have experienced Vietnam firsthand can really know what is going on. As such, the film is subtly hinting that any effort at secondhand interpretation is false. At the same time, however, the film is asked to be taken as representation, with the result that it "sacrifices its own validity for its belief in the primacy of experience" (Berg, 1986, p. 111). The problem with this element of the film's message was compounded by the fact that by the time it was released, a great deal of the public outcry against the war was from people who had experienced it firsthand, including the members of the Vietnam Veterans Against the War, who protested outside a New York theater showing *The Green Berets* ("Glory," 1968, p. 84).

A second problem for contemporary audiences was also one of the film's strongest elements—the narrative focus on the John Wayne persona. As stated previously, during the Vietnam era, Wayne had become more than just a movie star—he was a cultural icon. His image "more than any other single element . . . pervades all visions of Vietnam" (Scheurer, 1981, p. 152; Anderegg, 1991a). Whereas Audie Murphy was a war hero turned movie star, Wayne had "reversed the process" (Smith, 1975, p. 92) and became the man who "on film at least, has fought in most of the wars in the nation's history" (Rice, 1968, p. C17).

Unlike other American wars in which John Wayne "fought," however, Vietnam did not readily lend itself to clear images of good battling an overwhelming evil. Drawing on Moore's (1965) book and casting Wayne as a member of the Special Forces allowed him to offer a Manichean portrayal of outnumbered good against overwhelming evil, but it proved no match for the nightly barrage of images of "cold technological aggression against an agrarian society" (Hellman, 1986, p. 67).

Wayne's presence in the film also had a positive effect, however. His appeal was strongest to working-class America, which was also "bearing the brunt of the war's pain and suffering" (Hillstrom & Hillstrom, 1998, p. 144). At a time when American society was dramatically changing, Wayne was "unchanging—which was no doubt part of his appeal to an audience disoriented by change" (Wills, 1997, p. 279). His presence in Vietnam and the message of his film provided comfort to a great many Americans who, during that turbulent time, were unwilling to accept negative images of America coming out of Southeast Asia. Within the movie was "a memory of American greatness that many still wanted to live by" (Wills, 1997, p. 233). As Hillstrom and Hillstrom observed, *The Green Berets* "served as a salve [to working-class America], reassuring them that the cause of America—and their sons—in Vietnam was right and just" (p. 145).[20] Wayne maintained that the success of the film proved that the "so-called intellectual groups aren't in touch with the American people. . . . Instead of taking a census, they ought to count the tickets that were sold to that picture" ("John Wayne as the Last Action Hero," 1969, p. 56).

One final element to be considered here is that unlike much of the other Cold War rhetoric, the vision of America offered in *The Green Berets* is still available via the late movie on TV or the VCR. Although the Wayne persona has probably lost a measure of its influence, it is also the case that his message of "noble superpatriotism" retains its appeal to many people, some of whom were born after his death (Anderegg, 1991a). In the post–Cold War/September 11, 2001, environment, a major part of the political dialogue advocates American power as "a means of advancing the principles of a liberal civilization and a liberal world order" (Kagan, 2002, p. 11; see also Goldsborough, 2003, p. B13) and proclaims that Americans "can sometimes see themselves in heroic terms. . . . They will defend the townspeople, whether the townspeople want them to or not" (Kagan, 2002, p. 26). Actual or potential military involvement in places such as Afghanistan, Iraq, or the Korean peninsula are being defined as "tests of will," and there is a pronounced criticism of those Americans who threaten a domestic consensus concerning foreign policy (Pipes, 2002). In this contemporary political environment, it would be wise to keep in mind that although such simple messages of right versus wrong can provide comfort in times of confusion, there was another time when that comfort proved mistaken and costly.

NOTES

1. Wayne initially had trouble getting a major company to sign on for the picture. After Columbia and Universal backed out, Wayne finally agreed to "a lot rougher deal than I would normally have made" with Warner Brothers–Seven Arts (as cited in Carpozi, 1979, p. 219; Roberts & Olson, 1995; Windeller, 1967).

2. Several critics at the time of release noted that the film was "essentially argumentative at its base" (Adler, 1968b, p. D10). The movie has been labeled "more of a political object than an entertainment commodity" (Aufderheide, 1990, p. 101) and really only "a long lecture" (Berg, 1986, p. 111). Previous works have noted how popular films concerning Vietnam provided a "means by which civilians can relate to the war" (Edelman, 1979, p. 539; Dionisopoulos, 1990).

3. In a 1971 *Playboy* interview, Wayne said that he agreed with the critics who labeled the movie a propaganda effort: "It was an American film, about American boys who were heroes over there. In that sense it *was* propaganda" (p. 88). For more information on the use of popular media to address cultural sociopolitical concerns, see Nimmo and Combs (1983, 1990).

4. Anderegg (1991b) observed that unlike World War II, for which most of its characteristic descriptions were provided in novels, memoirs, and historical writings, Vietnam has "been given its imaginative life primarily through film. . . . Cinematic representations . . . seem to have supplanted even so-called factual analysis as *the* discourse of the war" (p. 1).

5. Ron Kovic (author of *Born on the Fourth of July*), Richard Nixon, Ronald Reagan, Newt Gingrich, and John Shalikashvili have acknowledged the influence Wayne's screen persona exerted on their political development (Wills, 1997). Indeed, some have said that it was America's "John Wayne politics" that got the United States involved in Vietnam in the first place, whereas others have maintained that we lost because we were not "John Wayne" enough.

6. Wayne goes on at some length about Vietnam and the dangers of communist expansion in a 1971 *Playboy* interview. Interviewer Richard Lewis asked Wayne, "[W]hat gives us the right to decide for the Vietnamese what kind of government they should have?" Wayne answered, "I don't want the U.S. to decide what kind of government they have. But I don't want the Communists to decide, either. And if we didn't help the South Vietnamese government, that's just what they'd do" (p. 86). It is illustrative that his response ignores the fact that the Communists were Vietnamese and instead refers to them solely as being Communists.

7. As he had said in 1967, "I can't believe that people in the U.S. don't realize that we are at war with international communism" (as cited in Roberts & Olson, 1995, p. 537).

8. *The Alamo* was the other movie Wayne produced, and it, too, was a "message film." As *Variety* observed, in 1960, "Wayne the political theorist and Wayne the filmmaker formed a merger . . . [and] Wayne produced, directed, and starred in *The Alamo*" ("John Wayne as the Last Action Hero," 1969, p. 55). He "hoped that the film would become a patriotic symbol, help elect Richard Nixon as president, and make a lot of money" (Roberts & Olson, 1995, p. 546). It failed on all counts.

9. Wayne had even let it be known that he wanted to shoot the movie in Vietnam. Of course, that was impossible because, as he said, "you start shooting blanks over there . . . they might start shooting back" (as cited in "Stars: The Duke," 1967, p. 67). Even the Soviet press felt moved to comment. The newspaper *Sovietskaya Kultura* called Wayne an extreme reactionary and warned that he "might find himself in the path of real bullets if he goes ahead with his plans to shoot a movie about the Green Berets in Vietnam. He is trying to glorify the heroic deeds of these insidious, specially taught soldier-killers. Mr. Wayne's previous films have been shot in the completely safe prairies of Texas or the hills of Colorado where his heroes play out their game firing at dummy targets. He will find real bullets if he goes to Vietnam" (as cited in Carpozi, 1979, p. 221).

10. Government assistance also saved Batjac a great deal of money. Movie producers are expected to reimburse the government for any expenses incurred, unless—as stipulated by Department of Defense Instruction 730.7, dated December 20, 1966—the final product is thought to be a "service furnished . . . the general public in the interest of public understanding of the Armed Forces" (Fulbright, 1970, p. 120). *The Green Berets* was considered to be just such a film, and a "grateful army eventually billed Wayne's production company a mere $18,623.64" (Smith, 1975, p. 128) for what Congressman Rosenthal estimated might have been more than $1 million worth of assistance (Madden, 1969). When the level of government assistance became a public issue, Wayne pointed out that Batjac had paid for the construction of a replica of a Vietnamese village at Fort Benning and was leaving it there to help train Army troops.

11. Government representatives did object to Barrett's first draft because it included a scene from Moore's (1965) novel in which the Special Forces entered North Vietnam to kidnap an official. The offending scene was rewritten by Barrett when he returned from a "research expedition" to Vietnam. There were also objections to the war being referred to as the "North against the South." The official view was as follows: "We do not see this as a civil war, and it is not. South Vietnam is an independent country, seeking to maintain its independence in the face of aggression by a neighboring country. Our goal is to help the South Vietnamese retain their freedom, and to develop in the way they want to, without interference from outside the country" (Department of Defense as cited in Suid, 1977, p. 114).

12. The dialogue from this scene was based on a briefing that the Central Intelligence Agency had given President Johnson in 1965. The purpose of the briefing was to highlight the idea that the war in Vietnam was not a civil war between Vietnamese but was instead a war of expansion by international communism. Ironically, much of the information presented during this briefing was falsified. The CIA had "intentionally misled President Johnson in order to make the case for ground intervention more compelling" (Roberts & Olson, 1995, p. 556; Slotkin, 1992).

13. As Paletz (1999) noted, it has become conventional wisdom that "untrammeled media coverage hampered and handicapped the war effort in Vietnam." Several studies refute this contention, however, and provide findings that indicate that with the exception of the period of the Tet Offensive in early 1968, most daily coverage was "closely tied to official information and dominant assumptions about the war" (p. 279).

14. The opening scene was evidently meant only for domestic audiences, who needed to understand and support American efforts in South Vietnam. According to Adair (1981), it was cut from several prints distributed to the overseas market.

15. Several writers remarked that the characters portrayed in *The Green Berets* seemed to indicate that Wayne's reference point for the film was not life but movie tradition. In Wayne's Special Forces A-Team, "the topkick is still named Muldoon" (Schickel, 1968, p. 8), there is a "lovable scrounger" named Peterson (Jim Hutton), a "dogface called Kowalski," and even "an enemy general, in the tradition of the suave celluloid Nazi, who flaunts fancy quarters, a French staff car, distinguished gray hair, a well-tailored uniform, and a decadent weakness for caviar, wine, and beautiful but helpless women" (Smith, 1975, p. 129; Carpenter, 1990).

16. In the novel, it was an American explosives expert who planted charges under ARVN machine gun positions in case some of the "friendlies" were actually Vietcong. In the movie, this was done by Captain Nihm.

17. Moore had complained earlier that many of the changes from the novel to the screenplay were "imposed on the scriptwriters by the Department of Defense," which was "trying to keep up an unpopular war" (Gold, 1967, p. 22).

18. Several critics noted that in the final shot of the movie, the colonel and Hamchuck walk off together down the beach as the sun sets in the east over the South China Sea.

19. Wayne (as cited in Suid, 1977) credited the critical "overkill" for the film's financial success when it returned its production costs and began turning a profit within 6 months of release (p. 122 Suid, 1981; Weiler, 1969). According to Wayne (as cited in Suid, 1977), most of the negative criticism of *The Green Berets* was from "irrationally liberal" reviewers who criticized his politics and the war instead of the film (p. 88). Indeed, Cook (1968) observed that many people were offended by "the kind of vituperation our foremost mass media have used in denouncing the film" (p. 453).

20. A 1980 survey by the Veterans Administration indicated that Vietnam veterans were favorable to the way they were portrayed in *The Green Berets* (Dionisopoulos, 1990; Freedman, 1985).

Part III

Rhetorics, Cultures, and Ideologies

Twenty years ago, Philip Wander (1983) called for an "ideological turn" in criticism. In defining this shift in criticism, he said,

> An ideological turn in modern criticism reflects the existence of crisis, acknowledges the influence of established interests and the reality of alternative worldviews, and commends rhetorical analyses not only of the actions implied but also of the interests represented. More than "informed talk about matters of importance," criticism carries us to the point of recognizing good reasons and engaging in right action. (p. 18)

Since Wander published his article, critics have debated what it means to do ideological criticism. The debates continue, but critics who practice ideological criticism expand the traditional Aristotelian definition of rhetoric as "an ability, in each [particular] case, to see the available means of persuasion" (Aristotle, 1991, pp. 36-37).

Ideological studies critique Western belief systems that frame constructions of class, ethnicity, gender, race, religion, and sexual identity. Critiques of these belief systems reveal that traditional critical approaches have focused on the rhetoric of privileged white men and, in turn, marginalized the voices of other groups. The ideological critic also serves as an advocate for social change. Wander (1996) extends his discussion of the ideological turn in criticism and elaborates on "rhetorical contextualization." Rhetorical contexualization implies that the critic has the responsibility to make links between theory and practice. In other words, Wander urges scholars to consider whether their criticism will make a difference in the real world. Wander echoes the views of many ideological critics who believe that their work leads them to serve as advocates for social change: "In a better world such questioning becomes more than an academic practice or humane activity. It becomes a civic responsibility" (p. 421).

The essays in Part III ask you to consider the role that rhetoric can play in fostering social change. These essays propose that you consider the implications of ideological criticism for studying issues associated with race, class, and gender. Consider the following questions as you read these essays: What is the relationship between rhetoric and ideology? What differences do these relationships make in rhetorical construction and interpretation? How might those particular readings differ from traditional interpretations and evaluations?

Dana Cloud's essay, "Fighting Words: Labor and the Limits of Symbolic Intervention at Staley, 1993-1996," enacts her vision of the ideological turn in criticism. In the essay, Cloud practices the type of criticism, a "project of critique," that she called for in a 1994 article. She cautioned that a project of critique, from an ideological perspective, requires that critics truly struggle with the meaning of the phrase "materiality of discourse" (p. 159). Thus, the intersection of the rhetorical and the material comes into clearer focus as a result of Cloud's essay. The critic must recognize that rhetoric alone does not oppress or liberate people. Rather, in our critical practices, we must "retain notions of the real; of the material; and of the structured, stable, and dominating" (p. 159).

"Fighting Words" speaks to the limits of rhetoric or symbolic agency in bringing about social change. Cloud uses a contemporary labor conflict as a case study to argue that the exploited, oppressed, and disenfranchised need more than symbolic agency to win confrontations with the materially powerful. She urges communication scholars to recognize that rhetorical and material resources must function together to bring about social change. As students of communication, you may be accustomed to thinking about rhetoric's power to transform the world. You may have read many examples of criticism that focus on the influence of a great speaker (e.g., Barbara Jordan, Martin Luther King, Jr., John F. Kennedy, and Elizabeth Cady Stanton). Cloud's study serves as a reminder that "great speaker" studies exaggerate rhetoric's influence. The laborers in Cloud's study needed more than rhetoric to change the conditions at their workplace.

Two other essays in this section also feature the limitations of rhetoric in bringing about social change. Kathryn Cañas and Mark Lawrence McPhail address rhetoric's potential to rectify inequities in U.S. culture. In "Demonizing Democracy: The Strange Career of Lani Guinier," a case study of responses to Lani Guinier, President William Jefferson Clinton's nominee to serve as assistant attorney general for civil rights, Cañas and McPhail argue that racism is a pathology that cannot be remedied through education and appeals to logic. Cañas and McPhail revisit an earlier work by McPhail (1994b), as well as the work of Condit and Lucaites (1993), and ask if an "actively nonargumentative discourse," a "rhetoric of coherence," or "a rhetoric of interbraiding" can challenge racist ideologies. Guinier's critics misrepresented her views and "demonized" her. Cañas and McPhail speculate that Guinier's nonargumentative rhetoric was threatening because it was revolutionary in challenging not only the symptoms of racism but also its deep structures. The authors conclude by suggesting that racial divisions will be healed only when white people make a commitment to self-reflection and recognize that racism is a white problem.

The concerns of Cloud and Cañas and McPhail are reiterated in "Racial Apologies." Dexter B. Gordon and Carrie Crenshaw ask whether rhetoric can remedy racism. Specifically, they explore whether racial apologies break and/or perpetuate our rhetorical silence about whiteness and white privilege in the United States. Crenshaw and Gordon compare and contrast the racial apology with the genre of apology as defined by rhetorical scholars, such as Ware and Linkugel (1973). They ask whether talk about race, specifically the racial apology, contributes to antiracist attitudes and actions.

Patricia A. Sullivan and Steven R. Goldzwig examine white privilege through an analysis of Frank McCourt's *Angela's Ashes* and *'Tis: A Memoir*. Autobiographical texts offer fruitful sites for studying issues associated with self-awareness and deserve more attention from rhetorical scholars. The authors argue that autobiographical discourse functions rhetorically to expose the constructions of race and class in the United States. As one critic noted in a review of *'Tis*, McCourt "sees through the most deep-seated American myths" (Schenk, 2000, p. 605). In turn, McCourt's texts can persuade readers to see through the same myths.

The essays represented in Part III are concerned with commenting on and effecting social injustice. They intentionally direct their analysis and evaluation toward intervention that can address inequities, and they suggest avenues for redress where issues of class, race, or gender seem to have been responsible for an uneven distribution of power and privilege.

9

Fighting Words

Labor and the Limits of Symbolic Intervention at Staley, 1993-1996

Dana L. Cloud

During the spring of 1993, workers at Staley Manufacturing in Decatur, Illinois, were embattled. They had been storing up grievances regarding wages and benefits as well as the company's plan to outsource—that is, to hire low-wage, nonunion workers at other plants to perform some of the corn sweetener plant's work. In addition, Staley required its employees to work mandatory, rotating 12-hour shifts. None of these features of workers' daily lives were open to negotiation.

In response to these hardships, the members of United Paperworkers International Union (UPIU) local 7837 pursued an "in-plant campaign" consisting of work slowdowns, "work-to-rule,"[1] and other efforts to hamper productivity. In June 1993, the company locked the workers out and began to run the plant using a staff of managers and others willing to cross the picket line. For more than 2 years, the union workers picketed, protested, and boycotted Staley in an effort to win back their jobs and a fair contract. They lost both.

To many progressives active in the labor movement, the Staley struggle, along with two concurrent labor disputes in the Decatur area at Bridgestone-Firestone and Caterpillar, marked a turning point for American labor. In the United States, union power has declined since

1981, when Ronald Reagan fired striking air traffic controllers, thus posing the threat of permanent replacement against any workers who would strike. The decline of union power has corresponded to measurable erosion of workers' standard of living in the United States even as corporate profits and executive pay have soared. The willingness of Decatur workers to fight back signaled hope that labor, long in the doldrums, might take action to reverse the past two decades' rollback of wages and benefits—in other words, to challenge the contemporary perception that workers are increasingly "disposable."[2] In the context of intensifying corporate downsizing and union busting, along with the growing income gap in the United States between workers and their bosses, the concessionary contract accepted by Staley workers in January 1996 after more than 2 years of struggle was a significant defeat; for the workers, it was a tragedy.[3] The contract allowed the company unlimited subcontracting, retained the mandatory 12-hour shifts, called for mandatory overtime, and provided no amnesty for fired union workers. Union jobs were cut by two thirds (Brecher, 1997, p. 357).

As a socialist active in the labor movement, I stood in solidarity with the Staley workers on a number of occasions and came to know several of the workers whose fighting words are the subject of this essay. My goal in analyzing and criticizing the consolatory rhetoric (Ochs, 1993) of the embattled workers is to honor their struggle by attempting to understand why it failed.

To that end, this chapter performs a narrative analysis of a newsletter published over 2 years by locked-out Staley workers. The analysis points to the significance of battle metaphors and their shifting deployment over time in this newsletter, called *News From the War Zone*. Interestingly, although the Staley workers rhetorically declared central Illinois a "war zone," they were constrained in their ability to match their fighting words with a material presence—pickets and plant occupations—that might have prevented the company from replacing the workers and sustaining production long enough to defeat the union. Early in the lockout, the workers rhetorically constructed themselves as warriors fighting a heroic battle. Later in the struggle, however, as defeat approached, the role descriptions in the newsletter emphasized the workers' victim, refugee, and, finally, martyr status. The consequences of speaking loudly but carrying a small stick in this instance call our attention to the limits of symbolic agency in the labor movement and, thus, to questions about the overemphasis on discursive power in organizational communication and social movement research in our field.

THE SYMBOLIC AND THE MATERIAL: COMMUNITY AND CONFRONTATION

This essay advances a materialist approach to social movements, particularly the labor movement, and to communication phenomena in general. Communication studies have long (and somewhat understandably) foregrounded the role of symbolic agency in building community and making social change, generally underemphasizing material conditions and the roles of economic and physical force constraining human actors. An exclusively symbol-oriented practice in communication studies of labor, however, risks ignoring the interplay of economic and rhetorical clout and constraint in worker confrontations with employers. Furthermore, an overemphasis on discourse risks assuming that workers and their employers are equally powerful in giving voice to their interests and equally included in decision making about work life, when in reality there are political, legal, and economic barriers to full equality in the workplace. In such a context, managerial strategies stressing employee participation and fellow-feeling often substitute an illusion of "voice" and "participation" for real workers' control over wages, benefits, work hours, profits, and work conditions or offer new participation programs even as the company is enacting layoffs, speedups, and "management by stress" (Parker & Slaughter, 1994).

Historical materialism (as opposed to other versions of materialism advanced in communication studies; see Greene, 1998) as a theoretical approach is insistent on the need for extradiscursive standards for critical judgment. It is optimistic about collective human agency but also critical and cognizant of constraints posed for such agency in a society marked by class and other polarized social relations (Cloud, 1994, 2001). At the same time, however, ideas and discourses can have a reciprocal influence on the making and distribution of resources (Gramsci, 1936/1971). As rhetorical scholar James Aune (1994) argues, we need to pay attention to rhetorics of struggle as well as to ideologies that reinforce structures of domination (p. 5).

Thus, a materialist approach does not suggest that the processes of meaning making and coming to voice among exploited and oppressed groups are insignificant, or that rhetoric is irrelevant to labor's strategy—only that we should include the economic dimension of analysis as one among several influential factors (Mann, 1993) in our studies of workplace discourses, especially because workplace conflicts often revolve around material concerns such as wages, work hours, benefits, and job stability. In this vein, critical organizational communication scholars have noted that employers often make symbolic offerings in the form of worker participation and involvement programs as a way of staving off future confrontation (Cheney, 1995; Cheney et al., 1998; Parker & Slaughter, 1994).

Social movement scholarship is another important starting point for this project. In 1972, Herb Simons called attention to the establishment bias inherent in privileging symbolic action over more coercive modes of "persuasion," such as sit-ins and strikes (or, from the employers' perspective, layoffs and benefit cuts). Simons charges rhetorical scholars of social movements with an establishment bias that results from assuming that conflicts are reducible to differences of opinion or ideas, and in which any notion of competing interests is displaced by assumption that only epiphenomena (beliefs or attitudes) are in dispute (p. 230). Furthermore, Simons argues that upholding a dichotomy between persuasion and coercion (assumed by most communication scholars to be morally and strategically inferior as a strategy) fails to recognize the possibility and necessity in some instances of coercive persuasion:

> Coercive persuasion applies to any situation in which at least one party sees himself in genuine conflict with another, has some coercive power over the other, and finds it expedient to establish, persuasively, any or all of the following: (1) his relative capacity to use coercive force, (2) his relative willingness to use coercive force, (3) the relative legitimacy of his coercive force, (4) the relative desirability of his objectives. (p. 232)[4]

Clearly, symbol use is instrumental in representing one's capacity, willingness, and legitimacy in using coercive force. It is the material potentiality of coercive force, however, that backs up such representations and makes them persuasive.[5]

Simons, Mechling, and Schrier (1984) write,

> We urge that rhetoricians abandon the myth of rhetorical determinism, the comforting but much too simplistic notion that a good rhetoric will win out. Just once we would like to see a study reported in which a movement or movement-related event is judged a great success and a leading figure in the movement is judged a rhetorical failure (or the reverse). (p. 830)

The Staley case is just such a reverse case, in which rhetorical savvy could not produce movement success and the deployment of other, materially coercive (although not necessarily violent)[6] action might have been more effective.[7]

As in the childhood game "rock, paper, scissors," those with scissors can shred paper combatants, and only a rock can stand up to the scissors. With regard to the current argument, the question is not whether Staley workers should have deployed rhetoric at all (of course they should have, and they did) but whether they settled for symbols too soon or too easily, when instrumental action in direct confrontation with the company was a real and necessary option.

TALK AND ACTION IN THE WAR ZONE

Staley Manufacturing, a subsidiary of multinational corporation Tate and Lyle, Incorporated, was well prepared economically to outwait and outpublicize the locked-out workers, who were widely discredited in the Decatur press.[8] The company also had the backing of the local police and courts, which imposed jail time and fines on activists. Within a context of heavily endowed corporate ruthlessness and a set of overwhelming material constraints, union bureaucrats and consultants, whose interests include not only winning the struggle but also maintaining their own power and credibility, are partially responsible for leading the workers to material defeat by arming the workers with only words, which could neither feed the activists nor prevent production from continuing at the Staley plant.[9] In such a context, fighting words were not enough.

Ordinary people, as opposed to their bosses or their political and labor leaders, leave less of a trace than those with access to institutional power and resources enabling the printing, videotaping, recording, distribution, and archiving of movement materials. The *News From the War Zone* publication, although thin in terms of numbers of published issues and pages, is a significant source of evidence for research on the labor movement. Indeed, it is the only bottom-up record of this event.[10] I turn now to an analysis of the newsletter published by unionized workers locked out at Staley, *News From the War Zone*, which was published regularly by the workers (significantly, not by union officials) from January 1994 until January 1996. The analysis proceeds more or less chronologically, documenting workers' shifting rhetorical personae—as strong warriors, as moral shamers, and, finally, as victims and martyrs. Rather than arguing that shifts in self-narration caused their defeat, however, the analysis suggests that material forces beyond the text and beyond their control had a determining influence on their self-narration.

Declarations of War: 1994

Militant members of UPIU 7837 started to publish *News From the War Zone* in January 1994, the sixth month of the Staley lockout.[11] Their goal was to reach out to other unions and workers to ask them to honor picket lines and to support the Staley workers' strike fund. At this early, promulgation stage of their movement, the workers narrated themselves as valiant heroes struggling alongside Caterpillar and Bridgestone-Firestone workers to turn the tide of the labor movement. In issue 1.2, for example, the front page of *News From the War Zone* features a photograph of the Staley plant's west gate blocked by a throng of workers. The headline reads, "Protesters Block Gates: The Battle of Decatur Escalates" (1.2; Hawking, 1994).[12]

In these early issues, the imagery of battle and war corresponded to a sense of autonomy and power on the part of the workers. For example, the writers labeled the Staley struggle "the battle of Decatur" (1.2), emphasizing the "force and determination" of the workers (Hawking, 1994). The narrative constructed the workers as warriors waging battle against the employers. The newsletter's cover and illustrations from this period reflect this warrior mentality, with images of fists raised in protest and of bombs raining down on the Staley plant. In February 1994, the workers built a large rally for their cause, drawing activists and workers from throughout the Midwest. Eric Jarosinski (1994), writing in the *Progressive* magazine, noted that "the fiery speeches, the chants of 'no contract, no peace,' and the enthusiasm of the crowd show a union ready and willing to do battle" (p. 30). Again, in this passage, it is the union doing battle, with the workers assuming the persona of active subject. Throughout 1994, issues of the *War Zone* continued to describe the struggle as a confident battle waged by workers. In April, the writers called for a "spring offensive . . . putting ourselves on the line" (1.2; Hawking, 1994). The workers sent a flyer to members and supporters of the local that read, "Call in the Troops: It's War!" (1.3; "Call in the Troops," 1994). At this point in the lockout, there is a sense in the materials that there are troops to be rallied and strengths to be tapped.

June 1994: The Retreat to Shaming

The sense of strength was short-lived, however. The use of police violence against union demonstrators, including the use of pepper spray mace during a June 1994 demonstration of 5,000 Staley supporters, put the workers on the defensive, initiating a shift to survivor and victim talk rather than warrior talk on the part of Staley workers. With issue 1.4 (August 1994), there is a clear shift in the newsletter away from the language of spring offensives and calling in the troops. Instead, under the headline "Police Violence Mars Staley Lockout Anniversary March," the text calls on Staley to "do what is moral and what is right," concluding that "those of us under attack here in Decatur represent a microcosm of the corporate aggression going on all over the country" (Sacco, 1994, pp. 1-2). Suddenly, in both reality and in self-narration, the workers were "under attack." Under such conditions, the workers began to take recourse in moral persuasion, begging Staley to "do the right thing." A photo essay regarding the June 25 instance of police violence focuses on how the workers survived the attack, with menacing images of police in riot gear holding billy clubs (1.4; Lane, 1994, p. 3). The text emphasizes people in pain, "blinded, lungs and skin on fire." Although the police crackdown on demonstrators was certainly worthy of coverage, this issue of *War Zone* reflects the effects of police in the construction of a revised, less warrior-like persona for the workers.

Although labor history shows that corporate executives will routinely turn to coercive force to break a strike or picket (Brecher, 1997), there is no necessary connection between corporate violence and workers' defeat. The key for workers at this point in a conflict is to match violence not with violence but with the very real power that workers hold to put corporate profits in jeopardy. In the Staley case, however, the workers began to talk about themselves as victims of and refugees from a war over which they had no control: "Why is it that we have to face brutal attacks at home, over our jobs, at the hands of police in our own country and communities?" (1.4; Lane, 1994, p. 3). The emphasis is on the brutality of corporate and police power and on the workers as victims of that power. The essay continues,

> The police have become the tools of corporate greed. We filled the streets and took peaceful action to protest the dog-eat-dog greed which grips our community. Without provocation, we were viciously gassed, many of us while sitting down with our backs to

> the cops. We were nonviolent. We stayed that way despite their brutal actions. . . . All of us in the front rows of that demonstration, including several children with thousands pressing in behind us, felt the sting and pain of the pepper gas they saturated us with. One worker was crawling blindly and the police turned him over on his back and sprayed him directly in the face as he lay still. People were in pain, blinded, lungs and skin on fire, but we refused to move. We stayed in place, nonviolent, but determined. (p. 3)

This text is accompanied by photos of police in riot gear using pepper mace against demonstrators, a distinct contrast from all previous covers featuring images of strong workers as warriors. The photoessay is double edged, however, because it also emphasizes the fact that the workers held their ground in the face of the police attack; the spread includes a photograph of workers standing up to the police. Therefore, this text represents a turning point within its own pages; from standing their ground as strong warriors, the workers are dramatically represented in this article as childlike, innocent, and completely vulnerable, as demonstrated by the image of the blinded man crawling, in vain, to escape the pepper spray. In addition, the descriptions of the police action make a rhetorical turn toward shaming and moralizing. The implication of the vivid description of righteous workers in pain lends the workers the moral, if not the material, high ground; even if they could not take the plant back, they could at least adopt the moral stance of "nonviolent," "peaceful," and "determined" martyrs.

By the fall and winter of 1994, the language of moral outrage and shaming had almost completely replaced confidence in the struggle. In the absence of workers' ability to stop Staley and regain their jobs, the newsletters began to foreground the moral condemnation of Staley and the police. In December, the workers put out a satirical Christmas tape as a fund-raiser: "Deck the Cops in Riot Gear" (1.5; McCall & Stauffer, 1994). Although workers' anger and political awareness of the role of the police in the corporate context are evident, satire seems the product of desperation, a small symbolic swipe at the police as a consolation for having been dispersed by them during the summer rally. This same issue of the *War Zone* declared, "Solidarity! This is the battle cry for the locked-out Staley workers, and when they yell it, they mean it" (1.5; "Messengers of Struggle," 1994). What could solidarity mean, however, in the absence of an actual strike or plant blockade? In this case, solidarity was redefined to emphasize emotional support for the boycotts of Staley and their customers, alongside shared moral and symbolic condemnation of Staley and its backers rather than shared willingness to block plant gates and honor picket lines.

Without direct action to back them up, the declarations of war and cries of solidarity on the part of Staley workers were empty threats. Although the Staley workers did staff symbolic pickets and held two large rallies at the plant in 1994, they never attempted, and may not have been able in any case, to stop replacement workers from entering the plant. The significance of this shift is that the recourse to rhetoric had a consolatory and conservative effect on the movement, encouraging workers to take the role of moralizing outsiders—gadflies on the corporate flank—rather than directly transformative agents.

The forces arrayed against them included not only Staley but also the Decatur city council, which ruled during the winter of 1994 and 1995 against allowing picketing workers to build temporary shelters from the bitter midwestern cold. Adding insult to injury, the AFL-CIO executive council refused a hearing to Staley workers during their meeting in February 1995 and refused to create a national wage-replacement fund to enable the workers to continue their protests. These setbacks generated an intensification of martyr language, providing evidence of the role of coercive power in shaping the conditions for public discourse. Therefore, I am not arguing that the workers' discursive shift was in itself responsible for the defeat at Staley. Clearly, the retreat enacted in the pages of the newsletter was the product of police violence and other material conditions beyond the workers' control. Union leaders and Ray Rogers, whose company, Corporate Campaign, Incorporated was a paid consultant to the union, however, instructed the workers at this point not to engage further in any materially obstructive actions, such as blocking the plant gate. Such a decision not to confront the company may have been warranted given the probability of additional police violence. At this point in the struggle, however, thousands of workers and their supporters were still mobilized and might have effectively challenged the police. Many among the rank-and-file wanted to continue to try more direct confrontations.

Instead, local union officials and Ray Rogers encouraged workers to settle for the symbolic act of sitting in the street. Such a demonstration can indeed send a powerful message. By shifting the venue away from the plant, however, they embraced the logic of martyrdom, which is characteristic of civil disobedience in general rather than struggle. Production resumed, removing any bargaining power the workers might have had in the form of a threat to ongoing profits. Thus, the Staley workers were in the position of having declared a war in which they were overwhelmingly outgunned, and declarations were no longer enough to sustain the fight. The corporate campaign may have prematurely ushered the movement into its final stages, practically skipping the more confrontational stages (e.g., the use of nonviolent direct action and the division of a movement into militant and pacifist factions) exhibited by most movements when they are met with resistance.

Telling the Story in 1995: Rhetorics of Victimage

Not coincidentally, as the workers became increasingly mired in defeat, they resorted increasingly to shaming strategies in which they appealed to public moral outrage by positioning themselves as innocent victims of corporate power. This strategy was the centerpiece of Ray Rogers's corporate campaign, which emphasizes shaming corporations into compliance with workers' demands. The idea is to chart and target for public vilification a company's network of financial backers, subsidiaries, insurers, customers, and dependent corporate enterprises. During 1995, the corporate campaign received front billing in the *War Zone*, displacing news about pickets and rallies, for which there was continuing support, to the back pages of the newsletter. Calls for boycotts and letters to the CEOs of Pizza Hut, PepsiCo, State Farm, KFC, and a number of smaller Staley customers and backers dominated these later issues, which could therefore be viewed as discouraging direct action in favor of symbolic attacks on Staley.[13]

In July 1995, the Staley workers rejected a contract offered by Staley, but rather than exhorting workers to back up this rejection with pickets, marches, and demonstrations as they did during 1993 and 1994, the workers called instead for a "PepsiPush weekend": "In the wake of the rejection, Local 7837 is escalating its campaign against Staley's customers" (2.4; "Union Rejects," 1995). Significantly, the *War Zone* no longer promoted a concrete battle of workers against Staley but reconstituted the movement's goal as the creation of indirect symbolic pressure against an abstract corporate network. Whereas 1994 issues proclaimed "The Battle of Decatur Escalates" and featured photographs of workers crowding plant gates in February (1.2, p. 1), the rhetoric of the 1995 issues was fraught with contradictions manifest between the goal of winning concrete gains for the workers and the strategy of abstract moralizing. For example, one article pled with readers (2.4; Watts & Lamb, 1995),

> We are writing to urge your continued support for this frontline battle against corporate greed. It is crucial that we immediately escalate our campaign against Pepsi. . . . We hold Pepsi accountable for its shameful role in this attack on American workers. We are persuaded that with your help, we will convince Pepsi to do the right thing by dumping Staley. When we win this fight, we will strike a blow for workers everywhere. (p. 4)

The irony of this passage is that in the absence of more direct action, the corporate campaign did not represent a "frontline battle"; rather, it consisted of behind-the-scenes maneuvering to create indirect pressure on Staley via Pepsi. Note that the writer is no longer even holding Staley accountable for the "attack on American workers." Rather than striking "a blow for workers," the Staley workers' struggle was on the downslide. In this case, an emphasis on shaming Pepsi into doing "the right thing" contradicted the militant battle language of escalated campaigns and successful fightback. In this light, it is notable that the demonstration held on the second anniversary of the lockout was labeled a "commemoration" rather than a rally or protest; a commemoration is a ceremonial rather than instrumental rhetorical occasion, better suited to mourning than organizing. Thus, the rhetoric of shaming serves a consolatory function for workers who held out little hope for real compensation.

By July 1995, workers consistently referred to themselves as Staley's lockout victims, and there is hardly any battle language at all in *News From the War Zone* after this time. For example, the front page of the August/September 1995 issue (2.5) shows workers at the west gate of the plant. In contrast to the 1994 photo, in which workers are apparently attempting to keep the gate closed and thus hamper Staley's ability to function, in the 1995 photo, four workers are shown chained to the gate. Their T-shirts and signs read "12-hour shifts kill workers," "Staley enslaves Decatur community," and "Staley destroys Decatur families." The emotionally intense references to enslavement, killing, and destruction paint the workers as completely victimized. Thus, although the image is one of workers engaged in action, it simultaneously reinforces their victim status. Rather than the presence at the gate hampering Staley, it is the workers whose movement is constrained.

As Kenneth Burke (1969b) noted, social conflicts produce rhetorics of victimage in which people ritually enact victim status as a means toward redemption and transcendence (p. 255). Burke argued that imagery of symbolic killings or violence dramatically depict a person's or thing's essence with powerful rhetorical effect (pp. 18, 260-261); consubstantiality, or rhetorical identification, "is established by common involvement in a killing" (p. 265). Ironically, however, the symbolic killing enacted in the Staley narratives is the killing, in stories and images, of self as transformative agent.[14] One gets the impression that this very dramatic act of civil disobedience was staged for cameras to deliver the moral message indicting Staley. The appeal is to reader sympathy for workers who display their victim status as a form of ironic protest. Indeed, the article's headline is "Chained Protesters *Symbolize* [italics added] Lost Freedom for Those Forced on 12-Hour Rotating Shift." It is clear at this point that the workers are substituting symbols and self-sacrifice for confrontation.

In addition to the corporate campaign, the Staley workers had initiated another new symbolic strategy late in 1994 emphasizing telling the story of the struggle rather than winning it. Having foreshortened the stage of direct confrontation during the summer of 1994, the workers began to send out teams of "road warriors" to tell groups of union supporters about "corporate greed and inhumanity in the 1990s. . . . We continue to tell and retell the story of our struggle here in Decatur" (2.2; "Road Warriors," 1995a, p. 7). The road warriors displayed exceptional dedication to the struggle and succeeded in building nationwide moral support for the workers. Their emphasis on storytelling as not only the means but also the end goal of their efforts, however, was a concession to material defeat and was explicitly justified as a substitute for traditional forms of labor protest in one article (2.4; "Road Warriors," 1995b):

> Pickets now are mere symbols of defense tactics that once were effective in labor disputes, especially during the 1930s and the 1940s. But during the 1990s and in the future we must work harder to draw attention to our plight . . . and form worldwide support networks to help stave off the brutalities of corporate warfare on workers. . . . We must go out and spread the word—tell the TRUE story. (p. 8)

Later, I take up the writer's claim that traditional tactics such as pickets are no longer effective tools of the labor movement. Here, I call attention to the ways in which this passage encourages readers, mainly participants in the struggle, to view their fightback as a purely symbolic or discursive one. Even so, there are a few lingering references to confrontation in the previous passage. At least the writer indicates an ongoing commitment to struggle against "the brutalities of corporate warfare."

Part of the purpose of the road warriors was to raise funds for the workers and to build nationwide networks of solidarity. In these ways, the "messengers of struggle" were not resorting exclusively to symbolism.

Even so, the previous passage foregrounds and emphasizes the symbolic rather than the material aims of this strategy. The writer suggests that the only thing to do now is to "draw attention to our plight," to "spread the word," and to "tell the true story." Hindsight allows us to see that the workers were already on the heels of defeat. Ironically, the writer called pickets "mere symbols" while exhorting militants to take up a strategy that really was "merely" symbolic.

The War Zone as Concentration Camp: 1996

In the end, the workers were able to tell the story only of their own martyrdom. The narratives emphasize the suffering and sacrifice of locked-out workers: "Even after being locked out of our jobs for more than 2 years, and subjected to unspeakable emotional and physical pain and suffering, our members are standing strong" (2.5; "S.O.S.," 1995, p. 3). Again, this statement contains a tragic irony. Rather than "standing strong," union militant Dan Lane was hunger striking as this issue went to press in a desperate attempt to shame Staley into talking with the locked-out workers. In January 1996, some of the exhausted union activists (under pressure from the international union and local leaders) voted to accept a contract no different from the one they had vowed to fight 3 years earlier.

Staley retained the prerogatives of outsourcing and enforcing rotating 12-hour shifts. The agreement cut the number of union workers in the plant from 760 to 250, eroding the union's power base, and 5,600 replacement workers who crossed the Staley picket lines remained on the job. One activist wrote (3.1; "Corporate Greed," 1996),

> For the embattled workers the price of resistance has been very high. Homes and livelihoods have been destroyed and previously held values forever altered. Decatur families, like so many everywhere, have been the victims of America's dirty big secret, that a one-sided class war is being waged by the rich and powerful against the rest of us. Important battles have been lost. (p. 1)

Here, the passive voice (e.g., "price has been high," "lives have been destroyed," "workers have been the victims," "war is being waged," and "battles have been lost") indicates a stance of passive resignation. The writing evokes an image of helpless workers as refugees from this war, without control, home, or livelihood. Likewise, this last issue of the *War Zone* referred to Decatur not as the site of workers' solidarity and struggle but as a "concentration camp," in stark contrast to the early issues' emphasis on workers' power. The images featured in the January 1996 overview of the struggle are univocally those of victimage: Three arrested workers hold signs that read "Punish Corporate Criminals, Not Their VICTIMS!" Small children hold a union sign that reads, "Our Children Are Victims Too." The repeated language of victimage is striking here. Furthermore, the photograph of the June 1994 police attack on workers with pepper mace is reprinted in this last issue; the moment when the workers were first victimized stands in for public memory of the lockout. Under the heading "A Struggle We Should Not Forget," two cartoon workers cower under a cartoon image of a gloved black hand holding a mace sprayer in the shape of a Pepsi can (3.1, p. 5). The sinister, overpowering glove and the exhortation to "not forget" reinforce the concentration camp metaphor and the analogy of these workers to history's ultimate victims. All these images construct the Staley workers as victims of corporate greed rather than as the warriors they started out to become.

One worker wrote of the defeat, "We can only hope that the painful lessons of the war on the workers here not be lost" ("Corporate Greed," 1996, p. 1). What are those lessons? What strategies might the Staley workers have deployed to win this struggle? For Local 7837, one lesson was the need for workers organization independent of UPIU leadership, which had supported the concessionary contract and refused material aid to the rebellious local (Weissman, 1996). Entrenched union leaders are sometimes more interested in preserving their own power behind the scenes with management than they are in militant action. The last issue of *War Zone* quotes union leaders as encouraging a "statesmanlike surrender." UPIU president Wayne Glenn overruled local leadership to force a vote on the final, concessionary contract; as a result, a number of workers questioned the corporate campaign strategy and condemned the union leadership's betrayal of the workers in the end ("Who Was the Enemy," 1996). Beyond noting the isolation of the local, it is difficult to assess the causal relationships in this defeat: Did the overreliance on discourse and the stalling out in the promulgation phase of the movement cause the defeat, or did early indicators of defeat (e.g., the police attack on demonstrators in June 1994) of necessity call a halt to the workers' mobilization, generating the consolatory strategies of a movement's abrupt but natural end? Given that there were two large and successful confrontational workers' rallies before the discursive and strategic shifts documented previously, it is likely that a combination of forces—awareness of the company's material power to control the outcome of the dispute and a premature retreat on the part of the union—came into play. In any case, the workers "spoke loudly but carried a small stick"; fighting words were necessary to building solidarity but insufficient to win the day.

The Staley workers had very little else but words with which to fight. Still, not only is the turn to the symbolic symptomatic of defeat but also it can persuade participants to end a struggle prematurely while the symbolic illusion of struggle goes on in a flurry of media stunts and press releases.[15] As the *Nation* noted in April 1996, a corporate campaign can have the effect of demobilizing the struggle, substituting moralizing rhetoric for direct action (Press, 1996).[16] As one union militant stated the issue after the defeat ("Paperworkers for Reform," 1996),

> We need to develop a strategy to put us on the offensive. . . . Utilizing tactics like corporate campaigns, in-plant strategies, can be part of this. But ultimately, the true test of strength is whether or not you are hurting a boss and that occurs when you hit their production. Isolated strikes in this day and age have proven to be ineffective methods, leading to defeat and busted unions. Multiple plant action, including strikes and sitdown strikes, has to be the order of the day. (p. 2)[17]

The discursive shifts in the Staley workers' narrative of their struggle were meaningful not as the sole cause of their defeat but as symptomatic of the effects of coercive power. The impact of coercive power on the outcomes of labor movement struggles demonstrates the necessity of materialist analysis to the study of corporate organizations and the labor movement.

MORE THAN A VOICE: IMPLICATIONS FOR COMMUNICATION SCHOLARSHIP

In 1968, Knapp and McCroskey noted that very little research had been devoted to labor unions, stating, "Clearly the writing and research in organizational communication has been largely management-oriented"

(p. 161). Even after the passage of three decades, this description of our field remains accurate. The rhetoric that is key to the labor movement, however, does not take the form of corporate campaigns or management team initiatives. Nor does it posit the crafting of shared identity as an end in itself. From studies of the speeches, pamphlets, newspapers, and conversations of workers on the ground floor of struggle, scholars can note the uses of rhetoric building worker confidence, identification, and solidarity as stages on the way to demonstrations of economic power. One Staley worker, Lorell Patterson (1995), made clear the continuing relevance of class and the material nature of worker demands:

> We've got to let them know we're not going to take this anymore. We want education. We want livable wages. We want decent housing. And we want health care for the rest of our lives, not the life of a contract. It's very simple—it shouldn't be hard to understand. Every human being has a right to those basic essentials. The only way I can see that we're going to get that is to start organizing and educating. We've got to start standing up and telling them no. I have a right to be treated as a human being. It's time to start believing that we have the power. (p. 6)

In this brief statement, Patterson (1995) sums up the relevance of the concepts of class interests and class power. The demands of workers for health care, wages, and education are basic and concrete, rooted in their collective interests as a class whose access to such basics has been threatened by downsizing, benefits reduction, outsourcing, and downward harmonization of wages as nonunion workplaces take over work once performed by union laborers. The notion that "we have the power" implies a sense of collective strength and solidarity necessary to win a better life.

The "new" strategies of worker empowerment—those heralded by communication scholars and corporate campaigners as giving workers a token voice—have encouraged workers to accept small opportunities for symbolic self-representation as a substitute for material compensation and security. As one Staley worker stated, "We need *more than a voice*! [italics added] We need a fist clenched in solidarity and, like our French union sisters and brothers, strategically ready to come down on those out to destroy us!" (3.1; "Corporate Greed," 1996, p. 1). These words, written after the Staley defeat, recognize the limits of discourse for labor. By implication, the image of a fist clenched in solidarity refers not to symbolic solidarity but to actual willingness to bring production to a halt to win "more than a voice."

This study of the Staley workers' increasing reliance on symbolic strategies during a struggle over extradiscursive interests shows that increasing recourse to communicative strategies may be partly responsible for rendering workers more "disposable." Paying attention to labor disputes from the perspective of workers and learning the history of the labor movement can educate communication scholars about the stakes of struggle and about the strategies that can win "more than a voice"—workplace democracy and economic justice, for real.

NOTES

1. Work-to-rule refers to a strategy in which workers protest by working exactly to job specifications and no more. According to Brecher (1997, p. 355), workers estimated that the work-to-rule cut production by one third to one half, directly provoking the lockout.

2. On the subject of "disposability," I refer readers to an issue of *Communication Research* (Conrad & Poole, 1997), which is dedicated to the roles of communication in reinforcing or challenging contemporary trends, such as downsizing and outsourcing.

3. For background, summary, and assessment of the Staley struggle, see Cooper (1996), Jarosinski (1994), "Labor Takes Its Lumps" (1996), Rachleff (1993), Uchitelle (1993), and Weissman (1996).

4. Simons adapted the concept of coercive persuasion from Schein (1961), who studied the brainwashing of American prisoners of war by Chinese communists in the 1950s.

5. The 1997 victorious UPS strike is a case in point. On July 8, 1997, Teamsters held a strike authorization vote. A flyer handed to me at my local hub's voting table read, "Ready to Strike if We Have To." Although solidifying workers' commitment to the potential strike was one rhetorical objective of this flyer, no doubt its message also put managers and owners of the company on notice that there was material power behind the fighting words of the leaflet.

6. "Coercion" and "violence" cannot be conflated because some coercive acts threaten power and profit without harming human beings. A strike is an example of a nonviolent but coercive action. Although the labor movement has a bloody history, too often accounts of that history elide the fact that it has been most often employers who initiate violence in response to nonviolent protest, sending in police, private thugs, or the National Guard to break picket lines. Notorious instances of corporate violence occurred in the Ludlow coal massacre in 1914 and in the textile uprising of 1934, in which seven striking mill workers were shot in Honea Path, South Carolina. According to Brecher (1997), "In the 29 months from January 1968 through May 1970, the National Guard was used on 324 occasions to suppress civil disorders—including many 'labor disturbances'" (p. 269). Brecher also notes, "When strikes seriously disrupt production for a significant period of time, they generally call forth state intervention" (p. 280).

7. Each stage of a social movement requires a different balance of material and rhetorical force (Bowers, Ochs, & Jensen, 1993). The stages of movement genesis and mobilization,

petition, promulgation, and solidification depend predominantly on rhetorical identification to win supporters to the cause and solidify their commitment. In the direct action (nonviolent or violent) involved in confrontations with establishment power, however, the balance of discourse and coercion shifts, requiring large numbers of participants along with other material resources, such as money to support agitators, media access for propaganda, and control over armed forces and weapons in case of establishment backlash (which has been historically commonplace in response to progressive movements). The denouement of a period of agitation once again calls forth symbolic strategies as participants either rejoice in victory or lick their wounds; either way, epideictic rhetoric closes out the movement. Strategies of confrontation and suppression both entail a measure of coercive force, without which agents attempting to confront or suppress will be unsuccessful. In encounters between agitation and control, therefore, the outcome depends not solely on rhetorical sophistication but also on variables of membership, commitment, and material power. Agents of social control can overwhelm agitators, no matter how rhetorically sophisticated, as long as control has force (in terms of resources, numbers, or capacity for violence) exclusively on its side (Bowers et al., 1993, p. 147).

8. According to one corporate campaign document, Tate & Lyle is a world leader in the production of sweeteners. In 1991, its profits were $400 million. Tate & Lyle acquired Staley in a $1.5 billion hostile takeover in 1988. Its chairman, Neil Shaw, earned $2 million in 1993 and 1994, and its CEO, Stephen Brown, lives in a mansion purchased by the company ("Crisis in Decatur," 1994).

9. Activist Lee Sustar (1997) writes, "Once locked out, leaders of UPIU Local 7837 had no plan to stop production. And although the workers eventually won the official backing of the AFL-CIO, building trades union members and Teamsters crossed picket lines throughout the lockout. Local leaders, facing court injunctions, actively discouraged mass pickets. . . . Such tactics would have been a serious undertaking. Police attacked a peaceful sit-in with pepper gas during a demonstration near the plant on June 25, 1994. But the union's failure to stop production allowed the company to wait until an exhausted workforce voted to accept management's original offer" (p. 24).

10. Like other informal, unofficial rank-and-file newsletters, such as Caterpillar workers' (United Auto Workers rank-and-file) *Kick the Cat*, UPS workers' *UPS Yours*, and the Teamsters for a Democratic Union's *Convoy Dispatch*, *News From the War Zone* provides rare access to ordinary workers' voices during the struggle. See Brecher (1997, pp. 305-365) and Moody (1997, pp. 269-292) for discussion of the importance of these rank-and-file publications to the movement for union democracy. Often, workers must struggle against the inherent conservatism and self-interest of union leaders to be effective in disputes with employers. It is important to distinguish between union bureaucrats and their interests, on the one hand, and workers, on the other hand, when analyzing the labor movement. For my purposes, the term *labor movement* refers to ordinary workers using unions as tools to pursue their interests in bargaining with employers. By no means should the term labor movement be taken to refer exclusively to the institutionalized power structure of American unions.

11. The workers published the newsletter from 1994 until January 1996, producing approximately 12 issues. They are cited and quoted in this chapter with permission from Mike Griffin, activist in the Staley struggle and founder of the War Zone Education Foundation (675 E. Hillshire Road, Decatur, IL 62521; e-mail: mgriffwzef@aol.com; phone: 217-428-6372). I am grateful to Mr. Griffin for providing me with issues of the newsletter

and for his steadfast promotion of workers' rights and union democracy in the United States.

12. I refer to issues of *News From the War Zone* by volume and issue; for example, 1.2 refers to volume 1, issue number 2. If the reference is attributable to a specific author or article title, I provide an author-date citation in addition to the volume-issue information.

13. Historically, boycotts have been much less effective at changing corporate behavior than strikes and protests. For example, the decades-long grape boycott called by the United Farm Workers has not challenged the growers' use of pesticides and the exploitation of migrant labor as intended. Boycotts are indirect strategies that position consumers, rather than workers, as the agents of social change. Objectively speaking, individuals or small groups of consumers in a society of mass consumption generally do not possess the power to damage corporate profitability. Even relatively small numbers of workers who strike and prevent production from ongoing can have an enormous impact on profits, however. The United Auto Workers (UAW) strike during the summer of 1998 at General Motors (GM) is another instance in which material strategies of pickets and plant occupations can shut down production and win the day for workers. As one reporter noted, "Because a strike at a crucial parts factory can shut down the company, GM has until now been leery of taking on the U.A.W." (Bradsher, 1998, p. A10). The GM strike lasted 39 days, shutting 27 of GM's main assembly plants, idling approximately 200,000 autoworkers in North America, and costing the company approximately $2.2 billion. As a result of the strike, GM agreed not to sell its five-plant Flint complex or Dayton, Ohio, brake plant (Evanoff, 1998).

14. Although concerned with the sinister uses of victimage and mortification in political contexts, Burke (1969b) was not a materialist in the classical sense. For him, the symbolic rewards were the aim of the rhetoric of victimage so that corporate leaders are not motivated by greed or material interest but by the symbolic magic that money represents (p. 260). Likewise, social movement agitators who employ a strategy of victimage would be seen as themselves constructing their own victimization in discourse; there is no place in this analysis to consider that they are actually, in reality, victims of corporate aggression. A materialist approach would observe that the Staley workers were in a real sense denied agency not by their narratives but, rather, by a powerful company, police, and city.

15. One might suggest as an alternative analysis that the problem was not the turn to rhetoric but, rather, that the Staley workers were simply bad rhetors who failed to garner potential support. This hypothesis is contradicted by the warm receptions received by road warriors and by the widespread accolades for the corporate campaign strategy (even though these same strategies had failed miserably in the 1989 P-9 strike at Hormel; Rachleff, 1993, pp. 58-59, 110-111).

16. The overall record of the corporate campaign is mixed. I am grateful to an anonymous reader of an earlier incarnation of this project for noting that the corporate campaign contributed to a labor victory by the Oil, Chemical and Atomic Workers (OCAW) at BASF in Geismar, Louisiana. The OCAW workers had been locked out from 1984 to 1989 under conditions similar to those of the Staley workers (Leonard, 1989; "OCAW Breaks BASF Lockout," 1990). Although I concede that the corporate campaign does not always or necessarily disable a labor struggle, I argue that its usefulness depends on other, material factors. In the case of BASF, it is possible that other factors besides the corporate campaign had determining force; the OCAW workers were more highly skilled and therefore more difficult to replace in a high-technology field. This clout provided a much different material context for the corporate campaign.

17. Not everyone involved in the Staley struggle shared these criticisms of the corporate campaign. Mike Griffin, a UPIU reformer and militant, called Ray Rogers a hero (personal communication, January 1997), blaming the defeat squarely on UPIU national leadership. For academic assessment of the corporate campaign strategy, see Craypo and Nissen (1993). For a more generous account of the use of the corporate campaign at Hormel, see Green (1990, pp. 16-22). For a narrative of the successes and (mostly) failures of Ray Rogers's Corporate Campaign International, see Hage and Klauda (1989, pp. 90-103).

10

Demonizing Democracy

The Strange Career of Lani Guinier

Kathryn Cañas and Mark Lawrence McPhail

In *The Strange Career of Jim Crow*, historian C. Vann Woodward (1974) articulated an anticipatory understanding of what would become one of the most significant struggles within African American politics and rhetorics in the aftermath of the Civil Rights movement. In the preface to the third edition of the book, Woodward commented on the paradoxical tension between the nonviolent strategies of the movement that had brought about seemingly significant social changes and an emerging need for the more oppositional and militant calls for black power, black unity, and black pride. He explained,

> Even the most complete victory over segregation would not satisfy that need, for few wished to deny racial identity or lose it in a white society. The ambivalence created a tension between those leaders of the race who were concerned mainly with protest against racial prejudice, injustice, and segregation and those mainly concerned with the preservation and fostering of racial identity, pride, and autonomy. (p. vi)

This emergent oppositionality came to the forefront in the late 1960s and early 1970s, and it redefined the exigencies and constraints of the rhetorical situation of race in America.

Two decades later, Celeste Michelle Condit and John Louis Lucaites (1993) noted a similar ambivalence in the tensions between heterogeneity and inclusivity, on the one hand, and essentialism and separatism, on the other hand. Indeed, as the century marked by "the problem of the color line" came to a close, many African Americans began to embrace a vocal oppositionality, one that reflected the belief that white Americans were unwilling or unable to commit to the black struggle for full racial equality and justice. Ironically, Condit and Lucaites argue, this oppositional stance further entrenched white racial resistance:

> [B]lack oppositional discourse has spawned successful white racist political commercials and tactics. Additionally, it has generated both a vehement defense of the elements of American culture derived from European antecedents, and a virulent attack on the claim that African culture has any valuable contributions to make to the Western world.(p. 221)

They suggest that this oppositionality has served to undermine the struggle for racial equality, and that an "interbraided rhetoric" is needed to sustain the political and economic advances made by the Civil Rights movement. They explain that "to preserve a democratic heterogeneity, we must envision a nonoppositional difference between cultures and groups" (p. 221). Our essay extends their analysis to illustrate how that nonoppositional difference has been theorized and the problems and possibilities it has revealed in practice.

In this essay, we reconsider the efficacy of nonoppositional discourse in addressing racial antagonisms through an examination of the failed nomination of Lani Guinier. We begin by illustrating how Guinier's writings on race exemplified an interbraided, nonoppositional rhetoric that called for an expanded and honest conversation about race in America and eloquently articulated an informed and accurate assessment of the institutional barriers that undermined civil and racial rights in this country. Next, we examine the response to Guinier's nomination in terms of the ways in which her writings on race were distorted and how she was personally attacked and demonized by her critics. Although Guinier's positions were explicitly nonoppositional, they were nonetheless defined as "antidemocratic" and even "racist." Finally, we illustrate how the attack on Guinier might usefully be understood in terms of existing research that explicates relationships between discourse, white privilege, and racial recovery. Our analysis calls for a revisiting of the rhetoric of racism that suggests the sobering possibility that racism may be beyond the reach of persuasion and might be better understood and addressed as a problem of social pathology.

AN AMERICAN INVITATION TO DIALOGUE: LANI GUINIER'S INTERBRAIDED RHETORIC

Following Condit and Lucaites (1993), Kathryn Anne Cañas (2002) argues that Guinier's rhetoric reflects both the principles and the practices of an interbraided rhetoric through its emphasis on dialogue: "Lani Guinier believed that dialogue was the vehicle and the value through which America could achieve participatory democracy—the foundation of the 1965 Voting Rights Act" (p. 51). Cañas suggests that Guinier draws on traditional American values to make the case for inclusivity and democratic heterogeneity: "As Guinier articulated a rhetoric of participatory democracy based on the value of dialogue, she interbraided Collectivist and Enlightenment values" (p. 157). Cañas's explication of Guinier's rhetoric illustrates how, contrary to the claims of her critics, Guinier's writings were neither undemocratic nor radical but drew directly on foundational principles of American democracy. It is this characteristic of Guinier's rhetoric that Mark McPhail (2002) explains reveals "a rhetorical consciousness" that "could have a potentially transformative effect on race relations, an explicitly nonoppositional and dialogic rhetoric" (p. 194). McPhail similarly suggests that Guinier's rhetoric exemplifies the underlying assumptions of the inclusive and interbraided rhetoric called for by Condit and Lucaites, and that her writings clearly reveal strong commitments to traditional notions of democracy that offer a powerful critique of racial identity and difference.

Guinier (1994) grounds her position "in the writings of James Madison and other founding members of our Republic" (p. 3), logically extending them beyond their original scope to their implications for a more diverse contemporary America. She explains,

> In a homogeneous society, the interest of the majority would likely be that of the minority also. But in a heterogeneous community, the majority may not represent all competing interests. The majority is likely to be self-interested and ignorant or indifferent to the concerns of the minority. (p. 3)

Guinier notes that because America is not a homogeneous society, there exists the need to hear and appreciate diverse political needs and provide alternatives to zero-sum, oppositional political practices and institutions. She explains,

> In an ideal democracy, the people would rule, but the minorities would also be protected against the power of majorities. But if a group is unfairly treated, for example, when it forms a racial minority, and if the problems of unfairness are not cured by conventional assumptions about majority rule, then what is to be done? The answer is that we may need an alternative to winner-take-all majoritarianism. (pp. 4-5)

Guinier's "radical" alternative is the principle of "taking turns," which she believes "in a racially divided society does better than simple majority rule if it accommodates the values of self-government, fairness, deliberation, compromise, and consensus that lie at the heart of the democratic ideal" (p. 5). The "undemocratic" character of Guinier's political philosophy is perhaps best revealed in her own words:

> In my legal writing, I follow the caveat of James Madison and other early American democrats. I explore decision-making rules that might work in a multiracial society to ensure that majority rule does not become majority tyranny. I pursue voting systems that might disaggregate The Majority so that it does not exercise power unfairly or tyrannically. I aspire to a more cooperative political style of decision making. . . . In looking to create Madisonian majorities, I pursue a positive-sum, taking turns solution. (p. 5)

Contrary to the claims of many of her critics in media and the government, Guinier (1994) believes that her legal writings reflect a commitment "to try to find rules that can best bring us together as a democratic society" (p. 6). Legal scholars Richard Briffault, Michael E. Lewyn, and Arthur Eisenberg, although differing in their interpretations of Guinier's writings, seem to concur with her on this issue.

Briffault, Lewyn, and Eisenberg explore in detail Guinier's discussions of the Voting Rights Act, cumulative voting, and supermajority voting. Unlike Guinier's media critics, these legal scholars read Guinier's positions against the historical context of race and representation in the United States. Although critical of some aspects of her philosophy, they nonetheless challenge the media's depictions of Guinier as "radical" and "undemocratic." Briffault (1995) argues that Guinier's position on voting rights could be deemed "radical only in a narrowly American context," and he notes that "semiproportional and proportional representation systems are the rule in most other democracies" (pp. 420-421). Briffault also observes that "there are 'consensus' democracies—democracies in which the majority limits itself, shares power, and acts only after it has obtained the consent of the minority" (p. 421). Briffault makes clear that Guinier's proposals are neither radical nor antidemocratic but quite the opposite: "In short, although Guinier would limit majority rule, her purpose is not anti-democratic, but pro-democratic—to perfect democracy by enabling the minority to join the majority in engaging in democratic self-government" (p. 455). Within the context of a system in which the majority systematically excludes minority voices, however, Guinier's proposals could be easily misinterpreted and misrepresented.

Lewyn (1994) agrees, noting that it is "unsurprising that her nomination stirred so much controversy" in light of her argument for a third generation of legislation that would police the legislative voting rules whereby "a majority consistently rigs the process to exclude a minority" (p. 928). Nonetheless, he maintains that "Guinier's writings never clearly state when, if ever, the Justice Department should pressure state and local governments to adopt cumulative voting or supermajority rules," and he questions "how radical a Guinier-led Civil Rights Division would have been, or whether a Guinier-led Civil Rights Division would require any more of state and local governments than a Civil Rights Division led by another Clinton appointee" (p. 928). Although Briffault and Lewyn are critical of Guinier's positions in terms of her interpretation and analysis of specific legal issues, neither suggests that her writings were essentially racial and antidemocratic.

Eisenberg (1994/1995) provides an even more explicit vindication of Guinier's critique of majority tyranny. Eisenberg explains that Guinier "does not call for the abandonment of majority rule; she does, however, propose electoral mechanisms designed to ameliorate the excesses of pure majoritarianism" (p. 626). He observes that Guinier "labors to fashion a system that is fairer to all who hold minority viewpoints regardless of race or ethnicity" (p. 626) and compares Guinier's model of representation to John Stuart Mill's 1861 philosophies. Eisenberg explains how Mill "observed that equal representation could be achieved . . . through a variety of electoral mechanisms, including what have come to be described as cumulative voting, limited voting, and proportional representation systems" (p. 618). In addition, he states that "both of Professor Guinier's most significant proposals, the increased use of cumulative voting and supermajority requirements, while undoubtedly animated by a desire to achieve racial fairness, seek to accomplish this end without the use of race-conscious mechanisms" (pp. 625-626). Because these same mechanisms had been advocated by Republican administrations in the past, he notes, "it was quite surprising that Professor Guinier's academic writings generated so much controversy when President Clinton nominated her to serve as assistant attorney general for civil rights" (p. 618). Eisenberg concludes that although Guinier's nomination "presented an opportunity for a serious national discussion of racial discrimination and its remediations," it "dissolved into one of name-calling and mischaracterization" (p. 632).

Even a cursory examination of her writings on race reveals that Guinier embraces the practice of dialogue and views it as the foundation for a more democratic rhetoric. She (1994) explains, "Decision making should incorporate a diversity of views to multiply the points of access to government, disperse power, and to ensure a rational, developed dialogue" (pp. 103-104). Ironically, it was her commitment to a democratizing of discourse that led to her demonization. She (1998) explains that "the irony here is that I am committed to dialogue and I am being silenced," noting that she was "simply remade" as an "elite group of opinion molders depersonalized and demonized" her (p. 122). Indeed, in both theory and practice, Guinier presented an interbraided rhetoric grounded in a coherent critique of oppositional practices. Hers was clearly a discourse that at once critically interrogated essentialized conceptions of identity and difference and at the same time drew on foundational assumptions and values of American society to offer a reconstructive vision of race and democracy.

Guinier's writings reflected a recognition of the concerns voiced by Condit and Lucaites (1993) concerning a nonoppositional heterogeneity and embodied the discursive strategies envisioned in the concept of rhetorical coherence. Guinier, however, was silenced by a chorus of angry voices, mostly but not exclusively white, who refused to hear in her words a remedy for the racial divisions that plague our society. Guinier clearly understood the ideological and epistemological foundations of those divisions. She (1998) wrote,

> Because so many people conceive of power as fundamentally oppositional and hierarchical, they understood me as a threat, as

> someone who was simply trying to give blacks a chance to rule over whites. Because power can only be seen in our culture as divided between winners and losers, someone had to lose. (p. 292)

Implicit in her position, however, was an underlying critique of such notions of power, division, and difference—a critique that, unfortunately, racialized her on both sides of the color line.

Guinier (1998) explains that

> by choosing to discuss democracy and race at the same time, I immediately became a racial partisan. That made me "too black" for those in the political mainstream, including the press. My ideas challenged the image of a country that has already achieved color blindness. They suggest that there is more work to be done. (p. 293)

She examines the complicity of people of color, including herself, in sustaining racial realities through commitments to racial essentialism and oppositional understanding of difference. She notes how, soon after her nomination, a young African American man opined that she was rejected because she was "too black" and also how Mexican American journalist Raoul Lowery Contreras argued that her positions "would simply steal this power from the fastest growing and more prosperous groups (Hispanics and Asian Americans) and hand it to less prosperous, yet numerous and geographically well-placed blacks" (p. 293). In the black and white, zero-sum game of race, Guinier's interbraided rhetoric was mischaracterized along various color lines as essentialized, oppositional, and even racist.

Guinier (1998) believes that it was her own failure to clearly articulate that rhetoric that fueled attacks of her opponents and revealed a discursive complicity that undermined her position and nomination:

> Those of us advocating racial justice were hamstrung because we were heard as advocating a strategy of "us" versus "them." In the words of the parking attendant, I was "too black." For many in the "political mainstream," that meant my thumb was on the scale to fix the results, not to improve the process of democracy. (p. 293)

When liberal "allies," such as Edward Kennedy and Carol Mosely Braun, failed to support her, and people of color, such as Contreras, openly attacked her, Guinier was easily characterized as a racial essentialist. She notes,

> They allowed the right wing to define me as a racial separatist, and then, consistent with a win/lose scorecard, seemed unable to see the story as anything other than one of "whites lose if blacks win, and Guinier favors blacks." (p. 293)

Nothing in her words or works, however, suggested that Guinier was an advocate of racial essentialism or separatism. To the contrary, in her writings, Guinier had explicitly critiqued rigid notions of racial identity and authenticity while emphasizing the extent to which race is deeply implicated in a diverse array of social and institutional realities.

In fact, it was her analysis of the racially antagonistic Reagan administration that eventually provided her critics the ammunition they needed to derail her nomination. In contrast to the racially divisive rhetoric of Reaganism, Guinier (1994) articulated an explicit commitment

> to move this country away from the polarization of the last 12 years, to lower the decibel level of rhetoric that surrounds race, and to build bridges among people of goodwill to enforce the civil rights laws on behalf of all Americans. (pp. 188-189)

Despite such good intentions, the road to her nomination was paved with distortions, caricatures, and a conscious misrepresentation of her voice and vision that was nothing short of character assassination. Guinier's words stand in stark contrast to the attacks of her critics: "I am a democratic idealist who believes that politics need not be forever seen as I win, you lose, a dynamic in which some people are permanent monopoly winners and others are permanent excluded losers" (p. 189). Perhaps it was her attempts to transform idealism into a realized democracy that rendered Guinier's rhetoric so dangerous to the systemic pathology of American racism: It attacked the disease and not simply its symptoms.

SPEAKING TRUTH TO POWER: REAGANISM AND THE TYRANNY OF THE WHITE MAJORITY

Guinier's most cogent critique of race is revealed in her analysis of institutional resistance to the Voting Rights Act under the Reagan administration, which she (1994) argues pursued policies based "not on consensus but confrontation" (p. 24). Guinier claims that this commitment to confrontation perpetuated political division by invoking the type of racial reasoning that would become instrumental in the demise of affirmative action and the destruction of the protections afforded African Americans by civil rights legislation. She notes,

> The polarizing philosophy of the Reagan years affected more than the administration's enforcement activities. Its legacy, engrafted upon Reconstruction era stereotypes about black elected officials, has perpetuated and accentuated a racially skewed reality in which blacks vote but do not govern, at least in majority white jurisdictions. (p. 24)

Guinier's critique of the Reagan administration's hostility toward civil rights is made even more compelling by research on the politics and rhetorics of contemporary racism. Robert L. Carter (1993) writes, "Conservative ideology has dominated the political and intellectual terrain for roughly the last 10 years, and that dominance became particularly pronounced during the Reagan administration. Concern for racial equality and justice for racial minorities has been downgraded" (p. 84).

Carter (1993) suggests that the ideological values cultivated under the Reagan administration revealed an underlying hostility to African Americans and the rights they had struggled to obtain:

> Although not a necessary consequence, these ideological values have been translated into hostility toward African Americans and contempt for their aspirations by activist ideologues and opportunistic politicians, and have generated the restrictive civil rights activities of the Reagan White House and its Department of Justice's efforts to turn the clock back to undo the gains achieved in the civil rights struggles of the 1950s and 1960s. (pp. 84-85)

The politics of Reaganism undermined existing civil rights laws such as the Voting Rights Act, and its rhetoric suggested that such laws were largely unnecessary by assuming that racism was no longer a problem in American society. Teun van Dijk (1993) explains, "This assumption gained wide acceptance in the United States as part of the conservative backlash in the 1980s associated with the Reagan administration" (p. 7). Van Dijk argues that traditional forms of racism have been replaced by more insidious discursive strategies that reify popular forms of racism and reflect an underlying commitment to the defense of white racial privilege. This "modern" or "symbolic" racism is the primary motivating force in the resistance of whites to demands for economic and political equality by African Americans in the post–civil rights era.

Modern racism is characterized by the "expression in abstract ideological symbols and symbolic behaviors of the feeling that blacks are violating cherished values and making illegitimate demands for change in the racial status quo" (McConahay & Hough, 1976, p. 38). It is reflected in the belief that "discrimination no longer exists and that the cherished values are those associated with 'equality' or 'equality of opportunity' (e.g., affirmative action laws or policies) rather than values associated with 'freedom of opportunity' (e.g., laws of policies prohibiting open discrimination)" (McConahay, 1986, pp. 95-96). Modern racism also explains the persistence of racial discrimination and hostility despite the demise of traditional forms of racial violence and racist sentiments. Robert Entman (1990) observes, "Even as it has become socially unacceptable to assert blacks' inherent inferiority or endorse legal segregation, a 'modern' form of racism has arisen" (p. 342). Entman argues that modern racism allows those whites "who are sensitive to the social disapproval of racism, to disguise their anti-black affect to themselves, thus preserving their self-image as unprejudiced" (p. 342). Modern racism symbolically masks white complicity in the perpetuation of racist institutions and practices by juxtaposing and rationalizing the negative representation of blackness expressed in "old-fashioned racism" with the positive representation of whiteness associated with traditional conservative values.

Empirical studies of symbolic racism confirm the existence of the three key indicators of the hypothesis: an "anti-black effect—a general emotional hostility toward blacks," "resistance to the political demands of blacks," and "a belief that racism is dead and that racial discrimination no longer inhibits black achievement" (Entman, 1990, pp. 332-333). Van Dijk (1987) notes that this hypothesis is "supported by much qualitative evidence and analysis, that social norms have changed toward racial tolerance, but that actual opinions, attitudes, and feelings may still be prejudiced" (p. 225). In addition to masking white tolerance of racism, these attitudes, beliefs, and opinions also sustain white power and privilege: "Indeed, this prejudice has a functional role in a society that still has important racist structures underlying its white group dominance in all fields" (p. 225). Van Dijk argues that the disappearance of blatant racial slurs from public discourse is less an indication of fundamental attitudinal or social changes than a remapping of the language of white racism.

Van Dijk's (1993) analysis of debates regarding the Civil Rights Bill of 1990 illustrates how this remapping is executed through the use of the "buzzword quota" as a rhetorical tactic for discrediting the bill's proponents. His analysis of the debates reveals a number of the same rhetorical moves that characterized the criticisms of Guinier. Conservative opponents argued that supporters of the bill were "against freedom, against equal opportunities for everybody" and characterized them as "establishing quotas," "fomenting racial strife," "leading the nation to destruction," and "expecting unfair competition" (p. 91). The parallels between the language of the debates and the attacks on Guinier are striking and suggest that the rhetorical moves revealed in each reflect the persistence of modern racism. Van Dijk concurs: "The prevailing political discourse of race is remarkably homogeneous, both as to topical content and as to rhetorical and argumentative strategies of persuasion, rationalization, and legitimation" (p. 114). He concludes with the sobering claim that "true ethnic-racial equality, justice, and multiculturalism have still not been realized anywhere in the West. Unfortunately, we have not found evidence that the dominant political elites in the West have such fundamental goals on their agendas" (p. 114). The disconformation of Guinier offers a strong confirmation of the symbolic and modern racism hypotheses.

Van Dijk's (1993) analysis of the ways in which the discourse of media elites sustains white racial privilege offers especially salient insights into the attack on Guinier:

> By paying special attention to white elite opinions about ethnic affairs, the press not only follows its own routines of newsmaking, namely by providing access of elites to its newsmaking, but at the same time literally silences minority opinion, especially when it is competent and critical. (p. 255)

Guinier was silenced because, in her own words, "she was made to embody America's worst fears on race" (as cited in Russakoff, 1993, p. 14). Those fears, articulated in the rhetorics of modern and symbolic racism, were reinforced by the press. Jane Rhodes (1994) writes,

> Consider the legacy of the term quota in the last 12 years. It is synonymous with the most hated aspects of affirmative action and reinforces the image of the undeserving poor (usually minorities) getting special favors while white males suffer disadvantages. Only

> a black woman could so perfectly embody these dual roles, and the news media were complicit in their creation and dissemination. (p. 2)

A closer analysis of the political and media discourse surrounding the Guinier nomination reveals the complicity of the press in misrepresenting her views, silencing her voice, and ultimately reinforcing the racial pathologies of what Aaron David Gresson (1995) describes as "white racial recovery."

FROM WELFARE QUEEN TO QUOTA QUEEN: THE RHETORIC OF WHITE RACIAL RECOVERY

The attack on Guinier began with the *Wall Street Journal* article by Clint Bolick (1993) that labeled her "Clinton's Quota Queen" and ended with the withdrawal of her nomination by Clinton, who confessed, "At the time of the nomination, I had not read her writings" (as cited in "Idea Woman," 1993, p. 5). In the aftermath of her failed nomination, it became clear that neither had many of her critics. Although it could be argued that the misrepresentation of Guinier was unintentional, Detine Bowers (1998) suggests that the attack on Guinier was "a classic example of structural strategies that silence African Americans by destroying credibility" (p. 191). Bowers's examination of the Guinier nomination reveals the ways in which elite discourse functions in the social and symbolic reproduction of racism. Bowers notes,

> The media labeled Guinier "welfare queen" and "quota queen" before she was officially nominated for the position or heard. In the aftermath of the bruhaha, Guiner (1993) expressed dismay over the ways in which she was quelled when she encountered the structures that had introduced her to the public. (p. 191)

Those structures served to misrepresent and silence Guinier in a manner that reduced her identity, her ideas, and her commitment to dialogue—to an essentialized understanding of racial difference.

Clint Bolick (1993), for example, claims that Guinier's ideas amounted to "a racial apartheid system" (p. A12). *The New Republic*

("Withdraw Guinier," 1993) describes her as a "firm believer in the racial analysis of an irreducible, racial 'us' and 'them' in American society" (p. 724), and Joe Klein (1993) describes Guinier's voting strategies as "race-based gimmicks" that will "further increase polarization" (p. 29). John Leo (1993) claims that Guinier described whites as a "racist political monolith" (p. 19), and Abigail Thernstrom (1993), a longtime critics of Guinier's, asserts that her starting point was a "total mistrust of white America" (p. 18). Although her critics find Guinier's writings to be antithetical to democratic political and legal principles and "racist," her supporters argue that her writings reflect a potentially transformative opportunity for understanding race in America. The *New Yorker* ("Idea Woman," 1993) notes,

> They do not show her to be an enemy of racial integration, a proponent of racial polarization, or an opponent of democratic norms. They show her to be a provocative, interesting thinker whose speculations could nourish what is a nascent debate in this country about alternative electoral systems. (p. 5)

Her speculations might also have moved the country beyond the polarizing and debilitating discourse of race that had emerged in the post–civil rights era.

According to David Corn (1993), however, she was "demonized in a fashion unequaled by an attack on a public figure since the pillorying of Anita Hill" (p. 856). Corn argues that the attack on Guinier was motivated both by "racism" and a desire "to paint even modest civil rights activism as dangerous" (p. 856). The attack, although initiated by conservative politicians and academics, was facilitated in the public sphere through the complicity of the U.S. media. Corn writes,

> On *Nightline* on June 2, Ted Koppell's interview with Guinier was framed by a taped introduction so distorted, so hostile, that Guinier had to waste time correcting basic facts. On June 3, the *New York Times*, which had run no editorials or columns supporting Guinier, published an Op-Ed piece criticizing her supposed advocacy of more legislative districts with black majorities in order to ensure minority seats. In fact, the whole thrust of Guinier's writings has been to oppose such redistricting. The media contributed to an inquisitorial, poisonous atmosphere in which every news report on Guinier served to perpetuate the senatorial smear job. (p. 856)

Like Clinton, few of Guinier's critics had actually read any of her law review articles, much less understood them. Furthermore, most members of the press simply repeated what had been said without investigating her works on their own. Laurel Leff (1993) notes that

> too many reporters uncritically accepted Bolick's and other conservatives' depictions of her views. And too many reporters substituted code words, such as "quotas," "affirmative action," and "reverse discriminations" for a genuine dialogue on the sensitive subject upon which her writings focus—the continuing effort to thwart blacks' effective participation in the political process. (p. 38)

Guinier's documentation of those efforts under the Reagan administration, under which Bolick had served, was either misrepresented or ignored by her critics, who instead echoed the rhetoric tropes of the Reagan revolution—the claims that racism was no longer a problem in America and that the real problem was "reverse racism."

These claims are central to what Aaron Gresson (1995) describes as "the white recovery project," a project that he explicitly associates with the Reagan administration: "'Reaganism' is the name for this recent period of recovery. Its significance as a rhetorical recovery movement can help to clarify the nationalist and racial aspects of the white recovery project" (p. 10). Gresson contends that "the need for this recovery of white power is the exigency" that has undermined post–civil rights African American emancipatory efforts, and he concludes that "white recovery accounts for the diffidence of racism" (p. 12). His analysis illustrates the ways in which white rhetoric mitigates and denies the existence of racial inequality and projects onto African Americans the responsibility of racism in much the same way that Guinier's critics projected it onto her. Gresson writes,

> Many whites have constructed personal racial stories that invert aspects of the black racial story. Because they see many of their own family and friends suffering, they believe white men have had to pay for black success. This is the new white racial story. In this new white racial narrative, moreover, the white male is the victim. (pp. 211-212)

Gresson's (1995) study examines the psychological impulses behind white recovery rhetoric, and he concludes that a reconstructive response to racial strife must embrace heterogeneity and inclusive dialogue, "but it requires, as well, that we acknowledge the persistence of racism, and that we collectively begin the systematic rebuilding of a healthier, more inclusive set of formative images" (p. 214). The attack on Guinier suggests, however, that the "new white racial story" may preclude this acknowledgment and collective rebuilding, precisely because it is a story premised on a vision of positive self-representation and white innocence. Stephen Carter (as cited in Guinier, 1994) notes,

> In this vision, we are united in common enterprise and governed by common consent. Although the nation has problems, some of them caused by racism, we are people of good will, aiming at a fairer, more integrated society, which we will achieve through the actions of our essentially fair institutions. (p. xiii)

Guinier's critique of the failure of these institutions under the Reagan administration to promote equal representation and fairness was also an implicit critique of the white majority's resistance to addressing racial injustice and inequality.

The rhetoric of racism that characterizes this story, and with which Guinier was demonized, reflects a fundamental incoherence in the minds and the messages of America's white majority. Its persistence indicates that although nonoppositional discursive strategies may be necessary for understanding the rhetorical dynamics of race relations, they are by no means sufficient for overcoming the diffidence of racism. Guinier's rhetoric was unsuccessful in convincing white Americans to reflect on the power and privileges of race that they have enjoyed for centuries at the expense of African Americans, and her failure signals a need to reconsider whether white racism is, as James Golden and Richard Rieke (1971) remarked more than 30 years ago, a problem of persuasion or psychiatry: "When forced to search deep into his own central belief system, the white man discovers he perceives himself as a white man and holds beliefs of a primitive nature, that whites are not only different but better than blacks" (p. 6). The assumption that these beliefs no longer define race relations is central to white racial recovery, and its unquestioned acceptance suggests an imperviousness to persuasion little different than that which Golden and Rieke theorized three decades ago.

Indeed, Golden and Rieke's (1971) examination of the persuasive attempts of black Americans to change white racial attitudes raises the question of whether American racism can be accurately understood as a rhetorical situation. Golden and Rieke write,

> When the black speaker tells his white audience to look deep inside their own belief systems and purge their racist ideas, he is confronting the most central, the most ego involving of all attitudes of the listener. The task may require a more intensive effort toward the restructuring of beliefs, attitudes, and values than can be accomplished through the ordinary channels of communication. (p. 7)

Golden and Rieke are troubled by the fact that, although African American rhetors offered eloquent and reasoned oratory and expertly used all the available means of persuasion, whites could not be induced to self-reflexively confront their own racism. On the one hand, this resistance to self-reflexivity raised serious questions about the efficacy and universality of rhetorical theorizing: If there were, indeed, effective strategies of discourse that could be categorized and delineated, why were they largely ineffective when the issue of race was involved?

On the other hand, it raised equally troubling questions about the contents of white consciousness. Golden and Rieke (1971) note, "As psychiatrists often observe, "in these cases the patient may have to purge himself of his damaging beliefs. In the case of black rhetoric, it may be that the white man must deal with himself and others like him" (p. 7). Golden and Rieke's exploration of black rhetoric suggests that the failure to rhetorically resolve this country's racial antagonisms lies less in the ability of African Americans to speak well than in the willingness of white Americans to listen. Their analysis indicates that rhetorical explorations of racial conflict and division that contrast the essentializing tendencies of oppositional discourse with the integrative impulses of dialogue must also address the persuasive and psychiatric impulses at work in the historical and contemporary resistance of whites to the legitimate needs and demands of African Americans.

When the extent and extensiveness of this resistance are taken into consideration, it becomes evident that the social transformations initiated by the Civil Rights movement cannot be sustained by the interbraided and coherent rhetorical efforts of African Americans alone but must inevitably be embraced by white Americans as well. Guinier and Torres (2003) concur:

> The hierarchy of power that is most effective in separating potential allies is race. Tackling the role that race plays in our social institutions is a way not just to improve the lot of people of color but to confront the ways in which power operates and circulates throughout our society and cultures. (p. 31)

The building of effective multiracial coalitions, however, will involve a commitment on the part of an increasingly resistant white majority to self-reflection and a relinquishing of racial privilege and self-interest. Ultimately, this requires an attack on the concept of whiteness.

Noel Ignatiev and John Garvey (1996) argue that "the key to fundamental social change in the United States is the challenge to the system of race privilege that embraces all whites, including the most downtrodden" (p. 1). They view racism as a peculiarly white problem, the solutions to which must come from the white community: Theirs is a "focus on whiteness and the struggle to abolish the white race from within" (p. 2). Ignatiev and Garvey believe that the reconstruction of racial realities must involve "a challenge to the institutions that produce race as a social category—a challenge that disrupts their normal operation" (p. 3). They call for a radical reconstruction of racial reality spearheaded by whites—"an assault on whiteness and all its ways, by a force including a detachment of renegades—race traitors—who believe that a new world, and nothing less, is worth fighting for" (p. 5).

Michael Novick (1995) similarly argues that white Americans must "build a culture of resistance, sustained through our daily lives and interactions, that enables us to carry that struggle forward to victory. Such struggle takes place not only between social groups and forces, but within individuals" (p. 15). Although Novick does not believe that racism is essentially a white problem, he implicitly recognizes the extent to which it is allied with white privilege, culture, and consciousness:

> We are up against a system whose survival depends on racism; a system that produces and reproduces racism in generation after generation, despite any contrary ideals it professes; a system that will in fact take desperate measures to defend, sustain, and perpetuate racism. (pp. 323-324)

Novick concludes that, although it is critical that people of color not be seduced into reifying the essentializing and oppositional tendencies of racist systems, it is equally imperative that whites, as "people of conscience," similarly call into question the legitimacy of racial politics, privilege, and power.

This is a vision essentially embraced by Guinier (1994), who had hoped to create through dialogue a discursive space within which Americans could collectively move "beyond the polarization and divisiveness of the past few years and the poison of racism that has so infected our society" (p. 190). The fact that so many white Americans were unwilling or unable to hear Guinier's message, however, seems to indicate that interbraided or coherent rhetorics may be no more effective in healing America's racial divisions than those rhetorics of "symbolic realignment" reflected in the oppositional discourse of black militants and millenarians (Goldzwig, 1989). If this is in fact the case, then the challenge for rhetors and rhetorical scholars committed to dismantling our nation's most enduring myth and exposing its fallacies may be greater than we ever imagined. If racism cannot be effectively addressed through dialogic and nonoppositional discourse, then we may have to seriously consider whether any type of rhetoric is capable of transforming the pathologies of color into the possibilities of conscience.

FROM THE COLOR LINE TO THE CONSCIENCE LINE: RACE, RHETORIC, AND THE NEW CAREER OF JIM CROW

The state of race relations in America in general, and the demonizing of Lani Guinier in particular, suggests that the problems of the twentieth century remain with us in the twenty-first century. Jane Rhodes (1994) notes, "It has been almost 100 years since William E. B. DuBois predicted that the problem of the color line would be the defining crisis of the twentieth century in America. The portrayal of Lani Guinier by the media bears out this prediction" (p. 1). DuBois was one of the last century's most vocal and thoughtful critics of the destructive legacy of racism in America, but his warnings went unheeded. The same could be said to be true of Guinier, whose analysis of the weakening of voting rights augured the central issue that would mark the beginning of the twenty-first century—the role of race in the 2000 presidential election. After the 2000 election, Bob Wing (2000) observed that "35 years after the passage of the Voting Rights Act, racist violations of election law are rampant," revealing "again just how central race is to U.S. politics and how racism is institutionally structured into the electoral system" (p. 1).

Wing (2000) argues, like Guinier, that the two-party system undermines democratic participation and racial equality: "The Civil Rights movement destroyed the monopoly over power by whites, but the tyranny of the white majority is still institutionalized in the winner-take-all, two-party, electoral college system" (p. 1). He gives voice to the sentiments of many African Americans, who viewed the failure to protect voting rights in the 2000 presidential election not as an indictment against one political party but of the political system, a system committed to the defense and protection of whiteness. Robert Allen, editor of *Black Scholar*, noted (as cited in Jordan, 2001),

> Of course, it was, first and last, about race: this stolen election. And then Gore didn't want to touch it because Gore didn't want to break with white supremacy—even though that meant he'd lose the election! That's how much white supremacy means to him. (p. 25)

Allen's criticisms were echoed by others in the African American community who understood that the right to vote came at great cost and recognized that the price of its destruction could be even greater. June Jordan (2001) remarked, "We have moved from the Invisible Man to the Invisible People. It's a raging and a sorrow at the terrible meaning of that discount—for us, and for democracy itself" (p. 25). Jordan contends that the media was instrumental in the disenfranchisement and silencing of African Americans: "Where is there record of any major national newspaper or TV channel attempting—before, during, and after The Stolen Election of 2000—to find out what black people were thinking, and why?" (p. 25). Jordan's questions remain unanswered with the exception of those progressive voices that were similarly silenced by mainstream media.

Those voices also invoked a trope of invisibility of black folk. In "Florida's 'disappeared' voters," Gregory Palast (2001) writes, "On November 7 tens of thousands of eligible Florida voters were wrongly prevented from casting their ballots—some purged from the voter registries and others blocked from registering in the first instance" (p. 20). He argues that the disfranchisement of African American voters was systematic, intentional, and reminiscent of the tactics used to deny African Americans access to the ballot before the Voting Rights Act became law:

> Three decades ago, George Wallace stood in a schoolhouse door and thundered "Segregation now! Segregation tomorrow! Segregation forever!" but he failed to block entry to African Americans. Governor Jeb Bush's resistance to court rulings, conducted at whisper level with high-tech assistance, has been far more effective at blocking voters of color from the polling station door. Deliberate or

> accidental, the error-ridden computer purge and illegal clemency obstacle course function, like the poll tax and literacy test of the Jim Crow era, to take the vote away from citizens who are black, poor, and coincidentally, almost all Democrats. No guesswork there: Florida is one of the few states to include both party and race in registration files. (p. 23)

Palast's (2001) analysis suggests that the strange career of Jim Crow has not yet ended, and that its impact on America's political and legal machinery remains intact. These, undoubtedly, were the machinations that Guinier had hoped to expose in her writings and transform through an inclusive and dialogic conversation about race in America. Her (dis)appointment is a clear indication that the debate over race in America has not yet abated but become more strange and paradoxical as the shifting and unstable characters of identity and difference have become more pronounced.

Those same strange paradoxes were recognized by Woodward (1974) three decades ago:

> In its tortuous course the debate suggested that the career of Jim Crow might become even stranger than it had been in the past. Black champions of separatism joined hands with white champions of segregation. Former integrationists accepted separatism as a viable compromise. (p. 218)

Woodward's observation anticipated the issues raised by contemporary rhetorical scholars who have attempted to theorize strategies that transform the rhetoric of racism from a discourse of negative difference to a dialogue capable of crafting a new vision of equality. By examining the ways in which African Americans might be implicated in white racial resistance through recourse to oppositional and antagonistic rhetoric, these scholars have attempted to reframe the rhetoric of race in ways that move it beyond the strange calculation of equality by which it has historically been measured.

Three decades ago, Woodward (1974) wondered if this strange calculation of equality represented "a new 'capitulation to racism,'" but he also realized that the white commitment to protecting racial privilege "made it increasingly difficult to answer some of the separatists' questions" (p. 219), especially questions about the problems and possibilities of racial integration:

> Are the cynics not right who define "integration" as the period between the time the first Negroes move in and the last whites move out? . . . Is integration worth the risk of accepting white values to the point of denying black identity? (p. 219)

The social, political, and economic realities of the past 30 years have shown Woodward's observations and the separatists' questions to be prophetic. White racial resistance to integration and equality in the post–civil rights era have undeniably proven to be empirical and rhetorical realities, and although the identity politics of blackness may have played a role in fueling this resistance, much evidence suggests that it may be rooted more deeply in the social politics and psychological pathologies of whiteness.

Like the strange career of Jim Crow, the even stranger career of Lani Guinier prompts a revisiting of the role of oppositionality and racial essentialism in the sustaining of racial antagonism. Guinier's message to America, unlike many of the so-called militant rhetorics of blackness that have emerged in the era after civil rights, was truly revolutionary. It affirmed the role of dialogue in the creation of new racial realities, reflected the fundamental principles of rhetorical coherence, and embodied the practice of a nonoppositional heterogeneity. She was silenced, however, by a society that seems committed to creating a new and even stranger career for Jim Crow. Had she been heard, perhaps the problem of the twentieth century, the color line, would have been crossed by people of conscience in ways that would have made Guinier's analysis of America's racial realities less painfully prophetic. The demonizing of Guinier demands that we rethink the roles of rhetoric, reason, and race in the social construction of difference and identity. Perhaps then we might be able to achieve what Guinier was never given the chance to do and craft a "public discourse on race in which all perspectives are represented and in which no one viewpoint monopolizes, distorts, caricatures, or shapes the outcome" (Guinier, 1994, p. 89).

11

Racial Apologies

Dexter B. Gordon and Carrie Crenshaw

The recurrent theme of accusation followed by apology is so prevalent in our record of public address as to be, in the words of Kenneth Burke, one of those "situations typical and recurrent enough for men (sic) to feel the need of having a name for them."

—B. L. Ware and Wil A. Linkugel (1973, p. 274)

Yet come to think of it can it not be that White folks are into denial bigtime themselves—that denial keeps us all as unaware as we wanna be. Denial is in fact a cornerstone of White European culture, and it has been called out by the major critical voices who speak to, for, and from the location of whiteness (Marx, Freud, Foucault). After all if we all pretend racism does not exist, that we do not know what it is or how to change it, it never has to go away.

—bell hooks (1995, p. 4)

Despite the immense successes of the civil rights movement, our society is still plagued by the ravages of racism. This is a system in which privileges and power are granted to Whites exclusively purely on the basis of the social category of "race." The economic, social, cultural, and individual manifestation of a White supremacist ideology that systemically permeates our society continues to privilege White people at the expense of people of color. Racism is recalcitrant, and the ongoing contestation of racism is a dynamic struggle against the hegemonic dominance of an ideology that is marked by strategic moves in the public political arena to preserve White privilege.

After 12 years of Republican attack on a progressive racial politics, William Jefferson Clinton was elected president. Beginning in his second term in office, President Clinton claimed to make the issue of "race relations" a major item on his agenda and began a project called his Initiative on Race. Clinton claimed that by talking with each other in forums throughout the country dedicated to the issue, Americans can transcend racism. If we can just talk about race, then we can become "One America." This interesting proposition has been foregrounded in our national discussion about race and deserves the attention of rhetorical scholars, who can contribute to our understanding of how communication practice functions in the crucible of race relations in modern-day politics. With Clinton's initiative as an important catalyst, our public political discourse about racism took an interesting turn. America wondered aloud, and sometimes contentiously, how to address its history of racial injustice as it tried to grapple with a future of racial justice. News stories of what we call "racial apologies," apologies offered for the existence of racism, were commonplace. In 1995, the Southern Baptist convention passed a "Resolution on Racial Reconciliation" apologizing for the role of the denomination in slavery, and in January 1997, President Clinton apologized for the racist treatment of soldiers during World War II by awarding the Medal of Honor to several African Americans whose brave deeds had been unjustly ignored. Outside the United States, examples include the Canadian government's apology for the nation's racist treatment of its native people and the Australian government's apology for the treatment of the Aborigines. So many of these racial apologies had been offered that one commentator noted that the 1990s "turned out to be the decade of the group apology" (Leo, 1997, p. 17). Given the increasing frequency and importance of the rhetorical practice of the racial apology in the last decade of the twentieth century, we believe it important to ask the following question: Does this kind of talk about racism contribute to antiracism? The end of the Clinton presidency also marked the end of any notion of a continued "national conversation on race." Race talk, however—and in some instances, high-profile, racist talk and racial apologies—still captures the American imagination.

This was demonstrated in striking fashion when Republican Senator Trent Lott of Mississippi praised the 1948 segregationist presidential bid of Senator Strom Thurmond at Thurmond's 100th birthday celebration on Capitol Hill on December 5, 2002. In comments broadcast live on C-SPAN, Lott declared,

> I want to say this about my state: When Strom Thurmond ran for president, we voted for him. We're proud of it. And if the rest of the country had followed our lead, we wouldn't have had all these problems over all these years, either.

These racist remarks created a firestorm in public debate. Although Lott offered multiple racial apologies, he was unable to prevent the political fallout. On December 20, 2002, under pressure, he resigned from his position as majority leader in the U.S. Senate. Thus, race and racial apologies remain a salient feature of U.S. life.

In this essay, we examine how the rhetorical construction of racial apologies function in our national discussion of race relations. Fundamentally, we are interested in exploring whether racial apologies make a contribution to antiracism—whether they break or perpetuate our rhetorical silence about White privilege in the United States. To illuminate the answer to our question, we compare our investigation of the notion of racial apologies to the traditional understanding of rhetorical apologia.

We provide two examples of racial apologies. In May 1997, President Clinton apologized for the Tuskegee syphilis study that refused treatment for several African Americans afflicted with the disease. In June of the same year, 12 U.S. Representatives submitted a concurrent resolution apologizing for the fact that slavery was sanctioned by the Constitution and laws of the United States until 1865. We start with a synthesis of several relevant literatures that inform our study, including ideological rhetorical criticism, whiteness studies, and apologia as a genre of public address.

We argue that these two examples are instances of racial apologies that are advanced as the kind of discourse about race relations that can "transcend" racism because of their resonance with traditional apologia. On closer examination, however, they function to perpetuate racism through their rhetorical silences about White privilege. Unlike traditional apologia, these apologies are made by a single individual or a few individuals on behalf of a group: the U.S. government, the Congress, the American people, and the nation. The fact that the group is White is always unmarked, unnamed, although it is always juxtaposed to the explicitly racially marked group of African Americans to whom the apology is offered. Moreover, these apologies construct racism as individual racist acts in the past to be transcended as a part of our effort to achieve racial reconciliation in the present and future. Their failure to acknowledge and, indeed, their implied denial of the fact that racism is a pervasive, ongoing, and systemic phenomenon function as a rhetorical strategy of "othering." This phenomenon occurs because the silence of these apologies about White privilege shifts the burden of transcending racism to African Americans. Also, the apologies are constructed so that the initiation of a break with the past can be completed only if African Americans forgive Whites for past racism.

We are not arguing that all racial apologies are bankrupt. We take a radically different stance from those who contend that issues of historical racism should be left in the past where they belong (D'Souza, 1995; Sowell, 1975; Steele, 1990). In contrast, we believe the past is always present among us and is often deployed to serve particular interests. We also distance ourselves from the notion that these apologies are useless and will achieve nothing. Indeed, grounded in our commitment to be part of the effort to shatter the silence about White supremacist ideology and White privilege, we strongly affirm that the issue of race, continued racism, and the United States' history of Black enslavement deserves careful, sustained, and widespread debate as part of our public discourse. We believe, however, that we must understand the limitations of certain rhetorical constructions of racial apologies to be able to distinguish them from those that do contribute to our antiracism progress. Much is at stake regarding the turn that these discourses will take. The debate over reparations, long viewed as "scalding hot, untouchable (as) public policy" from which even the most progressive politician runs, has had a vibrant revival of late, and in many instances this debate has represented reparation as a form of an apology (Merida, 1999). Randall Robinson's (2000) *The Debt: What America Owes to Blacks*, Roy L. Brooks's (1999) *When Sorry Isn't Enough: The Controversy Over Apologies and Reparations for Human Injustice*, Alfred Brophy's (2000) *Reconstructing the Dreamland: Contemplating Civil Rights Actions and Reparations for the Tulsa Race Riot of 1921*, and the Tulsa Race Riot Commission, which in February 2000 recommended restitution "in real and tangible form," are important markers in this debate signifying not only its revival but also its slow but significant emergence from the margins of American public discourse (see Appendix). The 2002 Reparations Rally and the filing of a lawsuit in federal court in Brooklyn on March 20, 2002, claiming damages against "FleetBoston Financial, the railroad firm CSX, and the Aetna insurance company, with a promise to name up to 100 additional corporations at a later date" mark the high point in the reparations effort (http://www.cnn.com/2002/LAW/03/26/slavery.reparations/). Because this debate is located in the context of a history of racial apologies, the fate of its revival and antiracist progress in general may be determined by whether we can astutely understand the difference between a racial apology that masks White privilege and one that does not.

WHITENESS, IDEOLOGY, AND OTHERING

As in most talk, White privilege, the social position of being White, remains unmarked and unnamed in the two texts we examine. Whiteness has both rhetorical and material dimensions in that it is both discursively constructed and accompanied by real material privilege (Hacker, 1992; van Dijk, 1993). There is nothing essential about whiteness; rather, it is a social location that is assigned value in a racist society. Many Whites sense that privilege accompanies whiteness (Feagin & Vera, 1995) but do not often acknowledge that privilege because they think of themselves as morally neutral nonracists. Instead, they differentiate themselves as nonracists by attributing racism to extreme White supremacists groups (Ezekiel, 1995, p. 1; McIntosh, 1992, p. 34). Whiteness is a strategic rhetoric that occupies the center of our culture and as such is invisible (Nakayama & Krizek, 1995). It maintains its invisibility through rhetorical silence. Silence about whiteness protects its unexamined status and sustains the assumption that to be White is the natural condition or norm (Crenshaw, 1997, p. 268). It is the rhetorical silence about and the lack of transparency of whiteness that put people of color in a double bind (Flagg, 1998). Racism becomes the problem of the other, and the moral force of the civil rights movement's "colorblind" rhetoric can be easily co-opted to prop up White privilege by perpetuating rhetorical silence about it (Crenshaw, 1998). In this sense, whiteness enjoys a privileged ideological status in our racist culture. It occupies that space that is taken for granted as the norm and protected by rhetorical silence.

Authors throughout the academy have been writing increasingly more in the area of "whiteness studies" (Clark & O'Donnell, 1999; Delgado & Stefancic, 1997; Frankenberg, 1993, 1997; Hill, 1997; Kincheloe, Steinberg, Rodriguez, & Chennault, 1991; Lipsitz, 1998; Lopez, 1996). Many are motivated by the desire to decenter the universality of whiteness by naming it and exploring how the often unspoken notion of whiteness in our culture operates to sustain White privilege in a racist society. The proliferation of such studies has generated many concerns and criticisms about the viability of the project to sustain its emancipatory impulse. Some critics fear that whiteness studies will serve to recenter White privilege because they will focus the discussion of racism on White people without supplying any alternative understanding of a liberatory racial politics. Clark and O'Donnell argue that this central conflict over "White fetishism" is the very threshold of the second wave of whiteness studies. The impulse to end the silence about whiteness for the purpose of decentering it and ending its universality has led to the often articulated question: What replaces the silence?

This is a material question and, thus, the answer must directly address the relationship between the symbolic and the material. Ideological rhetorical criticism does just that. Ideological rhetorical criticism asks what vested interests are protected by the selection of particular rhetorical constructions (Wander, 1983). It helps uncover the alliance between White material privilege and rhetorical silences about whiteness (Crenshaw, 1997). Because rhetoric is the medium of ideology, understanding how racist ideology works requires a rhetorical critic to question our taken-for-granted, naturalized assumptions. It requires questioning commonsense explanations that produce and reinforce our consent to the current social order and its power structures. A critical ideological approach illuminates our ongoing struggle over the meaning of race and makes room for oppositional consciousness by helping us to see the meaning of racialized constructions and the vested interests they protect.

In particular, a nonreductionist theory of hegemony informed by the insights of Antonio Gramsci can inform the way that we understand how racist ideology and ideologies in general operate to protect the powerful vested interests of a dominant class by preserving taken-for-granted frameworks that naturalize current power structures. Gramsci understood that a dominant group's protection of a self-serving ideology is not only maintained through coercive force but also preserved through gaining and maintaining consent to an ideology that legitimizes that coercive power. Hegemony is not simply a matter of economic determinism. Rather, his emphasis on the materiality of ideology helps us to understand how ideology is embodied in our institutions and cultural apparatuses (Laclau & Mouffe, p. 67). A hegemonic class articulates its ideology through these institutions and cultural apparatuses as in the self-interest of those whose consent it hopes to gain. Ideology is "a practice producing subjects" to gain consent based on the understanding that subjects are shaped by ideological discourse (Mouffe, Hegemony and Ideology in

Gramsci, p. 187). This practice is designed to gain consent to the current allocation of material privilege.

"Othering" is a commonplace rhetorical practice used to naturalize the dominant groups' protection of their position of privilege. Through othering, dominant groups rhetorically structure the social world to establish themselves as the normative, central subjects and those who are unlike them as marginal because of their presumed deviation from the norm. These "deviants" are rhetorically crafted as the "others." This move serves the important function of providing rhetorical cover for privileged groups by framing such privilege as natural. More insidiously, othering functions to silence those identified as being different. An important element of White supremacy is the effort to present whiteness as the norm and blackness as other. Important to this program is the silencing of voices critical of racial hierarchy and especially of White privilege.

Thus, when we ask whether a racial apology resists racism, we must ask the following: What replaces the silence about racism? What material arrangement does the apology preserve or change? We must ask if the apology maintains consent to the current material order or actually advocates a change in the material circumstances that mark White privilege. Otherwise, we are left with the possibility that our criticism of whiteness will simply recenter White privilege by focusing the issue on Whites by never asking the material question: What should replace it? Starting with this understanding of both the symbolic and the material dimensions of White privilege positions us to investigate what material arrangements racial apologies protect. Comparing racial apologies to our traditional understanding of apologia gets at this issue.

APOLOGIA

Rhetorical genres are dynamic constellations of rhetorical forms that strategically respond to the rhetor's situation and purpose (Campbell & Jamieson, 1978b, pp. 18-25). The study of rhetorical genres is useful for scholars because the concept is "an economical way of acknowledging the interdependence of purpose, lines of argument, stylistic choices, and requirements arising from the situation and the audience" (Jamieson & Campbell, 1982, p. 146). One genre that has received much attention is apologia. Apologia, or the speech of self-defense, is a distinct form of public address. Apologies in response to accusations recur so frequently that several scholars have argued for its importance as a distinct genre of public address worthy of specific attention and theoretical inquiry (Devreaux Butler, 1972; Kruse, 1981; Vartabedian, 1985; Ware & Linkugel, 1973). Ware and Linkugel note that an attack on a person's morality, motives, or reputation is qualitatively different from an objection to particular policies. They suggest that the only seemingly satisfying course of action demanded by this situation is a direct response, often in the form of a speech of self-defense or apologia (p. 274).

Thus, although scholars have limited apologia to a conceptual category including specific speeches of self-defense by an individual rhetor in a particular situation, we believe that what we know about apologia is relevant to our understanding of racial apologies. The accusation of racism or the attribution of a racist motive is a profoundly moral charge laden with negative implications for one's reputation and is widely thought to be so because of the successes of the civil rights movement. In some sense, these texts constitute an apology in response to the moral accusations of racism. There is one essential difference between these texts of racial apologies and the speeches that are traditionally categorized as apologia, however. In each instance, the rhetor is not really apologizing for himself or herself. Rather, he or she is apologizing for a group to which he or she belongs. We think that this difference is in part what makes these texts especially interesting. In the remainder of this essay, we explore the rhetorical and material implications of a White person apologizing for racism and/or a particular historical racist act or event on behalf of others who are White, despite the fact that whiteness and White material privilege are never truly made transparent in the discourse. They are statements of self-defense in response to a moral accusation but are made on behalf of the group to which the White rhetor belongs because of the existence of White privilege in a racist society.

RACIAL APOLOGIES

As a starting point for our inquiry into the nature of racial apologies, we examine two texts that constitute explicit apologies for past racist wrongs. The first is President Clinton's apology for the Tuskegee "experiment." In 1932, health researchers recruited 399 indigent, southern, Black men to participate in the "Tuskegee Study of Untreated Syphilis in the Negro Male" by leading them to believe that they would receive free medical treatment. These researchers then withheld treatment from these individuals and compared their health with that of Black men free of the disease. Chelala (1991) notes, "Although at the time the study began the treatment for syphilis was difficult, the study continued after penicillin was found to be effective in the 1940s, and even after serious doubts arose about the usefulness of the experiment" (p. 1529). By the time the experiment ended, approximately 100 men had died of syphilis, 40 wives had been infected, and 19 children had contracted the disease at birth (p. 1529). On May 16, 1997, 65 years after the study started and 25 years after its termination, President Clinton offered an apology for "one of the most scandalous experiments in the history of American science" (Rogers, Ward, Atkins, & Flynt, 1994, p. 503). Along with his apology, President Clinton announced a $200,000 grant to set up the Center for Bioethics in Research and Health Care at Tuskegee University (Samuel, 1997, p. 6C). The apology's timing was the result of a confluence of issues, including the urging of the presidential advisory board on race, the 25th anniversary of the government's hearings on the experiment, and the ethical issues raised by the National Institute of Health's and the Centers for Disease Control's support of a study of AIDS on the African continent. This study was labeled "Tuskegee Two," with comparisons made to the first Tuskegee experiment (Harter, Stephens, & Japp, 2000). The ethical questions raised by Black medical doctors and others, including the central claim of continued racist practices by the American government's health services, became part of the exigency for Clinton's apology. These developments also influenced the timing of the apology proposed by Representative Tony Hall's resolution. This resolution was in part a response to President Clinton's June 14, 1997, call for an initiative on race, less than 1 month after his Tuskegee apology.

The previous January, Clinton awarded the Medal of Honor to several African Americans whose brave deeds in World War II had been unjustly ignored. Although these apologies are part of the larger 1990s, international trend toward group apologies, they are also specific responses to contemporary American voices calling for an effective response to American slavery, including a call for reparations.

That American racism needs to be addressed is beyond reasonable question. Still undecided, however, is the mode of such address. Many worry whether it should be in the form of a public apology by the government. An apology for slavery would be a signal event in which the age-old practice of rhetoric would be employed by the head of state in an effort to repair the damage done by a nefarious institution previously sanctioned by the state. To understand the meaning and impact of these apologies, we need to know answers to the following questions: Who is making the apology? To whom is the apology made? What is being apologized for? and What is the function of the apology? We begin with an analysis of the Tuskegee apology.

The Tuskegee Apology

In the immediate sense, President Clinton made the apology for the Tuskegee syphilis study directly to the eight survivors and their families in the East Room of the White House. Five of the eight survivors were present: a Mr. Shaw, Charlie Pollard, Carter Howard, Fred Simmons, and Frederick Moss. The other three were represented by family members: Sam Doner was represented by his daughter, Gwendolyn Cox; Ernest Hendon was represented by his brother, North Hendon; and George Key was represented by his grandson, Christopher Monroe. The text of the speech, however, indicates much more (Clinton, 1997):

> To the survivors, to the wives and family members, the children and the grandchildren, I say what you know: No power on Earth can give you back the lives lost, the pain suffered, the years of internal torment and anguish. What was done cannot be undone. But we can end the silence. We can stop turning our heads away. We can look at you in the eye and finally say on behalf of the American people, what the United States government did was shameful, and I am sorry. The American people are sorry for the loss, for the years of hurt. You did nothing wrong, but you were grievously wronged. I apologize and I am sorry that this apology has been so long in coming.

Clinton indicates that he is sorry for the loss, that he apologizes, and that he is sorry that the apology has been too long in coming. His "we," however, clearly includes not only himself as an individual person expressing his apology but also himself as the representative of the American public and the U.S. government. Clinton is making the apology on behalf of the American people and the American government. Moreover, we argue that his references to "we" can be contextually understood as an unmarked reference to White people. His references to the public and government are references to a majority White public and an overwhelmingly White government. The word *we* has no clear referent in the text, although it clearly excludes those African Americans who were victims of the study and their families because it is juxtaposed to "you" in the text: "We can look you in the eye and say on behalf of the American people, what the United States government did was shameful, and I am sorry." The elision between we looking you in the eye at the beginning of the sentence becoming I am sorry at the end of the sentence is telling. Clinton is apologizing on behalf of White Americans.

This interpretation is also supported by a textual analysis of the rhetorical construction of the recipients of the apology. In addition to "the survivors, to the wives and family members, the children and the grandchildren," Clinton (1997) also addresses the apology "to Macon County, to Tuskegee, to the doctors who have been wrongly associated with events there." Most important, however, is the next sentence indicating that the apology is being made "to our African American citizens." Thus, contextually, African Americans are not included in Clinton's "we." Instead, they are recipients of the apology. Therefore, although Clinton acknowledges that the study was "an outrage to our commitment to integrity and equality for all our citizens," his apology is not directed to Whites: It is directed to African Americans.

The text of the apology also reveals clues to Clinton's (1997) construction of what the apology is for. The situation was constructed as an apology for the study. The text, however, reveals Clinton's understanding of why the study was a grievous wrong requiring an apology:

> So today America does remember the hundreds of men used in research without their knowledge and consent. We remember them and their family members. Men who were poor and African American without resources and with few alternatives, they believed they had found hope when they were offered free medical care by the United States Public Health Service. They were betrayed. Medical people are supposed to help when we need care, but even once a cure was discovered, they were denied help, and they were lied to by their government. Our government is supposed to protect the rights of its citizens; their rights were trampled upon. Forty years, hundreds of men betrayed, along with their wives and children, along with the community in Macon County, Alabama, the City of Tuskegee, the fine university there, and the larger African American community. The United States government did something that was wrong—deeply, profoundly, morally wrong. It was an outrage to our commitment to integrity and equality for all our citizens.

Clinton is apologizing because the study was a betrayal of trust, the victims were lied to by their government, and this lie resulted in the trampling of their rights. In addition, as the previously cited portion of the text indicates, Clinton is apologizing for the lives that were lost and the pain, suffering, torment, and anguish caused by the study. Interestingly, only one explicit mention is made of the racist motivation for these evils. Initially, the reference to rights is quite vague. Later in the text, however, Clinton (1997) addresses the apology "to our African American citizens, I am sorry that your federal government orchestrated a study so clearly racist." It is clear that Clinton is apologizing in part for the racism inherent in the event and the fact that the federal government could orchestrate a racist study. There is no explicit connection between the specific racist atrocity and currently existing fabric of systemic racism, however—no clear mark that this was an act perpetrated primarily by White people against African Americans.

This leads us to the important question: What is the rhetorical purpose of the apology? Clinton (1997) suggests that there are two major purposes for the apology: to ensure that we remember what happened and to provide a basis for "moving forward," for taking a first step toward rebuilding broken trust:

> The eight men who are survivors of the syphilis study at Tuskegee are a living link to a time not so very long ago that many Americans would prefer not to remember, but we dare not forget. It was a time when our nation failed to live up to its ideals, when our nation broke the trust with our people that is the very foundation of our democracy. It is not only in remembering that shameful past that we can make amends and repair our nation, but it is in remembering that past that we can build a better present and a better future. And without remembering it, we cannot make amends and we cannot go forward.

Clinton (1997) suggests that we dare not forget, that we must remember the shameful past to move forward—to make amends so that we can "build a better present and a better future." Moreover, it is essential to remember what happened so that it will "never be allowed to happen again. It is against everything our country stands for and what we must stand against is what it was."

Clinton (1997) also suggests that the apology is an essential first step to build one America, his term for his racial harmony agenda. He believes that the apology is a first step toward overcoming the racial divide in our nation:

> So let us resolve to hold forever in our hearts and minds the memory of a time not long ago in Macon County, Alabama, so that we can always see how adrift we can become when the rights of any citizens are neglected, ignored, and betrayed. And let us resolve here and now to move forward together. The legacy of the study at Tuskegee has reached far and deep, in ways that hurt our progress and divide our nation. We cannot be one America when a whole segment of our nation has no trust in America. An apology is the first step, and we take it with a commitment to rebuild that broken trust. We can begin by making sure there is never again another episode like this one. We need to do more to ensure that medical research practices are sound and ethical, and that researchers work more closely with communities.

Clinton (1997) implies that the apology should function to bring people together across America's racial divide. Although we have used the term *racial divide*, Clinton never explicitly did so. In the context of his reference to one America, however, this appears to be his meaning. Interestingly, in the entire text, there is only one reference to any term relating to race or racism. Clinton noted, "to our African American citizens, I am sorry that your federal government orchestrated a study so clearly racist."

The Slavery Apology

The resolution apologizing for slavery is simply stated "Resolved by the House of Representatives (the Senate concurring), that the Congress apologizes to African Americans whose ancestors suffered as slaves under the Constitution and laws of the United States until 1865" ("Concurrent Resolution," 1997). To understand the context and rhetorical implications of the resolution, we also examine Representative Hall's (1997) letter soliciting the support of members of Congress.

Hall's (1997) letter suggests that the resolution is one in which "we, on behalf of the United States Congress, apologize" for slavery. Congress is "a representative of the American people," who "share a common history, which includes a long era when slavery was acceptable." Despite the explicit nature of the apology, Hall undercuts his and the Congress' ownership of the apology by saying "no one alive today is responsible for slavery" and that "generations have passed since the end of slavery, and in that time Congress has done much to address the effects of that legacy." The apology is directly offered to "African Americans whose ancestors suffered as slaves." Thus, Hall conceives of the resolution as an apology offered by the U.S. Congress on behalf of the nation, the American people, to African Americans who are descendants of slaves. As in the previous text, there is no explicit reference to whiteness, despite the fact that the Congress continues to be mainly made up of members who are White, and that White privilege has resulted from our common history of slavery.

It is clear that Hall (1997) believes the Congress should apologize for slavery. There is not much detail about it, however. The resolution does not directly apologize for slavery. Instead, in its brevity, it merely apologizes to African Americans whose ancestors suffered as slaves. The resolution implies that the apology is for African American's ancestors' suffering under slavery, and the letter suggests that slavery was a "horrible wrong" (Hall) and that our common history "includes a long era when slavery was acceptable." Thus, the resolution and the letter indicate that the apology is for the past event of slavery, the suffering caused by it when it was in effect "until 1865," and the fact that it was a horrible wrong that it was ever acceptable "under the Constitution and laws of the United States" (Hall, 1997). The resolution does not apologize for the continuing effects of slavery in the form of currently existing racism. Hall's letter explicitly states that in the time "since the end of slavery . . . Congress has done much to address the effects of that legacy." Hall constructs the problem to be that "there was never an official apology for the horrible wrong" and that "this apology is long overdue."

Hall's (1997) apology is made by the Congress on behalf of the American people. Although there is never an explicit reference to whiteness, as in Clinton's (1997) apology, parts of the text suggest that the apology is made on behalf of Whites to African Americans. The clearest evidence for this position derives from an understanding of the rhetorically constructed purpose of the apology. The purpose of the apology is similar to the purpose of Clinton's Tuskegee apology. Hall acknowledges that "our resolution will not fix any lingering injustices resulting from slavery." Rather, he believes that the apology is necessary for reconciliation: "The reconciliation begins with an apology. We hope this apology will be a beginning of a new healing between the races." The apology is constructed as a confession of a past wrong and a request for forgiveness that will lead to a future of reconciliation: "This apology is long overdue, but it is never too late to confess that we were wrong as a nation and ask for forgiveness." The text establishes a dichotomy between "the races" that implies that the author views one race as giving the apology and the other race as receiving it. This dichotomy reflects the lingering impact of biological race talk in our culture, despite the fact that race and especially the concept of multiple races are a biological fiction. The overwhelming unity of human genetic makeup swamps any differences that have historically been attributed to the concept of race (Appiah, 1986, p. 21; Shipman, 1994, p. 269).

Functioning as ideological critics, one of our primary concerns in this undertaking is to interrogate the commonsense explanations offered for the apologies in question. In the words of Bill Clinton (1997), his apology is about moving the nation forward toward rebuilding a broken trust and becoming "one America." Congressman Tony Hall's (1997) measured expectations are revealed in his disclaimer that the resolution would not fix lingering injustices. He views an apology, however, as "the beginning of a new healing," a first step toward reconciliation. We question the functioning of these apologies and ask the following: If these efforts are not about fixing the lingering injustices resulting from slavery, why advance them? What are they truly about? Do we move forward toward becoming one America simply on the basis that these apologies are tendered? Indeed, we are unsure how we can "rebuild that broken trust," to use Clinton's words, without a thoroughgoing commitment to addressing the deep and ongoing issue of racism that was the basis for the rupturing of the trust in the first place. If these apologies are understood by White Americans as the fulfillment of their responsibility toward those who have suffered "the past injustices of American injustice," then it means that, having dispensed with this responsibility, they can move on. Indeed, within the context of such a perspective, the offering of one of these apologies becomes, for White Americans, an annoyance to be dispensed with. That many White Americans share this view is manifest from the President's town hall meetings on race during 1998. In these meetings, persons advancing these views received round applause of affirmation. Once the government presents such an apology, White Americans are then rhetorically empowered to confront African Americans in terms used by a White American on CNN concerning the Million Man March of 1995: "What more do they want?"

By stopping short of addressing the lingering injustices of racism in American society, these apologies are unable to function as effective antiracist documents. More than functioning to mask White culpability, they contribute to the United States' effort to ignore the fact that there are material benefits to racism. Beginning with slavery's unpaid labor, these benefits, gained at the expense of Black lives, have accrued for more than 300 years to other Americans. For example, Johnathan Kozol's work on the funding or lack of funding of America's public schools provides remarkable evidence that, unlike predominantly White communities, poor Black and Brown children have their future mortgaged as they continue to receive less than their fair share of America's material wealth.

Also, these apologies fail to address the stark reality of the continued material effects of racism on American lives in terms of material benefit to Whites and material loss to Blacks. In so doing, they squander the chance to help White Americans confront the difficult issues of White privilege directly resulting from racism. The apologies leave unchallenged the rhetorical foundation in which White Americans ground their oft used complaint that they "never had slaves." For these Americans, this is a favorite rejoinder to the observation that they are slavery's benefactors, thus sharing culpability for racism. These Whites tender such denial of responsibility and reject claims that they benefit from racism, even as they continue to reach into and make use of the contents of Peggy McIntosh's (1992) invisible knapsack that they wear, laden with White privileges as it is.

There is another facet to the issue of material consideration in these apologies: reparations. The $200,000 grant to set up a Center for Bioethics in Research and Health Care at Tuskegee University that accompanied President Clinton's (1997) apology for the Tuskegee experiment is woefully inadequate. It marked an important consideration as part of the process of addressing injustice of this nature, however: the issue of restitution. Grounded in biblical notions of justice, restitution has long been a part of America's puritanical traditions of correcting injustice. The renewed calls for reparations to African Americans represent an important aspect of any effective program seeking to address American racism.

Blacks in America have long challenged the nation to fulfill its moral ideal and do right. As early as 1829, David Walker confronted Whites with the challenge that Blacks should be treated as humans, and that one important step was open and official acknowledgment of the infliction on Blacks of slavery's injustices. Walker (1830/1965) stated, Americans have to "make a national acknowledgment to us for the wrongs they have inflicted on us" (p. 70). This charge has been expanded by Black nationalists such as Louis Farrakhan to a call for reparations. For example, the editor's preface to Walter Rodney's notable Black power thesis, *Groundings With My Brothers*, opens with an acknowledgment of the appalling conditions of Black people compared with Whites, declaring, "We, Black people, having realized this, demand from the White people economic and political power" (p. 5). The identification of the call for reparations with radical Black nationalism has resulted in the issue being ignored and conscripted to the margins of American public discourse. The question of reparations, however, continues to "challenge us to consider 380 years of history all at once, to tunnel inside our souls to discover what we truly believe about race and equality and the value of human suffering" (Merida, 1999). Despite efforts to detrude the reparations debate, efforts such as Robinson's (2000) *The Debt*, considered the boldest statement to date on the subject, will ensure its continuation as part of our public discourse. We contend that for the apologies under consideration here to function as an effective part of the antiracism programs seeking to create an America with "racial justice" for all, they need to be grounded in a broader program of reparations that will help us begin a long overdue but bold and imaginative program of doing the right thing about race and justice in America. Short of that, these apologies represent America's continued quest for racial harmony without racial justice.

CONCLUSION

The similarities and differences of the two texts discussed in this essay compared to traditional apologetic speeches of self-defense reveal some interesting implications of racial apologies. These apologies are similar to traditional speeches of self-defense in the sense that they are responses to specific accusations of a moral nature that impugn the character of the apologist. The Tuskegee study was "shameful" and "wrong." It was a moral "outrage." It was a racist "lie" that trampled the rights of U.S. citizens. Slavery was a "horrible wrong." It was unjust and caused much suffering. Both these apologies are offered for specific past racist events. There is no mention of the ongoing systemic and institutionalized racism that exists today or any real substantial advocacy of a change in material White privilege. Rather, the apologies are constructed as a response to an accusation about past immoral behavior. This is especially interesting given that the specified purposes of the apologies are the same. Each suggests that the apology should constitute a first step toward racial reconciliation, a way to overcome the racial divide in our country. Each apology also explicitly asks for forgiveness from African Americans. This similarity to traditional apologia might tempt the recipient to read these apologies just as the rhetors would have us read them—as transcendent. Clinton (1997) and Hall (1997) specify that the purposes of the apologies are to transcend the "racial divide," to "move forward," and cause "healing between the races." These apologies point to racial reconciliation resulting from apology and forgiveness as the way to transcend racism.

The differences of these texts from traditional apologetic form, however, reveal that this discourse is not truly transcendent but, rather, that it actually masks the denial of racism on the part of Whites. Both these apologies differ from the traditional characteristics of the apologia genre in an interesting way. A traditional speech of self-defense is made by a single person in defense of himself or herself. In both of these instances, the apologies were made by a single individual on behalf of the group to which they belong—the U.S. government, the Congress, the American people, and the nation. The fact that this group is White is always unmarked, although it is always juxtaposed to the explicitly racially marked group of African Americans to whom the apologies are offered.

These apologies draw on a symbolic resonance with a traditional rhetorical form, apologia, that makes them appear to be examples of "transcendent" discourse. When examined more closely, however, their differences from traditional apologetic form reveal that this resonance is really obscuring the protection of White material privilege. Therefore, racial apologies are similar to traditional apologia in the sense that they are speeches of self-defense. They are quite different, however, because they are constructed by White individuals in defense of Whites as a group to deflect personal responsibility for racism by masking White privilege. Rhetorical silences often protect the invisibility of the White norm in our culture and the material privilege that accompanies it (Crenshaw, 1997). In this instance, the denial of White privilege through rhetorical silence about whiteness is masked by its similarity to the traditional rhetorical form of apologia appealing to transcendence. By focusing on past events, these apologies construct racism as a reality of the past, not the present or future. The apology is constructed as the break with the racist past. If only African Americans will forgive Whites in response to the apology, racism can be transcended. This shifts the burden of making "racial progress" away from the advocacy of proposals for real material change and places it squarely on the shoulders of African Americans being asked to forgive Whites for past racist events.

Thus, although the voices demanding racial justice and a commitment to antiracism that created the exigency for the apologies were successful in eliciting a response, we contend that these racial apologies fall short of the demand. They contain yet another version of the rhetorical strategy of othering, which is the rhetorical practice of depicting people of color as having the characteristic of race while simultaneously assuming that White people are somehow not "raced." West (1993) notes that when Black people are "viewed as a them, the burden falls on Blacks to do all the cultural and moral work necessary for healthy race relations" (p. 3; see also Crenshaw, 1997, p. 264). These two apologies in their complete silence about White privilege shifted the burden of transcending racism to African Americans by constructing the apology as the break with the racist past if only African Americans will forgive Whites for past racism. Clinton (1997) concluded his apology with the explicit statement, "Today, all we can do is apologize. But you have the power, for only you—Mr. Shaw, the others who are here, the family members who are with us in Tuskegee—only you have the power to forgive." The rhetorical strategy of othering occurs all the time in our political discourse about racism. What is most interesting about this example of othering is that it was very effectively masked by its construction as an apology. The striking similarities to the traditional rhetorical form of apologia tempt us to read these apologies as transcendent when their real impact is the denial of White privilege. These insights have been generated in part through our comparison of current racial apologies to the traditional understanding of rhetorical apologia. Additional investigation of other racial apologies might make the case for the existence of a rhetorical genre of racial apologia and inform the answer to some interesting questions about the nature of postmodern apologia in general.

For now, however, we conclude that racial apologies that advocate no real material change in White privilege and construct racism as a past event to be transcended through the forgiveness of African Americans through a rhetorical practice of othering are inherently limited in their ability to contribute to antiracist progress. We also suggest that if the reparations debate is to make any serious progress, advocates for real material change will have to account for, if not outright confront, the recent historical context of how progress in race relations is currently being rhetorically constructed. Denial of White privilege is a powerful force in our culture, and to overcome it, any real apology must not be rhetorically constructed as a mask for the continuation of the racist distribution of material privilege. Rather, it must compel the recognition of the integral relationship between our symbolic constructions and the material experience of racism. In a broader sense, we also suggest that this criticism illustrates the productivity of using our understandings of traditional genre theory in ideological rhetorical criticism to reveal how the constellation of traditional rhetorical forms and similarities to them can function to mask White privilege in public political discourse. This approach may usefully guide us in negotiating the dangerous shoals of "White fetishism" as we work to make contributions to antiracist theory through the lens of critical whiteness studies.

APPENDIX

February 7, 2000

The Honorable Frank Keating

Governor of the State of Oklahoma

State Capitol Bldg.

Oklahoma City, OK 73105

Dear Governor Keating:

The Tulsa Race Riot Commission, established by House Joint Resolution No. 1035, is pleased to submit the following preliminary report.

The primary goal of collecting historical documentation on the Tulsa Race Riot of 1921 has been achieved. Attachment A is a summary listing of the record groups that have been gathered and stored at the Oklahoma Historical Society. Also included are summaries of some reports and the full text of selected documents to illustrate the breadth and scope of the collecting process. However, the Commission has not yet voted on historical findings, so these materials do not necessarily represent conclusions of the Commission.

At the last meeting, held February 4, 2000, the Commission voted on three actions. They are:

1) The Issue of Restitution

Whereas, the process of historical analysis by this Commission is not yet complete,

And Whereas, the archeological investigation into casualties and mass burials is not yet complete,

And Whereas, we have seen a continuous pattern of historical evidence that the Tulsa Race Riot of 1921 was the violent consequence of racial hatred institutionalized and tolerated by official federal, state, county, and city policy,

And Whereas, government at all levels has the moral and ethical responsibility of fostering a sense of community that bridges divides of ethnicity and race,

And Whereas, by statute we are to make recommendations regarding whether or not reparations can or should be made to the Oklahoma Legislature, the Governor of the State of Oklahoma, and the Mayor and City Council of Tulsa,

That, we, the 1921 Tulsa Race Riot Commission, recommend that restitution to the historic Greenwood Community, in real and tangible form, would be good public policy and do much to repair the emotional as well as physical scars of this most terrible incident in our shared past.

2) The Issue of Suggested Forms of Restitution in Priority Order

The Commission recommends

1) Direct payment of reparations to survivors of the Tulsa Race Riot.
2) Direct payment of reparations to descendants of the survivors of the Tulsa Race Riot.
3) A scholarship fund available to students affected by the Tulsa Race Riot.
4) Establishment of an economic development enterprise zone in the historic area of the Greenwood District.

5) A memorial for the reburial of any human remains found in the search for unmarked graves of riot victims.

3) The Issue of an Extension of the Tulsa Race Riot Commission

The Commission hereby endorses and supports House Bill 2468, which extends the life of the Commission in order to finish the historical report on the Tulsa Race Riot of 1921.

We, the members of the Tulsa Race Riot Commission, respectfully submit these findings for your consideration.

12

Autobiography, Rhetoric, and Frank McCourt's *Angela's Ashes* and *'Tis: A Memoir*

Patricia A. Sullivan and Steven R. Goldzwig

> *When I look back on my childhood I wonder how I survived at all. It was, of course, a miserable childhood: The happy childhood is hardly worth your while. Worse than the ordinary miserable childhood is the miserable Irish childhood, and worse yet is the miserable Irish Catholic childhood.*
>
> —Frank McCourt (1996, p. 11)

The Irish, especially Roman Catholic Irish, who arrived in the United States during the nineteenth and early twentieth centuries left behind oppression in Ireland but met a new type of oppression in the United States. The Irish were differentiated through language and visual representations as members of an inherently inferior race. As Jacobson (1998) observed, "Irishism" or "Celtism" in the middle of the nineteenth century was associated with "a fixed set of observable physical characteristics, such as skin and hair color, facial type, and physique" (p. 48). An article in *Harper's Weekly* in 1851 described the "Celtic physiognomy" as distinguished by the "small and somewhat upturned nose [and] the black tint of the skin" (as cited in Jacobson, 1998, p. 48). In the nineteenth century, the Irish were often depicted in cartoons, along with African Americans, as simians. The Irish were characterized as "lawless" in publications such as the *Atlantic Monthly*, and their eagerness to assimilate was perceived as a special threat to the Republic. As an *Atlantic Monthly* article in 1896 noted, "A Celt . . . lacks the solidarity, the balance, the judgments, the moral staying power of the Anglo-Saxon" (as cited in Jacobson, 1998, p. 49).

Ignatiev (1995) traced the changing fortunes of the Irish and "how they became white." He chronicled how Irish Catholics, "an oppressed race in Ireland, became part of an oppressing race in America" (p. 1). In *How the Irish Became White*, Ignatiev argued that the Irish, free blacks, and African Americans participated in "a common culture of the lowly" (p. 2). Jim Crow and Jim Dandy shared the antebellum stage with Pat and Bridget: All symbolized the inferiority of their race. The Irish, however, realized that they were living in a culture in which color was an important social marker, and Ignatiev claimed that they quickly adapted to that culture.[1]

Frank McCourt's autobiographical accounts speak to the assimilation of the Irish in the United States. *Angela's Ashes* (McCourt, 1996) and *'Tis: A Memoir* (McCourt, 1999) reflect the "transparency phenomenon." Because McCourt's narrator is white, he moves seamlessly through the world, and race is not an issue for him. As Lopez (1996) observed, "Within the logic of transparency, the race of non-whites is readily apparent and regularly noted, while the race of whites is consistently overlooked and scarcely ever mentioned" (p. 23). McCourt's narrator writes as "everyman" (every white man), and his story belongs to an American autobiographical tradition documented by scholars. In *Angela's Ashes* and *'Tis*, however, the narrator complicates matters by drawing attention to issues of class that informed his process of assimilation as an everyman who represents the immigrant experience.[2] Although "whiteness" is transparent in the autobiographical accounts, class issues are visible. McCourt's everyman foregrounds the class-based discrimination he faced. The accounts have resonated with many readers in the United States who see him as representing the triumphant immigrant experience, but his attention to class-based issues has been overlooked. *Angela's Ashes* and *'Tis* directly challenge the "myth of classlessness" in the United States. Critical attention to McCourt's popular narratives suggests they are more subversive than they may appear to be to the casual reader.

In this chapter, we provide an overview of scholarship on American autobiographical traditions and suggest a link between the rhetorical functions of traditional American autobiography and the construction of whiteness in the United States. Next, *Angela's Ashes* and *'Tis* are analyzed as texts that both uphold and subvert American autobiographical traditions. Finally, we explore implications of our study for exposing the transparency phenomenon as it functions for race and class in the United States.

EVERYMAN AND THE AMERICAN AUTOBIOGRAPHICAL TRADITION

Scholarship on autobiography has flourished during the past 30 years. Rhetorical scholars, however, have given limited attention to autobiographical discourse as a site of inquiry. For Benson (1974), Griffin (1990), and Solomon (1991), autobiographies are rhetorical when the writers are advocates. As Benson claimed, *The Autobiography of Malcolm X* "goes beyond the closed world of literary form towards the open forum of rhetorical address" (pp. 11-12). Griffin and Solomon identified the special ethos of the autobiographer as an advocate. Solomon observed, "The personal experience of the author becomes an almost indisputable refutation of those alternate stories" (p. 368). Oravec (1991), in responding to Solomon's analysis of the autobiographies of Elizabeth Cady Stanton and Anna Howard Shaw, suggested that the criticism failed to acknowledge "the ideological quality of autobiography" (p. 384). Bjorkland (1998), a sociologist, argued that autobiographers are aware of their roles as rhetoricians who are communicating with readers as audiences.

For our purposes in analyzing McCourt's work, scholarly efforts to define a distinctly American autobiographical tradition are significant. Sayre (1964, 1972, 1977, 1980) and Stone (1982) have defined an American autobiographical tradition that valued individualism and chronicled the lives of exemplary individuals. In his work, Sayre suggested the development of autobiography as a genre paralleled the development of the nation. Sayre (1980) stated, "In writing his or her story, the autobiographer becomes the known individual that most Americans would like to be" (p. 167). In explaining the American quest for individual "distinction," Sayre turned to John Adams. Adams believed that the American quest for distinction, for recognition from others, stemmed from the national choice to abandon titles and other aristocratic trappings. Sayre summarized the need for distinction as stemming "not only from a desire for praise but from a dreadful fear of being despised and obscure" (p. 153).

Sayre's discussion of distinction also identified, through analyses of autobiographical writing, a fundamental tension between individualism and conformity in the American character. The tension was explained through the writing of Adams. According to Sayre via Adams, an exemplary American sought distinction or fame through emulation rather than imitation. The exemplar emulated worthy models but also exceeded their accomplishments. American autobiographies thus reflect the American national character and American civilization. Stone (1982) echoed Sayre's observations and suggested that "autobiography is firmly rooted in our culture" (p. 3).

A number of scholars have responded to assessments such as Stone's by proposing that the culture described by Stone is male and European American. As Brodki and Schenck argued (1988), critics who view autobiographies as the lives of exemplary individuals have been defining a genre as practiced, for the most part, by men. They also addressed issues relative to class and the exemplary life by suggesting that "the class stance of the male autobiographer is summed up by a famous characterization of Henry Adams as a 'representative of the time, a mirror of his era'" (p. 2). Because women traditionally have not been public representatives of their times or eras, female autobiographers represent a different approach to chronicling their lives or selves.

The suggestion is that women have written autobiographies that are strongly rooted in their culture. Women were not occupying public positions of privilege that invited them to "write their lives large." The suggestion is that American autobiography as defined by scholars, such as Sayre and Stone, is the life of a public man of privilege.

Rosenblatt (1980) also challenged traditional definitions of autobiography and said that the genre of black autobiography is marked by two characteristics—the desire to exercise life choices and the recognition that black people's choices are limited in a racist society. He argued for "a special reality" that marks the autobiographies of minority voices. Thus, the black autobiographer's story is framed by an ongoing self-awareness of race.

Black autobiographers and others who write from the margins or borders of dominant culture write from autobiographical perspectives that make their "special realities" visible. In foregrounding their positionality, these autobiographers as rhetoricians, at least indirectly, draw attention to the transparency phenomenon that marks the autobiographical narrative of the exemplary individual—the male individual who writes from a position of privilege.

Berryman (1999) proposed that although critics have attempted to develop a coherent theoretical framework for studying autobiography, the multiple theories of autobiography reflect the diversity of the United States. Whereas scholars such as Sayre and Stone struggled to identify the characteristics that mark American autobiography as a genre, Berryman suggested that pluralism is the defining characteristic of American autobiography. The developments in autobiographical criticism also reflect the influence of postmodernism. Berryman noted, "With less worry about the rival status of fact and fiction, and less concern with formalist definitions, the critic of autobiography is empowered to be a self-reflexive, politically correct, cultural historian" (p. 12). Even as critics debate how autobiography should be defined as a genre, they agree that autobiographical texts offer fruitful sites for studying issues associated with self-awareness. A common message that emerges from whiteness studies is the urgency, in Flagg's (1993) terms, for whites to cultivate "a carefully conceived race consciousness, one that begins with whites' consciousness of whiteness" (as cited in Lopez, 1996, p. 22). Because autobiographical texts communicate dimensions of self-awareness, they demand critical attention from scholars who are urging white people to develop racial self-awareness.

WHITENESS STUDIES

At the beginning of the twentieth century, W. E. B. DuBois (1903/1990) published the *The Souls of Black Folk* and presented a case for "the color line" as the fundamental problem of the new century: "The problem of the twentieth century is the problem of the color-line—the relation of the darker to the lighter races of men in Asia and Africa, in America, and the islands of the sea" (p. 16). DuBois observed that one question had dominated discussions of race in the nineteenth century: "What shall be done with the Negroes?" (p. 16). Scholars who study whiteness have suggested that we are still asking the same question, although we have broadened it to ask, "What shall be done with non-white people?" Indeed, when DuBois posed the question, the fate of black people was an overt topic of discussion. With some exceptions, contemporary allusions to race tend to be covert.[3] White people, however, as in DuBois's time, rarely see race as their problem. As Johnson (1999) observed, "In addressing race, in the law, in literature, in popular culture, in communication studies, in religion or other areas of our lives, whiteness is privileged, normalized, deified, and raceless" (p. 1).

Wander, Martin, and Nakayama (1999) emphasized the importance of distinguishing the terms *race* and *white* from *whiteness*. In the eighteenth and nineteenth centuries, the terms race and white came to be associated with "an explicit assertion of superiority" (p. 14). Scientific studies were used to support prejudices and assumptions concerning the superiority of the white race. It was presumed that the natural world was ordered in a hierarchical fashion, and that whites were the most evolved race in "the great chain of being" (Webster, 1992, as cited in Wander et al., 1999, p. 15). Racial typologies, scientific assertions concerning inherent superiority and inherent inferiority, provided the basis for arguing that the social order was a natural outgrowth of the physical world. The term whiteness thus refers to the construction of "a historical systematic structural race-based superiority" (p. 15).

In an effort to (de)center whiteness and understand presumptions concerning white superiority, a number of scholars have documented the relationship between patterns of U.S. immigration and the legal construction of whiteness in the United States. For our purposes, assimilation of Irish immigrants as white is of particular importance. From a legal perspective, the Irish had advantages in the United States. In the early nineteenth century, U.S. law established blacks as noncitizens if they were free. According to the Naturalization Acts of 1790, 1795, and 1801, "free white persons" could be naturalized in American courts. As Lopez (1996) noted, although Irish immigrants faced discrimination, they were more likely to be defined as white based on a "commonsense" logic that informed court rulings. Courts defined white as a characteristic strictly based on physical appearance. This "commonsense" approach circumscribed white "as a purely physical phenomenon, an unchanging division of humankind that occurs in nature" (p. 25).

In the years prior to the Civil War, however, nativist sentiment prevailed and many politicians, writers, and ethnologists depicted the Irish as members of a "dark race" (Roediger, 1991, p. 133). When the Irish and blacks were compared on the basis of race, the latter were often cast in more favorable terms. Census records suggested confusion about how the Irish should be categorized. The Irish were not classified as either "native" or "foreign" (p. 133). In addition, African Americans and the Irish shared common ground as residents of the United States. They lived together in poor neighborhoods and did the hard work that native-born Americans did not want to do, particularly in domestic service and the transportation industry. Both groups were vilified and the targets of nativist rhetoric. Although the Irish shared historical bonds with African Americans, their interests diverged as the Irish came to identify themselves as white.

Through a history of labor and politics, Roediger and Ignatiev traced the construction of the Irish as white. The prefamine Irish arrived in the United States with enough resources to make some choices concerning employment and where they settled. These immigrants, however, were still poorer and less skilled than most native-born Americans and other European immigrants. The immigrants who arrived between 1845 and 1855, in the wake of the Great Famine, were even poorer and less skilled than their predecessors. Roediger (1991) observed, "Their numbers afforded them the possibility to become white. The desperate nature of their labor and their longings ensured that they would embrace that possibility to the fullest" (p. 139). In the midst of nativist sentiment, the Democratic Party mobilized the Irish to see themselves as white. When the Irish and free blacks were in competition for unskilled jobs, the Irish easily won these jobs. It was much easier for the Irish to defend their right to work based on their whiteness rather than their "Irishness." The Irish became white to work and avoid a "fierce backlash from native-born artisans" (p. 148).

As the Irish struggled to become accepted as white, they, along with immigrants from other countries, were viewed with suspicion by native-born citizens, who considered themselves the "real" Americans—those who would uphold American traditions. In the 1880s, observers such as James Russell Lowell expressed concern that the newly arrived immigrants would transform the character of America. Lowell reflected nostalgically on a time when the United States was home to true native-born Americans. He longed for a time before the arrival of the latest waves of immigrants, and the following observation revealed his concerns:

> While strolling through Boston's Public Garden he noticed two Irishmen looking at an equestrian statue of George Washington and

> wondering who was the personage thus commemorated. "I had been brought up among the living traditions of Lexington, Concord, Bunker's Hill, and the siege of Boston. To these men Ireland was still their country, and America a place to get their daily bread." (as cited in Kammen, 1991 p. 228)

Lowell questioned the wisdom of viewing the newly arrived immigrants as equal to "old stock Yankees" (p. 228). The newly arrived immigrants thus faced pressures to assimilate even as they identified with their homelands. The Irish responded to these pressures by "becoming white."

Wander et al. (1999) have cautioned that whiteness, like all categories, is "leaky" (p. 15). Because whiteness is a leaky category, "race can *only* be seen in relation to other categories, such as class, gender, sexuality, and so on, that render any category problematic" (p. 15). Through our case study of Frank McCourt's autobiographical writing, we enter the dialogue on "(de)centering whiteness" and foreground whiteness as a leaky category.

ANGELA'S ASHES AND 'TIS: NARRATIVES OF AN EXEMPLARY LIFE

The most apparent theme of Frank McCourt's narratives is one that is highly recognizable to readers from the United States. In a fundamental sense, the thread running through the narratives is newly arrived immigrant "makes it in the United States." In some respects, McCourt's story parallels the stories of other Americans whose stories are part of the larger search for a national culture. Mulford (1999), for example, explained the function that Benjamin Franklin's story played in providing standards for exemplary conduct and, in turn, providing "safeguards against social and economic instability" (p. 4). Franklin died in 1790, and early in the nineteenth century, segments of his autobiography were in print: "Stories of persons who had successfully completed that transition from dependence to independence in their own lives had an increasingly symbolic importance as the century wore on" (p. 5). Just as Franklin's autobiographical accounts served a didactic role for readers (immigrants, newly freed indentured servants, sharecroppers assuming freeholds, tinkers, and tailors), other autobiographical accounts have fulfilled a similar function.

In featuring a recognizable theme that served a didactic function, McCourt's autobiographical accounts thus parallel the recognizable tales of exemplary Americans such as Franklin. A more subtle theme, however, also binds together McCourt's narratives. McCourt's experiences in Limerick and New York were marked by class issues, and the narratives draw attention to these issues. McCourt's narrator complicates the story of the exemplary individual by chronicling how industriousness and skill were inadequate in the face of class differences that interfered with his ability to "get ahead." The narrator challenges the reader to recognize the class differences often denied in an American culture that foregrounds meritocracy. Attention to differences within whiteness invite the reader to address the myth of classlessness in the United States. *Angela's Ashes* (McCourt, 1996) and *'Tis* (McCourt, 1999) function as narratives that uphold the white male European American autobiographical tradition as defined by scholars such as Sayre and Stone. McCourt's narrator is an immigrant who makes it in America because of his intelligence, wit, cleverness, and industriousness. The narrator's story also speaks to other dimensions of the immigrant experience. In foregrounding class issues that made it more difficult for him to make it, the narrator reflects what Eakin (1991) called the "ongoing interplay between dominant and marginal texts" (as cited in Berryman, 1999, p. 82). Eakin, as a counterpoint to Sayre and Stone, suggested "the pluralistic nature of American culture has been decisive in the development of American autobiography" (as cited in Berryman, 1999, p. 82).

McCourt as the Ambitious Immigrant

When we read McCourt's autobiographical accounts, we were struck by the predictable elements of his story. The Irish had become white in McCourt's time, and his story is part of the larger American story of European immigrants who "made good." Indeed, the narrator casts the Limerick of his childhood as a wretched place where poor families lived under primitive conditions. In Limerick, the McCourt family endured rats, dampness, and the stench of communal lavatories. Throughout both narratives, life in New York City is cast as distinctly superior to life in Limerick.

Ultimately, the narrator enacts the claim that it is possible to make it in America if one is ambitious. *Angela's Ashes* (McCourt, 1996) and *'Tis* (McCourt, 1999) were published at a time of antiimmigrant backlash. As Gutierrez (1995) observed, legislation at the state and federal levels targets newly arrived immigrants. New arrivals to the United States thus encounter some of the same nativist sentiments that their predecessors faced when they arrived in this country.

During a time in which the United States is struggling with tensions over immigration issues, McCourt's narratives serve as a reminder that earlier immigrants assimilated. McCourt's narrator recounts how he became acculturated to life in the United States. *Angela's Ashes* (McCourt, 1996) opens with the narrator's observation that his "mother and father should have stayed in New York" (p. 11). The narrator thus sets the tone of the narrative by revealing the longing he felt for the United States. His parents, Angela and Malachy, were born in Ireland, but like so many generations of Irish citizens, they migrated to the United States. McCourt's parents met and married in the United States, and Frank was born in the United States. The family, including five children, struggled in Brooklyn.

Although jobs were not plentiful in the 1930s and 1940s, the narrator attributes the family's poverty to his father's problem with "the drink." As the narrator explains Malachy's failings, he casts them in stereotypes associated with the Irish. When Malachy does secure a job, he fails to bring home his wages. Angela, with her children in tow, goes from bar to bar trying to find her husband. Malachy is an engaging storyteller who regales his son with the story of Cuchulain (McCourt, 1996),

> a greater hero than Hercules or Achilles that the Greeks were always bragging about and he could take on King Arthur and all his knights in a fair fight which, of course, you could never get with an Englishman anyway. (p. 21)

He offers nickels to his children who "promise to die for Ireland" (p. 25).

Because Malachy was a "failure" in America, the family returned to Ireland after the death of a daughter, Margaret. Angela experienced a deep depression after the death of Margaret, and her Irish relatives living in the United States urged the return to Ireland. The Irish relatives, women who were married to men who were willing to work, composed a letter to send to Angela's mother in Limerick and asked her to send money so the family could return to Ireland. They suggested in the letter that Angela had married a misfit who would not make it in the United States. The relatives viewed Malachy as an "other" because he was from Northern Ireland rather than the Republic, and they observed (McCourt, 1996):

> That shows you what can happen when you marry someone from the North for they have no control over themselves up there a bunch of Protestants they are. He goes out for work every day but

> we know he spends his time in saloons and gets a few dollars for sweeping floors and lifting barrels and spends the money right back on the drink. (p. 45)

McCourt's narrator thus used the letter written by the Irish relatives to cast his father as someone who failed in the land of opportunity due to his own shortcomings. The United States, as depicted through the narrator's voice, welcomes those who are industrious and willing to work.

Throughout *Angela's Ashes* (McCourt, 1996), the narrator depicts himself as someone who is shocked by the conditions in Ireland and has what it takes to succeed in the United States. When the family returned to Ireland and stayed for a few days in the North with Malachy's family, the narrator expresses how shocked he was by the crowded conditions and the chamber pot. Clearly, the narrator suggests the conditions were much more primitive than the ones they experienced in New York:

> Mam snores hink, Dad snores honk. I get up and poke at Dad. I have to pee. He says, Use the chamber pot.
>
> What?
>
> Under the bed, son. The chamber pot. It has roses on it and maidens cavorting in the glen. Pee in that, son.
>
> I want to ask him what he's talking about for even if I'm bursting I feel strange peeing into a pot with roses and maidens cavorting, whatever they are. We had nothing like this in Classon Avenue where Mrs. Leibowitz sang in the lavatory while we clutched ourselves in the hall. (p. 49)

The narrator provides additional descriptions of the outhouse he used when he needed to "sit" on the chamber pot.

Of course, Malachy's job situation would not be any better in Ireland than it was in the United States because, as McCourt's narrator emphasizes, the problem with work was with his father, not with the country in which the family resided. Malachy's relatives assured him the economy in Ireland was much worse than in the United States, and that he should have stayed in the country where Mr. Roosevelt would make certain people had jobs.

The narrator thus casts his father as a man who lives by trying to get "something for nothing" (a violator against the American way). Malachy was as unambitious in Ireland as he was in the United States. The family was left with no recourse but to move to Limerick, where Angela's mother lived. Angela's mother helped the family get "set up," but she said that was all she could do. She emphasized that Malachy would need to take care of the family and, in the words of McCourt's narrator (McCourt, 1996), "get up off his arse, get a job, go on the dole, go for the charity at the St. Vincent de Paul Society or go on the relief" (p. 59). The family lived under miserable conditions, and a good portion of *Angela's Ashes* is devoted to chronicling those conditions. Malachy is cast as a proud man with "grand airs" (p. 98). For example, on Christmas the family is reduced to eating a pig's head for dinner. Frank carried the pig's head through the streets while his father sat at home by the fire, smoking a cigarette. The narrator observes, "Even if Dad came he wouldn't be much use because he never carries anything, parcels, bags, packages. If you carry such things you lose your dignity. That's what he says" (p. 98). In sum, the narrator of *Angela's Ashes* casts his father as a shiftless, irresponsible man.

In both autobiographical accounts, the narrator contrasts his own attitudes and conduct with those of his father. The narrator chronicles his bouts with typhoid and a serious eye infection but presents himself as a "self-starter" who was industrious even in the midst of trouble. The message from the narrator is that when he encountered adversity, he had the wherewithal to make it. He planned to return to America, and he worked to make that journey a reality. He also brought money to his mother, helped a man with arthritis make coal deliveries, and spoke with pride of his status as a working man. His classmates refrained from teasing him about his poverty when he had a job (McCourt, 1996):

> They don't call me names anymore. They don't laugh at my scabby eyes. They want to know how I got such a good job at 11 years of age and what I'm paid and if I'll have that job forever. They want to know if there are any good jobs going in the coal yards and would I put in a good word for them. (p. 264)

As he looked back over his life, the narrator took pride in drawing contrasts between his own work patterns and those of his father.

The diligence of the young McCourt recalls the diligence of the young Franklin. Every job in Limerick was part of McCourt's plan to return to America. The narrative suggests he was willing to endure humiliation to actualize his dreams. When he was 14 years old, he was preparing to begin a job delivering telegrams. He was so concerned about his shabby appearance that he removed his only set of clothing and stood in the backyard naked while washing the clothing with carbolic acid. Because he had nothing else to wear while the clothes were drying (and drying slowly in the damp Limerick air), he wore his grandmother's woolen dress. The narrator expresses shame over the circumstances and observes (McCourt, 1996),

> You're not supposed to wear your grandmother's old dress when she's dead and you're a boy but what does it matter if it keeps you warm and you're in bed under the blankets where no one will ever know. The dress has the smell of old dead grandmother and I worry she might rise from the grave and curse me before the whole family and all assembled. (p. 307)

McCourt, however, was a temporary telegram boy. When he had the opportunity to take the test to settle into a permanent job, he decided against it. He was mocked by people at the telegram office, who said he thought he was "too good" for such a job. Although Malachy was not industrious, his son as narrator presents himself as someone who has the industry to make it in America. When the narrator recounts his efforts to return to America, he echoes the virtues of Franklin's narrator, who emphasized industry and efforts to correct an "erratum" in his life. As a narrator framing his life story, he also parallels Franklin's "classic" American autobiographical account by adopting the sinner's tone of humility. As critics such as Sayre (1964) have suggested, the humble tone of Franklin's narrator served to magnify his accomplishments. The same might be said of McCourt's narrator.

Because McCourt's narrator has shortcomings, he is all the more exemplary because his story suggests others could overcome their errata and make it. For example, the narrator makes much of his "impure" adolescent thoughts and "interfering" with himself (McCourt, 1996, p. 292). He also expresses regrets about his sexual encounters with Theresa, a young woman who died from consumption. He delivered telegrams to her house, and they had the "excitement" (p. 324). After she died, he feared she was in hell because he had loved her and they had "tumbled naked and wild on the green sofa" (p. 325). He also confesses that he accepted a job writing threatening letters on behalf of Mrs. Brigid Finucane. Because he wanted to go to America, he accepted the job and stole paper and envelopes from Woolworth's so he would be able to write the letters.

Mrs. Finucane wanted to collect money that was owed to her, and she complimented McCourt on the sharp tone of the letters. The narrator notes that he became so taken with pleasing Mrs. Finucane and making money that "I begin to throw in words I hardly understand myself" (p. 333).

The narrator of *Angela's Ashes* thus emphasizes that the young McCourt would bend his ethical code to return to America. Finally, McCourt had enough money to book his passage to America, and his saga continues in New York and is recounted in *'Tis* (McCourt, 1999). The narrative of the industrious youth continues as McCourt makes his way with all the industry he demonstrated in Ireland. Of course, America held more opportunities for the industrious than Ireland ever did. He sailed for America in October 1949. From the opening of *'Tis*, the narrator suggests qualities that will help him actualize his dreams in America. He is open to meeting people, and he is a careful observer of character. A priest who McCourt met on the ship from Ireland chided him for talking to a deck hand about Dostoyevsky and neglecting to talk to rich Protestants who might have helped him find a job. McCourt, according to the priest, was wasting time because there would not be "many Help Wanted signs requiring a knowledge of Dostoyevsky" (p. 18). The narrator has offered a reminder of what he will become, a successful writer, and shares an "inside joke" with the reader.

The narrator casts himself as the typical immigrant who must learn the ways of his adopted country, but he also sets himself apart by drawing attention to his intellect. The priest, regardless of his criticism, was an important contact for McCourt and helped him find a job in New York City. He stayed in a room with the priest, who chided him for his primitive ways. The narrator's account, of course, cues the reader into how far he had come in America (McCourt, 1999):

> it's hard to know what to do when you make a mistake your first night in America but I'm sure in no time I'll be a regular Yank doing everything right. I'll order my own hamburger, learn to call chips french fries, joke with waitresses, and never again dry myself with a bath mat. (p. 21)

The priest made a connection with Boss Flynn, and McCourt, the newly arrived immigrant from Ireland, got a job at the Biltmore. He went through a series of jobs as a laborer, invariably comforted that on Third Avenue "there's hardly a block without an Irish bar" (p. 27). He emphasized that he was willing to do just about any odd job for an extra dollar to actualize his dream and have a better life.

The narrative theme featured thus far in our analysis is a recognizable one in American autobiography. McCourt, unlike his father Malachy, was industrious and would return to the land of opportunity. A clear message dominates McCourt's autobiographical writing: Industry will lead to success in America. From this perspective, McCourt is the exemplary male European American autobiographer as defined by scholars such as Sayre and Stone. Another theme, however, informs McCourt's autobiographical writing. As he narrates the story of the ambitious immigrant, the story is tempered by an awareness of class differences. Through his narratives, McCourt challenges the myth of classlessness in America.

McCourt as the Ambitious Immigrant From an Underclass

The narrator of *Angela's Ashes* (McCourt, 1996) recounts experiences with class differences in Limerick. As a boy, he was surrounded by rats, flies, fleas, and the stench from a communal lavatory. In describing the major drawback to his living arrangements as a child, the narrator says,

> We can chase the rats and kill them. We can slap at the flies and the fleas and kill them but there's nothing we can do about the neighbors and their buckets. If we're out in the lane playing and we see someone with a bucket, we call to our own house, Bucket coming, close the door, close the door, and whoever is inside runs to the door. In warm weather we run to close the door all day because we know which families have the worst buckets. (p. 211)

The narrator's living conditions reflected his class position, and he refers to the "other world," "the streets of respectable people" (p. 215).

Two other experiences recounted by the narrator also suggest, at least in hindsight, an awareness of class differences in Ireland. Because his parents were on the dole, McCourt did not receive appropriate treatment for an eye infection until it had become quite serious. The narrator recounts the humiliating experience of demonstrating "you're desperate enough for public assistance" (McCourt, 1996, p. 225). Women, with their children, behaved deferentially as they approached a Mr. Coffey and Mr. Kane and sought vouchers for medical treatment:

> Mr. Coffee and Mr. Kane love to have a good laugh with the women. They'll decide if you're desperate enough for the public assistance or if you're sick enough to see a doctor. . . . Mr. Coffee and Mr. Kane are funny men, they'd give Laurel and Hardy a run for their money. (p. 225)

The sarcastic tone of the narrative suggests Coffee and Kane functioned as a comedy duo whose routines played on the misery of the poor.

The biggest disappointment for the narrator, however, was the limitation his class placed on his education in Limerick. The headmaster at McCourt's school saw promise in him and wanted him to go to secondary school and the university. His mother was summoned by the headmaster to discuss the boy's future. She hesitated because she did not have "a decent dress or a proper coat" (McCourt, 1996, p. 288). The headmaster recognized that the "messenger boy trap" (p. 289) awaited McCourt, a boy who had abilities but no resources. Instead, the headmaster recommended to Angela that she take her son to the Christian Brothers for more schooling. Even with the headmaster's recommendation, the door was shut in McCourt's face. McCourt and his mother made themselves as presentable as possible and went to the Christian Brothers. The superior, Brother Murray, took one look at the pair and said there was no room for McCourt at the school.

Angela reminded her son that the Church had rejected him twice, once as an altar boy and once as a student, due to his economic circumstances. In *Angela's Ashes*, the narrator suggests that he did not care about school and just wanted to get a job and be a man—the man his father had never been. Of course, throughout both autobiographical accounts, the narrator said he had two dreams, America and education. Education was a dream he believed he could actualize in America.

The narrator thus delineated stark class differences in Limerick. In Limerick, the class differences were marked by differences in basic living circumstances—food, shelter, health care, and education. In America, the land of opportunity, the class differentiations were more subtle. Obvious class differences existed in Ireland and were taken for granted. As a newly arrived immigrant, the narrator encountered the myth of classlessness, and *'Tis*, at least in part, is the story of how the author's life unfolded using that myth as a reference point.

The narrator recounts his journey in 1949 on the *Irish Oak* and claims he knew his Limerick background would work against him in New York. The first officer on the ship was from Dublin and "sneered at Limerick"

(McCourt, 1999, p. 13). McCourt was dreaming of Limerick, "city of gray miseries," as he sailed to America (p. 15). The narrator, looking back, says his perspective at that time was that "smiles opened doors" in America, and his "destroyed teeth" would hold him back (p. 15). At that point, he seemed to assume that all Americans had perfect teeth.

'Tis indicates that the newly arrived immigrant soon became aware of class differences. He heard that the Irish "owe everything to the Democratic Party" (McCourt, 1999, p. 24), and the job he obtained as houseman at the Biltmore provided his first introduction to class differences. He was instructed to be "invisible" in his job cleaning the lobby (p. 31). The man who instructed him in playing the role of "the invisible man cleaning the lobby" (p. 31) also delineated the possibilities for a newly arrived immigrant from Ireland. None of those possibilities included education or a professional job:

> He tells me to keep my eye on the ball, don't forget to shower every day, this is America, stay sober, stick with your own kind of people, you can't go wrong with the Irish, go easy with the drink, and in a year I might rise to the rank of porter or busboy and make tips and, who knows, rise up to be a waiter and wouldn't that be the end of all my worries. He says anything is possible in America, Look at me, I have four suits. (p. 31)

As a lobby cleaner, McCourt had the opportunity to observe "golden" college girls (p. 32). He struggled with how to behave around golden girls from such a different social class than his own. Furthermore, he knew that if he opened his mouth, his teeth would frighten them. All he could do was lock himself "in a toilet cubicle and interfere with myself" (p. 33).

The job at the Biltmore was humiliating, and McCourt had constant reminders of his status in America. His eyes were infected and he had to "pull the lids apart with thumb and forefinger" (McCourt, 1999, p. 38). People stared at him "as if he were some class of leper" (p. 38). He noted, however, that according to the shop steward, he was above the Puerto Ricans or spics: "that's a new word, spics, and I know from the way he says it he doesn't like Puerto Ricans" (p. 38). The worst part about the job, however, was the constant contrast between his own position and that of the privileged college students who came to the Biltmore for drinks. He was invisible to them as a human being, but they did, on occasion, stare at his eyes. The narrator suggests that educated people should know better than to stare at those who are less fortunate:

> They shouldn't stare. They should know better the way their mothers and fathers are spending fortunes to make them educated and what's the use of all that education if you're so ignorant that you stare at people just off the boat with red eyes? (p. 40)

The ultimate humiliation for McCourt came when one of the female college students could not find a paper napkin with the phone number of a Princeton boy written on it. He was assured that the young lady was the daughter of an influential man and that he better find that napkin. He was ordered to go through all the trash he had swept away and to find the napkin in the midst of all types of waste, including "coffee grounds, bits of toast, fishbones, eggshells, grapefruit skins" (p. 41). When he could not find the napkin, McCourt played the role of the clever new arrival in America and made up a number and wrote it on a napkin. The maitre d' received a generous tip for forcing McCourt to find the napkin, and the narrator indicates "my only sorrow is that I won't be there when she calls that number" (p. 41).

The way the narrator explains it, he pondered why America was known as the land of the free. Due to his economic situation, Frank had limited possibilities, even though he was in the land of opportunity. Although he faced many humiliations in America, the narrator of *'Tis* casts him as someone who was curious and interested in improving himself through intellectual pursuits. He received a tip from a bartender, who told him he could get a library card and sit in the New York Public Library whenever he wanted to read. The bartender assured McCourt that visits to the library would improve him and set him apart from "the rest of the bogtrotters getting off the boat and stupefying themselves with the drink. Read your Johnson, read your Pope and avoid the dreamy micks" (McCourt, 1999, p. 28). The librarians were friendly, unlike the ones in Ireland, "who stood guard and protected the books against the likes of me" (p. 28).

Even when he went to the movies, he was reminded of his position in society. The narrator notes that in New York City, the ushers used big words, "consume" rather than "eat," when they told him he could not bring food into the theater. That meant he could not go to the movies and watch the Marx Brothers or *Hamlet* and eat the treats he brought in unless he concealed them under a raincoat. In Limerick, "you could bring in fish and chips or a good feed of pig's feet and a bottle of snout if the humor was on you" (McCourt, 1999, p. 35), but this was forbidden in places frequented by "Park Avenue" (p. 35). When McCourt tried to eat the food he had concealed, the people around him shushed him: "I know they're not the ordinary type of people who go to gangster films or musicals. These are people who probably graduated from college and live on Park Avenue and know every line of *Hamlet*" (p. 35).

Life in America was difficult, and in many respects, the narrator invites the reader to go beyond attributing those problems to immigrant status. Certainly, immigration issues are tied to the particular position McCourt occupies in *'Tis*, but in many respects class issues are prominently featured. From the humiliating experiences at work to the embarrassing experiences in his social life, the narrator recounts the challenges he faced based on his social class.

The class-based challenges are most apparent in the narrator's stories concerning his marriage to a woman from a different social class and his effort to find a teaching job after he graduated from New York University. The narrator says he became "so obsessed" with a young woman named Mike Small that he could not concentrate on his schoolwork. He hesitated to tell her much about his life, however, "because of the same and I don't think she'd understand especially when she grew up in a small American town where everyone had everything" (McCourt, 1999, p. 198). Mike Small was from New England, and the narrator says he remembered that, at one time, "No Irish Need Apply" signs had appeared in New England (p. 199). When he visited her family, they seemed aloof and unwelcoming:

> No one speaks to me and I'm wondering how Mike Small can go off and leave me standing here with the father and the grandmother ignoring me. I never know what to say to people at times like this. Should I say, How's the tugboat business? or should I tell the grandmother she did a wonderful job raising Mike. (p. 199)

In New York City, the class differences translate into Mike's interest in uptown life and McCourt's interest in Village life. The narrator claims he did not understand uptown cocktail parties at which people engaged in meaningless conversation and ate "little things on bits of stale bread and crackers" (p. 203).

McCourt's life as a student differed from Mike's as well. To support himself, McCourt worked on the docks and at a bank. He did not have time to be a "proper college student" who debated philosophical issues and discussed Camus and Hemingway. The major blow for McCourt came, in the narrator's terms, when he graduated from New York

University and had trouble finding a job. He passed the board of education exams and was certified to teach English. The bias he faced due to his Irish background was a problem, and when he finally landed a job at a vocational and technical school where a teacher had resigned, he was shocked by the salary. Furthermore, he dreamed of the status associated with teaching in a suburban school (McCourt, 1999):

> I wanted to work in one of their suburban schools, Long Island, Westchester, where the boys and girls were bright, cheerful, smiling, attentive, their pens poised as I discoursed on *Beowulf*, *The Canterbury Tales*, the Cavalier poets, the Metaphysicals. I'd be admired and once the boys and girls had passed my classes their parents would surely invite me to dinner at their finest houses. (p. 122)

His life as a new teacher was quite different. His brother was running a bar in New York, but his teacher's salary was too meagre to support decent housing and he lived in a cold-water flat, reminiscent of life in Limerick. For those without funds in New York City, heat and hot water were luxuries. The narrator says it was so cold in his flat that he often sat in the bathtub and read. Because he could not pay his bills, his heat was cut off. Eventually, McCourt's fortunes improved, and he taught at Stuyvesant, one of the most prestigious high schools in New York City.

The readers of *Angela's Ashes* and *'Tis* know McCourt is a successful writer. The autobiographical narratives recount difficult circumstances, but ultimately McCourt succeeds in the United States and actualizes his dream. Although the narrator chronicles the life of an ambitious immigrant, he also expresses frustrations based on class privilege. As we close this essay, we explore the role that autobiographical writing may play in exposing the transparency of whiteness and foregrounding class-based issues in the United States.

IMPLICATIONS

When we read *Angela's Ashes* and *'Tis: A Memoir*, we were impressed with McCourt's writing but struck by the stock story lines in his narratives. Readers from the United States recognize in McCourt's memoirs the patterns for making it in America. The author left miserable circumstances in Ireland and succeeded in his adopted land. McCourt's story is more complicated because he was born in America and presents himself as someone who longed to return to it. The basic story lines are recognizable, however, by readers in the United States. McCourt did what generations of immigrants have done. He came to America, a place where he could have a better life.

We have traced two thematic threads in the memoirs, the ambitious immigrant and the immigrant from an underclass. Here, we examine the potential of autobiographical writing for helping engaged readers address issues associated with the transparency of whiteness and class in the United States. Autobiographical writing, as noted earlier, communicates dimensions of self-awareness, which means that it may be an especially appropriate rhetorical form for raising racial self-awareness.

Whiteness is a leaky category, and we must understand it in relation to other categories, such as class. Until we examine structures of whiteness as articulated with structures of class, we will not be able to examine the differences in whiteness to expose its transparency. McCourt's narrator draws the reader's attention to class issues, but in keeping with popular themes in American autobiographical literature, it would be easy to overlook the tensions or gaps in the stories that speak to class issues. It is tempting, as a reader of an American success story, to overlook other elements of the narrative. Many of us have become acculturated to accept the myth of classlessness in the United States. When Kammen (1991) cited Lowell in *Mystic Chords of Memory*, he foregrounded the author's discomfort with the Irish immigrants' allegiance to their home country rather than America. Lowell also seemed concerned about class issues when he longed for "old stock Yankees." *Angela's Ashes* and *'Tis* are not exactly the stories, in Sayre's (1980) terms, that most Americans would like to emulate. When a reader carefully attends to McCourt's memoirs and reads resistively against the narrative of the ambitious immigrant, the narrative of the ambitious immigrant as a member of the underclass moves into the foreground. An autobiographer such as McCourt has constructed his stories self-consciously. He has reflected on his life and rhetorically shaped narratives that communicate his self-awareness. His memoirs are not "the truth of a life" in a literal sense but, rather, McCourt's perceptions of the truth of his life. Thus, *Angela's Ashes* and *'Tis* may encourage readers to examine the truths of their own lives in terms of issues related to "the logic of transparency" and the myth of classlessness.

Giroux (1997) argued that we need a "pedagogy of whiteness" that will help us "move beyond the view of 'whiteness' as simply a trope of domination" (p. 296). He proposed that we must develop pedagogical strategies that will help "rearticulate 'whiteness' as part of a broader project of cultural, social, and political citizenship" (p. 295). Giroux claimed that electronic forms of communication, particularly visual rhetorical texts, may make whiteness visible. We suggest that autobiographical narratives may serve a similar function because such writing invites the reader to identify with the writer on fundamentally human levels and therefore to make basic human connections. A memoir writer such as McCourt reminds us of the complexities of identity and invites us to consider how we position ourselves in society.

Autobiographical writing asks us to identify with the struggles of narrators who are trying to "make sense" out of their lives. It is this type of sense-making that we must all engage in if we are to go beyond articulating whiteness as domination. If we turn to autobiographical writing in an effort to understand how individuals have positioned themselves, we may also begin to understand how we have positioned ourselves. In *Beyond the Whiteness of Whiteness: Memoir of a White Mother of Black Sons*, Lazarre (1996), for example, emphasizes that her memoir is "told in many voices, the voice of the mother, of the teacher, of the Jewish woman, daughter of immigrants and American radicals; it also includes the voice of the wife of 27 years of an African-American man" (p. xix). She says that race had never been an issue in her marriage, and she only became aware of the privileges of whiteness through the eyes of her sons. When we read a memoir such as Lazarre's, we become aware of how we live as many voices and experience intersecting identities. Through the act of writing, Lazarre indicates that she became aware of her whiteness:

> I am an ordinary American woman protected by this whiteness (which, we all know, does not really exist yet is known and visible and powerful) into a precious invisibility of apparent belonging, and I am weighted down with the transforming shame this knowledge brings. (p. 18)

An engaged reader, as described by Travis (1998), accepts the invitation offered by texts such as those written by McCourt and Lazarre. She has identified the "disruptive effects of texts" (p. 5) and clarified what she calls "agency in reading" (p. 6). When a reader is an active agent, he or she engages in role playing and self-questioning through engagement with the text. As we grapple with challenging the logic of transparency and the myth of classlessness, active engagement with autobiographical texts may help us see the nuances of whiteness. An actively engaged reader brings an ideology to the reading experience but can "resist ideological determinisms" (p. 5). Thus, Travis has proposed that reading invites us to engage in the type of self-questioning that will help us lead more ethical lives.

When we challenge the logic of transparency and the myth of classlessness, we will lead more ethical lives. The narrator of *Angela's Ashes* and *'Tis*, by rhetorically weaving together the narrative threads of the ambitious immigrant and the ambitious immigrant from an underclass, invites us to engage in the type of self-questioning described by Travis (1998). Engaged readers of McCourt's work will learn as much about themselves as about McCourt. Although we talk about "racial divides" in the United States, particularly in our cities, we rarely engage in the self-questioning that could help us understand the historical patterns that inform the dynamics of contemporary race relations.

Discussions of divisions based on class are even more rare in the United States. President Bill Clinton's "On America" campaign is a good exemplar in this regard. Clinton's race initiative was criticized for failing to fully investigate and discuss the "roots of color consciousness" in America. As Berry (1999) noted,

> By discussing people of *color* without fuller analysis of the roots of *color* consciousness and its consequences, the race initiative has made it necessary for the rest of us [people of color] to do some hard analytical work. Any analysis of *color* consciousness also necessarily requires inclusion of the impact of gender roles, language, religion, and class. (p. 55)

In Clinton's race dialogue, class issues were largely shunted aside. As Dreier (1998) has argued, Clinton's attempts at racial reconciliation faced a "major obstacle"—the lack of a full discussion of "the widening disparities of wealth and income" (p. 43).

Autobiographical accounts, such as McCourt's, may prompt us to engage in self-questioning concerning our assumptions about race and class, and they may help us develop frames for understanding the complexities of race- and class-based tensions. *Angela's Ashes*, *'Tis,* and other personal narratives ask us to see the truth of a life as it relates to a larger historical context. For example, we might ask questions about politics, unions, and labor issues that provided the backdrop for McCourt's life in New York City.

If reporters asked such questions and gave more attention to historical context, they might offer more nuanced commentaries. For example, in covering community responses to Mayor Rudolph W. Guiliani's aggressive approaches to crime-fighting, many mainstream media accounts suggested community responses were divided along racial lines. Although responses to the deaths of Amadou Diallo, Abner Loiuma, and Patrick Dorismond were, to an extent, divided along racial lines, the picture was much more complicated. One newspaper article emphasized that many black people in New York City believe they could be the next Diallo, Louima, or Dorismond. Kweisi Mfume, president of the NAACP, said, "If four black police officers had fired 41 bullets at a white immigrant, it is unlikely that they wouldn't be found guilty of murder or reckless endangerment" (as cited in Gellman & Lynch, 2000, p. A1). We suspect, however, that responses were also divided along class lines, but mainstream media accounts focused on race rather than class.

Finally, we emphasize the power of including autobiographical elements in scholarly writing. Crenshaw (1997), for example, encouraged her readers to think about internalizing abstract ideas when she opened her study with an illustration from her own experiences as a professor. Before she offered a powerful rhetorical analysis of whiteness and the discourse of Senator Carol Moseley Braun and Jesse Helms concerning the renewal of a Confederate patent, she framed the study in relation to her own experiences. She described how she became aware of her own white privilege when a student assumed she was more "objective" than faculty members of color. The illustration forced readers to consider how they "live" their rhetorical scholarship in a material sense.

NOTES

1. McMahon (1997) questioned Ignatiev's argument that the Irish became unified only when they established solidarity with whites. She suggested that it was Irish nationalism and the experience of discrimination, rather than white solidarity, that united the Irish in America. In addition, she suggested that Ignatiev's "abstract Marxist theory" demands too much of the Irish, who arrived from a "precapitalist" society and were simply trying to survive in a "sometimes hostile society" (pp. 571-572).

2. We refer to McCourt as an immigrant because he tells his story from the vantage point of an immigrant. McCourt was born in New York City, the son of Irish immigrants.

His parents moved the family to Ireland after the death of their daughter, Margaret. As a young man, McCourt returned to New York City.

3. Speakers such as Patrick Buchanan (1991), of course, make overt statements about race: "I think God made all people good, but if we had to take a million immigrants in, say, Zulus, next year, or Englishmen and put them in Virginia, what group would be easier to assimilate and would cause less problems for the people of Virginia? There is nothing wrong with sitting down and arguing that issue, that we are a European country" (as cited in Lopez, 1996, p. 18). For Buchanan, non-white immigrants constitute "the problem." Studies of whiteness suggest, however, that many white people share Buchanan's attitudes but are more subtle in their expressions of those attitudes.

13

Communities, Identities, and Politics

What Rhetoric Is Becoming in the Twenty-First Century

Barry Brummett

Any attempt to identify new approaches to as ancient a topic as rhetoric has a tightrope act to perform. On the one hand, we must maintain semantic integrity by being careful, in our enthusiasm for discovery and change, not to call everything rhetoric. On the other hand, the observable actions, objects, and events that used to be drawn together under the rubric of rhetoric have changed. New forms of communication arise from new cultural, social, and economic practices. What people used to do so as to create a public dialogue in a public space is not what they do now. One must think carefully about why one would apply rhetoric to experiences that have not existed before.

Wobbling the balance between these two perils is the fact that a discussion of new forms of rhetoric necessarily involves consideration of emerging, sometimes barely understood, discursive practices. This collection of essays does not describe a fully formed twenty-first century rhetoric that is finished and complete. Instead, it points to what rhetoric seems to be becoming. This anthology, like any collection, also cannot attempt to do everything, to describe every form of emerging rhetoric. For these reasons, I take my task in this essay to lie in addressing the following questions: What particular vision of new rhetoric is embodied here? What makes it different from traditional views? What broad vision of rhetoric just over the horizon is adumbrated by these essays? Because a discussion of new approaches must necessarily point to what lies beyond, I note that this chapter comprises my own views of the new developments suggested by this anthology, but none of my conclusions can be found fully formed in any one of these essays. From the ground offered by the scholarship here, I leap off into either new territory or abyss—that is for the reader to judge.

My focus imposes on these essays a term scarcely used in them: I propose that the essays in this anthology are about what *political rhetoric* has become and will become in the twenty-first century. Political rhetoric has traditionally been conceived in terms of particular discursive forms or manifestations. When we think of political persuasion, we think of campaigns, debates, speeches, strikes, marches, sit-ins, perhaps even riots, and the broad social movements into which many of these forms are woven. I would not exclude all these traditional (and some not so traditional) manifestations from the house of political rhetoric, and all of them continue to be important forms of political influence. Many, if not all, of them are included in twenty-first century rhetoric by the essays in this anthology.

If we search for new twenty-first century rhetoric by focusing on manifestations or forms, we invite ourselves to search for discontinuities. We would inspect the essays here for evidence of breaks with how the political rhetoric of the past was done. A search for the new and discontinuous has its place, but it raises the problem mentioned previously: How are we justified in calling new forms by the old name of rhetoric?

I suggest instead that we ask ourselves what functions political rhetoric has performed and will continue to perform in the future: What work does it do in social contexts? I believe this question leads to the understanding that political rhetoric has historically performed certain key social functions, and that it continues to do so today, even in new and evolving forms or manifestations. A concern for functions leads us to search for continuities, and it justifies applying old terms such as rhetoric to new manifestations.

When we say political rhetoric, we are speaking of discourse, of symbolic and significant behavior, that creates, maintains, challenges, and overthrows power; of discourse that creates community in all its complexity; of discourse that creates identity; and of discourse that creates shared definitions of reality, even if increasingly fragmented and parochial communities congeal around those definitions. The functions of managing power, community, identity, and reality have always been key to what is called political rhetoric. Thus, my essay asks the following: What new manifestations of political rhetoric are emerging to perform these functions in the twenty-first century, or what will political rhetoric look like in these times? I base my answers on the essays in this anthology, but if I become silly or overreach, the fault must be assigned to me and not these good scholars.

Specifically, I argue that political rhetoric in the twenty-first century manifests four relative changes. Twenty-first century political rhetoric does not totally replace earlier manifestations. Furthermore, the four relative changes I suggest may not be entirely consistent with one another—nor is life in all its complexity. In general, I argue that twenty-first century political rhetoric is relatively more imaginary, commodified, local, and dialectic. In these changing forms, it carries out its ancient functions. After explaining what I mean by these claims, I show how the essays in this collection point toward such conclusions.

WHAT POLITICAL RHETORIC IS BECOMING

Imaginary

A popular definition of image in politics might be that it is the total package of verbal and nonverbal characteristics ascribed to a public figure or group by which people make emotional, aesthetic, and affiliative judgments about the figure or group. John F. Kennedy had the image of a brave, young, stylish, sophisticated, strong leader, by which people came to love or hate him. Image is the publicly presented style of a person or group.

Two characteristics of image are key. First, image is made up of signs or representations: pictures, voice recordings, newspaper and magazine articles, and television and movie coverage. Most people do not know public figures intimately and personally. Instead, they know a figure's image as embodied in signs: flickering pixels on a screen or edited sound bites on the evening news. Second, image is fundamentally aesthetic. It appeals first not to the public's powers of reason and analysis but to pleasure and entertainment, to an emotional sense of bonding or disgust with a figure. Image is thus carried in aesthetic material of narrative and pictures.

The image has always been part of political rhetoric, as orators gave thought to their appearance, gesture, diction, and so forth. Political rhetoric, however, was once carried out largely in manifestations of expositional discourse: reasoned argument, lengthy development of rationales for conscious decisions, and the chaining out of claims and proofs. The relative weight of image and appearance began to overtake reasoned discourse only as the age of cinema and television developed. Franklin Roosevelt took pains to hide his paralysis, and John Kennedy won his presidential debate (as everyone will tell you) because his youthful good looks trumped Richard Nixon's blue jowls. Politics shifted from the speaker's platform to the glowing screen. Today, the management of image is key to any political campaign, especially at the state or national level, where most candidates are encountered by most people only through mediated images. Beyond the campaign, however, politics is played on a field profoundly defined by the image.

Political rhetoric no longer uses the image; instead, the image is the site on which much political rhetoric is played out. Image is what is struggled over rather than being one tool by which struggle is done. Increasingly, politics is won or lost in the medium of sign manipulation. Evidence for these assertions may be found in any television broadcast or newspaper story about a current (especially national or international) political struggle. One will be hard-pressed to discover from these stories the substance of what the political combatants think. Instead, the coverage is concerned with who is winning or losing, with the rhetorical moves made by this one or that one, by strategies that move opinion polls up or down a few points. In other words, one will discover a politics of image. Increasingly, national and international political struggle stops at the screen and the page and has little to do with material conditions, such as the condition of the road in front of one's house, the security of one's job, or the condition of schools down the road. A political rhetoric that is increasingly focused on the image is increasingly simulational—increasingly a game played within the frame of the screen for its own sake.

Commodified

Something becomes commodified if it is reduced to the terms of the market. In late capitalism, two market factors are central: currency and pleasure. Currency refers to the need to understand actions, objects, and events in terms of a common denominator so that they may be compared and rationalized and, therefore, traded on a mass scale. Quantification is a sign of a preoccupation with currency. A culture in which "do the math" or "the bottom line" are sacred mantras, sports is understood largely in terms of statistics, the success of a synagogue is gauged by the number of seats filled, and plans and programs are disguised as budgets in a culture engrossed by commodification. Likewise, late capitalism cannot function unless the single-minded pursuit of pleasure is offered to people as the highest if not the only good in life. Markets would collapse were people to think about whether buying a new outfit is good for the community or the environment, whether it is the will of Allah, or whether it strengthens one's karma. Do we want it? This is what we are trained to consider. A culture that finds it difficult to assess the value of events outside of questions such as "did you have fun?," in which we have little to say to clerics after spiritually uplifting religious ceremonies besides "I really enjoyed it," and in which shopping is an end as much as it is a means is a culture engrossed by commodification.

Political rhetoric is increasingly played out in terms of commodification in several senses. The terms of struggle are collapsing into terms of the market. Preserving jobs and keeping the economy strong become ultimate values, replacing ideologically based values from earlier times, such as "honor" or "integrity." Pleasure becomes the ultimate motive; people will put up with anything, even war, if it can be made into an entertainment. Tellingly, the only joke told by comedian David Letterman upon returning to television after the destruction of the World Trade Center towers was to wonder whether Osama Bin Laden was motivated by an inability to "get cable."

The commodification of political rhetoric points to the distinct possibility that fundamental issues have been removed from the political arena by the success of international capitalism. People are allowed to debate what they want as long as there is no possibility that the rhetoric might produce an outcome that would stand in the way of the capitalist juggernaut. Commodification then loops back into the imaginary; one prime way to make sure that political struggle does not extend to the board room is to move it to the plane of signs and images, television and movies, and popular culture. Alternative, subversive political views are commodified as quickly as they arise: by the end of the week, you can buy the latest neo-Maost animal rights cell's T-shirt and black boots at the local Sears. Even political campaigns become an entertainment that cannot possibly produce a result that would threaten the capitalist structure.

The commodification of politics moves political rhetoric into the realm of the market and of the pleasures that drive it. Political struggle is carried out in television comedies and dramas more than in Senate deliberations. Social issues are worked out more in so-called reality programming than on talk shows featuring pundits (unless the latter can be made entertaining, as in *Politically Incorrect*). Market terms constrain what will be struggled over.

Local

This category seems contradictory with the others and contradictory within itself. So be it; life is complicated. Political rhetoric is local in the following two senses: It offers a personally engaged, material alternative to the imaginary, and (contradictorily) it creates the illusion of the local by stressing the personal and domestic, even at the national (and imaginary) level.

I located the move toward imaginary political rhetoric mainly at the national and international levels because these levels are distant to the ordinary political actor, although perhaps less so now than in earlier times. National and international politics are more imaginary now, however, largely because these are the levels at which the most powerful media intervene. The people in Cleveland might watch local news on television, but they watch the same news that everyone else watches when Peter Jennings or Dan Rather come on.

As people become increasingly attuned to the national and international levels of political rhetoric as played out through image, however, the lack of material involvement and real personal engagement in the imaginary demands a corrective. The public, heir of the local struggles with national importance characteristic of the Civil Rights movement, women's and reproductive rights, and environmental struggles, is in many ways living out the creed that politics is personal. At this writing, as the nation prosecutes a "war on terrorism," many ordinary citizens are expressing their political involvement through a wide range of local acts, from tying yellow ribbons to trees to marching on state capitols and walking with local Muslims in solidarity as they go to school or the grocery store. In many ways, today's local political rhetoric is a return to the involved citizenry imagined by the Sophists and by Cicero. With no hope of acting meaningfully on a national or international scale, however, many people have given these levels up to the imaginary and have moved their material political struggles to the local level.

Perhaps understanding a yearning for local involvement, media at the national and international levels have responded by a kind of imaginary localization, specifically the personalization of broad social and political issues. This is a form of metonymy, the trope of reduction, in which political problems too vast or distant to comprehend meaningfully are reduced to a more psychologically manageable set of signs. Thorny problems of U.S.-Cuba relations are metonymized into Elian Gonzalez and the other players in his drama. Issues of race relations and domestic abuse are reduced to the televised drama of O. J. Simpson. Hillary Clinton embodies social struggle over the role of women. The public believes that it knows and is intimate with Elian, O. J., and Hillary because the media have localized them through the image so as to metonymize important issues.

Dialectic

Dialectic is popularly understood as a discourse of "give and take," and an educated person might offer Plato's dialogues as examples thereof. There are three defining characteristics of dialectic that ground my assertion that political rhetoric today is increasingly dialectic. First, and of least importance, dialectic tends to proceed in question-answer format. It may be more accurate to say that it is a discourse in which exchange occurs freely, whether that be questions and answers or some other form. The monologic structure of the speech is not imposed on the communication. Second, participants in the dialectic are supposed to have no preconceived conclusion or axe to grind, although Plato casts this characteristic into doubt by resurrecting an obviously opinionated Socrates to conduct his dialogues. It may be more accurate to say that the participants in a dialectic are in a state of flux. They may have a notion of what they believe about the subject matter, but they and others are on unstable social, political, or linguistic ground and they know it. Third, and most important, dialectic is profoundly attuned to structure. A participant in dialectic is trying to determine how the world is organized and is using the organizing structure of language to help him or her do so by determining categories, genus, species, and definitions that will place an idea or entity into this box or that one.

It may seem perverse to claim that the political rhetoric of the twenty-first century will be increasingly dialectic when dialectic is an ancient discourse. Such an assertion calls our attention to times on a trajectory of waxing and waning when dialectic emerges more strongly. Dialectic becomes relatively more important in times of change and instability as established categories for organizing the world and our experiences in it are questioned. Dialectic is therefore a kind of political struggle in which participants work to rearrange a world in flux. For this reason, dialectic in times of change requires a relatively more open exchange of communication that pulls rhetors in from the margins of the old system so as to make the new one—it bespeaks if not a lack of preconceived ideas then a confusion over ideas—and it is preoccupied with how the world is organized through signs and symbols.

Political rhetoric is carried out dialectically all around us. News media are full of references to "Muslim terrorists," whereas millions protest the category that appellation creates, preferring instead two distinct categories, Muslim and terrorist. Whether terrorist attacks are "acts of war" or "crimes" is an ongoing dispute. Domestically, whether two gay parents and their children can be a species of the genus "family" is struggled over. Racial descriptors are destabilized as people demand the ability to define themselves outside the boxes offered by traditional categories of white, black, Asian, Latino, and so on. People call for more "prayer" and "faith" in the schools and elsewhere, but whether that can include Wiccan prayer or Pagan faith may be a matter of struggle. I call these struggles dialectic, and they characterize the political rhetoric of this emerging century.

WHAT THIS COLLECTION OF ESSAYS TEACHES US

I believe that we can see within the essays in this anthology evidence of a political rhetoric that is increasingly imaginary, commodified, local, and dialectic. Through these new forms, the ancient function of managing power, community, identity, and definitions of reality is carried out. I review the essays to examine the evidence—to use these four terms as ways to bridge the essays and to pull them together. We do not expect each essay to manifest all four dimensions equally, and no essayist should be held responsible for the structure that I impose.

James Darsey writes about James Baldwin's struggle to find a place between dogma and anarchy. Place was an elusive but vital issue for the expatriate, Baldwin. The poignancy of having no sense of place is signaled by the quotations with which Darsey begins from von Chamisso and Coleridge. Darsey notes, however, that, as Baldwin tells us, we are ultimately the creators of our places.

Baldwin's journey from place to place was a search for a site at which he could enact his politics locally. Baldwin yearned for one home place on which to stand even as he celebrated diversity, and the same can be said for Darsey, who calls for a sense of place as the site of real, lived experience even as he must understand that we all have our own, perhaps incommensurate, places. When Baldwin wished to intervene in the emerging civil rights struggle, he returned (if briefly) to the United States to act locally rather than simply writing from afar. The political rhetorics that most engaged Baldwin were involved in arranging and rearranging emerging, changing categories of his time. Baldwin, a writer on so many margins of categories, engaged in a dialectical rhetorical struggle. His writing addresses shifting definitions of race, sexual identity, and national allegiance. His work does so on the level of the imaginary, not the expositional or the polemic. Typical of so much emerging political rhetoric, Baldwin had his political say in producing entertainments for popular consumption (he and his agent hoped) in the form of novels.

One could hardly hope for a better example of the localization of political rhetoric than Kathryn M. Olson and G. Thomas Goodnight's study of the hearings in Prince William County. Wider issues of the encroaching commodification of everything, including history, framed a site for local political action. Olson and Goodnight study the ways in which ordinary people become locally engaged in meaningful ways. The strong implication in their essay is that community discourse is perforce native, natural, or untrained. In this sense, it is opposed dialectically to the polished, trained rhetoricians of Disney, who have bought their training and have sold their talents for a price.

These local heroes took on the multinational corporation, Disney, master of the imaginary. Disney's designs on the local history of Bull Run promised both a commodification of history by turning it into a theme park and a transformation of real history of the blood and death of local involvement into the encompassing simulational experience at which Disney excels. The earnest locals studied by Olson and Goodnight were engaged in local political rhetoric, but there is also a sense in which coverage of their struggle by the national media (how else did Olson and Goodnight find out about them?) metonymized them. Struggling locally, the good people of Prince William County become metonymies for all who struggle locally to control plans imposed by capital on our lives.

George Cheney's study of the Mondragón cooperatives may be the clearest example in this collection of the triumph of commodification. Cheney offers examples of the ways in which a language of business and trade edges out ethics and values. The citizen, who might speak in terms of the latter, becomes the consumer, speaking in terms of the former. Cheney's study is not hopeful about the possibilities for creating a rhetoric outside of the space of commodification, as the market consistently appropriates values.

A major site of commodification for most people is the place where they work, which is often a site of local political struggle. Within that place, discourse organizes the material and the discursive together; rules and corporate values create a particular way of categorizing experience, known in part as a corporate culture. Cheney's work invites us to think of corporate discourse as a site of dialectical struggle over how a particular organization will categorize experience.

Cheney reviews an interesting list of the things that a market can be. Of course, it used to be the place where a community would come together. It still is, on the level of the imaginary. People are increasingly a community because they wear, drink, or drive the same brand and because they purchase the same artist's music or buy tickets to see the same team. Political struggle can then be expressed in terms of which music or brand one buys or which team one follows.

Today, a major site of dialectical struggles over categories is the issue of identity. Ronald L. Jackson, II's cultural contract theory shows us how identity is worked out within the larger context of culture. Situating the self in relation to others is always dialectical because we work out who we are in terms of categories offered to us by a culture. There is struggle because these categories are often framed oppositionally. We live in an era of increasingly intercultural communication, and Jackson shows us how identity destabilizes under these conditions. His discussion of shifts in how people define themselves racially is a clear example of the centrality of dialectic for political struggle today because there is much at stake personally and socially in these definitions.

Jackson's terminology makes a segue from Cheney's chapter because the "contract" calls to mind the market. His theory is thus cast into terms of trade, which may well be an accurate framing of the problem if we live in a period of encompassing commodification. Jackson's essay invites us to consider the ways in which commodification trumps cultural difference; if capital reduces everything to a common currency, it must do so with culture as well. Cultural difference becomes just another commodity to market in the same way as a guayabero shirt or sagging pants. What becomes of identity when the dialectical categories available to one are all ultimately commodified?

Dialectic looms large in Marouf Hasian and Emily Plec's analysis of the rhetoric surrounding the Human Genome Diversity Project. The complaints against the project lodged by Third World rhetors are based on a dialectic of human categories. They claim that a rhetoric of humanity as one category, which has accompanied the announcement of genetic discoveries in the West, ignores diversity within that category. What it means to be human as a category, and whether that is a genus with clear species, seems to be at issue in this rhetoric. The politics of human categories are struggled over dialectically when it comes to the genome.

The genetic project is also a clear example of commodification. The rhetoric of DNA reduces humanity to that common denominator, which then becomes an infallible determinant of worth, just as reduction of all goods and services to a unit of currency makes the currency an infallible determinant of economic worth. Is someone accused of a crime? Consult his DNA. Might an employee prove sickly and fragile? Test her DNA. Should we get married? Let's have a blood test. Of course, there are groups and individuals who oppose such reduction to the currency of DNA, and of such disagreements are political struggles made.

Hasian and Plec also note the resentment that arises from the targeting of certain "indigenous" people for research on evolution, disease, and so on. The people are not consulted concerning this appropriation of their genes for research. This is another form of commodification, in which certain populations are made raw material for the march of Western science, just as the natural raw materials in their locales are appropriated for industry. The struggle to refuse such appropriation is a struggle against the whole project of commodification.

Finally, for most people, DNA is entirely in the realm of the imaginary. Although we all have such a thing, and at the cores of our beings, it is paradoxically not a part of everyday material existence. DNA is instead the stuff of movies and television shows—dramatic death row reprieves and shocking revelations on daytime trash television. We know about and we struggle over the essence of our material being by turning to images.

John M. Murphy and Thomas R. Burkholder correctly note the importance of specific decisions of location or personnel for party conventions. The strategic importance of meeting in this city or that city is widely discussed as the major parties make their convention decisions, and here we see the importance of the imaginary in political struggles. Convention location, keynote speaker, and even planks in the platform bear little relation to what will actually happen to real people on the street. Instead, they are a field of signs on which political struggle is carried out. On that field, Murphy and Burkholder note the ways in which party identity is created. Such an identity is largely imaginary, fashioned as it is of the signs and spectacles of the convention that is far removed from material existence.

Murphy and Burkholder's focus on the keynote address calls attention to its dialectical nature. Divisions asserted within the party during the primary must be overcome by stressing the greater importance of the overall category of party identity. Those who used to be McCain voters and Bush voters are invited to dissolve these species and become Republicans. In defining political realities, keynote speakers organize the political world for the party. As Murphy and Burkholder note, the speaker himself or herself must embody the dialectical synthesis that will unify disparate factions.

Museums seem to be on the edge between the local and the national. Often drawing a national audience because they commemorate widely known people, events, or movements, museums are also inherently of a place. One can hardly imagine the Martin Luther King, Jr. Memorial being located in Anchorage, Alaska, for instance. Victoria J. Gallagher studies the ways in which social memory is encoded in four civil rights memorials and museums. These museums are a site for local political action at the same time that they are destinations for tourists traveling from afar.

The focus on tourists calls our attention to the commodification of memory represented by these museums. Although they may be nonprofit, they either ask for donations or charge admission, and they have goods to sell. Not all public memorials are thoroughly commodified. For example, it is possible to walk into the King memorial and see the grave for free, but the shop nearby sells recordings of his speeches and other memorabilia. In an important sense, buying a tape or a T-shirt is a form of political action engaged in by many.

Politics is also shifted to the imaginary when racial struggle occurs in "cultural projection" more than in traditional forms of rhetoric, and Gallagher identifies this type of struggle in the memorials she studies. These are not material sites of struggle at the moment; instead, they represent struggles of the past in imaginary form. The memorials thus take their place among popular movies that reconstruct the Civil Rights movement with obvious political intent. Insofar as the museums attempt to create shared definitions of reality, they engage in a dialectic to define what race means and what it means to be American.

George N. Dionisopoulos highlights the imaginary as a site of political rhetoric in showing how John Wayne as icon and the film *The Green Berets* in particular played out one side in the rhetorical battle over the containment doctrine. Wayne was a field of images for most Americans, embodying a particular ideology and wild western myth in several of his films. Dionisopoulos analyzes the ways in which the cinematic images worked as political rhetoric in their time.

The struggles reviewed in Dionisopoulos's essay were more global than they might be today. At any rate, they speak of a time when local struggle seemed subordinate to more international movements. The dialectic of the Cold War looms large in Dionisopoulos's study. Was the conflict portrayed in the film between Vietnamese and the United States or between communism and democracy? The film engages in a rhetorical dialectic to define the terms of the struggle and how the world was organized. Whether the Vietnamese and Americans were seen as equals or as being in a colonial relationship is also an issue of dialectical struggle.

We must also remember that the film Dionisopoulos reviews was a commodity. People entered the theater to experience pleasure, and at the same time their entering was a form of political engagement. One would be hard-pressed to find hippies and antiwar protestors of the era lining up to see *The Green Berets*. Going to see the film, and other movies featuring Wayne, was a way to align oneself through purchasing a commodity with one side in a rhetorical struggle.

Dana Cloud's study of the Staley Manufacturing strike highlights very clearly the ways in which commodification sets the parameters for political rhetoric today. Her example raises the disturbing possibility that multinational corporations set the parameters within which political struggle may proceed. The fight may go so far but no farther—if it threatens the basic stability of the global economic system. So it seemed to have been at Staley, where rhetoric found its limits against a wall of economic and social structures. Workers are often given "a voice," Cloud notes, as a token replacement for real power.

The strikers at Staley were engaged in local rhetorical struggle but against a foe with wider resources. Cloud's study both affirms the importance of the local and reminds us of the limits of local effectiveness. She notes that local rhetorical struggle failed against broader "extradiscursive power."

The dismal dialectic of race is central to Kate Cañas and Mark Lawrence McPhail's study of the rhetorical struggle following the nomination of Lani Guinier. What they describe as Guinier's rhetoric of interbraiding can be seen as a dialectic of inclusion that attempts to recategorize a nation obsessed with racial categories. Like the strikers in Cloud's study, it failed—but perhaps not for extradiscursive reasons. The stage on which Guinier entered was constructed not so much of material as of sedimented discourses of race, in which entrenched categories proved difficult to overcome. Cañas and McPhail engage in their own rhetorical dialectic by casting the political Right as pathological and evil rather than misinformed. They identify an "ideology of innocence" held by whites in America—a categorical judgment within a dialectical rhetoric. They note the ways in which whiteness is constructed as a category, which is a kind of dialectical preoccupation.

Cañas and McPhail also identify a shift in political rhetoric from local, material engagement with racism to the imaginary plane of "symbolic" racism. This, too, is a dialectical problem: A nation taught to link racism with material conditions of who lives next door to whom, or who attains which job at what salary, may need to shift categories. Racism is now embodied in, and can thus be resisted in, the images constructed on television. As people throughout the nation passionately debated the Guinier case, they were talking about images on a screen, not the people who want to live next door.

Rhetorical struggles over race likewise claim the attention of Dexter Gordon and Carrie Crenshaw in their study of racial apologies. Dialectic is an important theme in their discussion as they consider what an apology is as a category and which groups of people apologize and to which other groups of people. What those groups are called and how they are constructed are dialectical questions having to do with organization of reality, such as when Crenshaw and Gordon discuss the ways in which whiteness is constructed as a morally neutral category. Whether an apology is something that can be done en masse, and on behalf of others, is a dialectical issue. The construction of racism as individual acts rather than broad social structures is a question of categories and how our thoughts about oppression are organized. In invoking Gramscian hegemony to explain how these categories support established structures of power, Gordon and Crenshaw call our attention to the power of the often subtle work of rhetorical dialectic.

Gordon and Crenshaw also claim that much is at stake in these struggles. I do not disagree, but at least until reparations are paid, consider the extent to which the whole issue of apologies is played out in the imaginary. If much is at stake, it is mostly in terms of image construction. An apology may address material wrongs, but it is about as far from a material action as any gesture can be. That an apology might satisfy millions who experience daily local affronts teaches us about the strength of the imaginary in trumping other categories of political rhetoric.

Patricia A. Sullivan and Steven R. Goldzwig continue a theme of examining the construction of whiteness, clearly a dialectical issue. It is instructive to learn from their study how the Irish in America began as a racially inferior category but "became white" through social and rhetorical struggle—a clear case of dialectical rearrangement of categories. This struggle is *transparent*, a term usefully employed in their essay. They note the ways in which the imaginary can occlude an understanding of some rhetorical processes, just as hegemony hides the active exercise of power in Gordon and Crenshaw's analysis. The imaginary in this case is literary, the writing of autobiography.

Through the construction of categories along lines of color, class, and national origin, privilege is maintained against the rhetorical assaults of the margins. The Irish entered social and political mainstreams as they reorganized those categories to include themselves within empowered groups. Sullivan and Goldzwig note the use of stock patterns in McCourt's work. This indicates the formulary nature of much image construction, which means that the terrain of imaginary conflict can be mapped and anticipated, and people can be trained to enter it.

In summary, the essays in this anthology provide evidence of a shift in political rhetoric toward increasing use of the imaginary, commodification, the local, and dialectic. They also provide evidence of the persistence of traditional forms of argumentative rhetoric. They point toward the limits of rhetoric in a materially straitened world. Although the focus of my essay is the narrow topic of political rhetoric, it may not be too much to suggest that political rhetoric as so defined is the ground toward which much or most rhetoric is moving in the twenty-first century. We are all—as scholars, activists, or ordinary citizens—becoming more aware of the rhetorical manipulation of power. As this discovery becomes more central in our lives, with more important consequences, we may all become political rhetoricians.

References

Abramson, D., Aldrich, J., & Rohde, D. (1999). *Change and continuity in the 1996 and 1998 elections.* Washington, DC: Congressional Quarterly Press.

Achenbach, J. (1993, November 12). Disney in the dell. *Washington Post*, pp. C1, C3.

Adair, G. (1981). *Vietnam on film: From "The Green Berets" to "Apocalypse Now."* New York: Proteus.

Adair, G. (1989). *Hollywood's Vietnam: From "The Green Berets" to "Full Metal Jacket."* London: Heinemann.

Adler, R. (1968a, June 20). Screen: "Green Berets" as viewed by John Wayne. *New York Times*, p. 49.

Adler, R. (1968b, June 30). The absolute end of the "romance" of war. *New York Times*, pp. D1, D10.

Allen, T. W. (1994). *The invention of the white race*. London: Verso.

Almond, G. A. (1991, September). Capitalism and democracy. *Political Science and Politics, 24*, 467-474.

Anderegg, M. (1991a). Hollywood and Vietnam: John Wayne and Jane Fonda as discourse. In M. Anderegg (Ed.), *Inventing Vietnam: The war in film and television* (pp. 15-32). Philadelphia: Temple University Press.

Anderegg, M. (1991b). Introduction. In M. Anderegg (Ed.), *Inventing Vietnam: The war in film and television* (pp. 1-14). Philadelphia: Temple University Press.

Anderson, M. (1998, March 29). Trapped inside James Baldwin. *New York Times*. Retrieved June 18, 2001, from http://www.nytimes.com/books/98/03/29/reviews/980329.29 anderst.html.

Appiah, A. (1986). The uncompleted argument: DuBois and the illusion of race. In H. L. Gates, Jr. (Ed.), *Writing and difference*. Chicago: University of Chicago Press.

Arendt, H. (1993). *Between past and future.* New York: Penguin.

Aristotle. (1991). *On rhetoric: A theory of civic discourse* (G. A. Kennedy, Trans.). New York: Oxford University Press.

Armada, B. J. (1998). Memorial agon: An interpretive tour of the National Civil Rights Museum. *Southern Communication Journal, 63,* 235-243.

Askew, R. (1972). Text of Gov. Askew's keynote address. *Congressional Quarterly Weekly Report, 30*, 1747-1749.

Auchincloss, E., & Lynch, N. (1989). Disturber of the peace: James Baldwin—An interview. In F. Standley & L. Pratt (Eds.), *Conversations with James Baldwin* (p. 80). Jackson: University of Mississippi Press. (Original interview conducted 1969)

Aufderheide, P. (1990). *Seeing through movies*. New York: Pantheon.

Aune, J. (1994). *Rhetoric and Marxism*. Boulder, CO: Westview.

Aune, J. A. (2001). *Selling the free market: The rhetoric of economic correctness*. New York: Guilford.

Auster, A., & Quart, L. (1979). Hollywood and Vietnam: The triumph of the will. *Cineaste, 9*, 4-9.

Auster, A., & Quart, L. (1988). *How the war was remembered: Hollywood and Vietnam*. New York: Praeger.

Ayres, B. D., Jr. (1994, February 22). Disney drums its fingers as Virginia debates the worth of a theme park. *New York Times*, p. A17.

Bailey, C. W. (1994, December). How Washington insiders ambushed Mickey Mouse. *Washington Monthly, 26*, 10-14. (WilsonSelectPlus. OCLC First Search: Full Text. 1/18/03)

Baker, H. (1976). Baker's address. *Congressional Quarterly Weekly Report, 30*, 2310-2312.

Baker, P. (1994a, February 11). Panel slaps Disney with ticket tax. *Washington Post*, pp. D1, D5.

Baker, P. (1994b, March 10). Allen offers new deal on Disney. *Washington Post*, pp. A1, A32.

Bakhtin, M. M. (1986). *Speech genres and other late essays* (V. W. McGee, Trans.). Austin: University of Texas Press.

Baldwin, J. (1984). *Notes of a native son*. Boston: Beacon.

Baldwin, J. (1985). *The price of the ticket*. New York: St. Martin's.

Baldwin, J. (1993a). *Another country*. New York: Vintage.

Baldwin, J. (1993b). *The fire next time*. New York: Vintage.

Baldwin, J. (1993c). *Nobody knows my name*. New York: Vintage.

Baldwin, J. (1995). *Going to meet the man*. New York: Vintage.

Balfour, L. (1999). Finding the words: Baldwin, race consciousness, and democratic theory. In D. McBride (Ed.), *James Baldwin now* (pp. 75-99). New York: New York University Press.

Baraka, A. (1987, December 20). James Baldwin: His voice remembered; We carry him as us. *New York Times*, p. 27.

Baranczak, S. (1994). Introduction. In W. Gombrowicz (Ed.), *Trans-Atlantyk* (C. French & N. Karsov, Trans.) (pp. ix-xxi). New Haven, CT: Yale University Press.

Barbour, A. G. (1974). *John Wayne: A Pyramid illustrated history of the movies*. New York: Pyramid.

Barker, J. (1999). *The discipline of teams: Participation and unobtrusive control*. Thousand Oaks, CA: Sage.

Barnet, R. J. (1990). *The rocket's red glare: When America goes to war, the presidents and the people*. New York: Simon & Schuster.

Barthel, J. (1967, December 24). John Wayne, superhawk. *New York Times Magazine, 4*, 22, 29-30.

Bass, J. D., & Cherwitz, R. (1978). Imperial mission and manifest destiny. *Southern Speech Communication Journal, 43*, 213-232.

Baudrillard, J. (1983). *In the shadow of silent majorities*. New York: Semiotext(e).

Bayh, E. (1996). We have an obligation. *Vital Speeches of the Day, LXII*, 715-716.

Beck, P. A. (1997). *Party politics in America*. New York: Longman.

Bellah, R. (1970). *Beyond belief: Essays on religion in a post-traditional world*. New York: Harper & Row.

Bellah, R., Madsen, R., Sullivan, W., Swidler, A., & Tipton, S. (1985). *Habits of the heart: Individualism and commitment in American life.* Berkeley: University of California Press.

Bennett, W. L. (1996). *The governing crisis: Media, money, and marketing in American politics.* New York: St. Martin's.

Benoit, W. L. (2000). Beyond genre theory: The genesis of rhetorical action. *Communication Monographs, 67,* 178-192.

Benson, T. (1974). Rhetoric and autobiography: The case of Malcolm X. *Quarterly Journal of Speech, 60,* 1-13.

Bentley, E. (1971). The political theater of John Wayne. *Performance, 1,* 154-159.

Bercovitch, S. (1978). *The American Jeremiad.* Madison: University of Wisconsin Press.

Berg, R. (1986). Losing Vietnam: Covering the war in an age of technology. *Cultural Critique, 3,* 92-125.

Berry, M. (1999). Color codes: Moving beyond Clinton's race initiative means facing black-white reality and building bridges. *Emerge, 10,* 55.

Berryman, C. (1999). Critical mirrors: Theories of autobiography. *Mosaic: A Journal for the Interdisciplinary Study of Literature, 32,* 71-84. Retrieved July 6, 2000, from http://proquest.umi.com/pqdweb?TS=9628954.

Bhabha, H. (1994). *The location of culture.* New York: Routledge.

Bitzer, L. (1968). The rhetorical situation. *Philosophy and Rhetoric, 1,* 1-14.

Bjorkland, C. (1998). *Interpreting the self: Two hundred years of American autobiography.* Chicago: University of Chicago Press.

Black, E. (1970). The second persona. *Quarterly Journal of Speech, 56,* 109-119.

Blair, C. (1999). Contemporary U.S. memorial sites as exemplars of rhetoric's materiality. In J. Selzer & S. Crowley (Eds.), *Rhetorical bodies* (pp. 16-57). Madison: University of Wisconsin Press.

Blair, C., Jeppeson, M. S., & Pucci, E., Jr. (1991). Public memorializing in postmodernity: The Vietnam Veteran's Memorial as prototype. *Quarterly Journal of Speech, 77,* 263-287.

Blair, C., & Michel, N. (2000). Reproducing civil rights tactics: The rhetorical performances of the Civil Rights Memorial. *Rhetoric Society Quarterly, 30,* 31-55.

Bolick, C. (1993, April 30). Clinton's quota queen. *Wall Street Journal,* p. A12.

Bowers, D. (1998). When outsiders encounter insiders in speaking: Oppressed collectives on the defensive. In J. Martin, T. Nakayama, & L. Flores (Eds.), *Readings in cultural contexts* (pp. 186-193). New York: Mayfield.

Bowers, J. W., Ochs, D., & Jensen, R. L. (1993). *Rhetoric of agitation and control.* Prospect Heights, IL: Waveland.

Bradley, P. (1994, May 12). Prominent historians join Disney foes. *Richmond Times-Dispatch,* pp. B1, B6.

Bradsher, K. (1998, July 13). High-level talks collapse in General Motors strike. *New York Times* [Late edition], p. A10.

Brecher, J. (1997). *Strike!* Boston: South End.

Breed, W. (1960). Social control in the newsroom. In W. Schramm (Ed.), *Mass communications* (pp. 178-194). Urbana: University of Illinois Press.

Briffault, R. (1995). Lani Guinier and the dilemmas of American democracy. *Columbia Law Review, 95,* 418-472.

Brodki, B., & Schenck, C. (1988). Introduction. In B. Brodki & C. Schenck (Eds.), *Life/lines: Theorizing women's autobiography.* Ithaca, NY: Cornell University Press.

Brooke, E. (1972). Keynote speech. *Congressional Quarterly Weekly Report, 30,* 2172.

Brooks, R. L. (Ed.). (1999). *When sorry isn't enough: The controversy over apologies and reparations for human injustice*. New York: New York University Press.

Brophy, A. L. (2000). *Reconstructing the dreamland: Contemplating civil rights actions and reparations for the Tulsa race riot of 1921*. Preliminary draft of a report to the Tulsa Race Riot Commission. Retrieved January 22, 2001, from http://www.okcu.edu/law/P-Broph.HTM.

Brower, V. (2002, December 2). HapMap to provide directions, signposts of worst human ills. *Biotechnology Newswatch,* 10.

Buchanan, P. (1991, December 8). *This week with David Brinkley* [Interview]. New York: American Broadcasting Company.

Bullis, C. A., & Tompkins, P. K. (1989). The forest ranger revisited. *Communication Monographs, 56,* 287-306.

Burke, K. (1962). *A rhetoric of religion*. Berkeley: University of California Press.

Burke, K. (1966). *Language as symbolic action.* Berkeley: University of California Press.

Burke, K. (1969a). *A grammar of motives*. Berkeley: University of California Press. (Original work published 1950)

Burke, K. (1969b). *Rhetoric of motives*. Berkeley: University of California. (Original work published 1950)

Burnham, W. D. (2000, April 17). Whole lotta shakin' going' on. *The Nation,* 11-13.

Burns, J. M., & Sorensen, G. (1999). *Dead center: Clinton-Gore leadership and the perils of moderation*. New York: Scribner.

Butler, D. (1995, October 5). Genetic diversity proposal fails to impress international ethics panel. *Nature, 377,* 373.

Call in the troops: It's war! (1994, June). *News From the War Zone, 1*(3), 3.

Calloway-Thomas, C., Cooper, P., & Blake, C. (1999). *Intercultural communication: Roots and routes.* Boston: Allyn & Bacon.

Campbell, A. E. (1986). The paradox of imperialism: The American case. In W. J. Mommsen & J. Osterhammel (Eds.), *Imperialism and after: Continuities and discontinuities* (pp. 34-40). London: Allen & Unwin.

Campbell, J. A. (1998). Rhetorical theory in the twenty-first century: A neo-classical perspective. *Southern Communication Journal, 63,* 291-308.

Campbell, K. K., & Jamieson, K. H. (Eds.). (1978a). *Form and genre: Shaping rhetorical action*. Falls Church, VA: Speech Communication Association.

Campbell, K. K., & Jamieson, K. H. (1978b). Form and genre in rhetorical criticism: An introduction. In K. K. Campbell & K. H. Jamieson (Eds.), *Form and genre: Shaping rhetorical action* (pp. 9-32). Falls Church, VA: Speech Communication Association.

Campbell, K. K., & Jamieson, K. H. (1990). *Deeds done in words: The genres of governance*. Chicago: University of Chicago Press.

Campbell, K. K., & Jamieson, K. H. (1995). Form and genre in rhetorical criticism: An introduction. In C. Burgchardt (Ed.), *Readings in rhetorical criticism* (pp. 394-411). State College, PA: Strata.

Cañas, K. (2002). *Barbara Jordan, Shirley Chisholm, and Lani Guinier. Crafting identification through the rhetorical interbraiding of value.* Unpublished doctoral dissertation, University of Utah, Provo.

Carpenter, R. H. (1990). America's tragic metaphor: Our twentieth-century combatants as frontiersmen. *Quarterly Journal of Speech, 76,* 1-22.

Carpozi, G. (1979). *The John Wayne story*. New Rochelle, NY: Arlington House.

Carter, R. (1993). Thirty five years later. New perspectives on *Brown*. In H. Hill & J. Jones (Eds.), *Race in America: The struggle for equality* (pp. 83-96). Madison: University of Wisconsin Press.

Cassidy, J. (2000, February 7). The price prophet. *New Yorker,* 44-51.

Cavalli-Sforza, L. L. (2000). *Genes, peoples, and languages* (M. Seielstad, Trans.). New York: North Point Press.

Cavalli-Sforza, L. L., Bodmer, W., & Dausset, J. (1997). Support for Genetic Diversity Project. *Nature, 390,* 221.

Cavalli-Sforza, L. L., Wilson, A. C., Cantor, C. R., Cook-Deegan, R. M., & King, M. C. (1991, October). Call for a worldwide survey of human genetic diversity: A vanishing opportunity for the Human Genome Project. *Genomics, 11,* 490-491.

Central Australian Aboriginal Congress. (1994, April). The vampire project: An aboriginal perspective on genome diversity research. *Search 25*(3), 88-90.

Charland, M. (1987). Constitutive rhetoric: The case of the Peuple Quebecois. *Quarterly Journal of Speech, 73,* 133-150.

Charland, M. (1991). Finding a horizon and telos: The challenge to critical rhetoric. *Quarterly Journal of Speech, 77,* 71-74.

Chatterjee, S., Conway, P., Dalziel, P., Eichbaum, C., Harris, M., Philpott, B., & Shaw, R. (1999). *The new politics: A third way for New Zealand.* Palmerston North, NZ: Dunmore.

Chelala, C. (1991, May 24). Clinton apologizes to the survivors of Tuskegee. *Lancet, 15,* 29.

Chen, G. M., & Starosta, W. J. (1998). *Foundations of intercultural communication*. Needham Heights, MA: Allyn & Bacon.

Cheney, G. (1995). Democracy in the workplace: Theory and practice from the perspective of communication. *Journal of Applied Communication Research, 23,* 167-200.

Cheney, G. (1997). The many meanings of "solidarity": The negotiation of values in the Mondragón Worker Cooperative Complex under pressure. In B. D. Sypher (Ed.), *Case studies in organizational communication 2* (pp. 68-83). New York: Guilford.

Cheney, G. (1999). *Values at work: Employee participation meets market pressure at Mondragón.* Ithaca, NY: Cornell University Press.

Cheney, G., & Christensen, L. T. (2001). Identity at issue: Linkages between internal and external organizational communication. In F. M. Jablin & L. L. Putnam (Eds.), *The new handbook of organizational communication* (pp. 231-269). Thousand Oaks, CA: Sage.

Cheney, G., & Frenette, G. (1993). Persuasion and organization: Values, logics, and accounts in contemporary corporate public discourse. In C. Conrad (Ed.), *The ethical nexus* (pp. 49-73). Norwood, NJ: Ablex.

Cheney, G., Straub, J., Speirs, L., Stohl, C., DeGooyer, D., Whalen, S., Garvin-Doxs, K., & Carlone, D. (1998). Democracy, participation, and communication at work: A multidisciplinary review. In M. E. Roloff (Ed.), *Communication Yearbook, 21*. Thousand Oaks, CA: Sage.

Christensen, L. T. (1997). Marketing as auto-communication. *Consumption, Markets and Culture, 1*(2), 1-31.

Christensen, L. T., & Cheney, G. (2000). Self-absorption and self-seduction in the corporate identity game. In M. Schultz, M. J. Hatch, & M. H. Larsen (Eds.), *The expressive organization* (pp. 246-270). Oxford, UK: Oxford University Press.

Clark, C., & O'Donnell, J. (Eds.). (1999). *Becoming and unbecoming white*. Westport, CT: Bergin & Garvey.

Clark, D. L. (1957). *Rhetoric in Greco-Roman education.* New York: Columbia University Press.

Clifford, J. (1992). Traveling cultures. In L. Grossberg, C. Nelson, & P. Treichler (Eds.), *Cultural studies* (pp. 96-112). New York: Routledge.

Clinton, W. J. (1997). *Remarks by the president in apology for study done in Tuskegee. White house: Office of the Press Secretary. May 16, 1997*. Retrieved April 20, 2001, from http://www.pub.whitehouse.gov/uri-res/I2R?urn:pdi://oma.eop.gov.us/1997/5/16/11.text.1.

Cloud, D. (1994). The materiality of discourse as oxymoron: A challenge to critical rhetoric. *Western Journal of Communication, 58*, 141-163.

Cloud, D. (1996, November). *Fighting for words: The limits of symbolic power in the Staley lockout, 1993-1996*. Paper presented at the annual conference of the National Communication Association, San Diego.

Cloud, D. (1997). Concordance, complexity, and conservatism: Rejoinder to Condit. *Critical Studies in Mass Communication, 14*, 193-196.

Cloud, D. (2001). Laboring under the sign of the new. *Management Communication Quarterly, 15*, 268-278.

Cohen, B. (1996, May 2). Population groups can hold critical clues. *Nature, 381*, 12.

Cohn, D., & Fears, D. (2001, March 13). Multiracial growth seen in census. *Washington Post*, p. A01.

Collier & Thomas (1988). Cultural identity. In Y. Y. Kim & W. B. Gudykunst (Eds.), *Theories in intercultural communication*. Newbury Park, CA: Sage.

Concurrent resolution. (1997, June 12). *Congressional Record*. Retrieved February 25, 2000, from http://rs9.loc.gov/cgi-bin/query/z?c105:H.+Con.+Res.+96.

Condit, C. (1997). Clouding the issues: The ideal and the material in human communication. *Critical Studies in Mass Communication, 14*, 197-200.

Condit, C., & Lucaites, J. (1993). *Crafting equality: America's Anglo-African word.* Chicago: University of Chicago Press.

Connor, S. (2001, September 10). How accusations of racism ended the plan to map the genetic diversity of mankind. *The Independent*, 3.

Conrad, C. (2002). *Notes on the Enron case*. Unpublished manuscript, Texas A&M University, College Station.

Conrad, C., & Poole, M. S. (Eds.). (1997). Communication in the age of the disposable worker [Special issue]. *Communication Research, 24*.

Conrad, J. (1988). *Heart of darkness* (R. Kimbrough, Ed.). New York: Norton.

Cook, P. (1968). Film reviews: The Green Berets. *Films in Review, 29*, 453-454.

Cooper, M. (1996, April 8). Harley-riding, picket-walking socialism haunts Decatur. *Nation*, 21.

Cooren, F. (1998, May 20). Personal communication with the author.

Cooren, F. (2000). *The organizing property of communication*. Amsterdam: Benjamins.

Corn, D. (1993). Sinking Guinier. *The Nation, 256*, 855-856.

Corporate greed and wimpy labor leaders team up to defeat Staley workers. (1996, January). *News From the War Zone, 3*(1), 1.

Coulmas, F. (1992). *Language and economy*. Oxford, UK: Blackwell.

Cox, H. (1999, March). The market as God: Living in the new dispensation. *Atlantic Monthly*, 18-23.

Craypo, C., & Nissen, B. (1993). *Grand designs: The impact of corporate strategies on workers, unions, and communities*. Ithaca, NY: ILR Press.

Crenshaw, C. (1997). Resisting whiteness' rhetorical silence. *Western Journal of Communication, 61*, 253-278.

Crenshaw, C. (1998). Colorblind rhetoric. *Southern Communication Journal, 63*, 244-256.

Crigger, B. J. (1995, January/February). The vampire project. *Hastings Center Report, 25,* 2.

Crisis in Decatur. (1994). New York: Corporate Campaign.

Cronen, V. E., Chen, V., & Pearce, W. B. (1988). Coordinated management of meaning. In Y. Y. Kim & W. B. Gudykunst (Eds.), *Theories in intercultural communication* (pp. 66-98). Newbury Park, CA: Sage.

Crouse, T. (1973). *The boys on the bus*. New York: Ballantine.

Cui, G., van den Berg, S., & Jiang, Y. (1998). Cross-cultural adaptation and ethnic communication: Two structural equation models. *Howard Journal of Communication, 9*(1), 69-85.

Cuomo, M. (1984). Keynote address. *Congressional Quarterly Weekly Report, 42,* 1781-1785.

Cyphert, D. (2001). Ideology, knowledge, and text: Pulling at the knot in Ariadne's thread. *Quarterly Journal of Speech, 87,* 378-395.

Dahler-Larsen, P. (1998). What 18 case studies of organizational culture tell us about counter-intentional effects of attempts to establish shared values in organizations. *Current Topics in Management, 3,* 151-173.

Daly, H., & Cobb, J. B., Jr. (1994). *For the common good* (2nd ed.). Boston: Beacon.

Darsey, J. (1999). Baldwin's cosmopolitan loneliness. In D. McBride (Ed.), *James Baldwin now* (pp. 187-207). New York: New York University Press.

Davis, J. W. (1983). *National conventions in an age of party reform.* Westport, CT: Greenwood.

de Certeau, M. (1984). *The practice of everyday life.* Berkeley: University of California Press.

de Rooy, P. (1990). Of monkeys, blacks, and proles: Ernst Haeckel's theory of recapitulation. In J. Breman, P. de Rooy, A. Stoler, & W. F. Wertheim (Eds.), *Imperial monkey business: Racial superiority in social Darwinistic theory and colonial practice*. Amsterdam: Vu University Press.

Delgado, R., & Stefancic, J. (Eds.). (1997). *Critical white studies: Looking behind the mirror*. Philadelphia: Temple University Press.

Derber, C., & Schwartz, W. (1983). Toward a theory of worker participation. *Sociological Inquiry, 53,* 61-78.

Derrida, J. (1976). *Of grammatology* (G. C. Spivak, Trans.). Baltimore: Johns Hopkins University Press.

Desilet, G. (1999). Physics and language—Science and rhetoric: Reviewing parallel evolution of theory on motion and meaning in the aftermath of the Sokal hoax. *Quarterly Journal of Speech, 85,* 339-360.

Devine, J. M. (1995). *Vietnam at 24 frames a second: A critical and thematic analysis of over 400 films about the Vietnam War*. Jefferson, NC: McFarland.

Devreaux Butler, S. (1972). The apologia, 1971 genre. *Southern Speech Communication Journal, 37,* 287.

Dewey, J. (1927). *The public and its problems.* Chicago: Swallow Press.

Dickson, D. (1996, May 2). Whose genes are they anyway? *Nature, 381,* 11-13.

Dievler, J. (1999). Sexual exiles: James Baldwin and *Another Country*. In D. McBride (Ed.), *James Baldwin now* (pp. 161-183). New York: New York University Press.

Dionisopoulos, G. (1990). Images of the warrior returned: Vietnam veterans in popular American film. In R. Morris & P. Ehrenhaus (Eds.), *Cultural legacy of Vietnam: Uses of the past in the present*. Norwood, NJ: Ablex.

Dionisopoulos, G., & Goldzwig, S. (1992). The meaning of Vietnam: Political rhetoric as revisionist cultural history. *Quarterly Journal of Speech, 78,* 61-79.

Disney: More dueling statistics [Editorial]. (1994, January 23). *Washington Post,* p. C6.

Disney: Now the real bargaining [Editorial]. (1994, March 8). *Washington Post,* p. A18.

Dow, B. J. (1996). *Prime-time feminism.* Philadelphia: University of Pennsylvania Press.

Dow, B. J., & Tonn, M. B. (1993). "Feminine style" and political judgment in the rhetoric of Ann Richards. *Quarterly Journal of Speech, 79,* 286-302.

Dreier, P. (1998). There's no justice without economic justice: Shortcomings of Clinton's race initiative report. *Social Policy,* 41-48.

D'Souza, D. (1995). The end of racism: Principles for a multiracial society. New York: Free Press.

DuBois, W. E. B. (1990). *The souls of black folk.* New York: Vintage/Library of America. (Original work published 1903)

Duff, D. (Ed.). (2000). *Modern genre theory.* Essex: Longman/Pearson.

Dupee, F. W. (1986). James Baldwin and "the man." In H. Bloom (Ed.), *James Baldwin* (pp. 11-15). New York: Chelsea House.

Durkheim, E. (1933). *The division of labor in society* (G. Simpson, Trans.). New York: Free Press.

Dutcher, P. N. (1976). The meaning of whiteness. In G. R. Bucher (Ed.), *Straight/white/male* (pp. 85-98). Philadelphia: Fortress.

Dyer, R. (1988). White. *Screen, 29,* 44-65.

Eakin, P. J. (1991). *American autobiography: Retrospect and prospect.* Madison: University of Wisconsin Press.

Edelman, R. (1979, November). Viet vets talk about Nam films. *Films in Review, 30,* 539-542.

Eisenberg, A. (1994/1995). The Millian thoughts of Lani Guinier. *New York University Review of Law & Social Change, 21,* 617-632.

Eisenberg, E. (1984). Ambiguity as strategy in organizational communication. *Communication Monographs, 51,* 227-242.

Eisner, M., & Schwartz, T. (1998). *Work in progress.* New York: Random House.

Entman, R. (1990). Modern racism and the image of blacks in local television news. *Critical Studies in Mass Communication, 7,* 332-345.

Evanoff, T. (1998, July 29). Terms of settlement between General Motors, union leave future uncertain. *Detroit Free Press,* p. 6A.

Evans, D. (1968). Keynote address. *Vital Speeches of the Day, 34,* 679-681.

Ezekiel, R. S. (1995). *The racist mind: Portraits of neo-Nazis and klansmen.* New York: Viking.

Fairhurst, G. T., Monroe Jordan, J., & Neuwirth, K. (1997). Why are we here? Managing the meaning of an organizational mission statement. *Journal of Applied Communication Research, 25,* 243-263.

Fanon, F. (1963). *The wretched of the earth.* New York: Grove Press.

Far from Viet Nam and green berets. (1968, June 21). *Time,* p. 84.

Farrell, T. B. (1978). Political conventions as legitimation ritual. *Communication Monographs, 45,* 293-305.

Feagin, J. R., & Vera, H. (1995). *White racism.* New York: Routledge.

Film maker opposes Civil War theme park. (1994, May 20). *New York Times,* p. A16.

Flagg, B. (1993). I was blind, but now I see: White race consciousness and the requirements of discriminatory intent. *Michigan Law Review, 91.* Retrieved April 19, 2003, from Lexis Nexis.

Flagg, B. J. (1998). *Was blind, but now I see: White race consciousness in the law.* New York: New York University Press.

Fogerty, B. (2000, September 16). A clear view to a nation's promise: Martin Luther King Memorial design draws its strength from Tidal Basin site; Cityscape. *Washington Post,* p. C01.

Fordney, C. (1994, November/December). Embattled ground. *National Parks, 68,* 26-31. (WilsonSelectPlus. OCLC FirstSearch: Full Text. 1/18/03)

Foss, S. (1986, Spring). Ambiguity as persuasion: The Vietnam Veterans Memorial. *Communication Quarterly, 34*(3), 326-340.

Foss, S. K., & Griffin, C. (1992). A feminist perspective on rhetorical theory: Toward a clarification of boundaries. *Western Journal of Communication, 56,* 330-349.

Foss, S. K., & Ray, E. B. (1996). Introduction: Theorizing communication from marginalized perspectives. *Communication Studies, 47,* 253-257.

Foucault, M. (1972). *The archaeology of knowledge*. New York: Pantheon.

Foucault, M. (1978). *The history of sexuality, Vol. 1* (T. Hurley, Trans.). New York: Vintage.

Foucault, M. (1984). *The Foucault reader* (P. Rabinow, Ed.). New York: Pantheon.

Frankenberg, R. (1993). White women. In R. Frankenburg (Ed.), *Race matters: The social construction of whiteness*. Minneapolis: University of Minnesota Press.

Frankenberg, R. (Ed.). (1997). *Displacing whiteness*. Durham, NC: Duke University Press.

Freedman, A., & Medway, P. (1994). Locating genre studies: Antecedents and prospects. In A. Freedman & P. Medway (Eds.), *Genre and the new rhetoric* (pp. 1-20). New York: Routledge.

Freedman, S. G. (1985, March 31). The war and the arts. *New York Times,* pp. 50-51, 54-57.

Frey, L. R., Pearce, W., Pollock, M. A., Artz, L., & Murphy, B. O. (1996). Looking for justice in all the wrong places: On a communication approach to social justice. *Communication Studies, 47,* 110-127.

Friedlaender, J. (1993). Update on the Human Genome Diversity Project. *Evolutionary Anthropology, 2,* 40.

Friedman, M. (1962). *Capitalism and freedom.* Chicago: University of Chicago Press.

Frye, M. (1983). On being white: Thinking toward a feminist understanding of race and race supremacy. In M. Frye (Ed.), *The politics of reality: Essays in feminist theory* (pp. 110-127). Trumansberg, NY: Crossing Feminist Series.

Frye, N. (1957). *Anatomy of criticism*. Princeton, NJ: Princeton University Press.

Fulbright, J. W. (1970). *The Pentagon propaganda machine*. New York: Liveright.

Gabriel, Y., & Lang, T. (1995). *The unmanageable consumer*. London: Sage.

Gallagher, V. J. (1995, Winter). Remembering together: Rhetorical integration and the case of the Martin Luther King, Jr. memorial. *Southern Communication Journal, 60*(2), 109-119.

Gallagher, V. J. (1999). Memory and reconciliation in the Birmingham Civil Rights Institute. *Rhetoric and Public Affairs, 2,* 303-320.

Gallois, C., Franklyn-Stokes, A., Giles, H., & Coupland, N. (1988). Communication accommodation in intercultural encounters. In Y. Y. Kim & W. B. Gudykunst (Eds.), *Theories in intercultural communication*. Newbury Park, CA: Sage.

Gandhi, L. (1998). *Postcolonial theory: A critical introduction*. New York: Columbia University Press.

Gaonkar, D. P. (1997). The idea of rhetoric in the rhetoric of science. In A. G. Gross & W. M. Keith (Eds.), *Rhetorical hermeneutics: Invention and interpretation in the age of science.* Albany: State University of New York Press.

Gedye, R. (1999, September). *Resistance to teamwork and customer service in a New Zealand public sector organization.* Unpublished manuscript, University of Waikato, Hamilton, New Zealand.

Gellman, B., & Lynch, C. (2000, February 26). Verdict renews city's divisions; minorities asking: What price safety? *Washington Post,* p. A1. Available: http://proquest.umi.com/pqdweb?TS=9928742,2-3.

Gibson-Graham, J.-K. (1996). *The end of capitalism (as we knew it): A feminist critique of political economy.* Cambridge, MA: Blackwell.

Giddens, A. (1979). *Central problems in social theory.* Berkeley: University of California Press.

Giddens, A. (1994). *Beyond left and right: The future of radical politics.* Stanford, CA: Stanford University Press.

Giddens, A. (1998). *The third way: The renewal of social democracy.* Cambridge, UK/Malden, MA: Polity Press/Blackwell.

Giles, H., Mulac, A., Bradac, J., & Johnson, P. (1987). Speech accommodation theory. In M. McLaughlin (Ed.), *Communication yearbook* (Vol. 10, pp. 13-48). Newbury Park, CA: Sage.

Gilliatt, P. (1968, July 6). The current cinema: Nanny run amok. *New Yorker,* pp. 44, 46-47.

Giroux, H. A. (1997). Racial politics and the pedagogy of whiteness. In M. Hill (Ed.), *Whiteness: A critical reader* (pp. 294-315). New York: New York University Press.

Gitlin, T. (1979). Prime time ideology: The hegemonic process in television entertainment. *Social Problems, 26,* 251-266.

Glantz, L. H., Annas, G. J., Grodin, M. A., & Mariner, W. K. (1998). Research in developing countries: Taking "benefit" seriously. *Hastings Center Report, 28,* 39.

Glendon, M. (1991). *Rights talk: The impoverishment of political discourse.* New York: Free Press.

Glory. (1968, June 29). *New Yorker,* 24-27.

Gold, R. (1967, November 1). Berets: Hawk-dove debate, Wayne hopes to avoid "politics." *Variety, 3,* 22.

Golden, J., & Rieke, R. (1971). *The rhetoric of black Americans.* Columbus, OH: Merrill.

Goldsborough, J. O. (2003, January 16). A difference in culture, not politics. *San Diego Union-Tribune,* p. B13.

Goldzwig, S. (1989). A social movement perspective on demagoguery: Achieving symbolic realignment. *Communication Studies, 40,* 202-228.

Goldzwig, S. R. (1998). Multiculturalism, rhetoric and the twenty-first century. *Southern Communication Journal, 63,* 273-290.

Goll, I. (1991). Environment, corporate ideology, and employee involvement programs. *Industrial Relations, 30,* 138-149.

Goodman, E. (2000, June 29). A stunning achievement, filled with warnings. *Boston Globe,* p. A27.

Gramm, P. (1992). Keynote address. *Congressional Quarterly Weekly Report, 50,* 2548-2550.

Gramsci, A. (1971). *Selections from the prison notebooks* (Q. Hoare & G. N. Smith, Trans.). Newark, NJ: New International. (Original work published 1936)

Graves, D. (1992). Representing the race: Detroit's monument to Joe Louis. In H. F. Senie & S. Webster (Eds.), *Critical issues in public art: Content, context, and controversy* (pp. 215-227). New York: HarperCollins.

Gray, H. (1989). Television, black Americans, and the American dream. *Critical Studies in Mass Communication, 6,* 376-386.

Gray, J. (1998). *False dawn: Delusions of global capitalism*. New York: Free Press.

Gray-Rosendale, L., & Gruber, S. (Eds.). (2001). *Alternative rhetorics*. Albany: State University of New York Press.

Green, H. (1990). *On strike at Hormel*. Philadelphia: Temple University Press.

Greene, R. W. (1998). Another materialism. *Critical Studies in Mass Communication, 15,* 21-41.

Greenstone, J. D. (1993). *The Lincoln persuasion: Remaking American liberalism*. Princeton, NJ: Princeton University Press.

Greider, W. (1997a). *One world, ready or not: The manic logic of global capitalism*. New York: Simon & Schuster.

Greider, W. (1997b). Planet of pirates: The manic logic of global capitalism. *Utne Reader,* 70ff.

Gresson, A. (1995). *The recovery of race in America*. Minneapolis: University of Minnesota Press.

Griffin, G. J. (1990). The rhetoric of form in conversion narratives. *Quarterly Journal of Speech, 76,* 152-163.

Guinier, L. (1993, November/December). A challenge to journalists on racial dialogue. *Extra,* 7-9.

Guinier, L. (1994). *The tyranny of the majority: Fundamental fairness in representative democracy.* New York: Free Press.

Guinier, L. (1998). *Lift every voice: Turning a civil rights setback into a new vision of social justice.* New York: Simon & Schuster.

Guinier, L., & Torres, G. (2003). The miner's canary. *Yes! A journal of positive futures, 24,* 28-31.

Gupta, A., & Ferguson, J. (1997a). Beyond "culture": Space, identity, and the politics of difference. In A. Gupta & J. Ferguson (Eds.), *Culture, power, place: Explorations in critical anthropology* (pp. 33-51). Durham, NC: Duke University Press.

Gupta, A., & Ferguson, J. (1997b). Culture, power, place: Ethnography at the end of an era. In A. Gupta & J. Ferguson (Eds.), *Culture, power, place: Explorations in critical anthropology* (pp. 1-29). Durham, NC: Duke University Press.

Gustainis, J. (1989). John F. Kennedy and the Green Berets: The rhetorical use of the hero myth. *Communication Studies, 40,* 41-53.

Gutierrez, L. (1995). The new assault on immigrants. *Social Policy, 25,* 56-63.

Gutin, J. C. (1994). End of the rainbow. *Discover, 15,* 70-75.

Gutman, A., & Thompson, D. (1996). *Democracy and disagreement.* Cambridge, MA: Harvard University Press.

Habermas, J. (1989). The public sphere: An encyclopedia article. In S. E. Bronner & D. M. Kellner (Eds.), *Critical theory and society: A reader.* New York: Routledge.

Hacker, A. (1995). *Two nations: Black and white, separate, hostile, unequal*. New York: Ballantine.

Hage, D., & Klauda, P. (1989). *No retreat, no surrender: Labor's war at Hormel*. New York: William Morrow.

Halal, W. E. (1996). *The new management: Democracy and enterprise are transforming organizations.* San Francisco: Berrett-Koehler.

Hall, S. (1981). The whites of their eyes. In G. Bridges & R. Brunt (Eds.), *Silver linings: Some strategies for the eighties* (pp. 28-52). London: Lawrence & Wishart.

Hall, T. (1997, June 17). Letter printed in race relations. *Congressional Record*. Available: http://rs9.loc.gov/cgi-bin/query/D?r105:1:./temp/~r105zMc7qH:e4190.

Hamilton, C. (2001). The Human Genome Diversity Project and the new biological imperialism. *Santa Clara Law Review, 41,* 619-643.

Hariman, R. (1995). *Political style: The artistry of power.* Chicago: University of Chicago Press.

Harris, C. I. (1993). Whiteness as property. *Harvard Law Review, 106,* 1707-1791.

Harris, J. F. (1993, November 12). In Disney visit, Allen finds mutual attraction. *Washington Post,* p. A18.

Harris, K., & Sanchez, J. (1994, September 29). Disney gives up plans for park at historic sight. *Los Angeles Times,* pp. A1, A30.

Harry, D. (1995, March 14). The Human Genome Diversity Project: Implications for indigenous peoples [On-line]. Available: http://www.hartfordhwp.com/ archives/41/024.html.

Hart, R. P. (1987). *The sound of leadership.* Chicago: University of Chicago Press.

Hart, R. P. (1999). *Seducing America: How television charms the modern voter.* New York: Oxford University Press.

Hart, R. P. (2000). *Campaign talk: Why elections are good for us.* Princeton, NJ: Princeton University Press.

Harter, L. M., Stephens, R. J., & Japp, P. M. (2000). President Clinton's apology for the Tuskegee syphilis experiment: A narrative of remembrance, redefinition, and reconciliation. *Howard Journal of Communications, 11,* 19-34.

Harvey, D. (2000). Cosmopolitanism and the banality of geographical evils. *Public Culture, 12,* 529-564.

Hasian, M. (1996). *The rhetoric of eugenics in Anglo-American thought.* Athens: University of Georgia Press.

Hasian, M., & Flores, L. A. (1996). Children of the stones: The Intifada and the mythic creation of the Palestinian state. *Southern Communication Journal, 62,* 89-106.

Hasian, M., & Plec, E. (2002). The cultural, legal, and scientific problems of the Human Genome Diversity Project. *Howard Journal of Communications, 13,* 301-319.

Hatfield, M. (1964). A program of faith. *Vital Speeches of the Day, 30,* 652-654.

Hauser, G. (1999). *Vernacular voices: The rhetoric of publics and public spheres.* Columbia: University of South Carolina Press.

Hawken, P. (1993). *The ecology of commerce: A declaration of sustainability.* New York: HarperCollins.

Hawking, C. J. (1994, April). The battle of Decatur escalates. *News From the War Zone,* 1(2), 1, 4.

Hecht, M. L., Jackson, R. L., & Ribeau, S. A. (2003). *African American communication: Exploring identity and culture* (2nd ed.). Mahwah, NJ: Lawrence Erlbaum.

Hegde, R. S. (2001). Global makeovers and maneuvers: Barbie's presence in India. *Feminist Media Studies, 1,* 129-133.

Heller, S. (1994, February 16). Disney recruits academic advisers to bring accuracy to new project. *Chronicle of Higher Education,* p. A10.

Hellmann, J. (1986). *American myth and the legacy of Vietnam.* New York: Columbia University Press.

Henry, D. (1988). The rhetorical dynamics of Mario Cuomo's 1984 keynote address: Situation, speaker, metaphor. *Southern Speech Communication Journal, 53,* 105-120.

Herr, M. (1977). *Dispatches.* New York: Knopf.

Hidalgo-Serna, E. (1983). *Ingenium* and rhetoric in the work of Vives (L. Ballew & H. Wilson, Trans.). *Philosophy and Rhetoric, 16,* 228-241.

Hill, M. (Ed.). (1997). *Whiteness: A critical reader*. New York: New York University Press.

Hillstrom, K., & Hillstrom, L. C. (1998). *The Vietnam experience: A concise encyclopedia of American literature, songs, and films*. Westport, CT: Greenwood.

Hilzenrath, D. S. (1993a, November 12). Disney's land of make-believe. *Washington Post*, pp. A1, A19.

Hilzenrath, D. S. (1993b, November 28). Disney bargains for a big piece of Prince William's Tomorrowland. *Washington Post*, pp. B1, B3.

Hirsch, E. D., Jr. (1987). *Cultural literacy*. Boston: Houghton Mifflin.

Hoffman, E. (2000, July/August). Wanderers by choice. *Utne Reader*, 46-47.

Hoffman, S. (1978). *Primacy or world order: American foreign policy since the Cold War*. New York: McGraw-Hill.

Hollihan, T. A. (1994). Evidencing moral claims: The activist rhetorical critic's first task. *Western Journal of Communication, 58*, 229-234.

hooks, b. (1995). *Killing rage: Ending racism*. New York: Holt.

Hsu, S. S. (1993a, November 12). Disney project runs into concern about traffic, pollution. *Washington Post*, p. A18.

Hsu, S. S. (1993b, November 23). Preservation group objects to Disney plan. *Washington Post*, pp. E1, E5.

Hsu, S. S. (1993c, December 21). Supporters of Disney park put together lobbying effort. *Washington Post*, p. C7.

Hsu, S. S. (1994a, January 5). Disney to release specifics of development plans. *Washington Post*, pp. B1, B5.

Hsu, S. S. (1994b, January 6). Disney's projections balloon. *Washington Post*, pp. A1, A10.

Hsu, S. S. (1994c, January 20). Disney's calls leave some ears burning. *Washington Post*, pp. B1, B6.

Hsu, S. S. (1994d, February 8). Could Disney become a drag? *Washington Post*, pp. B1, B4.

Hsu, S. S. (1994e, March 7). Disney picks all-star team to lobby for theme park. *Washington Post*, p. D3.

Hsu, S. S. (1994f, March 10). The ways of Disney. *Washington Post*, pp. VA1, VA3.

Hsu, S. S. (1994g, March 23). Disney development called threat to Va. farmland. *Washington Post*, p. D3.

Hsu, S. S. (1994h, April 14). Disney foes launch an "air" attack. *Washington Post*, pp. B1, B2.

Hsu, S. S. (1994i, May 11). Historians, writers organize against Disney theme park. *Washington Post*, p. B7.

Hughes, R. (1993). *Culture of complaint: The fraying of America*. New York: Oxford University Press.

Huxley, T. (1893). Evolution and ethics. *Popular Science, 44*, 18-35, 178-191.

Idea woman. (1993, June 14). *New Yorker, 69*, 4-5.

Ignatiev, N. (1995). *How the Irish became white*. New York: Routledge.

Ignatiev, N., & Garvey, J. (Eds.). (1996). *Race traitor.* New York: Routledge.

Ingenium. (1907). In *[Harpers'] A new Latin dictionary* (pp. 905-906). New York: American Book.

Ingenium. (1968). In *Oxford Latin dictionary* (p. 950). London: Oxford University Press.

Inouye, D. K. (1968). Commitment. *Vital Speeches of the Day, 34*, 709-711.

Iyer, P. (2000, July/August). Stranger in a strange land. *Utne Reader*, 43.

Jackson, R. L. (1999a). *The negotiation of cultural identity.* Westport, CT: Praeger.

Jackson, R. L. (1999b). White space, white privilege: Mapping discursive inquiry into the self. *Quarterly Journal of Speech, 55*(1), 1-17.

Jackson, R. L. (2000a). *Think about it! The question book for those curious about race and self-discovery*. Lincoln, NE: Writers Club Press.
Jackson, R. L. (2000b, February). So real illusions of black intellectualism: Exploring race, roles, and gender in the academy. *Communication Theory, 10*(1), 48-63.
Jackson, R. L., Morrison, C. D., & Dangerfield, C. (2002). Exploring cultural contracts in the classroom and curriculum: Implications of identity negotiation and effects in communication curricula. In J. Trent (Ed.), *Included in communication: Learning climates that cultivate racial and ethnic diversity* (pp. 123-136). Washington, DC: National Communication Association/American Association of Higher Education.
Jackson, R. L., & Simpson, K. (2003). White positionalities and cultural contracts: Critiquing entitlement, theorizing and exploring the negotiation of white identities. *International and Intercultural Communication Annual, 26*, 319-326.
Jacobson, M. F. (1998). *Whiteness of a different color: European immigrants and the alchemy of race*. Cambridge, MA: Harvard University Press.
James, D. E. (1989). *Allegories of cinema: American film in the sixties*. Princeton, NJ: Princeton University Press.
Jamieson, K. H. (1992). *Dirty politics*. New York: Oxford University Press.
Jamieson, K. H., & Campbell, K. K. (1982). Rhetorical hybrids: Fusions of generic elements. *Quarterly Journal of Speech, 68*, 146-157.
Jarosinski, E. (1994, February). Labor war zone in Illinois. *Progressive*, 30-33.
Jayaraman, K. S. (1996, May 2). Gene-hunters home in on India. *Nature, 381*, 13.
John Wayne as the last action hero. (1969, August 8). *Time*, 53-56.
Johnson, P. C. (1999). Reflections on critical white(ness) studies. In T. K. Nakayama & J. N. Martin (Eds.), *Whiteness: The communication of identity* (pp. 1-9). Thousand Oaks, CA: Sage.
Jones, G. (1986). *Social hygiene in twentieth-century Britain*. London: Croom Helm.
Jones, J. H. (1993). *Bad blood: The Tuskegee syphilis experiment* (Expanded ed.). New York: Free Press.
Jordan, B. (1976). Keynote address. *Congressional Quarterly Weekly Report, 34*, 1931-1932.
Jordan, J. (2001). The invisible people: An unsolicited report on black rage. *The Progressive, 65*, 24-25.
Judd, W. H. (1960). Best way to achieve good objectives and keep them. *Vital Speeches of the Day, 36*, 646-651.
Juengst, E. J. (1996). Self-critical federal science? The ethics experiment within the U.S. Human Genome Project. *Social Philosophy and Policy, 13*, 63-95.
Kagan, R. (2002, June/July). Power and weakness. *Policy Review, 113*, 3-28.
Kahn, P. (1994, November 4). Genetic Diversity Project tries again. *Science, 266*, 720.
Kammen, M. (1991). *Mystic chords of memory: The transformation of tradition in American culture*. New York: Knopf.
Kammen, M. (1993). *Mystic chords of memory: The transformation of tradition in American culture*. New York: Vintage.
Kean, T. H. (1988). Keynote address. *Vital Speeches of the Day, 58*, 7-10.
Kevles, D. J. (1985). *In the name of eugenics*. Cambridge, MA: Harvard University Press.
Kincheloe, J. L., Steinberg, S. R., Rodriguez, N. M., & Chennault, R. E. (Eds.). (1991). *White reign: Deploying whiteness in America*. New York: St. Martin's.
Klein, J. (1993, June 14). Principles or politics? *Newsweek*, 29.

Klumpp, J. F., & Hollihan, T. A. (1989). Rhetorical criticism as moral action. *Quarterly Journal of Speech, 75,* 84-97.

Knapp, M. L., & McCroskey, J. C. (1968). Communication research and the American labor union. *Journal of Communication, 18,* 160-172.

Korten, D. C. (1999). *The post-corporate world: Life after capitalism.* San Francisco, CA/West Hartford, CT: Berrett-Koehler/Kumarian.

Kotz, N., & Abramson, A. (1997). The battle to stop Disney's America. *Cosmos.* Retrieved January 18, 2003, from www.cosmos-club.org/journals/1997/disney.html.

Kruse, N. W. (1981). The scope of apologetic discourse: Establishing generic parameters. *Southern Speech Communication Journal, 46,* 278-291.

Kuttner, R. (1997). *Everything for sale: The virtues and limits of markets.* New York: Knopf.

Labor takes its lumps. (1996, March). *Progressive,* 8.

Lane, D. (1994, August). A June 25th [anniversary rally] photo essay. *News From the War Zone, 1*(4), 3.

Lane, R. E. (1991). *The market experience.* Cambridge, UK: Cambridge University Press.

Lane, R. E. (2000). *The loss of happiness in market democracies.* New Haven, CT: Yale University Press.

Larkin, T. J., & Larkin, S. (1994). *Communicating change: How to win employee support for new directions.* New York: McGraw-Hill.

Latour, B. (1993). *We have never been modern.* Cambridge, MA: Harvard University Press.

Laufer, R., & Paradeise, C. (1990). *Marketing democracy: Public opinion and media formation in democratic societies.* New Brunswick, NJ: Transaction Books.

Lazarre, J. (1996). *Beyond the whiteness of whiteness.* Durham, NC: Duke University Press.

Leff, L. (1993). From legal scholar to quota queen: What happens when politics pulls the press into the groves of academe? *Columbia Journalism Review, 32,* 36-41.

Lehrman, S. (1996, May 2). Diversity project: Cavalli-Sforza answers his critics. *Nature, 381,* 14.

Leo, J. (1993, May 17). A controversial choice at Justice. *U.S. News and World Report,* 19.

Leo, J. (1997, June 30). So who's sorry now? *U.S. News and World Report*, 17.

Leonard, D. (1989). New tactics responsible for union victory. *Labor Today, 28,* 6-7.

Lewyn, M. (1994). How radical is Lani Guinier? *Boston University Law Review, 74,* 927-951.

Linenthal, E. T. (1995). *Preserving memory: The struggle to create America's Holocaust Museum*. New York: Viking/Penguin.

Lipsitz, G. (1998). *The possessive investment in whiteness: How white people profit from identity politics*. Philadelphia: Temple University Press.

Lock, M. (1999). Genetic diversity and the politics of difference. *Chicago-Kent Law Review, 75,* 85.

Lopez, I. F. H. (1996). *White by law: The legal construction of race*. New York: New York University Press.

Lugar, R. (1972). Keynote address. *Congressional Quarterly Weekly Report, 30,* 2172.

Lyotard, J. (1991). *The postmodern condition: A report on knowledge.* Minneapolis: University of Minnesota Press.

Madden, R. L. (1969, June 27). John Wayne and the Army under fire. *New York Times,* p. 23.

Mann, M. (1993). *Sources of social power* (Vol. 2). Cambridge, UK: Cambridge University Press.

Mansfield, S. (1994, April 18). Eeeeek! A mouse! Step on it! *Washington Post,* pp. C1, C5.

Marks, J. (1995). *Human biodiversity: Genes, race, and history*. New York: de Gruyter.

Matthews, F. H. (1964). White community and "yellow peril." *Mississippi Valley Historical Review, 50,* 612-633.

Mathews, J. (1993, December 29). Disney in Virginia? Too early to decide [Opinion piece]. *Washington Post,* p. A19.

Mayer, J. (1930). Eugenics in Roman Catholic literature. In *Collected papers on eugenical sterilization in California*. Pasadena, CA: Human Betterment Foundation.

McBride, D. (1999). Introduction: "How much time do you want for your progress?" New approaches to James Baldwin. In D. McBride (Ed.), *James Baldwin now* (pp. 1-9). New York: New York University Press.

McCall, J., & Stauffer, B. (1994). *Christmas carols from the war zone* [Audio recording]. Washington, DC: Labor Heritage Foundation.

McCloskey, D. (1985). *The rhetoric of economics.* Madison: University of Wisconsin Press.

McConahay, J. (1986). Modern racism, ambivalence, and the modern racism scale. In J. Dovidio & S. Gaertner (Eds.), *Prejudice, discrimination and racism* (pp. 91-126). Orlando, FL: Academic Press.

McConahay, J., & Hough, J. (1976). Symbolic racism. *Journal of Social Issues, 32,* 23-45.

McCourt, F. (1996). *Angela's ashes*. New York: Scribner.

McCourt, F. (1999). *'Tis: A memoir*. New York: Scribner.

McCroskey, J., & Richmond, V. (2000). Applying reciprocity and accommodation theories to supervisor/subordinate communication. *Journal of Applied Communication Research, 28*(3), 278-289.

McGee, M. C. (1975). In search of "the people": A rhetorical alternative. *Quarterly Journal of Speech, 61,* 235-249.

McGee, M. C. (1990). Text, context, and the fragmentation of contemporary culture. *Western Journal of Speech Communication, 54,* 274-289.

McIntosh, P. (1992). *White privilege* (Working Paper No. 189). Wellesley, MA: Wellesley College, Center for Research on Women.

McKenzie, D. A. (1981). *Statistics in Britain, 1865-1930: The social construction of scientific knowledge*. Edinburgh, UK: Edinburgh University Press.

McKeon, R. (1973). Creativity and the commonplace. *Philosophy and Rhetoric, 6,* 199-210.

McKerrow, R. E. (1998). Corporeality and cultural rhetoric: A site for rhetoric's future. *Southern Communication Journal, 63,* 315-328.

McMahon, E. (1997). How the Irish became white. *American Historical Review, 102,* 571-572.

McPhail, M. (1994a). The politics of complicity: Second thoughts about the social construction of racial equality. *Quarterly Journal of Speech, 80,* 343-357.

McPhail, M. (1994b). *The rhetoric of racism*. Lanham, MD: University Press of America.

McPhail, M. (1998). From complicity to coherence: Rereading the rhetoric of afrocentricity. *Western Journal of Communication, 62*(2), 114-140.

McPhail, M. (2002). *The rhetoric of racism revisited: Reparations or separation?* Lanham, MD: Rowman & Littlefield.

Melanson, R. A. (1983). *Writing history and making policy: The Cold War, Vietnam and revisionism*. Lanham, MD: University Press of America.

Melanson, R. A., & Thompson, K. W. (1985). *Foreign policy and domestic consensus*. New York: University Press of America.

Merelman, R. M. (1995). *Representing black culture: Racial conflict and cultural politics in the United States*. New York: Routledge.

Merida, K. (1999, November 23). Did freedom alone pay a nation's debt? *Washington Post*. Online posting: BlackNews (blacknews@blacknews.net).

Messengers of struggle. (1994, December). *News From the War Zone, 1*(5), 1.

Miles, E. A. (1960). The keynote speech at national nominating conventions. *Quarterly Journal of Speech, 46,* 26-31.

Miller, C. (1994). Rhetorical community: The cultural basis for genre. In A. Freedman & P. Medway (Eds.), *Genre and the new rhetoric*. London: Taylor & Francis.

Miller, C. R. (1984). Genre as social action. *Quarterly Journal of Speech, 70,* 151-167.

Miller, Z. (1992). Keynote address. *Congressional Quarterly Weekly Report, 50,* 2116.

Mitchell, W. J. T. (1994). The violence of public art: *Do the Right Thing*. In *Picture theory: Essays in verbal and visual representation* (p. 395). Chicago: University of Chicago Press.

Mohr, C. (1968, June 20). U.S. Special Forces: Real and on film. *New York Times*, p. 49.

Molinari, S. (1996). A legacy of hope and opportunity. *Vital Speeches of the Day, 62,* 681-683.

Montagu, A. (1967). *Man's most dangerous myth: The fallacy of race*. Cleveland, OH: Meridian.

Moody, K. (1997). *Workers in a lean world: Unions in the international economy*. London: Verso.

Moon, D. (1999). White enculturation and bourgeois ideology: The discursive production of "good (white) girls." In T. Nakayama & J. Martin (Eds.), *Whiteness: The communication of social identity* (pp. 177-197). Thousand Oaks, CA: Sage.

Mooney, M. (1985). *Vico in the tradition of rhetoric*. Princeton, NJ: Princeton University Press.

Moore, R. (1965). *The green berets*. New York: Crown.

Moore-Gilbert, B. (1997). *Postcolonial theory: Contexts, practices, politics*. London: Verso.

Morgenstern, J. (1968, July 1). Affirmative? Negative! *Newsweek,* 94.

Morrison, T. (1987, December 20). James Baldwin: His voice remembered; Life in his language. *New York Times,* Late City Final Edition, Section 7, p. 27.

Morson, G. S., & Emerson, C. (1990). *Mikhail Bakhtin: Creation of a prosaics*. Stanford, CA: Stanford University Press.

Mouffe, C. (1992). Feminism, citizenship, and radical democratic politics. In J. Butler & J. M. Scott (Eds.), *Feminists theorize the political*. London: Routledge.

Moye, M. A. (1993). Mondragón facing 1992: Adapting co-operative structures to meet the demands of a changing environment. *Economic and Industrial Democracy, 14,* 251-276.

Moyers, B. (1966, January 18). Unpublished letter from Bill Moyers to John Wayne. Lyndon B. Johnson Library and Museum, Austin, TX.

Mulford, C. (1999). Figuring Benjamin Franklin in American cultural memory. *New England Quarterly, 72,* 415-443. Retrieved July 6, 2000, from http://proquest.umi.com/pqdweb?TS=9629190.

Murphy, J. M. (1998). Knowing the president: The dialogic evolution of the campaign history. *Quarterly Journal of Speech, 84,* 23-40.

Nakayama, T., & Martin, J. (Eds.). (1998). *Whiteness: The communication of social identity*. Thousand Oaks, CA: Sage.

Nakayama, T. K., & Krizek, R. L. (1995). Whiteness: A strategic rhetoric. *Quarterly Journal of Speech, 81,* 291-309.

National Party Conventions 1831-1992 (1995). Washington, DC: Congressional Quarterly.

National Research Council. (1997). *Evaluating human genetic diversity*. Washington, DC: Academic Press.

Newman, R. P. (1975). Lethal rhetoric: The selling of the China myths. *Quarterly Journal of Speech, 61,* 113-128.

Nimmo, D., & Combs, J. E. (1983). *Mediated political realities*. New York: Longman.

Nimmo, D., & Combs, J. E. (1990). *Mediated political realities* (2nd ed.). New York: Longman.

Novick, M. (1995). *White lies, white power: The fight against white supremacy and reactionary violence*. Monroe, ME: Common Courage Press.

Nussbaum, M. (1996). *For love of country: Debating the limits of patriotism*. Boston: Beacon.

Nussbaum, M. (1997). Kant and cosmopolitanism. In J. Bohman & M. Lutz-Bachmann (Eds.), *Perpetual peace: Essays on Kant's cosmopolitan ideal* (pp. 25-57). Cambridge: Massachusetts Institute of Technology Press.

OCAW breaks BASF lockout. (1990). *OCAW Reporter, 45,* 11-12.

Ochs, D. (1993). *Consolatory rhetoric: Grief, symbol, and ritual in the Greco-Roman era*. Columbia: University of South Carolina Press.

Odum, M. E. (1993, December 15). Strong land-use laws are urged for Disney project. *Washington Post,* p. D4.

Odum, M. E., & Hsu, S. S. (1993, December 2). Disney foes open campaign with little support in Haymarket. *Washington Post,* pp. D1-D2.

Ono, K. A., & Sloop, J. M. (1995). The critique of vernacular discourse. *Communication Monographs, 62,* 19-46.

Oravec, C. (1991). The ideological significance of discursive form: A response to Solomon and Perkins. *Communication Studies, 42,* 383-391.

Orbe, M. (1994). "Remember, it's always whites' ball": Descriptions of African American male communication. *Communication Quarterly, 42*(3), 287-300.

Ortega, K. P. (1984). Keynote address. *Congressional Quarterly Weekly Report, 42,* 2118-2119.

Osborn, M. (1986). Rhetorical depiction. In H. W. Simons & A. A. Aghazarian (Eds.), *Form, genre, and the study of political discourse* (pp. 79-107). Columbia: University of South Carolina Press.

Page, C. (2001, March 14). Piecing it all together: What the census should be asking about race, ethnicity. *Chicago Tribune* [On-line]. Available: http://www.chicagotribune.com/news/columnists/page.

Page, S. (1997, June 16). Starting the national discussion. *USA Today,* p. A1.

Palast, G. (2001). Florida's "disappeared voters": Disfranchised by the GOP. *The Nation, 272,* 20-23.

Paletz, D. L. (1999). *The media in American politics: Contents and consequences*. New York: Longman.

Paperworkers for reform. (1996). Reform now! *Paperworkers for Reform Newsletter, 1*(2), 2.

Parallax Pictures (Producer). (1997). *The ad and the ego* [Motion picture]. Berkeley: California Newsreel.

Parker, M., & Slaughter, J. (1994). *Working smart: A union guide to participation programs and reengineering*. Detroit, MI: Labor Notes.

Pastore, J. O. (1964). The democratic record. *Vital Speeches of the Day, 30,* 706-708.

Patterson, L. (1995, January 19). Lessons from the war zone [Interview]. *Socialist Worker,* 6-7.

Patterson, T. E. (1993). *Out of order*. New York: Knopf.

Pennisi, E. (1997, October 24). NRC oks long-delayed survey of Human Genome Diversity. *Science, 278,* 568.

Perelman, C., & Olbrechts-Tyteca, L. (1969). *The new rhetoric* (J. Wilkinson & P. Weaver, Trans.). Notre Dame, IN: University of Notre Dame Press.

Petit, C. (1998, February 19). Trying to study tribes while respecting their cultures. *San Francisco Chronicle,* p. A5.

Pipes, D. (2002, November 12). Profs who hate America. *New York Post*. Retrieved January 15, 2003, from http://www.nypost.com.

Pitts, M. R. (1984). *Hollywood and American history: A filmography of over 250 motion pictures depicting U.S. history*. Jefferson, NC: McFarland.

Plans unveiled for "Disney's America" near Washington, D.C. [News release]. (1993, November 11). Walt Disney Company, Orlando, FL. Retrieved January 18, 2003, from www.chotank.com/reledisn.html.

Powell, C. (2000, August 15). Moral strength and educatuon: Address to the Republican National Convention, Philadelphia, Pennsylvania, July 31, 2000. *Vital Speeches of the Day*, 66(21), 651-653.

Press, A. (1996, August 12). Students and union organizing. *Nation, 263*, 3.

Rachleff, P. (1993). *Hard-pressed in the heartland: The Hormel strike and the future of the labor movement*. Boston: South End.

Radley, A. (1990). Artifacts, memory, and a sense of the past. In D. Middleton & D. Edwards (Eds.), *Collective remembering* (pp. 46-59). Newbury Park, CA: Sage.

Ranney, A. (1975). *Curing the mischiefs of faction*. Berkeley: University of California Press.

Reardon, J. (2001). The Human Genome Diversity Project: A case study in coproduction. *Social Studies of Science, 31,* 357-388.

reconciliation. *Howard Journal of Communications, 11,* 19-34.

Resnik, D. B. (1999). The Human Genome Diversity Project: Ethical problems and solutions. *Politics and the Life Sciences, 18,* 15-23.

Rhodes, J. (1994). "Even my own mother couldn't recognize me": Television news and public understanding. *Federal Communication Law Journal, 47*. Retrieved April 12, 2002, from http://law.indiana.edu/fclj/pubs/v47/no1/jrhodes.html.

Rice, D. (1992). The Rocky dilemma: Museums, monuments, and popular culture. In H. F. Senie & S. Webster (Eds.), *Critical issues in public art: Content, context, and controversy* (pp. 228-236). New York: HarperCollins.

Rice, W. (1968, June 27). Wayne leads green berets into Vietnam. *Washington Post.* p. C17.

Richards, A. (1988). Keynote address. *Congressional Quarterly Weekly Report, 50,* 2061-2062.

Ritter, K. (1980). American political rhetoric and the jeremiad tradition: Presidential nomination-acceptance addresses, 1960-1976. *Central States Speech Journal, 31,* 153-171.

Road warriors: Burning rubber. (1995a, May). *News From the War Zone, 2*(2), 7.

Road warriors: Burning rubber. (1995b, July). *News From the War Zone, 2*(4), 8.

Roberts, R., & Olson, J. S. (1995). *John Wayne: American*. New York: Free Press.

Robinson, R. (2000). *The debt: What America owes to blacks*. New York: Dutton Plume.

Rochat, F. (2002, August). *Common decency facing political mass violence: How did some people come to protect persecuted minorities during World War II.* Paper presented at the University of Oslo Lecture Series on Genocide and Political Mass Violence in the 20th Century, Oslo, Norway.

Roediger, D. R. (1991). *The wages of whiteness*. New York: Verso.

Roediger, D. R. (1994). *Towards the abolition of whiteness: Essays on race, politics, and working class history*. New York: Verso.

Rogers, W. W., Ward, R. D., Atkins, L. R., & Flynt, W. (1994). *Alabama: The history of a Deep South state*. Tuscaloosa: University of Alabama Press.

Rokeach, M. (1973). *The nature of human values.* New York: Free Press.

Roloff, M., & Cloven, D. (1990). The chilling effect in interpersonal relationships: The reluctance to speak one's mind. In D. Cahn (Ed.), *Intimates in conflict: A communication perspective*. Mahwah, NJ: Lawrence Erlbaum.

Rosenblatt, R. (1980). Black autobiography: Life as the death weapon. In J. Olney (Ed.), *Autobiography: Essays theoretical and critical* (pp. 169-180). Princeton, NJ: Princeton University Press.

Rothschild-Whitt, J. (1979). The collectivist organization: An alternative to rational-bureaucratic models. *American Sociological Review, 44,* 509-527.

Rural Advancement Foundation International. (1996, March/April). *New questions about management and exchange of human tissues at NIH* [On-line]. Available http://www.rafi.ca/communique/fltxt/19962.html.

Russakoff, D. (1993, December 12). Lani Guinier's is still alive and talking. *Washington Post Magazine,* 15-19, 32-35

Sacco, M. (1994, August). Police violence mars Staley lockout anniversary march. *News From the War Zone, 1*(4), 1.

Said, E. (1979). *Orientalism*. New York: Vintage.

Salopek, P. (1997, April 28). Genes offer sampling of hope and fear: Cures possible, but groups worry about exploitation. *Chicago Tribune,* p. I8.

Samuel, T. (1997, May 21). Clinton tries to span nation's racial divide; Tuskegee is first step in his effort. *St. Louis Post-Dispatch,* p. 6C.

Satow, R. L. (1975). Value-rational authority and professional organizations: Weber's missing type. *Administrative Science Quarterly, 20,* 526-531.

Sayre, R. F. (1964). *The examined self: Benjamin Franklin, Henry Adams, Henry James*. Princeton, NJ: Princeton University Press.

Sayre, R. F. (1972). Autobiography and images of utopia. *Salmagundi, 19,* 18-37.

Sayre, R. F. (1977). The proper study—Autobiographies in American studies. *American Quarterly, 29,* 241-262.

Sayre, R. F. (1980). Autobiography and the making of America. In J. Olney (Ed.), *Autobiography: Essays theoretical and critical* (pp. 146-168). Princeton, NJ: Princeton University Press.

Schein, E. H. (1961). *Coercive persuasion*. New York: Norton.

Schenk, L. C. (2000). Review: Frank McCourt. *'Tis, 78,* 604-605.

Scheurer, T. E. (1981). Myth to madness: America, Vietnam and popular culture. *Journal of American Culture, 4,* 149-165.

Schickel, R. (1968, July 19). Duke talks through his green beret. *Life,* 8.

Schlesinger, A., Jr. (1992). *The disuniting of America: Reflections on a multicultural society*. New York: Norton.

Schmookler, A. B. (1993). *The illusion of choice: How the market economy shapes our destiny.* Albany: State University of New York Press.

Schudson, M. (1998). *The good citizen.* New York: Free Press.

Schutz, A. (1967). *The phenomenlogy of the social world.* Evanston, IL: Northwestern University Press.

Schwabe, K. (1986). The global role of the United States and its imperial consequences. In W. J. Mommsen & J. Osterhammel (Eds.), *Imperialism and after: Continuities and discontinuities* (pp. 41-48). London: Allen & Unwin.

Searle, G. R. (1976). *Eugenics and politics in Britain*. Leyden, UK: Woordhoff.

Sen, A. (1992). *Inequality reexamined.* Cambridge, MA: Harvard University Press.

Serna, E. H. (1980). The philosophy of *ingenium*: Concept and ingenious method in Baltasar Gracián (O. Olson, Trans.). *Philosophy and Rhetoric, 13,* 244-263.

Shepherd, D., Slatzer, R., & Grayson, D. (1985). *Duke: The life and times of John Wayne*. Garden City, NY: Doubleday.

Shipman, P. (1994). *The evolution of racism*. New York: Simon & Shuster.

Shome, R. (1996a). Race and popular cinema: The rhetorical strategies of whiteness in *City of Joy. Communication Quarterly, 44,* 502-518.

Shome, R. (1996b). Postcolonial interventions in the rhetorical canon: An "other" view. *Communication Theory, 6,* 40-59.

Shome, R. (1998). Caught in the term "post-colonial": Why the "post-colonial" still matters. *Critical Studies in Mass Communication, 15,* 204-212.

Shome, R. (1999). Whiteness and the politics of location: Postcolonial reflections. In T. K. Nakayama & J. N. Martin (Eds.), *Whiteness: The communication of social identity* (pp. 107-128). Thousand Oaks, CA: Sage.

Shome, R., & Hegde, R. S. (2002). Culture, communication, and the challenge of globalization. *Critical Studies in Media Communication, 19,* 172-180.

Silbey, J. H. (1994). The rise and fall of American political parties 1790-1993. In L. S. Maisel (Ed.), *The parties respond: Changes in American parties and campaigns* (pp. 3-18). Boulder, CO: Westview.

Simons, H. W. (1972). Persuasion in social conflicts: A critique of prevailing conceptions and a framework for future research. *Speech Monographs, 39,* 227-247.

Simons, H. W., Mechling, E. W., & Schrier, H. (1984). The functions of human communication in mobilizing for action from the bottom up: The rhetoric of social movements. In C. C. Arnold & J. W. Bowers (Eds.), *Handbook of rhetorical and communication theory* (pp. 792-867). Boston: Allyn & Bacon.

Singletary, M., & Hsu, S. S. (1993, November 12). Disney says Va. park will be serious fun. *Washington Post,* pp. A1, A18.

Sipress, D. (1999, November/December), Rancho. Il Wok de Paris, Tex-Mex Italian Asian French Cuisine. *Utne Reader*, 13.

Sleeter, C. (1994). White racism. *Multicultural Education, 39,* 5-8.

Sloan, G. (1993, November 12-14). History theme for Disney's D.C.-area park. *USA Today,* p. D1.

Slotkin, R. (1992). *Gunfighter nation: The myth of the frontier in twentieth-century America*. New York: Atheneum.

Smaglik, P. (2000, April 27). Genetic diversity project fights for its life. *Nature, 404,* 912.

Smith, A. (1986). *The wealth of nations.* London: Penguin. (Original work published 1776)

Smith, J. (1975). *Looking away: Hollywood and Vietnam*. New York: Scribner.

Smith, L. D., & Nimmo, D. (1991). *Cordial concurrence*. Westport, CT: Praeger.

Smith, T. (1986). American imperialism is anti-communism. In W. J. Mommsen & J. Osterhammel (Eds.), *Imperialism and after: Continuities and discontinuities* (pp. 41-48). London: Allen & Unwin.

Solomon, M. (1991). Autobiography as rhetorical narrative: Elizabeth Cady Stanton and Anna Howard Shaw as "new woman." *Communication Studies, 42,* 354-370.

Solomon, M. (1993). The things we study: Texts and their interactions. *Communication Monographs, 60,* 62-68.

Soros, G. (1997, February). The capitalist threat. *Atlantic Monthly,* 45-58.

S.O.S.: Save our solidarity. (1995, August/September). *News From the War Zone, 2*(5), 3.

Sowell, T. (1975). *Race and economics*. New York: McKay.

Spark, A. (1984). The soldier at the heart of the war: The myth of the green beret in the popular culture of the Vietnam era. *Journal of American Studies, 18,* 29-48.

Spivak, G. C. (1988). *In other worlds: Essays in cultural politics*. New York: Routledge.

Spivak, G. C. (1999). *A critique of postcolonial reason: Toward a history of the vanishing past*. Cambridge, MA: Harvard University Press.

Spretnak, C. (1999). *The resurgence of the real: Body, nature, and place in a hypermodern world*. New York: Routledge.

Starling, K. (2001, April 22). From Raleigh to Selma: A pilgrimage into the past. *News and Observer,* pp. 1D, 4D.

Stars: The Duke at 60. (1967, June 9). *Time,* 67.

Steele, S. (1990). *The content of our character: A new vision of race in America*. New York: St. Martin's.

Stevenson, J. (1995, December). James Baldwin: An appreciation. *Boston Book Review.* Retrieved June 18, 2001, from http://www.bookwire.com/bbr/interviews/baldwin.html.

Steyn, M. (2001). *"Whiteness just isn't what it used to be": White identity in a changing South Africa*. Albany: State University of New York Press.

Stoler, A. L. (1989). Making empire respectable: The politics of race and sexual morality in 20th-century colonial cultures. *American Ethnography, 16,* 634-660.

Stoler, A. L. (1997). *Race and the education of desire*. Durham, NC: Duke University Press.

Stone, A. E. (1982). *Autobiographical occasions and original acts: Versions of American identity from Henry Adams to Nate Shaw*. Philadelphia: University of Pennsylvania Press.

Suid, L. (1977). The making of The Green Berets. *Journal of Popular Film, 5,* 106-125.

Suid, L. (1981). Hollywood and Vietnam. *Journal of American Culture, 4,* 136-148.

Suit seeks billions in slave reparations. (2003, April 14). Available: http://www.cnn.com/2002/LAW/03/26/slavery.reparations.

Suleiman, S. R. (1983). *Authoritarian fictions: The ideological novel as a literary genre*. New York: Columbia University Press.

Supriya, K. E. (1996). Confessionals, testimonials: Women's speech in contexts of violence. *Hypatia, 11,* 92-106.

Sustar, L. (1997, Summer). A new labor movement? *International Socialist Review,* 19-26.

Taylor, P. L. (1994). The rhetorical construction of efficiency: Restructuring and industrial democracy in Mondragón, Spain. *Sociological Forum, 9,* 459-489.

Terkel, S. (1989). An interview with James Baldwin. In F. Standley & L. Pratt (Eds.), *Conversations with James Baldwin* (p. 15). Jackson: University of Mississippi Press. (Original interview conducted 1961)

Interdisciplinary Study of Literature, 32, 71-84. Retrieved July 6, 2000, from http://proquest.umi.com/pqdweb?TS=9628954.

Thernstrom, A. (1993, June 14). Guinier miss. *The New Republic,* 16-19.

Thomas, E. (1975). Editor's preface. In W. Rodney (Ed.), *Groundings with my brothers*. London: Bogle/L'Overture. (Original work published 1969)

Thompson, W. N. (1979). Barbara Jordan's keynote address: Fulfilling dual and conflicting purposes. *Central States Speech Journal, 30,* 272-279.

Thornton, A. P. (1977). *Imperialism in the twentieth century*. Minneapolis: University of Minnesota Press.

Ting Toomey, S. (1999). *Communicating across cultures*. New York: Guilford.

Tompkins, P. K., & Cheney, G. (1985). Communication and unobtrusive control in contemporary organizations. In R. D. McPhee & P. K. Tompkins (Eds.), *Organizational communication: Traditional themes and new directions* (pp. 179-210). Beverly Hills, CA: Sage.

Toulmin, S. (1964). *The uses of argument*. Cambridge, UK: Cambridge University Press.

Tousignant, S., & Hsu, S. S. (1994, September 11). Speakers split evenly at Disney hearing; Prince William Commission delays decision. *Washington Post*, p. A1.

Travis, M. A. (1998). *Reading cultures: The construction of readers in the twentieth century*. Carbondale: Southern Illinois University Press.

Trent, J. S., & Friedenberg, R. V. (1991). *Political campaign communication*. Westport, CT: Praeger.

Turner, R. (1993, November 12). Disney outlines plan for a theme park at site in Virginia. *Wall Street Journal*, pp. A2, A8.

Tuttle, K. (2000, January 4). Martin Luther King Memorial approved: The National Capital Planning Commission announced. *Speakin' Out News, 20*(9), 1.

Twomey, S. (1993, November 15). It's history, Abe—Liven it up a bit. *Washington Post*, pp. D1, D7.

Uchitelle, L. (1993, June 29). 800 workers locked out by Staley. *New York Times*, p. D6.

Union rejects concessionary pact. (1995, July). *News From the War Zone, 2*(4), 1.

Upton, D. (1999). Commemorating the Civil Rights movement. *Design Book Review, 40*, 23-33.

Valenti, J. (1966, January 6). Unpublished memorandum from J. Valenti to President Lyndon B. Johnson. Lyndon B. Johnson Library and Museum, Austin, TX.

van Dijk, T. (1987). *Communicating racism: Ethnic prejudice in thought and talk*. Newbury Park, CA: Sage.

van Dijk, T. (1993). *Elite discourse and racism*. Newbury Park, CA: Sage.

Vartabedian, R. A. (1985). Nixon's Vietnam rhetoric: A case study of apologia as generic paradox. *Southern Speech Communication Journal, 50*, 366-381.

Virginia approves Disney subsidies. (1994, March 13). *New York Times* (National ed.), p. A27.

Vlastos, S. (1991). America's "enemy": The absent presence in revisionist Vietnam war history. In J. C. Rowe & R. Berg (Eds.), *The Vietnam War and American culture* (pp. 52-74). New York: Columbia University Press.

Wakefield, D. (1968). *Supernation at peace and war: Certain observations, depositions, testimonies, and graffiti gathered in a one-man fact-and-fantasy finding tour of the most powerful nation in the world*. Boston: Little, Brown.

Walker, D. (1965). *David Walker's appeal, in four articles; Together with a preamble to the colored citizens of the world, but in particular, and very expressly, to those of the United States of America* (C. M. Wiltse, Ed.). New York: Hill & Wang. (Original work published 1830)

Wander, P. (1983). The ideological turn in rhetorical theory. *Central States Speech Journal, 34*, 1-18.

Wander, P. (1996). Book review: Marxism, post-colonialism, and rhetorical contextualization. *Quarterly Journal of Speech, 82*, 402-426.

Wander, P., Martin, J. N., & Nakayama, T. K. (1999). What do white people want to be called? A study of self-labels for white Americans. In T. K. Nakayama & J. N. Martin (Eds.), *Whiteness: The communication of identity* (pp. 27-50). Thousand Oaks, CA: Sage.

Ware, B. L., & Linkugel, W. A. (1973). They spoke in defense of themselves: On the generic criticism of apologia. *Quarterly Journal of Speech, 59,* 273-283.

Watson, T., Jr. (1963). *A business and its beliefs: The ideas that helped build IBM.* New York: McGraw-Hill.

Watts, D., & Lamb, G. (1995, July). Open letter to supporters of locked out Staley workers. News From the War Zone, 2(4), 4.

Wayne, J. (1965, December 28). Unpublished letter from John Wayne to President Lyndon B. Johnson. Lyndon B. Johnson Library and Museum, Austin, TX.

Wayne, J. (1966, February 18). Unpublished letter from John Wayne to Mr. Bill Moyers, Special Assistant to the President. Lyndon B. Johnson Library and Museum, Austin, TX.

Wayne, J. (1971, May). Playboy interview: John Wayne with Richard W. Lewis, interviewer. *Playboy,* 75-76, 78, 80, 82, 84, 86, 90, 92.

Weber, M. (1978). *Economy and society* (G. Roth & C. Wittich, Trans.). Berkeley: University of California Press.

Webster, D. (1989). On the compromise measures: The seventh of March speech. In J. Andrews & D. Zarefsky (Eds.), *American voices: Significant speeches in American history, 1640-1945* (p. 191). New York: Longman. (Original work published 1850)

Webster, Y. (1992). *The racialization of American.* New York: St. Martin's.

Weiler, A. H. (1969, January 3). John Wayne's "Green Berets" a box-office triumph. *New York Times,* p. 20.

Weisberg, J. (1998, January 25). United shareholders of America. *New York Times Magazine,* pp. 29-31.

Weissman, R. (1996, January/February). A bitter defeat at A. E. Staley. *Multinational Monitor,* 39-40.

Werhane, P. H. (1991). *Adam Smith and his legacy for modern capitalism.* Oxford, UK: Oxford University Press.

Wesseling, H. L. (1986). Imperialism and empire: An introduction. In W. J. Mommsen & J. Osterhammel (Eds.), *Imperialism and after: Continuities and discontinuities* (pp. 1-10). London: Allen & Unwin.

West, C. (1993). *Race matters.* Boston: Beacon.

White, D. M., & Averson, R. (1972). *The celluloid weapon: Social comment and the American film.* Boston: Beacon.

White, H. C. (1981). Where do markets come from? *American Journal of Sociology, 8,* 517-547.

White, J. B. (1985). *Heracles' bow: Essays on the rhetoric and poetics of the law.* Madison: University of Wisconsin Press.

White, T. H. (1961). *The making of the president 1960.* New York: Pocket Books.

Whitt, L. A. (1998). Resisting value-bifurcation: Indigenist critiques of the Human Genome Diversity Project. In B. Bar On & A. Ferguson (Eds.), *Daring to be good: Essays in feminist ethico-politics.* New York: Routledge.

Who was the enemy . . . the real Staley story. (1996, January). *News From the War Zone, 3*(1), 2.

Wilkinson, A., & Willmott, H. (1995). Introduction. In A. Wilkinson & H. Willmott (Eds.), *Making quality critical: New perspectives on organizational change* (pp. 1-32). London: Routledge.

Wills, G. (1997). *John Wayne's America: The politics of celebrity.* New York: Simon & Schuster.

Wilson, M. O. (1999, Fall). Between rooms 307: Spaces and memory at the National Civil Rights Museum. *Harvard Design Magazine,* 28-31.

Windeller, R. (1967, September 27). Defiant Wayne filming "Green Berets." *New York Times,* p. 41.

Wing, B. (2000). The color of election 2000. *Colorlines.* Retrieved April 12, 2002, from http://www.alternet.org/story.html?StoryID-10201.

Withdraw Guinier. (1993, June 14). *The New Republic,* 7.

Woodward, C. (1974). *The strange career of Jim Crow* (3rd ed.). New York: Oxford University Press.

Wray, M., & Newitz, A. (1997). *White trash: Race and class in America.* New York: Routledge.

Wright, M. (1999). "Alas, poor Richard!": Transatlantic Baldwin, the politics of forgetting, and the project of modernity. In D. McBride (Ed.), *James Baldwin now* (pp. 208-232). New York: New York University Press.

Xu, Q. (1999). TQM as an arbitrary sign for play: Discourse and transformation. *Organization Studies, 2,* 659-681.

Yardley, J. (1993, November 15). All ears—And that's the problem. *Washington Post,* p. B2.

Young, J. (1992). The counter-monument: Memory against itself in Germany today. *Critical inquiry, 18,* 267-296.

Zarefsky, D., Miller-Tutzauer, C., & Tutzauer, F. E. (1984). Reagan's safety net for the truly needy: The rhetorical uses of definition. *Central States Speech Journal, 35,* 113-129.

Zbaracki, M. J. (1998). The rhetoric and reality of total quality management. *Administrative Science Quarterly, 4,* 602-636.

Zorn, T. E., Christensen, L. T., & Cheney, G. (1999). *Do we really want constant change?* (Beyond the Bottom Line booklet series, Vol. 2). San Francisco: Berrett-Koehler.

Index

About the Editors

Steven R. Goldzwig, Ph.D., is Professor of Communication Studies at Marquette University. He is coauthor of *"In A Perilous Hour": The Public Address of John F. Kennedy*. He has written numerous scholarly articles and teaches a variety of courses on politics, ethics, and rhetoric.

Patricia A. Sullivan, Ph.D., is Professor at State University of New York, New Paltz. She is coauthor of *From the Margins to the Center: Contemporary Women and Political Communication* and coeditor of *Political Rhetoric, Power, and Renaissance Women*. Her articles have appeared in *Quarterly Journal of Speech*, *Western Journal of Communication*, *Communication Quarterly*, and *Women and Politics*.

About the Authors

Barry Brummett, Ph.D., has taught at Purdue University and the University of Wisconsin at Milwaukee and is now Charles Sapp Centennial Professor of Communication and chair of the communication studies department at the University of Texas at Austin. He is author of several articles and books, including *Rhetorical Dimensions of Popular Culture, Contemporary Apocalyptic Rhetoric, Rhetoric of Machine Aesthetics*, and *The World and How We Describe It: Rhetorics of Reality, Representation, Simulation*.

Thomas R. Burkholder, Ph.D., is Associate Professor in the Hank Greenspun School of Communication at the University of Nevada at Las Vegas. He teaches and studies American public address, rhetorical criticism, and rhetorical theory. His work has appeared in *Communication Studies* and *Southern Communication Journal*. He is coauthor of the second edition of *Critiques of Contemporary Rhetoric*.

Kathryn M. Cañas, Ph.D., is Associate Professor and Lecturer in the David Eccles School of Business at the University of Utah. Her primary responsibilities include developing and integrating communication-based management courses into the business curriculum at the undergraduate and graduate levels. Her areas of research include the rhetoric of democracy, the rhetoric of minority women in the public arena, and understanding and managing diversity as a competitive advantage in business.

George Cheney, Ph.D., is Professor of Communication at the University of Utah and Adjunct Professor of Management Communication at the University of Waikato, Hamilton, New Zealand. His teaching and research interests include corporate public discourse, identity and power in organizations, quality of worklife, corporate social responsibility and sustainability, the marketization of society, and the rhetoric of war. The author or editor of four books and more than 70 articles and chapters, he has been recognized for teaching, research, and service. He has lectured in Europe and Latin America.

Dana L. Cloud, Ph.D., is Associate Professor of Communication Studies at the University of Texas at Austin. She has written one book, *Consolation and Control in American Culture and Politics: Rhetorics of Therapy* (Sage, 1998) and numerous articles on Marxist theory; race, gender, and culture; and the rhetoric of social movements. Currently, she is working on a book-length project about the union democracy movement during the 1990s at Boeing.

Carrie Crenshaw, Ph.D., is an independent scholar living and writing in Birmingham, Alabama. She is author of numerous articles on feminism, critical race studies, and argument theory and criticism. She has received several grants in support of her research and debate outreach efforts. Her current focus is on integrating scholarly endeavors with her personal and political activism and the important position of being a primary caregiver to two small children.

James Darsey, Ph.D., is Associate Professor of Communication at Georgia State University. His essays on the rhetorics of radical and marginalized groups have appeared in *Quarterly Journal of Speech, Communication Monographs, Communication Studies, Western Journal of Communication*, and various anthologies. His 1997 book, *The Prophetic Tradition and Radical Rhetoric in America*, received several awards and was named by *Choice* as an outstanding academic book for 1997.

George N. Dionisopoulos, Ph.D., is Professor in the School of Communication at San Diego State University. His research interests include political communication in the 1960s and presidential rhetoric.

Victoria J. Gallagher, Ph.D., is Associate Professor in the Department of Communication at North Carolina State University. Her research on the rhetoric of civil rights leaders and civil rights-related commemorative sites has appeared in *Quarterly Journal of Speech, Rhetoric and Public Affairs, Southern Communication Journal,* and several edited collections. Her current research projects include a book length comparative analysis of civil rights museums and memorials and a rhetorical examination of selected photographs and paintings featured in *Life* and *Look* magazines during the 1960s. Professor Gallagher teaches courses in rhetorical theory, criticism, and communication ethics.

G. Thomas Goodnight, Ph.D., is currently a Professor, Annenberg School for Communication, University of Southern California. He has also been a professor and director of graduate studies, the Department of Communication Studies, Northwestern University.

Dexter B. Gordon, Ph.D., is Professor in the Communication Studies Department and Director of African American Studies at the University of Puget Sound. He is author of *Black Identity: Rhetoric, Ideology, and Nineteenth-Century Black Nationalism* (2003) and articles on rhetoric and culture.

Marouf Hasian Jr. Ph.D., is Associate Professor in the Department of Communication at the University of Utah. He is author of *The Rhetoric of Eugenics in Anglo-American Thought* (University of Georgia Press, 1996) and numerous articles on the law and rhetoric, postcolonial studies, and critical rhetoric.

Ronald L. Jackson II, Ph.D., is Associate Professor of Culture and Communication Theory in the Department of Communication Arts & Sciences at the Pennsylvania State University. He is author of *The Negotiation of Cultural Identity, Think About It!, Understanding African American Rhetoric* (with Elaine Richardson), and *African American Communication: Identity and Culture* (with Michael Hecht and Sidney Ribeau). He is editor of *African American Communication & Identities: Essential Readings* (Sage, 2003). His theory work includes the development of two paradigms called cultural contracts theory and black masculine identity theory.

Mark Lawrence McPhail, Ph.D., is Professor of Interdisciplinary Studies in the Western College Program at Miami University, Oxford, Ohio. He is author of *Zen in the Art of Rhetoric: An Inquiry Into Coherence* and *The Rhetoric of Racism Revisited: Reparations or Separation*? His scholarship has been published in *Quarterly Journal of Speech*, *Critical Studies in Mass Communication*, and the *Howard Journal of Communications*, and his creative work has appeared in *Dark Horse Magazine* and *The American Literary Review*. His research interests include rhetorical theory and epistemology, language and race relations, and visual communication.

John M. Murphy, Ph.D., is Associate Professor of Speech Communication at the University of Georgia. He studies contemporary public address. His work has appeared in *Quarterly Journal of Speech*, *Rhetoric and Public Affairs*, and *Presidential Studies Quarterly.*

Kathryn M. Olson, Ph.D., is Associate Professor of Communication at the University of Wisconsin–Milwaukee. Her research agenda revolves around rhetoric that constitutes community or involves social controversy. She approaches the related issues from perspectives of argumentation, rhetorical criticism and theory, and public address scholarship. Her work appears in academic journals including *Quarterly Journal of Speech* and other publications on rhetoric, argument, and communication.

Emily Plec, Ph.D., is Assistant Professor of Speech Communication at Western Oregon University. Her research interests include the rhetoric of science and sport, environmental communication, and critical approaches to social justice.